Wissenschaftliche Untersuchungen
zum Neuen Testament · 2. Reihe

Herausgeber / Editor
Jörg Frey (München)

Mitherausgeber / Associate Editors
Friedrich Avemarie (Marburg)
Judith Gundry-Volf (New Haven, CT)
Hans-Josef Klauck (Chicago, IL)

243

V. Henry T. Nguyen

Christian Identity
in Corinth

A Comparative Study of 2 Corinthians,
Epictetus and Valerius Maximus

Mohr Siebeck

V. Henry T. Nguyen, born 1977; B. A. Life Pacific College (USA); M. A. Talbot School of Theology, Biola University (USA); PhD University of Aberdeen (UK); currently teaching at Loyola Marymount University and Biola University in Los Angeles, USA.

BR
166
.N48
2008

ISBN 978-3-16-149666-0
ISSN 0340-9570 (Wissenschaftliche Untersuchungen zum Neuen Testament, 2. Reihe)

The Deutsche Nationalbibliothek lists this publication in the Deutsche Nationalbibliographie; detailed bibliographic data is available in the Internet at *http://dnb.d-nb.de*.

The book was printed by Laupp & Göbel in Nehren on non-aging paper and bound by Buchbinderei Nädele in Nehren.

Printed in Germany.

To my Wife

Preface

This book is a revision of my doctoral dissertation submitted to the University of Aberdeen (Scotland, UK) in August 2007. This work would not have been completed without the encouragement and support of many people. It is a privilege to be able to express my gratitude to each one of them. First of all, I owe a debt of gratitude to my doctoral supervisor, Dr. Andrew D. Clarke, for his careful, patient, and gracious supervision throughout the time it took me to complete the dissertation. His attention to detail and valuable insights have greatly influenced and improved this study. In addition, I am thankful for his example of humility as a biblical scholar, and for all his academic and personal encouragement. I am also indebted to Dr. Bruce Winter for taking such a great interest in this research project and for his supervision during my six-month stay at Tyndale House (Cambridge, UK). At an early stage of this project, a visit to the archaeological site of Corinth with him provided countless rich discussions that helped to shape this study. I am also grateful for all his academic, personal, and spiritual guidance throughout my doctoral programme. I also would like to extend my thanks to my examiners, Dr. Peter Oakes and Professor I. Howard Marshall, for their helpful comments and valuable suggestions of improvements.

I am very grateful to Prof. Dr. Jörg Frey for his prompt acceptance of the manuscript for publication in the *WUNT* series II, and to Dr. Henning Ziebritzki and the editorial team at Mohr Siebeck for their kind and efficient assistance.

Going through my doctoral programme allowed my family and me the wonderful opportunity of living in Cambridge and Aberdeen. During our time in Cambridge, I benefited from the valuable fellowship with the readers, residents, and staff members at Tyndale House. In Aberdeen there are many people I owe a warm word of thanks. In particular, I am thankful for our friends at Bridge of Don Baptist Church, especially those in our house church group in Deeside. I am also grateful for the friendships that were forged while being a part of the postgraduate community at the University of Aberdeen. Very importantly, our time in the United Kingdom would not have been possible without the prayers and financial support of our dear families and friends. I am especially indebted to my mother for her constant sacrifice and support, not only during my doctoral programme but throughout my life. I also wish to express my debt of gratitude to Dr. Joseph Hellerman for his encouragement in my maturation as a person and as a student of the New Testament.

Our two children, Olivia and Carson, have enhanced the experience of researching and writing this book by being a constant source of joy, life, and motivation. My life and research have only been enriched by their many interruptions and diversions. They have richly contributed to the completion of my 'dissertation', which happens to be the biggest word that Carson knows!

I save my final words of gratitude and appreciation for my lovely wife and best friend, Adriana, who often had to put up with a distracted, tired, and grumpy husband. Her endless patience, encouragement, love, support, and humour have made me a better person throughout the trials and woes of researching and writing a dissertation/book. It is difficult to imagine the completion of this book without her by my side. I dedicate this book to her.

March 2008   V. Henry T. Nguyen

Table of Contents

Chapter 1

Introduction

1.1 The Object and Rationale of the Study

This study developed from an initial research interest in exploring 'identity', especially Christian identity, in the social world of the New Testament. In a recent study, David Horrell states, 'Identity has become something of a buzz-word in recent social science and in studies in early Christianity'.[1] Also, Philip Esler reflects on the difficulty of discussing identity issues because the term 'identity' has become a 'plastic word' and so elastic in definition.[2] Esler advises that it makes sense for one to use the term, provided that he or she defines it. Thus, to clarify, this present study is interested in what is considered 'social identity' – that is, an individual's identity in society, and how that identity was perceived and used in social relations. In particular, this study is interested in looking at the social relations involving Christian identity. In his study, *Social Identity*, Richard Jenkins provides a helpful definition for this present study: 'Social identity is our understanding of who we are and of who other people are, and reciprocally, other people's understanding of themselves and of others (which includes us)'.[3]

Some New Testament scholars have employed the modern 'social identity theory', which was developed by Henri Tajfel and others in the 1970s, to interpret the New Testament, especially with the use of modern scientific models.[4] However, the aim of this study is to employ a basic understanding of 'social identity' (as given above) to evaluate the primary sources that reveal

---

[1] Horrell, *Solidarity*, 91. For studies of 'cultural identity' in the Roman empire, see e.g. Laurence & Berry, *Cultural Identity*; Huskinson, *Experiencing Rome*. For historical studies of Christian identity, see e.g. Lieu, *Neither*; idem, *Christian Identity*. Additionally, many studies of Christian identity have employed modern social scientific approaches: e.g. Malina, *NT World*; Esler, *Conflict*; Buell, *New Race*; Horrell, *Solidarity*.

[2] Esler, *Conflict*, 19. Cf. Lieu, *Christian Identity*, 11–17, who evaluates the anachronistic idea of 'identity' in the first- and second-century contexts.

[3] Jenkins, *Social Identity*, 5.

[4] For more on this modern theory which considers the social psychology of identity, see Tajfel, *Human Groups*; Robinson, *Social Group*. For recent NT studies that incorporate this modern theory, see e.g. Esler, *Galatians*; idem, *Conflict*; Asano, *Community-Identity*.

dynamics of social relations in the ancient Graeco-Roman world; this understanding, in turn, will shed some light on the New Testament texts and the social aspects of Christian identity. In other words, given the overlap with studies using the social identity theory and their application of a *modern* model or grid, this study can be perceived as attempting to construct an *ancient* model or grid in order to interpret the New Testament writings.

This study began with a particular interest in looking at social identity in Paul's letters in order to grasp how he approaches Christian identity in his church communities. After surveying the Pauline corpus, there appeared to be some important texts that indicated issues relating to social identity. One notable text was 2 Cor 5.12, in which Paul explains that he gives the Corinthians an opportunity to boast against those who boast in 'outward appearance' (πρόσωπον) and not in the heart. Commentators have rightly explained that Paul is reacting here against a boasting in external and worldly things that were used for social advantages (e.g. social status, eloquence in speech, and physical appearance).[5] However, commentators have not provided much explanation for Paul's use of πρόσωπον here, and how it might be used to express aspects of social identity. In addition to this verse, the initial survey of the Pauline writings revealed that there were other instances of πρόσωπον and its cognates that also seemed to indicate some features of social identity. For instance, in 2 Cor 10.7 Paul writes τὰ κατὰ πρόσωπον βλέπετε, and in Gal 2.6 he asserts that unlike humans, God does not look on man's outward appearance (πρόσωπον) (cf. Gal. 6.12). Given these examples, this study became interested in examining whether Paul could be communicating aspects of social identity with some of his uses of πρόσωπον and other related concepts.

From an early immersion in the literary and non-literary sources of the Graeco-Roman world in and around the first century CE, followed by a survey of pertinent secondary literature, I found an ancient concept – the concept of *persona* (or social *persona*) – which seemed to explain aspects of social identity.[6] Interestingly, the modern English usage of *persona*, which is a loanword from Latin, does have a colloquial meaning of the 'aspect of a person's character that is displayed to or perceived by others'.[7] Given this modern definition the idea of *persona* can somewhat be already understood by modern readers; nevertheless, this concept still needs to be properly grasped in its ancient context. Furthermore, although scholars occasionally use the

---

[5] See Chapters Five and Six for an analysis of this verse.

[6] Unless otherwise noted, the texts and translations of ancient Greek and Latin literary sources are taken from the Loeb Classical Library, and in some cases the translations may have been slightly modified in order to highlight certain Greek and Latin terms (e.g. πρόσωπον and *persona*).

[7] *The Oxford English Dictionary* (2nd ed.; Oxford: Oxford University Press, 2005), ad loc.

term *persona* (often in its modern sense) there has been no study that has extensively explored the social significance of the ancient concept of social *persona* in the Graeco-Roman world. In fact, scholars of the New Testament and of ancient history have significantly overlooked this important social concept. One reason why New Testament interpreters have not given much attention to it is because they have not picked up on the equivalence of the Latin word *persona* and the Greek word πρόσωπον, and have usually understood the latter as merely denoting the 'face'. This study seeks to demonstrate that πρόσωπον has an additional overlooked meaning of social identity and a relation to the concept of *persona*.

In an early stage of this study, extensive searches of the Latin term *persona* and the Greek term πρόσωπον were conducted with the aid of electronic databases of ancient sources (e.g. the Thesaurus Linguae Graecae [TLG] and the Packard Humanities Institute [PHI]). A preliminary observation of the results from these searches revealed that although the terms have a wide range of meanings, both terms often indicated aspects of social identity. In particular, the features of rank and status were involved in many of these instances that expressed notions of social identity. Since rank and status are important components of one's socio-political identity in the Graeco-Roman social world (see Chapter Two), they were used to help decide which material would be pertinent for this study. This survey also showed that there were many significant uses of the terms *persona* and πρόσωπον by many authors during this time period. Two of these figures – Valerius Maximus and Epictetus – were selected for further examination since: they had significant uses of *persona*/πρόσωπον, they provided valuable details relating to social identity, and the size of their literary works are manageable.[8] Their works were read as a whole in order to grasp fully their awareness and understanding of the concept of *persona*. After reading through their works, it was clear that they dealt with issues of social identity (e.g. rank and status), and would be able to illuminate some of the Pauline texts concerning social identity. In addition to these ancient figures, a survey of the Pauline material revealed that about half of the instances of πρόσωπον occurred in 2 Corinthians. Moreover, a survey of the Corinthian correspondence revealed numerous texts that describe conficts in the church involving issues of social status and Christian identity. With this concentrated use of πρόσωπον and the valuable social description, the Corinthian correspondence (more specifically, 2 Corinthians) was chosen as a suitable focus of this Pauline study.

---

[8] The small amount of secondary literature on Valerius and Epictetus, and the manageable size of their literary works, make it feasible to consider them in detail within this comparative study. Also, see Chapter Seven for a brief suggestion of some other figures who are worth considering for further studies on this research topic of social identity (e.g. Seneca, Plutarch, and Dio Chrysostom).

The particular rationale for selecting these three figures is that, as the following chapters will show, they all indicate some reflection on this common theme of social *persona*. There are, moreover, further benefits in comparing these three figures. For instance, their works offer a diachronic and geographic trajectory for this study: Valerius wrote in Rome during the early first century CE, Paul lived in Corinth during the mid-first century and later wrote on a number of occasions to the church there, and Epictetus lived in Rome and then in Nicopolis in the Greek East during the late first and early second century. That is, Valerius provides insights into the outworking of social identity in Rome, and Epictetus provides details of its outworking in the Greek East; the information gleaned from these two figures, then, will provide the necessary backdrop for understanding the social context of Paul's letters to the Christians in Corinth, which is a Roman colony in the Greek East. Another benefit is that since New Testament scholars, and even classicists have largely neglected Valerius and Epictetus, this study will provide further knowledge of them that will help to illuminate the New Testament and its social world.[9]

This study proposes to fill in the lacuna of this prominent ancient social concept in both classical and New Testament studies by delineating the concept of *persona* and its importance in the Graeco-Roman social world and particularly in the church at Corinth. The thesis is that Paul, Epictetus, and Valerius all react against a preoccupation with superficial displays of *persona* in the early imperial period. In 2 Corinthians, in particular, Paul reacts against the Corinthian Christians' assimilation of the conventional values of *persona* into their conception of Christian identity, and challenges their superficial assessment of one another based on these conventional values. In order to correct their misconception of Christian identity, Paul promotes and embodies a new and subversive Christ-like identity.

This argument will be developed by first addressing, in the remainder of this chapter, some introductory issues concerning method. Then, in Chapter Two, the concept of *persona* will be elucidated with the use of literary and non-literary sources. In Chapters Three to Six, Valerius Maximus, Epictetus, and Paul will be examined, respectively, for their understandings and critiques of *persona*. As mentioned above, Valerius will provide an understanding of

---

[9] It should be noted that this study's interest in these two figures contributes to the small number of studies that has considered their comparative value for New Testament studies – though none of the studies has examined aspects of social identity. For Valerius, there are only two: Hodgson, 'Gospel Criticism'; idem, 'Social World'. For Epictetus, see Bonhöffer, *Epiktet und NT*; idem, 'Epiktet und NT'; Bultmann, 'Epiktet'; Sharp, *Epictetus*; Schrage, 'Stellung'; Sevenster, 'Education'; Braun, 'Indifferenz'; Klauck, 'Dankbar leben'; Jagu, 'Morale'; Oakes, 'Epictetus'; Winter, *Philo*, 113–22; Yieh, *One Teacher*, 185–236; Engberg-Pedersen, 'Self-Sufficiency'.

social *persona* in the city of Rome, and Epictetus will provide an understanding of social *persona* in the Greek East; accordingly, the gleaned insights will be helpful for interpreting Paul's correspondence to the Christians in the Roman colony of Corinth in its proper social context. Given that this is a New Testament study, Paul's critique of social identity will be given special attention, especially his approach to Christian identity in 2 Corinthians. Furthermore, some comparison will be made at the end of each of these three chapters between their critiques and the conventional outworking of *persona*, and also between the critiques of the three figures themselves. Finally, conclusions will be drawn together in Chapter Seven.

1.2 Method

Scholars have been interested in what has been called *Antike und Christentum* – the intersection of ancient history and early Christianity, and the use of ancient sources to illuminate early Christianity.[10] New Testament scholars interested in this intersection have conducted comparative and linguistic studies that search for 'parallels' in ancient literary and non-literary sources.[11] However, some scholars have drawn attention to the hazards and problems involved with the use of such 'parallels' – for example, the narrow focus only on terms that are the same.[12] Given that this study is concerned with comparing parallel material, some issues regarding method need to be addressed.

1.2.1 Social Concept

Since this study is stimulated by some of Paul's uses of πρόσωπον, it is important to indicate that this study should be regarded as a 'social concept study', rather than a 'word study'. Although the word or lexical study has been a popular and useful method to ascertain the meaning of words in the New Testament, there are some shortcomings to its use. Since this study is interested in a particular meaning of πρόσωπον, which happens not to be

---

[10] For more on this topic, see Judge, 'Antike', 3–58. See also Winter, '*Christentum*', 121–30, who discusses in the reverse direction, *Christentum und Antike,* suggesting that scholars of ancient history should consider early Christian sources (e.g. the New Testament) as illuminating sources for studies in ancient history. It is also the goal of this present study to contribute knowledge to scholarship in ancient history. See e.g. Engels, *Roman Corinth*, 107–16, who notably examines Paul's Corinthian correspondence for his study of Roman Corinth.

[11] See White & Fitzgerald, 'Quod est comparandum', 13–39, for a recent overview of the use of 'parallels'.

[12] For the problems of 'parallels', see White & Fitzgerald, 'Quod est comparandum', esp. 27–32; Sandmel, 'Parallelomania', 1–13.

given explicitly in any of the Greek lexicons, it is important to focus on the current state of Greek lexicography.[13] Recent studies have drawn attention to and demonstrated the inadequacies of many of the standard lexicons used in studying the Greek language – such as Bauer and Danker's *A Greek-English Lexicon of the New Testament and Other Early Christian Literature* and Liddell-Scott-Jones' *A Greek-English Lexicon* (LSJ).[14] For instance, although LSJ is the most popular and a heavily relied upon Greek lexicon, it is essentially focused on Classical Greek and not the Greek of the post-Classical period – the latter period being more pertinent for New Testament studies. Some faults in Greek lexicons, which have been demonstrated, are: the gaps in coverage; the reliance on glosses instead of providing definitions; that most lexicons are built upon the material of predecessors and a great number of the entries have been uncritically accepted by subsequent lexicons; and the contamination from translations such as the Latin Vulgate.[15] Also, John Lee has expressed that reading through texts of the post-classical period, 'you will sooner or later come across something poorly dealt with, or not covered at all, by LSJ and any other available tool'.[16] In view of Lee's comment, this present study suggests that this is the case with the term πρόσωπον. Therefore, this study heeds the caution in using lexicons and aims to study the term πρόσωπον in a different fashion.

In addition to the problem of Greek lexicography, there is the improper use of 'parallels' in word studies. New Testament scholars often investigate a word by searching for and compiling other instances with the aid of electronic databases of ancient texts such as the TLG. Often times, though, scholars will only make a narrow use of the ancient sources by being fixated on the particular term and only searching for instances of it. Additionally, they often will use the results for statistical purposes or merely as proof texts for their arguments. This superficial use of parallels to describe a term found in the New Testament runs the risk of missing out on the context of the ancient source and other synonymous language and expressions used in it. L. Michael

---

[13] The lexical entries will be mentioned in the next chapter.

[14] Liddell, Scott, & Jones, *A Greek-English Lexicon*; Bauer & Danker, *A Greek-English Lexicon*. For some critiques, see e.g. Chadwick, *Lexicographica Graeca*, who presents copious examples of the shortcomings of LSJ; Lee, *History*, for an excellent study of the history of NT lexicography; idem, 'Present State', 66–74, for the present state of Greek lexicography; and other essays in Taylor, Lee, Burton, & Whitaker, *Biblical Greek*.

[15] See the more detailed discussions and examples in Lee, *History*; idem, 'Present State', 66–74. Also, Johnson, 'Resources', 77, after looking at the somewhat more adequate Latin lexicons, shifts his attention to the Greek lexicons and describes their situation: 'We have not walked into a slum exactly, but the buildings are more closely spaced, the porch banisters often rickety, the lawns not so well kept. Approaching the dictionary, a Hellenist must remain cautious and light on the feet'.

[16] Lee, 'Present State', 72.

White and John Fitzgerald convey that 'one must deal with the nuances and differences among the moralists and other non-Christian writers based on their context, backgrounds, and intentions – in precisely the same way that we need to be aware of the drastic differences among the New Testament writing themselves'.[17] Therefore, New Testament scholars should treat properly not only their New Testament texts, but also other ancient sources – that is, to consider sources in their proper context.

Scholars have recently taken on the task of providing new directions to study New Testament words, such as considering a term's semantic domain and synonyms.[18] White and Fitzgerald promote:

In future studies of this type it will be crucial to investigate such terms, not simply in isolation from one another, but as part of the conceptual 'linkage group' to which they belong and with increased attention to the social worlds in which they are used. Similarly, attention will need to be given to combinations of Greek words as well as to equivalent terms and similar expressions in Latin and other languages. While there is thus a need to expand the linguistic horizons of research, the data used in making comparisons must not be restricted to instances of verbal identity or similarity. Some of the most striking parallels between Christian and non-Christian texts are primarily conceptual and involve little or no verbal agreement between the two.[19]

This study aligns with their suggestions, and will take a more robust approach by investigating both the Greek term πρόσωπον and the equivalent Latin term *persona*. Additionally, this study will also consider those other 'concepts' that are related to the social feature of *persona*.

Furthermore, rather than searching ancient sources for a wooden meaning of a term or concept, this study will consider its dynamic meaning by examining the concept of *persona* and related concepts (e.g. rank and status) within the larger arguments of the works of Paul, Epictetus, and Valerius. For instance, in the case of Epictetus, who has some significant uses of πρόσωπον, rather than only collating the relevant instances of the term, this study additionally will explore his work as a whole for other similar expressions and concepts that could be missed if the study was only fixated on the term πρόσωπον. Peter Oakes similarly points out the 'danger of jumping straight into seeking to compare Epictetus with the New Testament':

---

[17] White & Fitzgerald, 'Quod est comparandum', 38, which is commenting on a statement by Malherbe, 'Hellenistic Moralists', 275–6.

[18] See Lee, *History*, 155–75, who considers Louw & Nida, *Greek-English Lexicon* and its approach to semantic domains as 'the breakthrough' in NT lexicography. See also Winter, 'Lexical Handbook', whose paper promotes his new lexical project that considers 'ancient' rather than 'modern' semantic domains, the latter being used by Louw and Nida. I am grateful to him for a copy of the paper.

[19] White & Fitzgerald, 'Quod est comparandum', 31. Cf. Horst, 'Corpus', 1157–61, who overviews the project *Corpus Hellenisticum Novi Testamenti*, which has a main emphasis on conceptual parallels, rather than lexical parallels.

Documents clearly need to be read as a whole, in their context, and the significance of the parts only deduced once the argument of the whole has been grasped. If instead we jump straight into comparison with the New Testament, we will probably address the document with an agenda other than its own, leading to an analysis of the ideas of the document using an inappropriate, and hence distorting the grid.[20]

Therefore, this study should not be regarded merely as a lexical study, but more as a 'social concept study' that will consider the concept of *persona* within the context and framework of a number of ancient documents.

1.2.2 Social History

Many scholars who are interested in comparative studies have given special attention to the 'background' of a concept by considering its historical socio-cultural context. By looking at this context, information can be gathered about the social practices, beliefs, behaviour, values, and ideals of the people in their own contexts – which would shed light on how people perceived and valued certain concepts. The acceptability of this method is evinced from the many studies of the Graeco-Roman social world by Roman social historians.[21] Also, the widespread use of the socio-historical method to understand the social world of the New Testament, especially of the Corinthian correspondence, testifies to the acceptability of the method for New Testament studies.[22] In order to grasp the concept of *persona* in the Graeco-Roman social world, this study employs this descriptive-historical perspective by exploring the literary and non-literary sources in their contexts. White and Fitzgerald aptly concludes: 'In order for us to understand fully how a Paul – or any other writer of the time, whether pagan, Jew, or Christian – might have appropriated these semantic and social conventions, we must continue to examine closely the parallels in their contexts. *Quod est comparandum* ("Thus should it be compared")'.[23]

---

[20] Oakes, 'Epictetus', 39.

[21] It will suffice to list here a few studies that are used in the next chapter: Garnsey & Saller, *Roman Empire*; Lendon, *Honour*; Saller, 'Status'; Barton, *Roman Honor*.

[22] See e.g. those on the Corinthian correspondence: Clarke, *Leadership*; idem, *Serve*; Chow, *Patronage*; Dutch, *Educated Elite*; Welborn, 'Discord'; Pogoloff, *Logos*; Litfin, *Proclamation*; Winter, *After Paul*; idem, *Philo*; Marshall, *Enmity*; Horrell, *Social Ethos*; Savage, *Power*; Ebel, *Attraktivität*; Meggitt, *Poverty*. Also worth noting are the studies of Philippians, which concerns the socio-historical setting of another Pauline church in a Roman colony: Oakes, *Philippians*; Hellerman, *Reconstructing*.

[23] White & Fitzgerald, 'Quod est comparandum', 39.

1.2.3 Heuristic Comparison

Even though comparative studies are common in New Testament scholarship, one final issue to address is the comparative approach of this study.[24] A problem of some comparative studies is that the different sources are often simply reduced to show that there is some sort of dependency, relationship, or shared tradition. This study, however, will compare the different sources heuristically. Philip Alexander has recently given a helpful explanation of his employment of a heuristic comparison:

> it is intended to sharpen our understanding of what each text is saying, whether in agreement or disagreement. It is not meant to establish literary dependence...Since the comparison is heuristic, differences of date, place, tradition, literary genre and language are immaterial. What we are comparing and contrasting are *ideas* circling round a common theme.[25]

Although Paul, Epictetus, and Valerius offer a variety of dates, places, traditions, literary genres, and languages, they all show concerns with the common theme of social *persona*. Therefore, the same interpretative lens will be placed on these three individuals in their own contexts to examine this common theme. By placing Paul in the same discussion with Epictetus and Valerius, insights would be gained that in return would illuminate Paul's own understanding and critique of *persona*.[26]

---

[24] See e.g. the comparative studies in Fitzgerald, Olbricht, & White, *Early Christianity*. See above for a list of NT studies of Valerius and Epictetus, most of which employ a comparative method.

[25] Alexander, 'Qumran', 353 (italics his).

[26] Cf. Malherbe, 'Hellenistic Moralists', 299, who writes in his study of Paul and the Hellenistic moralists, 'It is potentially fruitful, and certainly more realistic, to place Paul in the context of these discussions...'

Chapter 2

Social Identity and *Persona*

2.1 Introduction

Social identity, as noted in the previous chapter, 'is our understanding of who we are and of who other people are, and reciprocally, other people's understanding of themselves and of others (which includes us)'.[1] In order to grasp how aspects of identity affect social relations in the Graeco-Roman world, this study focuses on the ancient concept of *persona*. As will be seen, *persona* is a rich term that has a long history. In modern times, the word is commonly used in reference to the 'aspect of a person's character that is displayed to or perceived by others'.[2] Although this modern definition of *persona* is helpful for the present study, this definition needs to be explored whether it was existent or prevalent in ancient times, particularly during the New Testament era.

Having come across the possible significance of the concept of *persona*, this study conducted direct searches of the Latin term *persona* and also the Greek word πρόσωπον – which is commonly considered to be the Greek counterpart of *persona* – in the Graeco-Roman primary sources. The results revealed many instances of the terms that do connote aspects of social identity. Interestingly, the social features of rank and status, which are important elements of identity in Graeco-Roman society, were seen to be connected to these instances and were helpful in deciding which instances were relevant for this study. The recognition of the relationship between *persona* and the social features of rank and status further confirmed the possible importance of the concept of *persona* for the understanding of social identity in the ancient sources.

Although scholars of the New Testament and ancient history have made passing references to the term *persona*, there has been no substantial study of its social significance. This chapter, then, will establish the concept of *persona* and its significance in the Graeco-Roman social world – especially in Roman society. In order to understand this social concept, this chapter

---

[1] Jenkins, *Social Identity*, 5.
[2] *The Oxford English Dictionary* (2nd ed.; Oxford: Oxford University Press, 2005), ad loc.

proposes: first, to demonstrate that the terms *persona* and πρόσωπον can convey a sense of social identity; secondly, to consider the Roman stress on *persona*; and thirdly, to assess the conventional (or popular) projection of social *persona* in the first-century Graeco-Roman social milieu.

2.2 *Persona* and Πρόσωπον

A suitable place to begin this study of the concept of *persona* is with an examination of the Latin term *persona*. In addition to this Latin word, equal attention will be given to πρόσωπον because New Testament scholars have largely ignored the correlation between the terms. Attention will first be given to the state of research on the two terms, followed by an analysis of them.

2.2.1 *The State of Research on* Persona/Πρόσωπον

Research on the term *persona* (and πρόσωπον) can be seen in the numerous studies of the modern interest in defining human identity, the person, human personality, or the human self. With different interests (e.g. philosophical, psychological, moral, biological, and legal), these studies have investigated in part the term *persona* and its developed meanings in order to gain further understanding of the notion of a 'person'. Although this present study is not interested in the understanding of *persona* in the modern sense of the human person or personality, the studies of that modern sense are helpful in providing information that have bearing on the social dimension of *persona*. Therefore, this section on the state of research of *persona* will consider these studies of the 'concept of the person' in order to grasp better the ancient social 'concept of *persona*'.

In his seminal study of the 'concept of the person', which gives consideration to *persona* and πρόσωπον, Marcel Mauss remarks on

comment une des catégories de l'esprit humain, – une de ces idées que nous croyons innées, – est bien lentement née et grandie au cours de longs siècles et à travers de nombreuses vicissitudes, tellement qu'elle est encore, aujourd'hui même, flottante, délicate, précieuse, et à élaborer davantage.[3]

Since that important study, scholars have continued to elaborate on the concept and have further complicated the understanding of it. Christopher Gill introduces his edited work on the same concept by acknowledging, 'The subject of the person is one of the most discussed, and most controversial, in modern philosophy'.[4] Troels Engberg-Pederson, in the same volume,

---

[3] Mauss, 'L'esprit humain', 263.
[4] Gill, 'Introduction', 2.

expresses, 'Like so many other time-hallowed concepts, that of the person is constantly under attack in modern philosophy, and one may be rather tempted to give it up altogether'.[5] In particular, the terms *persona* and πρόσωπον have posed difficulties for research into this subject, as noted by P.W. Duff: 'The word *persona* has a long and complicated history. Its various meanings, and those of its Greek equivalent, πρόσωπον, and of its modern derivatives, have been the subject of much controversy among philologists, lawyers, philosophers, and especially theologians'.[6] Max Turner, a New Testament scholar, also affirms the difficulties with the terms in his recent quest for an understanding of 'personhood': 'For New Testament scholars there could thus be some excuse to shrug our shoulders and walk away from the problem [of "personhood"], not least because the troublesome words *persona* and *prosōpon* (in the sense "person") do not appear in our Scriptures, nor in their contemporary literature'.[7]

Many modern studies, like those above, that are interested in the concept of human identity have managed to give brief consideration to the meanings of *persona* and πρόσωπον. However, with the varied interests of scholars examining the concept of the person and the meaning of *persona* and πρόσωπον, there has been no conclusive understanding of human identity.[8] Given the difficulty of too many competing definitions, Amélie Rorty, in her essay on human identity, 'Persons and *Personae*', indicates the problem: 'As inheritors of the Judaeo-Christian, Renaissance, Enlightenment, and Romantic traditions, we want the concept of the person to fill a number of functions'.[9] With so many modern interests in human identity – including moral, legal, theological, metaphysical, social, biological – these concerns tend to colour and inform the meanings sought. She argues that it is not possible to have *the* concept of person, since some of these functions overlap and may even cause tension with others.[10] Consequently, she underscores the necessity to accept the tensions and conflicts of the various functions, and to abandon any 'metaphysical longing' for only one concept.[11]

Rorty's comments are helpful for any study attempting to trek through the difficult terrain of the terms *persona* and πρόσωπον, and even the uncharted terrain of the social concept of *persona*. Thus, to clarify, this study does not

---

[5] Engberg-Pedersen, 'Stoic Concept', 109.

[6] Duff, *Personality*, 1.

[7] Turner, 'Personhood', 211.

[8] Cf. Gill, 'Introduction', 7.

[9] Rorty, 'Persons', 22. See her pp. 22–35 for a list of seven functions, one of which is pertinent to this present study (#4): 'Social persons are identified by their mutual interactions, by the roles they enact in the dynamic dramas of their shared lives' (28).

[10] Rorty, 'Persons', 35.

[11] Rorty, 'Persons', 37–8.

attempt to establish *the* identity of an individual in Graeco-Roman society, especially in light of Rorty's caution for a more complex understanding, nor does it attempt to describe comprehensively one's 'personal' or 'human' identity. This study, rather, is only exploring the terms *persona* and πρόσωπον for a circumscribed meaning of one's 'social identity'.

2.2.2 Social Identity: A Meaning of Persona/Πρόσωπον

There have been a few studies that have analysed both *persona* and πρόσωπον, and have provided useful insights for understanding the terms in the sense of social identity. In 1906, Siegmund Schlossmann produced a substantial study, *Persona und ΠΡΟΣΩΠΟΝ im Recht und im christlichen Dogma*,[12] which analysed both terms and the history of their development, especially the development of their legal meaning as found in the legal and Christian sources. Then in 1938, Mauss presented a significant essay, 'Une catégorie de l'esprit humain: La notion de personne, celle de "moi"',[13] which discussed the concept of the person by considering the notions of the 'person' (*personne*) and the 'self' (*moi*). In his socio-anthropological analysis of the ancient Greeks and Romans, he found similar conclusions to Schlossmann on the development of the terms' meanings and their relation to the concept of the person. Mauss, however, goes beyond a mere legal meaning and considers an enriched moral and socio-political meaning of *persona*, which he suggests was influenced by Late Stoicism and Christianity. Finally, Maurice Nédoncelle also produced a useful study of the etymology of both terms in 1948 entitled, 'Prosopon et Persona dans l'antiquité classique'.[14] In it he draws similar conclusions to the other two studies, yet places a stronger emphasis on *persona*/πρόσωπον as denoting the actual social being, that is, 'l'individu qui se promène dans la rue et que vous y apercevez en ouvrant les yeux'.[15]

The comprehensive studies of Schlossmann, Mauss, and Nédoncelle, along with some other illuminating studies on aspects of *persona*, provide a strong foundation for this study's interest in social identity. Given the lack of need for an exhaustive treatment of the meanings of *persona* and πρόσωπον, the goal of this section is to build on the relevant conclusions from these valuable studies in order to grasp a meaning of 'social identity' and a correlation of the two terms.[16] Before exploring the terms *persona* and πρόσωπον and the

---

[12] Schlossmann, *Persona*.

[13] Mauss, 'L'esprit humain', 263–81. See Carrithers, Collins, & Lukes, *Category*, for an English translation and a collection of essays reflecting on Mauss' essay.

[14] Nédoncelle, 'Prosopon', 277–99.

[15] Nédoncelle, 'Prosopon', 299.

[16] This section will not provide exhaustive details from primary sources concerning the

theme of social identity, it is important to bear in mind that both terms (as will be seen) are very malleable, since they often carry such a varied range of senses, such as 'mask', 'face', 'front', 'person', 'social status', and 'legal status'.[17]

2.2.2.1 Persona

The Latin word *persona* exhibits a range of meanings:[18] (1) a mask, especially worn by actors; (2) a character in a play or dramatic role; (3) the part played by a person in life (a position, role, character); (4) the actual being of someone, individual personality, or one's person; (5) in a legal context, referring to an individual in a case, or the person in respect of the individual's rank or importance; (6) in the grammarians, a person. Besides the term's wide semantic range, scholars have indicated the difficulties of understanding its etymology. Nédoncelle, for instance, comments on the difficulty: '*Persona* mérite de nous retenir plus longuement. Son importance est obvie. C'est un mot difficile: l'étymologie en est obscure, le développement sémantique en est compliqué'.[19]

Despite the complication, the consensus is that the term had an original meaning of 'mask'.[20] Interestingly, Gellius recounts a witty explanation, given by Gavius Bassus, that *persona* was formed from the verb *personare*, whereby the mask has a hole for the voice 'to sound through' (*per/sonare*) (*Noct. att.* 5.7). Although the validity of this explanation is uncertain, it was an early meaning of 'mask' that consequently influenced the term's development into the meaning of 'person'. Nédoncelle asserts that 'personus (= qui résonne) et persona ont dû confluer de bonne heure dans l'inconscient des Romains'.[21] This development is observed through the common use of various expressions that have the word *persona* linked with certain verbs, such as *personam gerere* ('to conduct a role'), which became associated with

---

developed meanings of the terms. See the major works discussed in this section for further references to primary sources.

[17] Since these complex terms are used in a variety of ways in different contexts, they will often not be translated in this study.

[18] These meanings are selected from Glare, *Oxford Latin Dictionary*, ad loc; Lewis & Short, *A Latin Dictionary*, ad loc. Although the shortcomings of lexicons were highlighted in Chapter One, the lexical definitions are given in this chapter to highlight both of the terms' wide semantic range.

[19] Nédoncelle, 'Prosopon', 284.

[20] E.g. Mauss, 'L'esprit humain', 274. See Nédoncelle, 'Prosopon', 286–93, who argues that *persona* derives either from the proper name 'Persepona', or from the ancient Etruscan word *phersu* ('mask'). Cf. Altheim, 'Persona', 35–52.

[21] Nédoncelle, 'Prosopon', 293. Cf. Schlossmann, *Persona*, 14–15.

a role in a drama (*dramatis persona*).[22] Schlossmann explains that *persona* itself does not mean 'role', but it is the qualification in the various expressions that dictate 'die Rolle spielen'.[23] He continues to show the theatrical imagery 'spilling over' into the social interactions of public life: 'Endlich heißt *personam gerere etc.* häufig nicht blos soviel wie eine Rolle auf der Bühne, im Drama spielen, sondern auch im Leben irgend eine Funktion verrichten'.[24] Similarly, Carlin Barton explains this understanding of *persona*, 'The Latin *persona* was not only the mask but also the part expressed by that mask'.[25] Since it is natural for the mask to represent, essentially, the individual and his or her role, 'the self cannot be the mask alone...nor can it be the man alone...so it must be some fusion of mask and man'.[26] Thus, the word *persona* has a meaning of a role played in life, which is derived from a role played in the theatre.

In his study, Nédoncelle lists seven variant meanings of *persona* used by Cicero beyond the mere theatrical meaning:[27] 'rôle en justice' (e.g. *De or.* 2.102); 'personnage ou rôle social' (*Inv. rhet.* 1.52.99); 'réalité ou dignité collective' (*Off.* 1.124); 'personnalité murquante ou constituée en dignité' (e.g. *Off.* 1.97); 'personne juridique par opposition aux choses' (*De orat.* 3.53); 'personnalité ou caractère concret d'un individu' (e.g. *Amic.* 1.4; *Q Rosc.* 20; *Inv. rhet.* 1.34); 'notion philosophique de personne' (*Off.* 1.107). His presentation of Cicero's usage is significant because it shows that by the time of Cicero, the term clearly developed meanings beyond the semantic domain of the theatre and is reflecting the socio-political identity of the individual. Mauss similarly recognises the expansion of the term's meaning beyond its original theatrical meaning, and suggests that Roman law influenced the developed meaning of *persona* by making it synonymous with the true nature of the individual.[28] He demonstrates the legal meaning by pointing out how *persona* conveyed certain qualifications (e.g. citizenship, the Roman name, and property) and how slaves did not have this right of *persona* (*servus non habet personam*).[29] This understanding is clearly evident in the legal writings of the Roman jurists, who, to some extent, established the

---

[22] See Schlossmann, *Persona*, 19–20, 22–4; Emmet, *Roles*, 175.

[23] Schlossmann, *Persona*, 19.

[24] Schlossmann, *Persona*, 20.

[25] Barton, *Roman Honor*, 82.

[26] Hollis, 'Masks', 222.

[27] Nédoncelle, 'Prosopon', 297, comments on the large development of the word by Cicero's time: 'Mais avec Cicéron, d'un seul coup, elles apparaissent toutes'. See his pp. 297–8 for more references.

[28] Mauss, 'L'esprit humain', 277.

[29] Mauss, 'L'esprit humain', 275–7. Emmet, *Roles*, 176, also follows Mauss: 'A *persona* has *Conditio* (his family ranking), *Status* (his civil position) and *Munus* (his functions in civil and military life)'.

technical meaning of a legal *persona*. In Roman law, there are only *personae*, *res*, and *actiones* (Gaius, *Inst.* 1.3.8), and slaves are regarded as *res* (things or property) and not legal persons with rights to ownership.[30] The Roman socio-political world, then, can be seen as one of the major influences on the notion of *persona*.[31] In fact, Mauss intimates that 'les Romains, les Latins pour mieux dire, semblent être ceux qui ont partiellement établi la notion de *personne*, dont le nom est resté exactement le mot latin'.[32]

This section has highlighted the developed meaning of the term *persona* and pointed out a particular nuance of 'social identity' that existed, at least, since the time of Cicero. The term had an original meaning of mask, which functioned as a portrayal or reflection of a particular identity. With the influence of several factors, *persona* expanded in meaning and was often used to represent the social identity of the individual. Anthony Long, in his study of the concept of the person, aptly states, 'Persona is not primarily what a human being is, but rather a role or status a human being has or maintains or undertakes or bears or assumes...'[33]

2.2.2.2 Πρόσωπον

The Greek word πρόσωπον is commonly identified as the equivalent to the Latin word *persona*. Interestingly, Greek lexicons also reveal a wide range of meanings:[34] (1) face, countenance: in front, facing; in person; (2) one's look, countenance; (3) a mask: dramatic part, character; (4) person: legal personality ['standing, social position'];[35] (5) a feature of a person. Even though πρόσωπον displays some similarities to *persona* in its range of meanings, its etymology is not as difficult to ascertain as that of *persona*.[36] The earliest identifiable meaning is found in Homer, which refers to the 'face' – for example, 'the old woman hid her face (πρόσωπα) in her hands'

---

[30] Cf. Mauss, 'L'esprit humain', 274.

[31] Another later influence on the meaning of the term was the early church debates over Christian dogma, especially concerning the person of Christ. See e.g. Tertullian, *Adv. Prax.* 7.11–12; Boethius, *Contra Eutychen* 3.4–5.

[32] Mauss, 'L'esprit humain', 274.

[33] Long, 'Persons', 13.

[34] The list of meanings are selected from Liddell, Scott, & Jones, *A Greek-English Lexicon*, ad loc; Bauer & Danker, *A Greek-English Lexicon*, ad loc.

[35] Interestingly, the *LSJ Supplement* replaces the legal meaning with a meaning of social standing which is relevant for this study's interest in social identity. The legal sense, nevertheless, will be established below.

[36] Nédoncelle, 'Prosopon', 293, does not see a common root for both *persona* and πρόσωπον, nor does he believe that the former derived from the latter.

(*Od.* 19.361). Aristotle also gives a definition for the term, 'The part below the skull is named the πρόσωπον' (*Hist. an.* 1.8.491b.9).[37]

Developing from this original meaning of 'face', the term was also used in reference to the theatrical mask, τὰ τραγικὰ πρόσωπα (Aristotle, *Protr.* 31.7.958a.17),[38] which gave the term a sense of the surface or *façade* of the individual. The word πρόσωπον was consequently used interchangeably with the Greek word for a theatrical mask, προσωπεῖον. Conversely, the term προσωπεῖον was used in reference not only to the mask, but also to the social role of an individual. Josephus, for instance, recounts Antipater's scheme of assuming the role (προσωπεῖον) of a devoted brother to Herod (*BJ* 1.471). Like the case of *persona*, this meaning was a natural development, since a mask is basically a representation of a person being portrayed, and could function as a synecdoche for the whole person.[39] In addition, there was a strong Latin influence on the term.[40] By the imperial period πρόσωπον took on similar meanings to the Latin *persona*, especially the meaning of a social role in life which also developed from the meaning of a theatrical mask.[41] Mauss observes that πρόσωπον did have the same meaning as 'mask', but similarly signified 'le personnage que chacun est et veut être, son caractère...la véritable face'.[42] Nédoncelle also elucidates that the term emerged into a meaning which represented the social being: 'nous sommes à la fois au théâtre et dans la vie. Le mot, peu à peu, deviendra synonyme de personnalité sociale et finalement d'individu ou de personne en général'.[43]

Comparable to *persona*, the meaning of πρόσωπον was also influenced by Roman law.[44] In addition, Mauss suggests that Late Stoicism with its personal ethics had enriched not only Roman law but also the meaning of the person.[45] With their contribution of personal ethics, the Stoics helped to shape the ethical duties and virtues of one's social identity. For example, Epictetus uses the theatrical sense of πρόσωπον to show how God has assigned an individual a certain social role (πρόσωπον) in life to play out well

---

[37] See Lohse, 'πρόσωπον', 769, for more references.

[38] For the meaning of mask, see Nédoncelle, 'Prosopon', 279–81; Schlossmann, *Persona*, 37. See also Lohse, 'πρόσωπον', 769–70, for more references.

[39] Cf. Schlossmann, *Persona*, 35–8.

[40] See Nédoncelle, 'Prosopon', 282.

[41] Schlossmann, *Persona*, 42.

[42] Mauss, 'L'esprit humain', 277.

[43] Nédoncelle, 'Prosopon', 281.

[44] See Schlossmann, *Persona*, 50–62, for πρόσωπον in legal sources. Also, like *persona*, the christological and trinitarian debates of the early church also influenced the later meaning of the term. See Lohse, 'πρόσωπον', 778–9; Schlossmann, *Persona*, 73–88.

[45] Cf. Mauss, 'L'esprit humain', 277; Long, 'Persons', 14–15. On the Stoics' concept of the person and its moral development, see Gill, 'Human Being', 137–61; Engberg-Pedersen, 'Stoic Concept', 109–35.

(*Ench.* 17). Moreover, Cicero presents the four-*personae* theory (*Off.* 1.107–21), which is an ethical treatise on the various *personae* of an individual that is believed to be based on the theory of the Greek philosopher, Panaetius, and his understanding of the πρόσωπα (cf. Epictetus, *Diss.* 1.2).[46] Cicero's theory not only identifies a correlation between *persona* and πρόσωπον, but also describes the four various types of *personae*/πρόσωπα that an individual has, which is significant for social identity.

Other important sources to survey for their usage of πρόσωπον are the New Testament and Jewish writings – including the LXX and the later Jewish writers, such as Philo. It is important to bear in mind that these writings were produced in the context of the Graeco-Roman world, which would have possibly influenced the writers' understanding and employment of the word. In the LXX, πρόσωπον is predominantly used to translate the Hebrew term פָּנִים ('face'), which is theologically significant in regard to God's countenance – for example, 'the Lord lift up his πρόσωπον upon you, and give you peace' (Num 6.26).[47] The term was also used as a synecdoche for the individual and as a reference to the features or appearance of the individual, which would have implications of social identity. In Sirach 19.29, for instance, πρόσωπον is used to signify the perception of a person by initial meeting and sight. Interestingly, the following verse states that 'a man's attire and hearty laughter, and the way he walks, show what he is' (19.30). Also, in Sirach 10.5 the πρόσωπον of an individual is qualified by a social position: προσώπῳ γραμματέως. Moreover, in 2 Macc 6.18 the term appears to be referring to Eleazar's social position: 'Eleazar, one of the scribes in high position, a man now advanced in age and of a noble πρόσωπον (τὴν πρόσοψιν τοῦ προσώπου κάλλιστος), was being forced to open his mouth to eat swine's flesh'.

Philo, the Hellenised Jew from Alexandria, has an important discussion of πρόσωπον in his *Legum allegoriae*. He employs allegorical exegesis in an examination of humanity and the significance of the number seven: 'And the πρόσωπον, the living creature's noblest part, is pierced by seven apertures...' (1.12). While discussing God's creation of man, Philo ponders why God had formed man and breathed εἰς τὸ πρόσωπον (1.33). He elucidates that the πρόσωπον functions as a synecdoche for the whole body: 'for this part of the body is beyond other parts endowed with the soul...As the πρόσωπον is the dominant element in the body' (1.39). Elsewhere, he uses πρόσωπον to refer to the social identity of various individuals. For instance, in his treatise *De posteritate Caini*, he elaborates how there is appropriate speech for particular individuals:

---

[46] See Gill, 'Personhood', 175, 187–90, for Panaetius and Cicero's theories.

[47] See Lohse, 'πρόσωπον', 771–4, for a good survey of πρόσωπον in the LXX.

For we have to talk in one way to an old man, in another to a young one, and again in one way to a man of importance and in another to an insignificant person, and so with rich and poor, official and nonofficial, servant and master, woman and man, skilled and unskilled. What need to make a list of innumerable sorts of πρόσωπα, in our conversation with whom our talk varies, taking one shape at one time, another at another?[48]

Here Philo lists a variety of social persons, and their physical features and attributes of social identity.

The New Testament corpus also has instances where the term appears to convey a sense of social identity – a meaning that has been often overlooked by New Testament scholars.[49] Significantly, Paul has some significant uses of πρόσωπον. For example in 2 Cor 5.12 he writes, ἵνα ἔχητε πρὸς τοὺς ἐν προσώπῳ καυχωμένους καὶ μὴ ἐν καρδίᾳ, and in 2 Cor 10.7 he writes, τὰ κατὰ πρόσωπον βλέπετε.[50] In addition to πρόσωπον, there are also cognates of πρόσωπον that occur in the New Testament. In Gal 6.12, for instance, Paul uses εὐπροσωπέω to refer to a particular social marker and identity, which in this case is circumcision and Jewish identity: 'It is those who want to make a good showing (εὐπροσωπῆσαι) in the flesh that try to compel you to be circumcised – only that they may not be persecuted for the cross of Christ'. Also, there is the set of Greek expressions found in the Septuagint and New Testament that builds upon the term πρόσωπον, for example λαμβάνειν πρόσωπον, which is probably a translation of the Hebrew phrase נשא פנים, an expression of showing partiality.[51] Despite its Hebrew origin, the Greek expression was used to denote aspects of identity in social relations. For example, in Gal 2.6 Paul addresses the problem of partiality being given to the social position of certain leaders by stating that πρόσωπον [ὁ] θεὸς ἀνθρώπου οὐ λαμβάνει. There are additional terms that are derived from the phrase λαμβάνειν πρόσωπον, such as προσωπολημψία.[52] Dorothy Emmet explains that προσωπολημψία is employed in the New Testament 'in the sense of looking snobbishly at the special status and not through it at the human being'.[53] This preferential treatment is clearly seen in Jas 2.1–5, where the Christians are admonished not to show favouritism (προσωπολημψίαις) towards individuals with a high social standing. These New Testament texts, which reveal social

---

[48] 109–10.

[49] For more on NT usage, see Lohse, 'πρόσωπον', 775–9.

[50] The NT texts listed here will be examined in greater detail in Chapters Five and Six.

[51] See Lohse, 'πρόσωπον', 779–80. Cf. Gen 32.21; Deut 1.17; 10.17; 2 Chron 19.7. Lohse explains the meaning of this expression, along with other similar ones: 'They are to be explained in terms of the respectful oriental greeting in which one humbly turns one's face to the ground or sinks to the earth. If the person greeted thus raises the face of the man, this is a sign of recognition and esteem' (779).

[52] See Lohse, 'πρόσωπον', 779–80.

[53] Emmet, *Roles*, 180.

description of Christians in the Graeco-Roman world, do show the term πρόσωπον used in reference to features of social identity.

This section has shown that the Greek word πρόσωπον did have a sense of social identity in the writings of the Graeco-Roman world. This nuance developed from its earlier meanings of 'face' and 'mask', whereby πρόσωπον was used to express a role played in a theatrical setting. Eventually the term was commonly used to refer to a person's social role in life, thus giving the term a synecdochical function of expressing the person and his or her social identity.

2.2.2.3 The Correlation Between Persona and Πρόσωπον

Having identified a particular meaning of 'social identity' for the terms *persona* and πρόσωπον, one further issue to clarify is the relationship between the two terms. Six points will be listed here that suggest a correlation between *persona* and πρόσωπον. First and foremost, there has been no contention made against the consensus that both terms are equivalent to each other. Secondly, the comparison of the lexical entries of *persona* and πρόσωπον indicated some similarities in both their wide semantic ranges. Thirdly, they both have a similar developed meaning from 'mask' to a representation of one's social role in life. Fourthly, Cicero's presentation of the four-*personae* theory is understood to be influenced by Panaetius' theory of the πρόσωπα (cf. Epictetus, *Diss.* 1.2).[54] Fifthly, the rhetorical technique of προσωποποιία ('speech-in-character'; *fictio personae*) is associated with *persona*/πρόσωπον, whereby the speaker takes up a 'rhetorical *persona*' by speaking in the *persona* of another individual (Quintilian, *Inst.* 3.8.49–54; 9.2.29–37; cf. 1.7.3). Finally, the Vulgate has instances where *persona* is used to translate πρόσωπον (e.g. Acts 10.34; Rom 2.11; Gal 2.6; Jas 2.9; Jude 16.).[55] Given the evidence, it is correct to observe a correlation between *persona* and πρόσωπον, and their equivalent meaning of 'social identity' in the Graeco-Roman social world. Importantly, this section has underscored this particular meaning of πρόσωπον that has been virtually ignored by New Testament scholars.

---

[54] Gill, 'Personhood', 175, 187–90. Also, in Epictetus' discourse concerning πρόσωπον (1.2), he exhibits parallels to Cicero's four-*personae* theory.

[55] See Nédoncelle, 'Prosopon', 282. Also, it is worth noting Boethius' assertion, 'et πρόσωπον, id est persona' (*Contra Eutychen* 3.81).

2.3 The Roman Stress on *Persona*

Building on the foundation of *persona*/πρόσωπον[56] as a term that could refer to one's social identity, the intention of this section is to qualify that particular meaning further within the first-century context of the Roman empire. One could argue that the social concept of *persona* can be observed differently in various settings – such as Roman, Greek, or Jewish. In fact, this study demonstrates that there were many shades of *persona* (i.e. *personae*) in the Graeco-Roman world. Although this study recognises this possible diversity,[57] the primary focus is on the Roman stress on *persona*, especially since the dominant social, cultural, and political force in the Graeco-Roman world is Roman. As will be seen, the Roman social hierarchy and Roman law fossilised a certain conception of *persona* in the Roman social world. Also, it should be emphasised that the above analysis of *persona* and πρόσωπον did consider in part the terms' meaning of social identity in their Roman context. The aim here, then, is to demonstrate the existence and general contours of the Roman stress on *persona* in the Roman world – especially as a traditional and elite ideal.

Michael Carrithers describes the 'Roman version of the *personne*, the *persona*', as follows: 'The Roman *persona* was such, a matter of functions, honours, duties, and rights, precisely by virtue of being a citizen of a concretely conceived political group, a collectivity'.[58] Despite this helpful description, a difficulty in attempting to conceptualise the concept of social *persona* is that there is no explication of *persona* in the extant source material of the early imperial period. In order to describe further this social concept, this study will construct somewhat of a 'heuristic fiction' of the concept of *persona* and the Roman emphasis on it.[59] That is, the copious instances from ancient sources that use *persona*/πρόσωπον in the sense of social identity within a Roman context will be collated in order to glean a description of *persona*, which will be used to redescribe the social reality of *persona*. In addition, it should be pointed out that the description of social *persona* in this

---

[56] Having established a correlation of both terms, the remainder of the study will use either *persona*, πρόσωπον, or *persona*/πρόσωπον to refer to the same meaning of social identity, unless noted otherwise.

[57] In particular, the following chapters on Paul and Epictetus will highlight some diversity in the concept of *persona* in the Roman Greek East, but will still accentuate the Roman stress on *persona*.

[58] Carrithers, 'Alternative', 250.

[59] Ricoeur, *Interpretation Theory*, 67, uses the construction of a heuristic fiction to help explain the concept of a metaphor, with which there is a 'redescription that occurs through the transference of this fiction to reality'. However, the use of the label 'heuristic fiction' for this study does not imply that the social concept of *persona* was fictional.

section will be a generalisation and not a comprehensive understanding of *persona*.

An appropriate source to begin exploring the Roman stress on social *persona* is Cicero's 'four-*personae*' theory (1.107–21),[60] which is found in *De officiis*, a work explaining the appropriate duties of individuals. Cicero begins his philosophical treatise on *persona* by expounding on the first two *personae* that Nature has allotted. The first *persona* is universal in that all humanity has the capacity to reason, which makes humans more superior than other creatures. This *persona* is the source of 'morality' and 'propriety', and is where man can ascertain his 'duty' (1.107). The second *persona* is assigned to particular individuals, such as physical endowments, personal gifts, and talents (1.107–14). Cicero advises that one should live consistent to the given traits and not imitate or take on others' traits (1.110–14). He then continues with the other two *personae* (1.115–21). The third *persona* is based on circumstances and chance, and consists of social positions such as 'regal powers and military commands, nobility of birth and political office, wealth and influence' (1.115), which are all significant for knowing one's social standing. The fourth *persona* is sustained by one's free choice in matters such as career, whereby some engage in philosophy, others in civil law, and others in oratory (1.115). Cicero further elucidates this *persona* by giving examples of individuals who exemplified it through their choice of career or 'calling in life' (1.116–21). Although he refers to a philosophical understanding of one's *personae*, with all the various references to social roles throughout this text, an individual's social *persona* is recognised, in many regards, to be associated with rank and status in Roman society.

After his discussion of the four *personae,* Cicero discusses social roles (1.122–5), which are key components of the Roman conception of *persona*. Cicero, for example, discusses the 'duties of the magistrates, of private individuals[, of native citizens,] and of foreigners' (1.124–5). For the magistrate, as the leader of the state, he is to uphold the state's honour and dignity, and to maintain law and justice. Concerning the private individual's duty in regard to the state, he is to labour for her peace and honour, which results in him being esteemed and called a 'good citizen'.[61] For the foreigner, however, he is to mind his own business and not be involved in politics. Consequently, Cicero concludes that 'we shall have a fairly clear view of our duties when the question arises what is proper and what is appropriate to each *persona*, circumstance, and age' (1.125.5). In this text, an individual's social

---

[60] For more on this theory, see Gill, 'Personhood', 166–99; Dyck, *De Officiis*, 269–95.

[61] Cf. *Off.* 3.43.10, where Cicero explains the importance of one's friendship, except when it conflicts with duty to one's country. He further writes that in a situation of being a judge in a friend's case, one has to lay aside the *persona* of a friend when he assumes that of a judge.

duties are determined by his or her social status – a magistrate, private individual, or foreigner.

Elsewhere, Cicero lists various orators and describes their social status. He discusses Lucius Paullus who 'sustained easily by his eloquence the *persona* of first citizen (*personam principis civis*)' (*Brut.* 80.2). The epithet of first citizen (or 'leading citizen') that qualifies his social identity shows another instance where the term *persona* is associated with a person's social status in Roman society. This meaning can also be found in Cicero's *De haruspicum responso*, where he addresses the Senate: 'not that it lay beyond my duty or my power to sustain my present *persona* or character, honoured as I have been with the offices which are at the bestowal of the Roman people, and with many distinctions conferred by you' (61.11). Here Cicero is drawing attention to his social *persona* – the offices and distinctions which he received in Roman society.

The Roman historian, Suetonius, also associates *persona* with Roman rank and status. In his work on Julius Caesar, he mentions the emperor's enforcement of a certain dress code: 'he denied the use of litters and the wearing of scarlet robes or pearls to all except those of designated *personae* and age, and on set days' (*Iul.* 43.1.7) This text reveals that an individual's dress is a social indicator of the rank and status of his or her *persona*, and serves to delineate the various statuses in the Roman social spectrum. Suetonius also discusses Tiberius' interactions with many people of high rank and status, and describes him as one who 'showed equal modesty towards those with *personae* of lower rank' (*Tib.* 32.2.1). Additionally, in his work on grammarians, Suetonius describes the *persona* of Marcus Valerius Probus as one who had a few followers and 'never taught in such a way as to assume the *persona* of a master (*magistri personam*)' (*Gram.* 24.4.3).

Plutarch also demonstrates this association of πρόσωπον with a social identity by using the theatrical meaning behind the social concept. Plutarch recounts a time when Phocion pleaded to Antipater and had 'tried to conceal his power under the πρόσωπον of a common man of mean attire and simple mode of life' (*Phoc.* 29.3.3). Antipater, having a significantly high rank and status, attempted to take on a different πρόσωπον by pretending to be a common person – an individual of no significant rank and status. Plutarch also mentions a certain Timocleia, who made a daring move in killing a Macedonian. Upon hearing this, the Macedonians arrested her and brought her to the king, but the king 'seeing in the composure of her πρόσωπον and her unhurried step an indication of high rank and noble blood, questioned her as to who she was among the women' (*Mor.* 260C). Significantly, the king was able to glance at Timocleia and determine that she had a certain high rank and status.

This sampling of texts helps not only to substantiate further the understanding of *persona*/πρόσωπον as 'social identity', but also to show specifically the term's relationship to the Roman social distinctions of rank and status. This association between *persona* and the features of rank and status in Roman society can be explained by two major factors – the Roman social hierarchy and Roman law. It is these two factors that clearly show the Roman emphasis on social *persona*.

2.3.1 *The Roman Social Hierarchy and Social* Persona

The Roman social hierarchy was a significant feature of Roman society. With its orderly stratification of rank and status, the social hierarchy delineated one's social identity in Roman society. E.A. Judge defines rank and status as follows:

> 'Rank' is meant to denote any formally defined position in society, while 'status' refers to positions of influence that may not correspond to the official pattern of the social order. Status tends to convert itself into rank, and rank is the fossilised status of the past, defending itself against the aspirations of those who have only status, often newly acquired.[62]

Roman society functioned on a hierarchy of ranks (*ordines*), and the social stratification throughout Roman society evolved around a system of inequality – an unequal distribution of scarce values, goods, power, and prestige.[63] This social structuring around inequality can be observed in the expressions that reveal the dichotomy of a bifurcated society, with one group controlling the social and economic resources: such as elite/non-elite, rich/poor, freed/slave, *honestiores*/*humiliores*.[64] It is important to bear in mind that this system of inequality benefited and protected the minority group of the elite, which suggests that social *persona* was essentially an elite concept that was used to promote the elite ideals and virtues of being a Roman.

For this study, a suitable place to begin a survey of the Roman social hierarchy is with Augustus' social and moral reforms, which restored the traditional and ideal values of Roman rank and provided sharper distinctions between them.[65] Through his reforms, the senatorial order in the imperial

---

[62] Judge, *Rank and Status*, 9.

[63] For an overview of this, see Hellerman, *Reconstructing*, 3–5; Garnsey & Saller, *Roman Empire*, 109–12. There have been socio-economic studies of the Roman social hierarchy that have explained Roman society as an agrarian society, which displays the highest degree of inequality.

[64] On this social demarcation, see Hellerman, *Reconstructing*, 6–9. Regarding the legal classification of *humiliores*/*honestiores*, see Garnsey, *Social Status*, 222, who suggests that the understanding of *persona* should be supplied with it.

[65] On the importance of Augustus and his social reform, see Garnsey & Saller, *Roman Empire*, 107–25; Nicolet, 'Augustus', 89–128.

period remained the most prestigious of the elite social categories, consisting of several hundred families that were perceived to be worthy by traditional standards of birth, wealth, virtues, and moral excellence.[66] Augustus restored the elite honour of the senators by fixing a higher qualification of money to the senatorial order and implementing legislation that maintained the moral excellence and virtues of the senators, such as prohibiting the marriage of senators to freedwomen and performance in public spectacles.[67] The equestrian order was the second tier of the aristocratic ranks, which had similar, but lower, requirements for membership than the senatorial order: noble birth, wealth, and moral excellence. This group was much larger than the senatorial group, consisting of thousands of members. The third tier of the elite orders consisted of the decurions or councillors of the towns across the Roman empire. Membership of this group also required the possession of noble birth, wealth, and moral worth, but the requirements were lower than members of the equestrian order. Below the three aristocratic orders of the Roman social hierarchy were the mass of the population: the humble free, and below them were the slaves. Also, among the free individuals of the Roman world, there were distinctions of freeborn and freedman, and citizen and non-citizen.[68]

Within the upper and lower strata of Roman society, there existed further stratification and distinctions according to social status.[69] The need to grade and identify status occurred within the smallest categories of individuals, which helped to distinguish those individuals with honour from those without honour. For instance, even the gladiators of the arena, who were associated with *infamia* ('ill repute'), had their own ranking system based on experience and talent.[70] Thus, there was an 'ubiquitous tendency in the Roman world to divide and subdivide into groups and subgroups, in order to clearly define the social pecking order'.[71]

Status, in addition, challenged the ordering of rank and provided social mobility for many individuals. One particular group that reflected this fluidity of status was the Roman freedmen.[72] Through their experience as slaves, these freedmen could have been well-trained, accumulated great wealth, and achieved greater social status – and in some cases, they could have gained even greater social standing than the humble freeborn.[73] Nevertheless, since

---

[66] Garnsey & Saller, *Roman Empire*, 112.

[67] Garnsey & Saller, *Roman Empire*, 113.

[68] For Roman citizenship, see the classic study by Sherwin-White, *Roman Citizenship*.

[69] Garnsey & Saller, *Roman Empire*, 118–23.

[70] See Edmondson, 'Dynamic Arenas', 95–6.

[71] Hellerman, *Reconstructing*, 11.

[72] For more on the Roman freedmen, see Duff, *Freedmen*.

[73] See Saller, 'Status', 831, 834–5; Garnsey & Saller, *Roman Empire*, 124–5.

the system of rank and status served the Roman elite, the freedmen's servile origins would have socially stigmatised them regardless of their achieved honour.[74] Pliny the Younger, for instance, expresses his indignation at a monument of Pallas, who was one of Claudius' influential freedmen. The monument describes how the Senate rewarded him for his fidelity and affection to his patrons with the insignia of a praetor and also a great amount of money, but he was contented with accepting only the honour. Pliny reviles:

> I was forcibly reminded by this inscription, how farcical and ridiculous are those honours, which are thus sometimes thrown away upon dirt and infamy; which such a rascal in short, had the assurance both to accept and to refuse, and then set himself forth to posterity as an example of moderation![75]

This brief overview of the Roman social hierarchy has depicted a society that carefully graded and distinguished all individuals by rank and status. In fact, Meyer Reinhold intimates that 'Roman society evolved into one of the most hierarchic and status-conscious social orders in mankind's history'.[76] It is this social ordering that caused the whole populace to become aware and conscious of the Roman values of identity, and of their own place in the social ladder. This is especially true since certain privileges and honours were linked according to the various ranks and status. Given the ability and motivation for social mobility, there was a need to recognise and assess one's social *persona* in light of others'.

2.3.2 *Roman Law and Social* Persona

It was observed above that the establishment of inequalities was fundamental for Roman social stratification. Peter Garnsey and Richard Saller explain, 'Inequalities, deriving from uneven property distribution that was confirmed or accentuated by imperial policies, were underpinned by Roman law'.[77] Roman law provided the stipulations and criteria for the ordering of rank and status, which gave individuals an understanding of their social identity and legal privileges. In his seminal study, *Social Status and Legal Privilege in the Roman Empire*, Garnsey conveys the significance of *persona* by assessing that since legal discrimination and privilege were usually determined by one's *persona*, 'The notion of *persona*, then, is primary'.[78]

The significance and consequences of one's legal *persona* are demonstrated in some fragments found in Herculaneum in the dossier of a legal case that took place in 75 CE between two women: Calatoria Themis

---

[74] For the social stigma of slavery, see Jones, '*Stigma*', 147–8.
[75] *Ep.* 7.29.
[76] Reinhold, 'Usurpation', 275.
[77] Garnsey & Saller, *Roman Empire*, 110.
[78] Garnsey, *Social Status*, 222.

and Petronia Iusta.[79] The dispute is over the legal status of Petronia, who claimed she was born after her mother's manumission from Calatoria, which would make her freeborn rather than a freedwoman; Calatoria, on the other hand, claims that Petronia is her freedwoman. Since both parties could not produce any documentation supporting their claims, they sought witnesses for *testimonia*. For Petronia, the difference between having the legal status of freeborn or freedwoman would have critical consequences for her future life in Roman society.

In his influential study, *Law and Life of Rome*, John Crook has drawn attention to the overlooked and misused legal sources as critical source material for information about life in Roman society.[80] He explains that Roman law was enmeshed in society, and the Romans lived within this complex socio-legal environment – even while unconscious of most of these laws.[81] It is important to recognise that although Roman law has a primary prescriptive function, it can be used as a social commentary. Keith Hopwood observes:

...the laws themselves are an important historical source for the ideology of their time and the compromises legislators were forced to make with customs and established interest groups to ensure that the laws were enforceable: legal history becomes general history, and general history is richer if it takes legal history into account. The laws passed are an invaluable source for the ideology of their period: they may or may not tell us what people were doing; instead, they tell us what the ruling groups wanted people to be doing and what they wanted them not to do.[82]

Since Roman law shaped and under-girded Roman society, historians should recognise the relationship of law and life in the Roman world. Accordingly, Roman law should not be treated as existing in a social vacuum, but as deriving from and reflecting its social environment. The majority of the source material for Roman society, then, should be regarded as reflecting a world where public and private life was intertwined with legal concepts and understandings. Consideration will now be given to two basic types of sources for their description of Roman law and explanation of *persona*: the Roman literary sources and Roman legal sources.

---

[79] *Tab. Herc.* XIII–XXX. See Crook, *Law and Life*, 48–50; Gardner, 'Proofs', 1; Lintott, 'Freedman', 555–65.

[80] Crook, *Law and Life*, esp. 7–35. Almost three decades later idem, 'Legal History', 31–6, still comments on the improper use of Roman law by general historians. For positive studies of the integration of Roman law and society, see McKechnie, *Thinking*; Aubert & Sirks, *Speculum Iuris*.

[81] Crook, *Law and Life*, 7–8.

[82] Hopwood, 'Violent Crime', 65. Cf. Crook, 'Legal History', 34.

2.3.2.1 Roman Literary Sources

Whether the Roman literary sources were written by historians, orators, philosophers, poets, satirists, or philosophers, they inevitably reflect legal concepts in their portrayal of everyday life, and also express 'mere legal allusions', for all of which a knowledge of law was required to elucidate them.[83] The Roman literary works are, then, an excellent source to find concepts and descriptors of the socio-legal realities of Roman society. It will suffice here to give only a few examples in the literary sources of the legal overtones of social identity.

In *De inventione rhetorica*, Cicero's handbook on the composition of arguments, he remarks, 'Inferences may be drawn from the *persona* of the accused if the attributes of the *personae* are carefully taken into account' (2.28.7). Quintilian also indicates the importance of the attributes of an individual's social identity in a legal context: 'The *persona* of the adviser also makes a lot of difference. If his illustrious past, his noble family, his age, or his fortune raises expectations, we must take care that what is said is not out of keeping with the man who says it' (*Inst.* 3.8.48). *Persona* here, again, is related to the various social distinctions one has in society. Moreover, as will be seen below, the legal aspects of one's social identity has major implications for the outcome of legal proceedings, since those with an elite *persona* received greater privileges, such as undeserved acquittals or less severe punishments.

As a Roman lawyer, Pliny the Younger would often have used the legal meaning of *persona*. He recounts a particular speech given in court: 'Tis my plea on behalf of Accia Variola, noteworthy from the high rank of *persona* (*dignitate personae*) concerned...For here was a high-born lady, wife to a man of Praetorian rank...' (*Ep.* 6.33.8). Appropriately, the *persona* here is qualified by her high rank, which is established from her birth and husband's rank. Also, in a letter to Maximus, Pliny discusses a case he has to take up before the court and the difficulties involved, one of which was the issue concerning the rank of *personae* (*personarum claritate*) (*Ep.* 2.14; cf. 1.23.5). Although the term *persona* seems tantamount to 'person' in these texts, the contexts do indicate that the term is concerned with one's social rank and status.

---

[83] See Crook, *Law and Life*, 18.

2.3.2.2 Roman Legal Sources

One of the oldest known sources of Roman law is the *Twelve Tables* (450 BCE).[84] In addition, there is plenty of known legal material from the later Republic and imperial periods that existed in various forms – such as edicts of the praetors, statutes, constitutions by the emperors, and public opinion.[85] A major legal source is Gaius' *Institutes* (c. 160 CE), which was a handbook used to introduce Roman law. Later on, the works of the Roman jurists became popular, such as those by Ulpian and Paulus. Consequently, in about 530 CE Justinian's codification of Roman laws, which were from the works of the jurists of the mid-first century BCE to the third century CE, resulted in two significant Roman legal sources: the *Institutes* and *Digest*.[86]

A formal legal meaning of *persona* is clearly found in Gaius' *Institutes*, a second-century CE handbook on Roman law: 'All our law is about *personae*, things or actions' (*Inst.* 1.3.8).[87] From the major legal works, such as Gaius' *Institutes*, classicists have often demonstrated the legal identity and privileges of all individuals living in Roman society.[88] For some scholars, however, the later dating of the legal material poses a major obstacle for recognising the legal concept in first-century Roman society. Eduard Lohse, for instance, in his study of the Greek πρόσωπον word group, rejects the existence of its legal sense in the New Testament era.[89] Thus, the aim here is to make an argument for the validity of the legal understanding of *persona* within the first-century Roman world.

Archaeological discoveries, like the legal waxed tablets from Pompeii and Herculaneum, have added more verity to the later legal sources' relevance for earlier social contexts. Through these findings, Crook has demonstrated how

---

[84] For the importance of this legal source for Roman society, see Cicero, *De or.* 1.195–7; Livy 3.34.6.

[85] For a good overview of the various extant legal sources, some of which are often overlooked and neglected by historians, see Johnston, *Roman Law*, 1–24; Crook, *Law and Life*, 18–35. Crook, 'Legal History', 34, advises that 'the general historian needs to take into account that the law is never the only, and is often not the most significant, factor in the nature of society: "unwritten law", custom public opinion can be at least as, or even much more, determinant, and the general historian must not isolate or privilege the law as a factor'.

[86] Although some of these laws were adopted from much earlier sources, the majority of the sources are from the late classical jurists.

[87] The legal *persona* is often understood in the technical sense of 'legal personality', which is a specialised term of jurisprudence. See Duff, *Personality*, 1–25, for 'legal personality' in Roman law. He defines the 'legal person' as the one who has 'the capacity for legal rights and duties' (1). He also discusses the Latin term *caput* and its relationship to this legal concept.

[88] See e.g. the studies by Crook, *Law and Life*; Garnsey, *Social Status*; idem, 'Legal Privilege'; Garnsey & Saller, *Roman Empire*; Treggiari, 'Social Status'; Saller, 'Status'.

[89] Lohse, 'πρόσωπον', 770.

certain legal concepts, which were only known previously in later legal sources, did exist in the first century.[90] He reflects:

[These examples] help to show that many, at least, of the complications of Roman law were not just professional 'overkill'; by and large, the whole system, as we learn of it, was a living and practised one and – this is the important point for the general historian – can therefore be used to illustrate Roman society.[91]

There are additional reasons for the validity of using these 'later' legal sources, particularly Gaius' treatment of *persona*, to illuminate the first-century Roman world. Will Deming has recently argued that an early conception of Gaius' 'law of *personae*' (*ius personarum*) can be found earlier in Paul's letter to the Romans.[92] Although Deming presents only a plausible case for the 'law of *personae*' as the legal backdrop for ὁ νόμος τοῦ ἀνθρώπου in 7.1, he does provide convincing arguments for understanding the *ius personarum* as a developing legal concept which existed prior to the mid-second century. For instance, Gaius does not explain the term *persona*, which allows the possibility that the idea of a legal *persona* was already conceptualised. By showing the diversity within Gaius' work, Deming concludes, along with other scholars, that the *ius personarum* brings together 'various patterns of conceptualization that go back prior to the *Institutes*'.[93] It is, moreover, quite tenuous to imagine Gaius as innovating these laws in a social vacuum, rather than deriving them from existing legal concepts that were already conceptualised in Roman society. Along with the evidence seen above of the legal connotation of *persona* in the first-century literary sources, the reasons presented here suggest that Gaius' presentation of *persona* offers some reflection of the legal realities of *persona* that were, at least, conceptualised in the first-century Roman social milieu.[94]

In section three of Gaius' first book of his *Institutes*, he provides a succinct classification of the various legal statuses of people (male and female):

All our law is about *personae*, things or actions. We turn first to *personae*. The main classification in the law of *personae* (*iure personarum*) is this: all men are either free or slaves. Again, among free men, some are free-born while others are freed. Free-born are those who were born free; freedmen, those who have been manumitted from lawful slavery. Again there are three classes of freedmen; for they are either Roman citizens, or Latins or in the

---

[90] Crook, 'Legal History', 34. See idem, 'Working Notes', 229–39, and Cloud, 'Pompeiian Tablets', 231–46, for some interactions with the Pompeiian tablets and their significance for Roman law and society.

[91] Crook, 'Legal History', 34.

[92] Deming, 'Paul, Gaius', 218–21, for his argument.

[93] Deming, 'Paul, Gaius', 219.

[94] Deming, 'Paul, Gaius', 227–9, also intimates that Paul was aware of the 'law of persons' from his experiences in Corinth. If this is true then it would have implications for the existence of the concept of *persona* in the Corinthian correspondence (see Chapter Five).

category of capitulated aliens. Let us examine each of these in turn, beginning with capitulated aliens.[95]

Throughout this section on *persona*, Gaius discusses the legalities of the various social distinctions of *personae*, which provides the legal foundation for the Roman social stratification of rank and status. Deming reflects on Gaius' law, 'As several scholars have remarked, under *ius personarum* Gaius understands not rights and duties of persons, but the rules governing how a person attains and loses various positions of status in Roman society'.[96] By understanding the 'law of *personae*' as essentially a treatment of the 'law of status', the concept of *persona* can be understood to be largely dependent on social status.

Another legal source that sheds light on the concept of social *persona* and the relationship of Roman law and society is the *senatus consultum de Cn. Pisone patre*.[97] This large bronze tablet reports the Senate's decisions in 20 CE regarding the trial of Cn. Calpurnius Piso and his associates, who were all blamed for the death of Tiberius' adopted son, Germanicus.[98] Among the many significant details in this legal inscription, there are a couple of relevant features worth pointing out for illumination on the Roman stress on *persona*. First, is the portrayal of the *personae* of the two parties involved in the supposed 'trial': Piso and the deceased Germanicus. For instance, Piso is described as a savage, while Germanicus is described as having remarkable forbearance and restraint (26–7). Being guilty, Gaius' *persona* is now affected through the social practice of *damnatio memoriae*, which is the process of expunging a person's existence from the memory of Roman society. Piso received six penalties for his punishment, which included: the prohibition of public mourning by members of his family (lines 73–5; cf. 76–82), the removal of any statues and images that are erected (75–6), the erasure of his name from the public inscriptions honouring Germanicus (82–4), and the confiscation and destruction of his property (84–108).[99] The punishments in this legal decree are aimed at publicly destroying the prestige and honour of Piso's elite *persona*.

---

[95] 1.3.8–12. Translation by Gordon & Robinson, *Institutes*, 23–5, with slight modifications. Gaius' text served as a foundation for Justinian's codification of his *Institutes* (1.2.12–1.3) and the *Digest* (1.5).

[96] Deming, 'Paul, Gaius', 226. Cf. Zulueta, *Institutes*, 23; Crook, *Law and Life*, 36; Zimmermann, *Obligations*, 25.

[97] See the entire first issue of *American Journal of Philology* 120 (1999), which is devoted to this inscription.

[98] This text is related to the *Tabula Siarensis*, which decrees the honours that Germanicus is to receive in commemoration of his death in 19 CE. The events leading up to the death of Germanicus are recounted in book 2 of Tacitus' *Annals*, and the trial of Piso is in book 3.

[99] See Bodel, 'Punishing Piso', 43–63, for more on Piso's punishment.

Secondly, the inscription is very significant in its demonstration of the widespread impact of Roman law for the vast Roman empire:

> That in order that the sequence of the entire transacted affair could more easily be handed down to the memory of future generations and they might know what the Senate had thought both about the exceptional restraint of Germanicus Caesar and about the crimes of the elder Cn. Piso, it was [the Senate's] pleasure that the speech our *princeps* read out and likewise these decisions of the Senate be set up, inscribed in bronze, in whatever place seemed best to Ti. Caesar Augustus; likewise [that] this decree of the Senate, inscribed in bronze, be affixed in the most frequented city of every province and in the most frequented place of that city...[100]

These lines from the senatorial decree are informative of the ubiquitous influence of Roman law throughout the Roman provinces. Like many legal decrees, this *senatus consultum* was inscribed on a bronze tablet, a material that accentuated the decree's sense of permanence and authority.[101] Furthermore, in order to propagate the condemnation of Piso, this legal material was to be erected in the most conspicuous place within the public sphere of Roman society. Assuming that other legislative material would have circulated in a similar fashion as this *senatus consultum*, the Roman populace would have been exposed to and aware of Roman law as they would have walked through the streets and encountered these legal declarations. As in Piso's case, the damnation of his social *persona* was determined and disseminated through the effective medium of Roman law.

In summary, Roman law permeated Roman society and was an integral part of its social structures. By examining the data of Roman law within the legal and non-legal sources, one can understand more about the social realities of life in the Roman world. Roman society was highly stratified through a system of rank and status, which was determined and maintained by Roman law. Roman law, then, affected one's social identity because it defined the legal status of everyone in society. The Roman populace was aware of the legal *persona* because of the privileges involved with Roman social stratification. That is, with opportunities for social mobility, individuals were conscious of the social hierarchy and its legal overtones, since the attainment of a higher social status meant greater privileges and prestige. The Roman social hierarchy and Roman law, then, shaped one's social identity in the Roman empire. Additionally, with greater privileges given to those with an elite *persona*, this concept of *persona* should be regarded as an elite ideal.

---

[100] 165–72. Translation from Potter & Damon, '*Senatus consultum*', 39, 41.

[101] Meyer, *Legitimacy*, 35: 'bronze tablets in particular conveyed a message of eternal existence and validity' (cf. 27). Pliny the Elder explains how bronze was used to secure the 'perpetuity of monuments, by means of bronze tablets on which records of official enactments are made' (*Nat.* 34.21.99). Meyer also cautions: 'This fact, however does not mean that its converse is true, that tablets not of bronze must therefore have been intended to be, and were seen as, "only" temporary or less authoritative' (35).

Therefore, the Roman hierarchy and Roman law promoted and protected the Roman traditional/ideal values and virtues of *persona*.

2.4 The Conventional Projection of *Persona*

Having delineated the Roman stress on *persona*, attention will now be given to the 'conventional' or 'typical' outworking of social identity – that is, how it was commonly projected – within the Roman social milieu in the early imperial period. The above section explored the concept of *persona* by collating certain instances of *persona*/πρόσωπον within a Roman context. This section will continue to discern the concept, but will not focus exclusively on the terms *persona* and πρόσωπον. Since this study is a social concept study rather than a lexical study, consideration will be given also to social descriptions that reflect the concept of social *persona* – such as honour, rank, and status.[102]

2.4.1 The Visual Expressions of Persona

Barton writes, 'For the Romans, being was being seen'.[103] Also, John Lendon explains the importance of social visibility for the Romans: 'No quality was honourable in and of itself. Honour was mediated through the perceptions of others, and even a superfluity of worthy qualities was of no use unless these qualities were publicly known, and approved by other aristocrats'.[104] Seneca accordingly reveals the common view that, 'In order to constitute renown, the agreement of many distinguished and praiseworthy men is necessary' (*Ep.* 102.8). With this necessity to fashion and display one's social *persona* for public approval, life in the Roman world was a grand spectacle, where individuals would parade their social identity before the gaze of others.[105] This idea of a visible *persona* is consistent with the term's original meaning of a theatrical 'mask', which denotes *persona* as 'the manifestation of one's being,

---

[102] There have been several studies that have focused on certain social features which have bearing on the Roman stress on *persona*. See e.g. those studies on Roman honour: Lendon, *Honour*; Barton, *Roman Honor*; Hellerman, *Reconstructing*.

[103] Barton, *Roman Honor*, 58.

[104] Lendon, *Honour*, 37. Cf. MacMullen, *Social Relations*, 62: 'What most magnified honor, however, was the degree to which city life was lived publicly, in the open. Thus, whatever one was or did, everyone knew at once'; Garnsey & Saller, *Roman Empire*, 118: 'A Roman's status was based on the social estimation of his honour, the perception of those around him as to his prestige'; Eck, 'Self-Representation' 129–67.

[105] Bergmann, 'Introduction', 9: 'Societies and people define themselves through spectacle'. See Bergmann & Kondoleon, *Ancient Spectacle*, for a collection of essays highlighting the various spectacles in Roman culture.

the thing presented to view, the spectacle, form, or aspect'.[106] Barton describes how social *persona* expresses itself visibly: 'One's face was one's *persona*, one's mask...The *persona* and the role expressed by it were the very boundary and definition of one's being, the *sine qua non* of existence. For the Romans there was no depth without surface'.[107]

In order to maintain the pedigree of the various ranks and statuses, there were a set of socially determined status symbols and behaviour that were appropriate to the various social distinctions of *persona*.[108] These self-displays of status and honour were visible ways of differentiating and assessing individuals, which maintained social order in the Roman world. Garnsey and Saller aptly comment on the impact of this visual differentiation:

Putting everyone in his proper place was a visual affirmation of the dominance of the imperial social structure, and one calculated to impress the bulk of the population of the empire...The impoverished may have resented this principle, even as public event after public event imprinted it in the communal consciousness.[109]

In fact, legal regulations were established in order to protect the moral excellence and prestige of certain elite ranks – such as the public expressions of privileged attire, special seating at public spectacles, and legal privileges. Beyond these expressions of privilege there were also social conventions that an individual could use to project vividly his or her social *persona* in public.

This section will explore several of these visual expressions of *persona* that caused life in Roman society to be a grand spectacle, where individuals 'observed and were observed'.[110] There are, however, four issues to address concerning this survey of the public expressions of social identity. First, scholars have expressed a certain degree of scepticism for using the extant source material because these sources were chiefly produced by members of the elite who could be biased and only portrayed the values of elite culture. However, by showing that there were common conventional expressions that

---

[106] Barton, *Roman Honor*, 56.

[107] Barton, *Roman Honor*, 57.

[108] The idea of behaviour that is consistent with a particular *persona* can be seen in: Plutarch's account of how Aristphanes should assign proper words to different πρόσωπα: 'to a king his dignity, to an orator his eloquence, to a woman her artlessness, to an ordinary man his prosaic speech, to a market-lounger his vulgarity' (*Vit.* 853D); and Philostratus' description of the sophist Antipater – 'like a brilliant tragic actor who has a thorough knowledge of his profession, his utterances were always in keeping with the Imperial πρόσωπον (Βασιλείου προσώπου)' (*Vit. soph.* 2.607.15).

[109] Garnsey & Saller, *Roman Empire*, 117. See also the seminal study by Zanker, *Images*, for the power of images (esp. imperial images) and their role in shaping Roman society.

[110] Space does not allow for a thorough discussion of the various expressions of social *persona*. There have been numerous studies that have shown different expressions of social distinctions, which relate to *persona*. This section has greatly benefited from these studies, esp. Hellerman, *Reconstructing*, 11–32; Saller, 'Status', esp. 827–34.

visibly depicted *persona*, it can be grasped that individuals throughout the various strata of Roman society would have been aware of the values of *persona*. Secondly, this survey will give attention to material that will present 'history from below'. John Clarke, in his recent study, *Art in the Lives of Ordinary Romans*, explores the 'non-elite art' to portray the values of the 'ordinary' (non-elite) Romans, who have adopted and practised the elite values of social identity.[111] Thirdly, since the ancient sources do not give a catalogue that describes social *persona*, this survey of the visible expressions will be beneficial for understanding the contours of the Roman stress on *persona*. Fourthly, although there are many visible social features that visibly project social identity, this study will focus only on those expressions that involve social behaviour and in particular the exaggeration of certain elements of *persona* (esp. social status).

2.4.1.1 Attire

Emmet writes, 'In ancient and mediaeval times different social roles were associated with special dress, perhaps a carry-over from drama and ritual'.[112] A Roman's attire, then, was a visual expression of his or her social *persona*. In his study of the Romanisation of central Spain, Leonard Curchin has a discussion about 'cultivating a Roman image', in which he remarks on Roman attire, 'The adoption of Roman dress and hairstyle was an important step in constructing a Roman persona'.[113] All Roman citizens were given the privilege of wearing the *toga virilis*. Suetonius described that Augustus reinstated the public donning of the toga, and required individuals to display this attire in certain contexts (*Aug.* 40). Among the upper elite orders, the attire was conspicuously different. Members of the senatorial rank were privileged to bear on their togas the *latus clavus* (the broad purple stripe), while those of equestrian rank were privileged to bear the *angustus clavus* (the narrow purple stripe). There were also further distinctions in the accoutrement of the elite, such as the gold rings of the equestrians, and special crowns. Non-elite groups also had their symbolic attire. Freedmen, for example, wore the *pilleum* ('cap of liberty') which signified their manumission.[114] Dio Chrysostom vividly relates the individuals' attire to their occupation, especially those of the non-elite Romans:

---

[111] Clarke, *Ordinary Romans*. He is among a number of scholars who have been interested in this neglected material culture of the Roman 'non-elite', which lies outside of elite circles. See also Petersen, *Freedman*. This section's treatment of the expressions from the non-elite sector is indebted to Clarke's insightful study.

[112] Emmet, *Roles*, 175.

[113] Curchin, *Romanization*, 217.

[114] Cf. Valerius Maximus 8.6.2.

Why on earth is it that, whenever men see somebody wearing a tunic and nothing more, they neither notice him nor make sport of him? Possibly because they reason that the fellow is a sailor and that there is no occasion to mock him on this account. Similarly, if they should spy some one wearing the garb of a farmer or of a shepherd – that is, wearing an exomis or wrapped in hide or muffled in kosymba[115] – they are not irritated, nay, they do not even notice it to begin with, feeling that the garb is appropriate to the man who follows such a calling. Take our tavern-keepers, too; though people day after day see them in front of their taverns with their tunics belted high, they never jeer at them but, on the contrary, they would make fun of them if they were not so attired, considering that their appearance is peculiarly suited to their occupation.[116]

Significantly, there would have been a vast difference between the projections of *persona* by the Roman elite and non-elite, since the former group had attire that was more distinct and vivid than the latter group. Thus, for the elite, attire served as a visual means of announcing their possession of an ideal and reputable *persona*.

2.4.1.2 The Arena and Public Spectacles

Garnsey and Saller write, 'Romans paraded their rank whenever they appeared in public, and nowhere more conspicuously than at public spectacles in theatre, amphitheatre and circus'.[117] The arena provided a dynamic place for self-displays of power and prestige, and could be regarded as a synecdoche of Roman society and its social order (Cicero, *Q Fr.* 2.15.2; *Sest.* 106, 116).[118] A particular visible expression of social identity is seen in the social stratification of seating in the *cavea*. Legislation enshrined that members of the elite were privileged to the best seats that were separated from those of the commoners.[119] The senators were given the front row seats, with the equestrians' seats behind them. With this, and other conspicuous self-representations of power and prestige – such as the senators parading into their seats, and their distinguishable attire representing their elite social standing – the spectacle was greater in the *cavea* than on stage. Horace indicates that, 'He would look more closely at the crowd than at the games, since the crowd offers lots more spectacle' (*Epist.* 2.1.197–8). The Romans attended the arena not only to observe the spectacles, but to be observed for the presentation of their *personae*. Ovid describes, 'They come to see, they

---

[115] The *exomis* and *kosymba* are clothing that were suitable for manual labour.

[116] *Or.* 72.1–2. For a study of Roman identity and work, see Joshel, *Work*.

[117] Garnsey & Saller, *Roman Empire*, 117.

[118] See Nguyen, 'Execution' 38–9, for my discussion of the Roman arena as an embodiment of Roman society.

[119] For the social stratification within the *cavea*, see Rawson, '*Discrimina Ordinum*', 83–114; Parker, 'Observed', 163–7. The social stratification also affected the performers on stage, who were associated with *infamia* for appearing before the gaze of others.

come that they be seen' (*spectatum veniunt, veniunt spectentur ut ipsae*) (*Ars am.* 1.99), and Tertullian similarly articulates, 'Why, nobody going to the games (*spectaculo*) thinks of anything else but seeing and being seen (*videri et videre*)' (*De spect.* 25). With the grand spectacle within the *cavea* being so elaborate, visiting foreigners were taken to the arena to observe the size and ordering of the population and classes (Tacitus, *Ann.* 13.54). Given the arena's reflection of the Roman social order, the Roman concept and values of *persona* would have been cemented in the consciousness of the Roman populace. Saller intimates about this function of the arena, 'Knowledge of the seating at the spectacles was knowledge of the Roman system of rank'.[120]

2.4.1.3 Private Banquets

The private banquet was an expression that took place within the home (*domus*), which was a location that should not be seen as a retreat from the public's gaze because 'the domus provided an owner with a site for entertaining, conducting business, partaking in religious and political activities, and it was thus instrumental in shaping his public persona.'[121] The private banquet was a social event where a host would invite guests who would enhance the host's social rating. The guests were seated at the table according to the rating of their *persona*, with the host occupying the most visible seat of honour. Not only was the seating graded by social standing, but also was the food – the finer quality of food was allotted to those of honour, while those of lower status were given food of poor quality. Pliny the Younger describes his experience at a banquet:

It would take too long to go into details (which anyway don't matter) of how I happened to be dining with a man – though no particular friend of his – whose elegant economy, as he called it, seemed to me a sort of stingy extravagance. The best dishes were set in front of the host and a select few, and cheap scraps of food before the rest of the company. He had even put the wine into tiny little flasks, divided into three categories, not with the idea of giving his guests the opportunity of choosing, but to make it impossible for them to refuse what they were given. One lot was intended for himself and for us, another for his lesser friends (for all his friends are graded) and the third for his freedman.[122]

Pliny's description also reveals the common practice of hosts inviting people of lower status in order to accentuate their social prestige. Juvenal describes the quality of food given to a client who was invited to fill in an empty spot at the lowest couch:

But what a dinner! You get wine that fresh wool wouldn't absorb...bread that is hardly breakable, hunks of solid dough that are already mouldy, to keep your molars busy without

---

[120] Saller, 'Status', 820.
[121] Petersen, *Freedman*, 123.
[122] *Ep.* 2.6.

letting you bite. But for the master is reserved soft snowy-white bread kneaded from fine flour.[123]

This dining experience highlighted the difference in privileges for the various grades of social identity, which clearly placed the spotlight on those with prestige and honourable status.[124] With members of lower status being involved in these banquets, they would have been aware of status gradation and the privileges of having an honourable *persona*. In addition, in his study of the art of the non-elite Romans, Clarke explores the Pompeiian homes owned by the non-elite and has found evidence from domestic art and architecture that they adopted this elite practice of hosting banquets and seating their guests according to their social status.[125] Therefore, this Roman dining practice vividly illustrates the social behaviour of distinguishing individuals based on certain values of *persona* (e.g. rank and status).

2.4.1.4 The Legal System

It was explained above that the concept of *persona* has a strong legal connotation. For instance, the *persona* of the individual on trial had a critical role in the Roman judicial system and would often predetermine the verdict.[126] The Roman legal system reinforced the hierarchy of social inequalities, and individuals were often treated based on their *persona*. Cicero instructed a protégé, 'make it your business to enable him to conclude his negotiation...in a manner befitting the justice of his case and his own position (*pro causae veritate et pro sua dignate*)' (*Fam.* 13.57.2). In a letter to Calestrius Tiro, who would be taking up provincial office as a governor in Spain, Pliny the Younger praised his preferential treatment of justice that is given to the elite members of that society:

You have done splendidly – and I hope you will not rest on your laurels – in commending your administration of justice to the provincials by your exercise of tact. This you have shown particularly in maintaining consideration for the best men (*honestissimum quemque*), but, in doing so, winning respect of the lower classes while holding the affection of the superiors. Many men, in their anxiety to avoid seeming to show how excessive favour to men of influence, succeed only in gaining a reputation for perversity and malice. I know there is no chance of your falling prey to that vice, but in praising you for the way you tread the middle-course, I cannot help sounding as if I were offering you advice: that you maintain the

---

[123] 5.24–5, 67–71.

[124] See Dio Chrysostom, *Or.* 30.29–30, who uses the hierarchy within the banquets as a metaphor.

[125] See Clarke, *Ordinary Romans*, 223–45.

[126] See Garnsey, *Social Status*, 209–10, 221–2.

distinctions between ranks and degrees of dignity. Nothing could be more unequal than the equality which results when those distinctions are confused or broken down.[127]

Given the accustomed practice of partial treatment, Valerius Maximus reflects on how the legal system was different for two general classes of people (e.g. elite/non-elite; patrician/plebian): 'so the laws tied up the humble and the poor (*humiles et pauperes*), but did not bind the rich and the powerful (*divites et praepotentes*)' (7.2. *ext*. 14). This preferential treatment can also be observed in the demarcation between citizens and non-citizens. For example, in the Book of Acts, Luke recounts Paul's disclosure of his identity as a Roman-born citizen to avoid the severe punishment that he was about to receive, which was not appropriate for Roman citizens (22.24–9; cf. 16.37–9). Another example of this is seen in 17 CE, when the Senate attempted to banish the practice of astrology, by exiling the citizens (πολῖται) and putting to death foreigners (ξένοι) (Dio Cassius 57.15.8). From these two instances, a privileged group (citizens) was exempted from certain forms of punishments. Finally, this dual-penalty system can be seen clearly in the second-century legal bifurcation of *honestiores*, those individuals with higher status, and *humiliores*, those with lower status – whereby the latter group received the severer penalties.[128]

2.4.1.5 Salutatio

The *salutatio* was a morning ritual that reflected the Roman patron-client relationship. It involved clients and friends crowding at the doors of certain elite members (patrons). The clients waited for the opportunity to be admitted inside according to their social standing in order to greet their patrons in exchange for favours – such as dinner invitations, food, or small sums of money.[129] Besides the enhancement of the clients' social status, the 'rivalry and jostling' at the doors (Dio Cassius 58.5) also accentuated the social rating of the patrons and their *persona*. The clients, in addition, could accompany the patron on his rounds of public business during the day and applaud his speeches in court, because the patron's social rating would increase if he was

---

[127] *Ep.* 9.5. Translation from Garnsey, 'Legal Privilege', 144–5. Cf. Gellius, *Noct. att.* 7.14.3, 9; 14.2.

[128] On the *honestiores/humiliores*, see Garnsey, *Social Status*, 219–76. Garnsey, 'Legal Privilege', 160, points out the suggestion that the *honestiores/humiliores* distinction took over the distinction of citizens/non-citizens. Although the *honestiores/humiliores* distinction is first found in the second century, there is enough evidence here suggesting that there was a conceptualised idea of preferential treatment for the Roman elite in the first century.

[129] See *CIL* 8.17896, which is a mid-fourth century CE inscription that carefully lists the order in which individuals were admitted to the governor's morning *salutatio*; cf. Lendon, *Honour*, 234.

seen with a flock of clients trailing him.[130] With Roman society's competitive environment for status, individuals sought opportunities to amplify their *salutatio* spectacle. According to Plutarch, Marius returned home to Rome after many years of military service and relocated near the Forum in order to increase the morning attendance at his house (*Mar.* 32.1). Given its regularity and visibility, the *salutatio* became a vivid image to describe the lengths individuals would go to achieve and enhance their status. Plutarch, for instance, refers to aristocrats in search of high office as those who 'grow old haunting the doors of other men's houses' (*Mor.* 814D).

In his examination of non-elite homes in Pompeii, Clarke has identified a particular home owned by two freedmen brothers, the House of the Vettii, that demonstrates the non-elite's imitation of *salutatio*.[131] Within the largest reception space of the house there is a large and elaborate frieze that depicts cupids and psyches working and playing.[132] This room is identified to be the reception area where clients and peers would wait for the patrons and be able to behold and examine the frieze. Analysing the frieze, Clarke suggests that the Vettii's friends would have recognised the frieze 'as the best in fashionable decorative painting of the time – a mark of the Vettii's improved social and financial status'.[133] Clarke further explains that for other viewers who were former slaves it was 'a sign of what they had left behind and a trophy of their new status', and also 'a way of sanitizing the viewers' servile past even while advertising the Vettii's new gentility and good (elite) taste'.[134]

2.4.1.6 Roman Statuary

The erection of statues is another means of visually projecting one's social *persona*.[135] Peter Stewart has recently produced an informative study that explores the significant function of Roman statues for the self-representation of identity.[136] Interestingly, the lifelikeness of the statue is intensified by the

---

[130] Cf. Garnsey & Saller, *Roman Empire*, 151; Tacitus, *Ann.* 3.55. Also, see the negative examples in Plutarch, *Mor.* 615D; Lucian, *Nigr.* 13.

[131] See Clarke, *Ordinary Romans*, 98–105.

[132] For photos, see Clarke, *Ordinary Romans*, 99, 102–4.

[133] Clarke, *Ordinary Romans*, 105.

[134] Clarke, *Ordinary Romans*, 105.

[135] There have been recent interests in examining Roman art and material remains to understand their significance from the perspective of the ancient viewer. Besides those discussed below, see also Newby & Leader-Newby, *Art*; Elsner, *Roman Eyes*. Also, funerary statues and inscriptions are not discussed here, but are further public expressions of *persona*. Also, for non-elite funerary inscriptions that imitate those of the elite, see Clarke, *Ordinary Romans*, 181–219. See also Bodel, 'Death', 259–81, who examines Roman funerals as elite self-advertisement.

[136] Stewart, *Statues*. See also Eck, 'Self-Representation', 129–67; Smith, 'Cultural Choice', 56–93.

Hellenistic view that a statue was the actual representation of the individual depicted. Stewart writes on this ancient understanding, 'The likeness of a statue to a living person, and more importantly perhaps the idea that a statue is intended to stand in for people, give rise to the fantasy that the statue might do human things'.[137] More significantly, Stewart relates the meaning of *persona/* πρόσωπον, in the sense of face or mask, to Roman statuary and points out, 'The vast quantity of portrait busts or heads surviving from Roman antiquity and attested in written sources is ample evidence that the face could stand as a sufficient marker of an individual's identity'.[138] The statue's face or head as an expression of individual identity can be seen in the common use and reuse of statues with slots for removable heads, whereby any particular head could be set into the various generic torsos which would then give the statue its proper visual representation of a person.[139] In addition to the face of the statue, other aesthetic markers within the statue could further indicate one's distinguished *persona* – such as certain crowns and rings, the toga, and elaborate hairstyle.[140] Stewart remarks on the effectiveness of the portrait statues' presentation of the individuals' social *persona*:

Of course, there are degrees of likeness, and Roman portraits were highly conventional, appealing to physiognomical assumptions, displaying symbolic markers of social persona or character...So it is that portraits are often said to perpetuate the memory of the dead, make present those who are absent, or lend insight into the personalities of those who have never been seen before. And like the human face, the realistic portrait was a conspicuous sign of individual identity.[141]

There also appears to be a hierarchy of various statue types, such as location, size, pose or mount, material, and attire, all of which inform something about the status of the individual.[142] Regarding the location, statues were erected in strategic locations in order to attract the attention of the public. In Pompeii, there is an honorific statue of M. Holconius Rufus that was erected in the junction of a busy thoroughfare, so that the crowds would

---

[137] Stewart, *Statues*, 43. For more on this ancient understanding, see Steiner, *Images*, 79–134.

[138] Stewart, *Statues*, 47. Cf. Pliny, *Ep.* 2.5.11, and Juvenal 10.62–4, for the significance of the statues' head.

[139] See Stewart, *Statues*, 47, who points out that the portrait faces on mass-produced sarcophagi were commonly left unfinished until use. See also Smith, 'Cultural Choice', 56–93, who explores the portrait monuments in the Greek East as projecting particular cultural and political identities.

[140] See Smith, 'Cultural Choice', 63–70.

[141] Stewart, *Statues*, 79.

[142] Stewart, *Statues*, 80.

not have missed it.[143] Also, under the reign of Antoninus Pius, L. Fabius Severus was honoured with the following decree:

> that a gilded equestrian statue should be erected to him, and at the earliest opportunity, in the most frequented part of our forum, and that this consensus of ours and this decree should be inscribed on its base, so that both the face and the deeds of the most esteemed of men should endure to posterity...[144]

Through their high visibility, these statues reinforced the values of identity within Roman society. Consequently, there was a degree of excessiveness in displaying these status symbols for others' gaze that resulted in a congestion in many areas of the city due to an overpopulation of statues.[145] Dio Cassius reports that Claudius had to remove the statues 'in view of the fact that the city was becoming filled with a great multitude of images (for any who wished were free to have their likenesses appear in public in a painting or in bronze or marble)' (60.25.2–3).[146]

Besides enhancing an individual's *persona*, inscriptions and statues also had the social function of disparaging it, which occurred through the process of *damnatio memoriae*.[147] In the *senatus consultum de Cn. Pisone patre*, for instance, Piso's statues were to be removed (lines 75–6) and his name was to be erased from the inscriptions of Germanicus (82–4). Given the former popularity of the individual, the ancient viewers could possibly identify the name of the individual who was being 'erased'. Even modern viewers can often identify the victim of *damnatio* by looking at the context and from other sources. There, then, lies a paradox in *damnatio memoriae* – one's memory is to be removed, yet still displayed in a manner to remind others of the individual to be erased from memory, which is necessary for the victim to be an example for deterring future crimes. Thus, when the ancient viewers read the inscription they would see the condemned individual's name effaced, thus denouncing the individual's social identity.

Regarding the non-elite, there appear to be similar elite practices of erecting portrait statues and honorary inscriptions.[148] For example, a stone altar erected by *vicomagistri*[149] at a crossroads in Rome depicts the status of

---

[143] See Stewart, *Statues*, 136–7.

[144] *CIL* 5.532. Translation from Stewart, *Statues*, 138.

[145] See Stewart, *Statues*, 129–36, for more on the overpopulation.

[146] Cf. Suetonius, *Calig.* 34. For a similar problem outside of Rome, see *CIL* 8.7046; Stewart, *Statues*, 135.

[147] For more on *damnatio memoriae*, see Stewart, *Statues*, 267–78; Flower, *Forgetting*. Given the significance of the statues' face and head, it often would be sufficient to topple only the head of the statue and replace the torso with a new head.

[148] See Clarke, *Ordinary Romans*, for several other examples of non-elite statues that resemble elite practices.

[149] Clarke, *Ordinary Romans*, 81–5. The *vicomagistri* were minor officials who

the freedmen, who are wearing togas. Although the inscriptions indicate their servile origins, the overall presentation indicates the representation of their reputable status as *vicomagistri*. Clarke remarks on their public displays of status, 'One can imagine the competition for the rank of vicomagister within Rome's crowded popular wards, where it was difficult for anyone to gain the public visibility and social importance that were such significant measures of a man's personal distinction (*gloria*)'.[150] He consequently concludes that this non-elite altar 'imitated the elite monuments of the state religion'.[151]

2.4.2 The Preoccupation with the Superficial Aspect of Persona

Although the above sampling of expressions could be expanded, the expressions presented sufficiently demonstrate the *persona*-conscious nature of Roman society. By visibly presenting certain elements of *persona*, especially social status, individuals were attempting to announce their possession of an ideal and honourable *persona*. Lendon summarises how honour incited these, and many other, expressions of social identity:

> The elements that elicited the community recognition that was honour – that is, the qualities that would be perceived as honourable – included high birth in an illustrious home town, wealth (provided it came from reputable sources, and preferably in the form of landed estates) legal status (that of a senator or an equestrian, or at least a citizen, not that of a freedman or slave), a great house, a grand procession of slaves and clients on the street, expensive clothes. And there were more subtle qualities, all the signs of a proper upbringing and education and an aristocratic manner: the proper accent, words, posture, bearing – in short elegance. Two aristocrats never needed to enquire of genealogies to realize that they were both gentlemen; *all they needed was a glance.*[152]

The last sentence of the quotation highlights the social importance of parading and assessing one another's visible *persona*, hence the need to flaunt the accoutrements of a distinguished *persona*. Clarke expresses the concern for these visible displays by both the elite and non-elite:

> For the elite as well as the non-elite, who you were depended on how people perceived you in public spaces. Everyone noted your dress, your walk, your gestures, and your speech – and from these markers understood your place in society. Given the importance of such external signs of status, it is little wonder that visual representation in the public sphere was so important for non-elite Romans.[153]

---

administrated the small wards (*vici*) of Rome that were demarcated by Augustus in 8–7 BCE. Their responsibilities included watching over the traffic, crime, and fires, and sacrificing to the Lares and the Genius of Augustus.

[150] Clarke, *Ordinary Romans*, 84.
[151] Clarke, *Ordinary Romans*, 85.
[152] Lendon, *Honour*, 36–7 (emphasis mine).
[153] Clarke, *Ordinary Romans*, 69, 71.

Therefore, it is evident through these visual expressions that a proper *persona* was a pivotal component of identity in Roman society.

Since individuals in Roman society only needed 'a glance' in order to ascertain another's social identity, these visual expressions became the prime criteria used to establish and evaluate each other. Within the above discussion of the association of *persona* with status symbols, and the discussion of the visible expressions of it, there appeared to be an obsession with the superficial or outward elements of *persona*. Although there were individuals who displayed what were held to be noble or ideal aspects of *persona*, there were others who exaggerated and exploited certain external elements of an ideal and honourable *persona*. Consequently, these individuals solely relied upon their superficial presentation of *persona* as the primary attestation of their possession of a reputable *persona*; accordingly, the Roman populace chiefly evaluated individuals based on their outward projection of it. This exploitation and distortion of the ideals of *persona* engendered a preoccupation with the shallow displays of *persona*. Two specific social features will be presented here, which illustrate this social problem that resulted from the plethora of visual expressions: conspicuous consumption and social usurpation.

Conspicuous and lavish consumption provides evidence of an obsession with the external presentation of *persona*. Seeing that Roman society was inflamed by a competition for honour, not only was it crucial for individuals to present certain displays of status and prestige, but it was also paramount to have more lavish and extravagant displays.[154] For example, the *salutatio* provided patrons with a visual display of their status, yet many individuals were not satisfied with their displays and found ways of amplifying their *salutatio* spectacles in order to enhance their social rating. This was the case of Marius, as mentioned above, who returned home to Rome after many years of military service and relocated near the Forum in order to multiply the attendance at his house in the morning (Plutarch, *Mar.* 32.1). This Roman excess is also witnessed in the desire for elaborate homes and numerous slaves. For instance, Seneca mentions an individual who had four hundred slaves (*Ep.* 41.7). That excess can be contrasted to Apuleius' fictional narrative of a prominent and wealthy individual, Milo, who was not highly regarded by others because he only had a small home, kept one slave, and wore plain clothing (*Met.* 1.21).

The preoccupation with the outward displays of identity can also be seen in the problem of social usurpation. Given the *persona*-consciousness of Roman society, individuals would conceal their actual social status and pretentiously portray a higher one – that is, a false projection of a noble *persona* – in order to achieve social mobility. Since there was an engrossment with the

---

[154] For a study of lavish consumption, see Dalby, *Pleasure*.

superficial type of outward appearance, it was not uncommon to achieve this pretence through fraudulent means.[155] Moreover, the non-elite often performed these deceptive acts of *usurpatio*. They tried to attain the privileges of the elite by pretentiously exhibiting the superficial elements of a prestigious *persona*, which were typically displayed by those of genuine high status. Accordingly, through a number of pieces of legislation, the Roman elite attempted to maintain the distinctions of the elite ranks and statuses by punishing those who were guilty of *usurpatio* of rank, privileges, and status insignia.[156] Despite these attempts to curb usurpation, there are copious instances of individuals falsely and pretentiously displaying a higher-rated *persona*. For instance, Pliny the Elder reports of slaves and freedmen who wore cheap gold-plated rings in order to pass off as belonging to the equestrian order (*Nat.* 33.6.23; cf. Petronius, *Sat.* 32.3).[157] Martial, moreover, provides examples of low status individuals who imitated the elite cultural practice of extravagantly displaying a wealth of antiques, by parading their own cheap forgeries.[158] Martial also writes of a freedman who sat in the front row of senatorial seats in the theatre in order to conceal his servile origins (2.29). These acts of usurpation, then, highlight the preoccupation with the superficial features of *persona*, since these acts of social usurpation typically involved the false and ostentatious displays of external status symbols.[159]

Therefore, given that only 'a glance' was needed to determine social identity, the features of conspicuous consumption and social usurpation both manifest the common and popular view of *persona* at the time – a preoccupation with its superficial dimension. Moreover, this shallow projection essentially was an exploitation and exaggeration of the Roman traditional ideals and values of *persona*. The remainder of this study will particularly concentrate on this social problem of individuals solely focusing and relying on the status symbols that outwardly display a reputable *persona* in order to achieve honour and privilege. In fact, as will be seen, there existed in the Graeco-Roman social world a small number of social commentators who criticised this pervasive social problem of an outward focus on *persona*.

---

[155] See Reinhold, 'Usurpation', 275–302, for an excellent study exploring these fraudulent practices of usurping status and status symbols.

[156] E.g. Paulus, *Sent.* 5.25.12, who asserts the punishment for impersonating a high-ranking military member. See Reinhold, 'Usurpation', 276.

[157] See Petronius' *Satyricon* for a fictional story of a freedman, Trimalchio, and his friends, who constantly make fools of themselves in their attempts to display their new social status as Roman citizens.

[158] See 4.61; 5.39; 8.6; 9.59; 10.87; 12.69. See Reinhold, 'Usurpation', 284, who points out the thriving and lucrative market of imitations of jewellery and antiques.

[159] Reinhold, 'Usurpation', 285, mentions that Martial even indicates the difficulty at times to tell the difference between the genuine and false displays.

2.5 *Persona* in the Context of Oratory, Rhetoric, and Sophistry

Before concluding this chapter on the concept of *persona* and the Roman emphasis on it, it is critical to survey the social concept within the Graeco-Roman context of oratory/rhetoric/sophistry, since it will provide a necessary backdrop for the following chapters which interact with this context. In addition, this specific context also demonstrates the obsession with the superficial displays of *persona*.

During the Republic, oratory had an important role in the Roman judicial and political system, and especially for elite members of society. Despite the socio-political changes during the imperial period, oratory remained an integral part of society and became more accessible to the general populace. In addition, Roman oratory was influenced through the cultural adoption of Greek rhetoric and rhetorical skills, such as declamation,[160] which were integrated into Roman education.[161] Greek rhetoric, consequently, promoted and intensified the importance of public speaking skills among the elite, since eloquence was an indication of one's elite social class and education. George Kennedy writes, 'Rhetoric played an important part in the intellectual and aesthetic life of the Augustan Age: it maintained its dominant position in the educational system...'[162] Ramsay MacMullen explains the rewards of being trained in rhetoric for the elite, 'Those who went on to advanced training in rhetoric and a career of eloquence were hailed by crowds of supporters and laudatory decrees, by claques and plaques'.[163]

In addition, oratory was important for the Roman elite because, 'Good speech was appropriate to one's role and expressive of one's persona'.[164] Similarly, Catherine Steel comments on how oratory served as a self-representation of *persona*, 'Oratory was a place where the Roman elite was visible, and was a place where its members articulated to one another and to the Roman state more widely what identity they did and should have'.[165] Erik Gunderson also elaborates how declamation expressed one's identity:

---

[160] On declamation, see Bonner, *Roman Declamation*; Kennedy, *Rhetoric*, 312–22.

[161] Steel, *Roman Oratory*, 64, differentiates oratory from rhetoric by explaining that oratory refers to speeches delivered orally in a variety of situations and, by extension, to the texts which purport to record these words; and rhetoric is the name for the techniques through which people might speak more effectively. For Greek rhetoric within Roman education, see Bonner, *Education*.

[162] See Kennedy, *Rhetoric*, 301–2. See also his pp. 378–427, for more on eloquence in Augustan Rome.

[163] MacMullen, *Social Relations*, 107.

[164] Cf. Barton, *Roman Honor*, 161.

[165] Steel, *Roman Oratory*, 54. She also intimates that it is no surprise that the Romans would respond with enthusiasm to polished speech when exposed to it (68).

For the speakers in declamation selves are assumed and borrowed. One speaks wearing a persona. But one is also very careful about these personae. They are not to be donned lightly, and the 'self' that speaks as a character in a declamation never diverges too far from the self that is instructed to take up this mask and make good use of it.[166]

Living in a *persona*-conscious and competitive society, the Romans inevitably would place more emphasis on rhetorical skills than on content, such as philosophy which originally had an influence on Greek rhetoric.[167] Consequently, orators would be judged according to their eloquence and the use of oratorical gestures.[168] Seneca the Elder relates the trial of Vatinius, who, in reaction to the masterful oratory of the prosecutor, asked the jurors, 'Am I to be condemned, gentlemen of the jury, because he is eloquent (*disertus*)?' (*Controv.* 7.4.6) Cicero also explains that, 'There are some men who stammer so in their speech, or are so discordant in tone, or so uncultivated and rustic in their appearance or gesture that even if their talents and skills are sufficient, still they are not able to join the ranks of orators' (*De or.* 1.115).[169] Related to the admiration of eloquence is the conventional preoccupation with the external appearance and displays of oratory, all of which contributed to the theatricality of oratory.[170] This can be observed in Plutarch's statement that although the sayings of Cato are based on the premise that men's characters are revealed much more by their speech, the conventional view was they are revealed 'by their πρόσωπον' (*Cato Mai.* 7.3.5).

Thus, the valuation of the externals of oratory and rhetoric resembles the prevalent social condition of a preoccupation with the superficial side of *persona*. Gualtiero Calboli and William Dominik explain how rhetoric reflected its cultural context: 'For rhetoric, like any other field of activity, is constructed socially, politically and cognitively in ways that reflect, express and extend – through its rules, structures, processes and values – the culture that produces it'.[171]

A phenomenon that intensified the preoccupation with the exterior displays of *persona*, in regards to rhetoric and philosophy, was the Second Sophistic – a movement that occurred throughout the first three centuries CE in the Greek speaking parts of the Roman empire, whereby crowds would gather to hear

---

[166] Gunderson, *Declamation*, 144.

[167] See Calboli & Dominik, 'Roman *Suada*', 5. Cf. Steel, *Roman Oratory*, 48.

[168] On Roman eloquence, see the essays in Dominik, *Eloquence*. For oratorical gestures, see Quintilian, *Inst.* 11.3.65–184; Cicero, *De or.* 3.220; Graf, 'Gestures', 36–58; Hall, 'Gestures', 143–60.

[169] For 'rustic' speech, see Connors, 'Field', 71–89. Cf. Quintilian, *Inst.* 1.11.16; 6.3.17, 107.

[170] For more on the theatricality of oratory, see e.g. Gotoff, 'Oratory', 289–313.

[171] Calboli & Dominik, 'Roman *Suada*', 11.

professional orators performing oratorical declamations.[172] With the Roman governance of the Greek East, and the influence of the Roman social hierarchy and Roman law, the sophistic performance became a valuable tool for competitions of status.[173] Sophistry, like oratory and rhetoric, was commonly used to express and parade one's status before their peers, as Tim Whitmarsh points out:

> At the heart of the social role of sophistry lay the concept of competition...Competition for status was the foundation upon which the entire edifice was built: sophistry was at once a collective celebration of the exclusivity of elite culture, and a forum within which individual members of the elite could vie for personal prominence.[174]

These sophistic performances were popular and drew great crowds. Aristides accounts that in a particular performance 'the council chamber was so full that it was impossible to see anything but men's heads' (*Or.* 51.32). These showings were also dynamic because of the two-way performances between the speaker and audience: the speakers performed great visual and audible performances, while the audiences judged and evaluated them according to the speaker's sophistry.[175] Also, the importance of physical appearance in the sophist's performance can be grasped in Polemo's cry from his deathbed: 'give me a body, and I shall declaim' (*Vit. soph.* 544).

Interestingly, the sophists were distinguished from most philosophers by their outward appearance, as seen in Philostratus' recount of the career change of Aristocles of Pergamum, 'As long as he was a student of philosophy he was slovenly in appearance, unkempt and squalid in his dress, but now he began to be fastidious, discarded his slovenly ways, and admitted into his house all the pleasures that are afforded by the lyre, the flute, and the singing voice' (*Vit. soph.* 567–8).[176] Also, due to the pressures of having to produce grandiose sophistic performances, sophistry became associated with the 'showmanship and smoke-and-mirrors trickiness' of epideictic oratory.[177] Hence, 'when fully embodied in performance, the sophist's declamation

---

[172] See Whitmarsh, *Second Sophistic*, 4–5, for a definition of the Second Sophistic. For more on the Sophists, see Bowersock, *Greek Sophists*; idem, *Approaches*; idem, 'Philosophy'; Kennedy, *Rhetoric*, 553–613. A good source for knowledge of the Second Sophistic is Philostratus' *Vitae sophistarum*, which documents the lives of famous sophists.

[173] On the Sophistic movement and the relationship between Rome and Greece, see Whitmarsh, *Second Sophistic*, 10–13.

[174] Whitmarsh, *Second Sophistic*, 38–9.

[175] Cf. Whitmarsh, *Second Sophistic*, 25–6: 'The role of the audience, however, was not simply to analyse language and intellectual content, but also to scrutinize the sophist's physical person'.

[176] Cf. Bowersock, 'Philosophy', 161–2.

[177] Whitmarsh, *Second Sophistic*, 16. For more on the sophistic performance, see his pp. 23–40.

would have been dynamized by clothing, props, gesture, intonation, vocal texture, complemented by the surroundings, and framed by an ongoing dialogue with the audience'.[178] The Roman satirist Lucian composed the voice of a rhetoric instructor who advises his students not to bother with difficult material, but to focus instead on their shallow appearance:

Bring with you, then, as the principal thing, ignorance; secondly, recklessness, and thereto effrontery and shamelessness. Modesty, respectability, self-restraint, and blushes may be left at home for they are useless and somewhat of a hindrance to the matter in hand. But you need also a very loud voice, a shameless singing delivery, and a gait like mine. They are essential indeed, and sometimes sufficient in themselves. Let your clothing be gaily-coloured, or else white, a fabric of Tarentine manufacture, so that your body will show through; and wear either high Attic sandals of the kind that women wear, with many slits, or else Sicyonian boots, trimmed with strips of white felt. Have also many attendants and always a book in hand.[179]

These accoutrements of the sophist were pivotal if one expected to impress and receive accolades from the audience. The crowd's hobbyhorse of the sophist's outward appearance is clearly seen in Philostratus' description of a speech by the sophist Alexander: 'The Athenians thought he was so well turned out that even before he had spoken a murmur they went around praising his good style' (*Vit. soph.* 572). Like many aspects of Roman culture, sophistry was a means of visually expressing one's *persona*. Whitmarsh writes, 'Identity was not an inner being fixed inside the sophist: it was rather, linked to his public persona, and shifted with his fortunes'.[180] Thus, the sophistic movement, along with oratory and rhetoric, was an integral part of Roman culture, which embraced and promoted shallow presentations of *persona*.

2.6 Conclusion

This chapter has surveyed the development of the meanings of *persona* and πρόσωπον, and demonstrated that in both these malleable terms there existed a meaning of 'social identity' in the Graeco-Roman world. Although the general concept of *persona* can be broadly seen in the Graeco-Roman world, this chapter focused on the Roman context since the dominant social, cultural, and political force during the New Testament era was Roman. In fact, it was demonstrated that there was a clear Roman stress on the concept of *persona*, a stress which would have impacted the majority of individuals

---

[178] Whitmarsh, *Second Sophistic*, 24.

[179] *Rhet. praec.* 15.

[180] Whitmarsh, *Second Sophistic*, 34; see his pp. 32–4 for sophistry and its expressions of identity.

living in Graeco-Roman society. This Roman emphasis on *persona* was influenced by the Roman social hierarchy, which stratified society according to rank and status, and by Roman law, which framed and maintained that social hierarchy. Moreover, it was shown that although the Roman stress on *persona* impacted individuals from both the elite and non-elite social strata in the Graeco-Roman world, the concept of *persona* was primarily a traditional and elite ideal, which served to portray and protect the honour and privileges of the elite.

Furthermore, *persona* was discerned to be a significant feature of Roman society, as evident from the various visual expressions of *persona*. Individuals (elite and non-elite) exhibited these outward displays in order to announce their possession of an ideal and honourable *persona*. Moreover, these outward expressions, which exaggerated particular elements of an honourable *persona*, conveyed the conventional projection of *persona* in the early imperial period. It was consequently determined that the predominant understanding of *persona* in society at the time was a preoccupation with its superficial dimension, as seen in the social behaviour of conspicuous consumption and social usurpation. As a result, the conventional outworking of *persona* was essentially a distortion of the ideal notions of a proper *persona*. This pervasive problem of shallow presentations of one's social identity, was also observed in the specific social context of oratory/rhetoric/sophistry, where orators produced spectacular performances in order to impress the crowds who were fixated with the orator's appearance and eloquence.

With the social condition of a preoccupation with the outward features of social identity, there arose a number of moralists, philosophers, and satirists who reacted and voiced their criticisms against this social problem. These social commentators deemed these shallow presentations and assessments of *persona* as inappropriate social behaviour. Seneca, for instance, expresses criticisms against the enthusiasm for these ostentatious projections:

As he is a fool who, when purchasing a horse, does not consider the animal's points, but merely his saddle and bridle; so he is doubly a fool who values a man from his clothes or from his rank, which indeed is only a robe that clothes us.[181]

Seneca's denunciation of this conventionally projected *persona* is representative of other social critics in the Graeco-Roman world. Saller writes, 'Philosophers and satirists railed against these and other status symbols, on the grounds that they did not reveal a man's true worth as measured by virtue'.[182]

The remainder of this study will concentrate on three individuals – Valerius Maximus, Epictetus, and Paul – who all belonged to this minority

---

[181] *Ep.* 47.16.
[182] Saller, 'Status', 829.

group of social critics of *persona*, especially the Roman stress on *persona*.[183] More specifically, they are critics of the commonly projected *persona* at the time, and also the related social behaviour of a preoccupation with its superficial aspect. Examining these three social critics and their works not only will affirm and further demonstrate the significance of *persona* in their social worlds, but also will reveal three different critiques of the Roman emphasis on *persona*. The next three chapters will consider, respectively, each of these three figures and their critiques of social identity and *persona* in their social worlds. Also, at the end of each chapter their critiques will be compared with each other's. As mentioned in the previous chapter, a benefit of comparing these three individuals is that Valerius provides an understanding of social identity in Rome and Epictetus provides an understanding of it in the Greek East; the insights from these figures, accordingly, will illuminate Paul's approach to Christian identity in his second letter to the Christians in Corinth, which is a Roman colony in the Greek East.

---

[183] Although these three individuals will accentuate the Roman emphasis on *persona*, they will also show somewhat of a diverse understanding of *persona* – for example, Epictetus and Paul will highlight the concept of *persona* in the Roman Greek East.

Chapter 3

Valerius Maximus and Identity in Rome

3.1 Introduction

As mentioned in Chapter One, in an early stage of research for this study, an extensive search of the terms *persona* and πρόσωπον was performed. While searching for instances of the term *persona* in the Roman literary sources, Valerius Maximus was observed to have some significant uses of the term *persona* in his work, *Factorum et dictorum memorabilium* ('Memorable Deeds and Sayings'),[1] that were relevant to this study of social identity. Rather than just presenting these instances, Valerius' work was read as a whole for more insights into his understanding of social identity. By reading through his work in light of his social setting and looking beyond the instances of the lexical term *persona* for related terms and expressions, more pertinent information concerning social identity and the concept of *persona* was found. As in the research on the terms *persona* and πρόσωπον, the use of the social features of rank and status were helpful in deciding which evidence counted as part of Valerius' understanding and critique of social identity. While organising the evidence, a preliminary look at the data gave an impression that Valerius had both a negative and a positive critique of Roman identity. Moreover, a survey of the secondary literature on Valerius Maximus and his work confirmed the possible dual aspects of his critique of Roman social identity.

Having described the social concept of *persona* in the previous chapter, this present chapter will provide a profile of Valerius, the first individual of this study, and his understanding and critique of social identity and the concept of *persona*. The profile will explore the importance of Valerius and his work, *Facta et dicta* for describing the concept of *persona*, and especially the Roman stress on *persona*, in the social milieu of the city of Rome in the first-century CE. Before Valerius' perception of social *persona* can be properly scrutinised, it is necessary to be briefly acquainted with Valerius, his audience, and his work.

---

[1] Hereafter, '*Facta et dicta*'.

3.1.1 *Valerius Maximus*

There is no reasonable objection to Valerius' authorship of *Facta et dicta*. There is, however, little information on his life, and the few existing external details are insufficient to provide any convincing biographical knowledge.[2] The only exception is that he lived during the reign of Tiberius (14–37 CE), a fact which is known from the preface of the work.[3] In Valerius' work, there are minimal amounts of first-person biographical material, and scholars have explored these few internal details for further illumination on his identity. For instance, Valerius recounts the suicide of an elderly woman of the highest rank on the island of Cea, during his journey to Asia in the company of Sex. Pompeius and other Romans (2.6.8). Debate exists over the identity of Sex. Pompeius, who has been suggested to be Pompeius, the consul of 14 CE, and later, the proconsul of Asia in the mid-20s.[4] In opposition to this identity, David Wardle has suggested that 'the casual way he [Pompeius] is mentioned would make V. seem a very ungrateful client; Pompeius may thus become a humble unknown and any date for the episode be lost'.[5] However, Shackleton Bailey has provided a summary of points that refutes Wardle's scepticism:

A humble unknown was unlikely to be traveling to Asia with Valerius and a company of Romans – actually ex hypothesi his suite (*cohors*). And a lady of the highest station would not have been so anxious for the honour of his presence at her deathbed 'to add lustre to her passing'. The *seemingly* casual introduction of the episode, along with a generous dose of flattery, probably appeared to Valerius as a graceful maneuvre, the dedication of his work having gone to the Emperor, not to Pompeius.[6]

This story, then, would have had the opposite effect of portraying 'ungratefulness', by positively portraying the nobility and prestige of Pompeius, Valerius' patron. In fact, elsewhere, Valerius gives fulsome praise of Pompeius as 'a most illustrious and eloquent gentleman' (4.7 *ext.* 2b).

---

[2] There are three external details worth noting. First, see Skidmore, *Practical Ethics*, 113–14, for a brief discussion of a 1494 Venice edition of Valerius' work containing a *Life*, which gives biographical information based on inferences from the work itself. Second, Valerius Maximus' surviving name presents difficulties in regard to his identification. Skidmore speculates that Valerius is related to the prestigious *gens* Messallae (115–17); however, Wardle, *Valerius Maximus*, 1, rightly assesses that 'no more than conjecture is possible'. Third, other literary authors do refer to Valerius and his work, but these brief references do not add any significant insights into Valerius' identity: Gellius, *Noct. att.* 12.7.8; Plutarch, *Brut.* 53.4; *Marc.* 30.4.

[3] For arguments of an early dating towards the beginning years of Tiberius' reign, see Bellemore, 'When?', 67–80; Millar, *'Domus Augustus'*, 4. For a later dating of the early 30s, see Wardle, *'Domus Augusta'*, 479; Briscoe, 'Notes', 398–402.

[4] See Briscoe, 'Notes', 395–408, for a substantial argument that aims to refute any scepticism against this identity.

[5] Wardle, *Valerius Maximus*, 1.

[6] Bailey, *Valerius Maximus*, I:2 (italics his).

Thus, the small amount of evidence does suggest a strong possibility that Sex. Pompeius was Valerius' patron, which indicates that Valerius had direct associations with the Roman elite.

Attention has also been given to various details in *Facta et dicta* that possibly indicate the social position of Valerius. There have been proposals made that Valerius' remark of 'our meagre substance' (4.4.11) suggests his status as a man of limited wealth.[7] However, the phrase could be regarded, as some scholars have suggested, as a 'human generalisation, not a description of Valerius' personal means'.[8] The phrase, 'my petty self', in his dedicatory preface to Tiberius (1.1 *praef.*) has also been probed. Although the language here could be consistent with the language of a client, this language does not disprove one's noble birth,[9] and the primary tone of the dedication is to show 'abject humility' to the emperor, to whom the work is dedicated.[10] Lastly, Clive Skidmore has determined Valerius' preface to his chapter 'Of fraternal devotion' (5.5) as indicative of Valerius' glorious ancestral linkage: 'Before I was born I dwelt in the same domicile, I spent my time of infancy in the same cradle, called the same persons parents...I drew equal pride from the masks of our ancestors (*maiorum imaginibus*)'. He argued that Valerius is of 'senatorial extraction', since only those of senatorial rank were entitled to display these ancestral busts.[11] However, even if Valerius did have a senatorial pedigree he should not be assumed *ipso facto* to have possessed a senatorial career himself, especially since there is no evidence of Valerius' rank as a senator. This text, nevertheless, does convey Valerius' pride in having a noble birth.

In summary, there are no attestations of Valerius having a significant public life or career,[12] and the only possible evidence for determining the social status of Valerius is his likely patronage by the consul Sex. Pompeius. Even if he was a client of Pompeius, it is still unclear as to what his social standing was in the Roman hierarchy. Importantly, although there is only conjecture that places him within the upper strata of the Roman elite, there also is no explicit evidence suggesting that he should be classified among the lower strata of Roman society. It would thus be conceivable to locate Valerius, at the very least, somewhere within the margins of the Roman elite.

---

[7] So Helm, 'Valerius Maximus', 90.

[8] Carter, 'Valerius Maximus', 34; cf. Wardle, *Valerius Maximus*, 1. The pronoun 'our' is probably used in a generic sense to describe his audience, which would not necessarily include himself.

[9] Cf. Skidmore, *Practical Ethics*, 114–15.

[10] Wardle, *Valerius Maximus*, 1.

[11] Skidmore, *Practical Ethics*, 115. However, Bailey, *Valerius Maximus*, I:1, claims that this is an imaginary person and not Valerius himself.

[12] Wardle, *Valerius Maximus*, 1: 'That he followed no public career is almost certain – at least no trace of one has survived'.

In addition, his personal narrative in 2.6.8 is indicative that he did have interaction with the nobility.[13] This notion is further strengthened by his literary work, which is highly descriptive of the Roman elite, and also is dedicated to the emperor. Therefore, it seems appropriate to classify Valerius as on the fringes of the elite circles. In other words, if the Roman social hierarchy is to be viewed as bifurcated, then Valerius could be located in the upper sphere of the lower ranks, or more likely, in the lower sphere of the upper ranks.

3.1.2 Valerius' Audience

To understand Valerius and the nature of his work, it is important to consider the identity of his audience. The question concerning the identity of Valerius' audience is as complex as the question of his identity.[14] In *Facta et dicta*, which is essentially a compilation of literary *exempla*, Valerius gives no explicit descriptors of his audience, which leaves room for speculation as to the social status of his target audience. The proposed views for the identity of Valerius' audience have been declaimers, lawyers, the social elite, and also a wider audience. For instance, Skidmore uses the rhetorical device of 'unlikely example' to identify the social status of Valerius' audience as belonging to a high social status.[15] Quintilian explains the use of 'unlikely examples' to persuade individuals through the examples of lower status (*Inst.* 5.11.10). Skidmore accordingly identifies Valerius' audience to be of greater rank and status than the most elevated 'unlikely example' found in *Facta et dicta* – a centurion (3.8.7). Although, this approach offers some insights, it is still not a conclusive approach for determining the identity of his audience. In addition, with the variety of topics that Valerius communicates, it is also difficult to identify a particular group. For example, the chapters concerning legal matters (e.g. 7.7–8.6) could suggest lawyers being part of Valerius' audience, and the chapters on military matters (e.g. 2.7) could also suggest members of the Roman military. Additionally, various questions arise when attempts are made to discern to whom these varied topics would be pertinent. For instance, with his inclusion of foreign *exempla*, is he targeting foreigners at Rome? Also, with a discussion of those born of humble conditions who rose among the nobles (3.4), would Valerius be addressing those of humble means or the nobles?

Nonetheless, by surveying the majority of the themes, it is clear that these topics would have been pertinent for the Roman elite.[16] It is plausible, then, to

---

[13] *Contra* Maslakov, 'Roman Historiography', 455.
[14] See Wardle, *Valerius Maximus*, 12–15, for a brief overview.
[15] Skidmore, *Practical Ethics*, 87–9, 103–7.
[16] Cf. Skidmore, *Practical Ethics*, 104–5.

include the Roman elite among Valerius' intended audience because his work would be of great use in affirming traditional Roman virtues as witnessed by his presentation of the great Roman (and foreign) examples of the past. For instance, in the preface to his discussion 'Of electoral defeats' (7.5), he indicates the social status of the potential readers interested in this topic: 'A presentation of what happens on the Campus will be a useful preparation for those entering on the path of public office'. However, Valerius' work of memorable deeds and sayings would also have been relevant for the general Roman populace, since *Facta et dicta* does contain worthwhile themes for encouraging and motivating individuals of any social status to aspire and live virtuously.[17] It is right, therefore, not to limit Valerius' audience to any specific social status or group, but to regard the work as intended for a 'wide audience'.

Valerius, as an individual on the fringes of the Roman elite, would be a suitable candidate for producing a work directed to a wide Roman audience. His understanding of Roman elite culture would give him the necessary knowledge to address the members of the upper strata; yet, his social place on the lower margins of the Roman elite would give him an awareness to address the needs and concerns of the general Roman populace.[18]

3.1.3 *Valerius' Work:* Facta et dicta

Facta et dicta is a neglected work in both classical and New Testament studies.[19] In the work, Valerius presents some one thousand *exempla*, which are structured into nine books and a little less than ninety chapters. *Facta et dicta* has five major components of its structural framework: the whole work, the book, the chapter, the preface, and the historical *exemplum*.[20] Previous studies of *Facta et dicta* have primarily concentrated on its historicity or Valerius' usage of other literary sources.[21] In recent studies, the focus has shifted away from *Quellenforschung* and *Quellenkritik*, to analysing the function and purpose of his work. In his groundbreaking monograph, *Valerius*

---

[17] Cf. Wardle, *Valerius Maximus*, 12–13.

[18] Cf. Wardle, '*Domus Augusta*', 493.

[19] Bloomer, *New Nobility*, 3, supposes that scholars tend to focus on the literature written during the eras of Augustus and Nero, and generally characterise the Julio-Claudian as a period of 'decline' in literature. For NT studies, there are only Hodgson, 'Gospel Criticism'; idem, 'Social World'. Also, some recent contributions to scholarship on Valerius are: Wardle, *Valerius Maximus*, which is a commentary and translation of Book 1; Bailey, *Valerius Maximus*, which is the first English translation of the entire work; Walker, *Valerius Maximus*, which is another English translation.

[20] See Wardle, *Valerius Maximus*, 6–15.

[21] See the bibliographic details in Maslakov, 'Roman Historiography'; Bloomer, *New Nobility*; Mueller, *Roman Religion*.

Maximus and the Rhetoric of the New Nobility, which is the first serious analysis of *Facta et dicta* in modern times, W. Martin Bloomer argues that the work is a rhetorical handbook for declaimers and rhetoricians.[22] Skidmore, in his seminal study, *Practical Ethics for Roman Gentlemen,* argues that the work is not a mere rhetorical handbook, but a handbook providing guidance for the social elite on how to live a virtuous life.[23] Subsequent scholars have continued Skidmore's focus on Valerius' moral and social intention in order to shed further light on the pertinence of Valerius' work for Roman society.[24] This present study follows this trend of identifying the social and moral purpose behind Valerius' work for his social setting. Although *Facta et dicta* has only been introduced here in part, the remainder of this chapter will continue to examine the nature and structure of the work in order to understand Valerius' perception and critique of social *persona.*

3.2 The Preoccupation with the Superficial Aspect of *Persona*

The previous chapter depicted not only the concept of *persona* as an elite ideal, but also the commonly projected *persona* at the time. Moreover, the Roman stress on *persona* was demonstrated, which is relevant for this chapter since Valerius is Roman, is writing in the city of Rome, and, as will be seen, is concerned with a crisis of Roman identity. Since the conventional (or popular) presentation of Roman identity exaggerated and emphasised certain superficial elements of *persona,* the traditional ideals and virtues of *persona* became distorted, which resulted in a preoccupation with its shallow features. Significantly, the titles of some of Valerius' chapters mirror this preoccupation with the superficial aspect of Roman identity. Some of his chapters deal with the problems of wealth and conspicuous living, such as 'Of luxury and lust' (9.1). Others highlight the engrossment with visual displays and eloquence in oratory: 'How great is the force of eloquence' (8.9), and 'How much importance lies in elocution and apt bodily movement' (8.10). Valerius also discusses the legal aspect of *persona* and the commonplace

---

[22] Bloomer, *New Nobility,* e.g. 1–2, 255–6. Cf. Sinclair, 'Declamatory', 141–6. For criticisms of the declamatory background for Valerius' work, see Römer, 'Aufbau', 99; Winterbottom, 'Bloomer', 50–2; Skidmore, *Practical Ethics,* 107; Loutsch, 'Procédés', 32, 39; Wardle, *Valerius Maximus,* 13–14. Although Wardle would see the work being useful for declaimers, he holds that the bulk of Valerius' work and the material of his *exempla,* are different from standard declamatory treatments.

[23] Skidmore, *Practical Ethics,* e.g. xvii. Cf. Römer, 'Aufbau', 99 n. 2, who regards the work as a 'Lehrstück'; Lehmann, 'Revendications', 26, 'monographie moralisatrice'.

[24] So David, *Valeurs*; Weileder, *Valerius Maximus*; Mueller, *Roman Religion*; Wardle, 'Sainted Julius'; idem, '*Domus Augusta*'.

exploitation of legal privilege in 'For what reasons ill-famed defendants were acquitted or condemned' (8.1). Furthermore, Valerius positions two chapters together to draw attention to the correlation between social status and virtue: 'Of those born in a humble situation who became illustrious' (3.4) and 'Of those who degenerated from famous parents' (3.5). More significantly, his following chapter, 'Of which men of mark indulged themselves in dress or other style more freely than ancestral custom permitted' (3.6), is a penetrating discussion into a particular problem of individuals being obsessed with the conspicuous displays of their social standing.

In addition, the final two chapters of *Facta et dicta* sufficiently highlight the preoccupation with the external dimension of *persona*, particularly the problem of usurpation of the Roman social order. 'Of physical likeness' (9.14) is a curious discussion of the issue of individuals having no dignified status, yet who were socially accepted into more noble positions because they physically resembled those of higher status and, conversely, those of high status were socially degraded due to their physical resemblance to others of low status. In the chapter, Valerius presents the *exemplum* of two freedmen, who resembled a noble Pompeius Magnus, and how 'they drew people's eyes to themselves, as everybody noticed the appearance of the great man in their mediocre *personae* (*in personis mediocribus*)' (9.14.1).[25] The problem clearly being addressed here is the assessment of one's social identity based on the sole criterion of the surface appearance of *persona*. After giving several examples concerning the issue of physical likeness, Valerius summarises: 'Let this choice of domestic examples be abundantly sufficient, they being outstanding in *personae* and of fairly common notoriety' (9.14.5). Also, the next and final chapter in *Facta et dicta* is on the issue 'Of persons born in the lowest station who tried by falsehood to thrust themselves into illustrious families' (9.15). Like Valerius' previous chapter, this chapter highlights the problem of social usurpation, which was probably a concern for Valerius and his audience.

Since there was a preoccupation with the shallow features of *persona* that engendered what Valerius considered inappropriate social behaviour, he produced a work reacting to this social condition. It is important to bear in mind that in *Facta et dicta* there is no indication that Valerius is reacting against the Roman social structures (e.g. the social hierarchy), diminishing the value of status symbols, or criticising the idea of being 'Roman'. In fact, Valerius and his readers appreciated the elite conventions of rank and status since his *exempla* are typically of high rank and status, and express the virtues

---

[25] Valerius' uses of *persona* in 9.14 are associated with the social status markers of the *exempla* – e.g. 'noble birth' (9.14.3), 'aristocratic Consulship' (9.14.4), and 'ex-Consul and ex-Censor, and Curio, holder in abundance of all high offices' (9.14.5).

which traditionally characterised the Roman elite. In other words, Valerius positively portrays many of these *exempla* as indeed possessing and projecting the heroic conventions of Rome's traditional past – that is, the traditional notions of what he considers to be an 'ideal' Roman *persona* – which is in contrast to the conventionally projected *persona* in his day. Significantly, he devotes a whole chapter to the theme of social distinctions being awarded to individuals who acted according to virtue (8.15). Valerius is reacting, then, particularly against what he considered to be the inappropriate exploitation and exaggeration of the ideals and virtues of Roman identity for personal gain.

Valerius' critique can be seen clearly in a set of chapters that were mentioned above, in which he juxtaposes the chapter 'Of those born in a humble situation who became illustrious' (3.4) with the chapter 'Of those who degenerated from famous parents' (3.5) to draw attention to the link between social status and virtue.[26] At the end of the preceding chapter (3.3), Valerius gives introductory remarks on these two chapters:

So virtue, once aroused, is not disdainful in admitting men, and allows vigorous characters to approach. Nor does it offer a generous or grudging taste of itself according to distinction of *personae*, but it is accessible to all on an equal basis, and values you rather by how much desire for virtue than by how much status you possess.[27]

These introductory remarks give the interpretative key for understanding his objective in 3.4–5. Valerius reacts to the notion that virtue is received on the sole basis of one's rank or status. By denouncing this viewpoint, Valerius announces that virtue does not merely consider the status of one's *persona*, and that virtue is available to any individual who lives by an appropriate set of social ethics. Consequently, these two chapters would encourage his readers of low status to attain virtue, and more importantly, would prevent his more elite readers from complacently thinking that the public and shallow projection of high social status is a sufficient qualification and guarantee of virtue.[28]

After exhibiting the *exempla* of those who had a low social rating, yet were still able to achieve great honour by their virtuous deeds and sayings (3.4), and those who failed to live up to the glory and honour of their parents (3.5),[29]

---

[26] Valerius often makes a contrast to exhort his readers to live according to Roman virtues – such as the contrast between the chapter 'Of the grateful' (5.2) and the following chapter 'Of ingrates' (5.3). He articulates, 'I have chosen to set in view signs of gratitude and acts of ingratitude so that due reward may accrue to vice and virtue through the very comparison of judgment' (5.2 *praef.*).

[27] 3.3 *ext.* 7. Translation from Skidmore, *Practical Ethics*, 88–9.

[28] Cf. Skidmore, *Practical Ethics*, 89.

[29] Valerius transitions from 3.4 to 3.5 by writing, 'The part of my twofold promise that follows must be delivered after the masks of illustrious men have been veiled, since I have to

Valerius realises how negative it would be for him to continue discussing individuals who did not live up to their social pedigree. So he shifts to another related social problem that engendered a false impression of Roman identity: 'It is better to relate which men of mark indulged themselves in some degree of innovation in their costume and other mode of living' (3.6 *praef.*). This next chapter, 'Of which men of mark indulged themselves in dress or other style more freely than ancestral custom permitted' (3.6), as noted above, is a penetrating discussion into a particular problem that was relevant to Valerius and his audience. All the given examples in this discourse are historical individuals of rank and status who were obsessed with publicly portraying themselves before others. For Valerius, this would be an abuse of privilege. Valerius again emphasises the urgency for appropriate social ethics, since Roman society was plagued with individuals from both ends of the social spectrum who were conventionally portraying their Roman identity by certain means that were incongruous with the traditional virtues of an ideal Roman *persona*.

In short, Valerius' critique of *persona* was primarily aimed at resolving the conflict of identity in Rome. In particular, he was against the popularly projected Roman *persona* at the time, which was a warped and corrupted presentation of the traditional and ideal values of Roman identity. As noted above, Skidmore has set a precedent for understanding Valerius' work as promoting a moral agenda of how to be a Roman gentleman. This present study continues this interpretation by submitting that Valerius not only reacted against the shallow presentation of social *persona* in his day, but that he also aimed to restore and promulgate the authentic and traditional values of what he considered to be an ideal Roman *persona*. This proposal will be developed by examining the moral intention of *Facta et dicta*, and also Valerius' promotion of the traditional and ideal Roman *persona*. Moreover, this examination of the ideal Roman *persona* will fill in the previous chapter's broad outline of the Roman stress on *persona*.

3.3 The Moral Intention of Valerius' Work

In order to examine the moral purpose of Valerius' work, attention will be given to the work's preface which informs of his task and style, and also of his authority for compiling *Facta et dicta*. Attention will then be given to Valerius' use of the *exempla* tradition to show the formative attributes of what he considers to be the ideal Roman *persona*.

---

tell of those who degenerated from their splendour, noble monsters steeped in the foulest filth of sloth and rascality' (3.5 *praef.*).

3.3.1 Valerius' Task and Style of Compiling Facta et dicta

Valerius' preface to his entire work is a central text for understanding the nature of the work. Examining its details will also reveal insights relating to Valerius' perception of the ideal Roman *persona*. He commences the work by articulating to his readers how he composed *Facta et dicta*:

> I have determined to select from famous authors and arrange the deeds and sayings worthy of memorial of the Roman City and external nations, too widely scattered in other sources to be briefly discovered, to the end that those wishing to take examples may be spared the labour of lengthy search.[30]

Valerius undertook the difficult task of researching and sifting through the historical materials, and compiling a work documenting historical *exempla* of worthy 'deeds and sayings' *(facta et dicta)*.[31] The fundamental value of the memorable deeds and sayings for his work is evident in how often he links 'deeds' and 'sayings' together to recall explicitly the purpose of the work (4.1.12; 6.2 *praef.*; 7.2 *praef.*; 7.3. *praef.*; 9.3 *praef.*; 9.11 *praef.*; 9.11.12).[32] Valerius was among other contemporary writers and historians who also preserved historical exemplary materials of the greatest and most noteworthy deeds (e.g. Herodotus, *praef.*; Thucydides 1.1.1; Sallust, *Cat.* 4.2).[33] Valerius, then, was not innovative in his task of compiling deeds and sayings of utmost worth for his readers, since he accepted a conventional literary task, and his work would have been accepted among other contemporary works.

Having explained his literary task, Valerius continues his preface by indicating the difference between his work and similar previous works:

> Nor am I seized with ambition to be all-embracing. Who should comprise the transactions of all time in a moderate number of volumes? Or who in his right mind should hope to transmit with closer care or superior eloquence the procession of domestic and foreign history recorded by the felicitous pens of predecessors?[34]

This portion of the preface indicates two important features of Valerius' literary venture: brevity and eloquence. The examination of these two aspects will show some characteristics of Valerius' literary style, and possibly reveal more particulars of the purpose of *Facta et dicta*.

First, Valerius expresses that he does not desire to be 'all-embracing', nor see the possibility of covering all historical transactions from every age.

---

[30] 1.1 *praef.* 1–6.

[31] Cf. Frontinus, *Str.* 1 *praef.*

[32] See Wardle, *Valerius Maximus*, 66–7. Interestingly, in the preface of Acts (1.1) Luke informs that in his first book he has written of all that Jesus began ποιεῖν καὶ διδάσκειν. It would be worthwhile to explore this text in light of Valerius' preface, esp. since studies in Luke's preface (e.g. Alexander, *Preface*) have not yet considered Valerius' preface.

[33] Cf. Wardle, *Valerius Maximus*, 66.

[34] 1.1 *praef.* 6–11.

Brevity is a necessary motivating factor for him because previous works were often too lengthy and impractical.[35] Vitruvius in the preface to his *De architectura* (5 *praef.* 2–5) explains that given the busyness of his readers, who were overstrained by public and private business, his use of brevity would assist them in remembering his information more conveniently (cf. Frontinus, *Str.* 1 *praef.*; Plutarch, *Tim.* 15.6).[36] Valerius similarly had in mind the busyness of his readers, which led him to take on the task of researching and compiling a work that was brief and convenient. Despite its brevity, *Facta et dicta* comprehensively contains material from the earliest Greek literature through the reign of Tiberius (cf. Vitruvius, *De arch.* 5 *praef.* 5). Thus, *Facta et dicta* should be viewed as a brief, convenient, yet comprehensive work, which would be accessible and practical for 'everyday' use.[37]

Secondly, Valerius indicates that he is not seeking to improve on others' style with 'closer care' or 'superior eloquence'. By stating this, he announces that he is not innovating or adding anything new to the subject.[38] To explain what Valerius possibly could have meant in attempting not to be more elaborate, Bloomer differentiates Valerius from other popular literary authors: 'His initial "program" defined what he is not, an antiquarian historian (Varro), a historian and stylist (Livy) or a great stylist (Cicero)'.[39] On the basis of comparison between Valerius and other authors, various scholars have examined *Facta et dicta* and expressed negative remarks about Valerius' literary ability.[40] Although this study is not concerned with Valerius' use of sources, there are some particulars worth noting. Source critics evaluating Valerius' usage have generally commented on the differences in his presentation of the historical details to the presentation in the sources he used. However, by closely evaluating some of the deviations in *Facta et dicta* –

---

[35] Cf. Wardle, *Valerius Maximus*, 67, who lists some large-scale works on the history of Rome. E.g. see Livy's preface of his work, which is compiled in 142 books. See also Skidmore, *Practical Ethics*, 31–4, for further discussion of the brevity and convenience of Valerius' work.

[36] For more discussion, see Skidmore, *Practical Ethics*, 31–4.

[37] Cf. Wardle, *Valerius Maximus*, 14–15; Bloomer, *New Nobility*, 237–8. Also Mueller, *Roman Religion*, 15, comments that Valerius' provision of some one thousand *exempla* was 'to illustrate conduct in a variety of situations'.

[38] Cf. Wardle, *Valerius Maximus*, 68.

[39] Bloomer, *New Nobility*, 254. Valerius has rarely been analysed properly because scholars are quick to compare him to prior works of history. See Wardle, *Valerius Maximus*, 14–15, who comments on the complexity of Valerius' literary role.

[40] See e.g. Bloomer, *New Nobility*, 149; Maslakov, 'Roman Historiography', 454; Carter, 'Valerius Maximus', 30, 47. For more remarks, see Wardle, '*Domus Augusta*', 479; Mueller, *Roman Religion*, 5.

such as word order, and the synonyms used – certain insights can be seen.[41] For instance, in his article on the texts concerning Juno, Hans-Friedrich Mueller observes Valerius' remoulding of stories to associate intimately both religion and behavioural conduct.[42] Additionally, G. Maslakov assesses Valerius' *exempla:*

They are best seen as a phenomenon of a special kind – as the product of a widespread general interest in the ideals and actions of the nobility...[T]hese *exempla* mirror not so much the ideals of the *nobiles* themselves (though they do that to a certain extent), [but] as public attitudes to those ideals and the level of understanding in the community as a whole of the goals and accomplishments of those individuals.[43]

Also, in regard to his choice of language and use of synonyms in comparison to his sources, Bloomer assesses Valerius' diction as the vernacular: 'In the terms of his contemporaries Valerius avoided obscenity, Grecisms, and vulgarisms. Everyday words he certainly employed'.[44] From these insights, Valerius' statement of seeking not to be more eloquent should be understood as describing his choice of employing a simple and practical style, which would be relevant and obtainable by a wide audience, and not just the Roman elite.

3.3.2 *Valerius' Authority for Compiling* Facta et dicta

Valerius continues his introductory preface by dedicating the work to the emperor Tiberius:

Therefore I invoke you to this undertaking, Caesar,[45] surest salvation of the fatherland, in whose charge the unanimous will of gods and men has placed the governance of land and sea, by whose celestial providence the virtues of which I shall tell are most kindly fostered and the vices most sternly punished. Orators of old rightly began from Jupiter Best and Greatest, the finest poets took their start from some deity. My petty self shall betake me to your goodwill all the more properly in that other divinity is inferred by opinion whereas yours is seen by present certainty as equal to the star of your father and grandfather, through whose peerless radiance much far-famed lustre has accrued to our ceremonies. For other gods we have received, the Caesars we have bestowed.[46]

Facta et dicta is a critical work for classical studies because it reflects the Roman milieu during the reign of Tiberius.[47] Augustus, through his great

---

[41] See further discussion by Wardle, *Valerius Maximus*, 16–18; Bloomer, *New Nobility*, 233–43.

[42] Mueller, '*Vita*', 257–8. He also assesses, 'Moreover, by removing chronology, Valerius removed time. They are present, not ancient, examples'.

[43] Maslakov, 'Roman Historiography', 445.

[44] Bloomer, *New Nobility*, 237–8.

[45] There is no dispute that Tiberius is the referent of 'Caesar'.

[46] 1.1 *praef.* 12–25.

[47] Although this present study is not dependent on this crucial time period of the Roman

political and moral reform, transformed Rome from its Republican past to its imperial future. With the death of such a historic figure, Tiberius assumed control of this crucial age of transition. Mueller comments on the importance of Valerius' work as a witness for this time period:

> Valerius is very much a denizen of that new society and his peculiar literary perceptions of the republican past offer insight into his view of the contemporary scene. Indeed, because Valerius Maximus comes so close on the heels of Augustus' efforts at religious revival and moral reform, his views of religion and personal morality in the context of Tiberian Rome are essential.[48]

The importance of *Facta et dicta* yields the appropriate social context for understanding Valerius' invocation to the emperor, which is paramount for understanding Valerius' work. From this dedication, which is concerned about virtues and vices, 'the essentially moral purpose of the work becomes clear'.[49] The invocation will now be analysed to determine the contours of Valerius' 'moral purpose'.

It is not unusual for prose writers to dedicate their works to the emperor, but Valerius is the earliest extant prose writer to invoke the emperor.[50] Valerius' dedicatory language used for Tiberius is flattering and suggestive of the importance of the emperor to Roman society.[51] In his dedication, Valerius lauds Tiberius, 'by whose celestial providence (*caelesti providentia*) the virtues of which I shall tell are most kindly fostered and the vices most sternly punished'. Valerius implicitly conveys the emperor's divine origin by using the important term *providentia*, which is often attributed to Tiberius.[52] Wardle writes that Valerius 'imputes a divine origin for Tiberius' forethought [*providentia*] in language which all but states that Tiberius was a god'.[53] Moreover, Valerius affirms the ancient tradition of orators and poets beginning their works with some great divine power, such as Jupiter, who was worshipped as the chief god in the Roman pantheon.[54] Valerius, however, deviates from the tradition by starting off his work with a greater divine

---

empire, a brief overview is necessary for a proper analysis of the purpose of Valerius' composition.

[48] Mueller, '*Vita*', 3, cf. 222. See also Bloomer, *New Nobility*, 3; Maslakov, 'Roman Historiography', 439.

[49] Wardle, *Valerius Maximus*, 13.

[50] Wardle, *Valerius Maximus*, 68.

[51] See Wardle, *Valerius Maximus*, 68–74, for commentary on the various expressions in the preface. E.g. Valerius addresses Tiberius as 'Caesar, surest salvation of the fatherland'. *Salus* ('salvation' or 'safety'), which first appears on the imperial coins during Tiberius' reign, is often attributed to Tiberius by Valerius (cf. 2.9.6; 8.13 *praef*.; 9.11 *ext*. 4).

[52] See Charlesworth, 'Providentia', 110–13, who analyses the numismatic evidence expressing the *providentia* of Tiberius.

[53] Wardle, *Valerius Maximus*, 69.

[54] Cf. Wardle, *Valerius Maximus*, 70; Mueller, *Roman Religion*, 1, 11.

power – the emperor Tiberius. That is, 'Rather than invoke this traditionally most powerful member of Rome's pantheon, Valerius mentions Jupiter, only to invoke Tiberius instead'.[55] Furthermore, Valerius' self-denigration of 'petty self', which has been discussed above, is to be understood as an expression of his humility before the splendour and divinity of Tiberius. Wardle comments, 'Because his talents are humbler than those of the great orators and poets, he needs a greater power to assist him, the superior, present divinity of the emperor'.[56] The implicit stress on the divinity of Tiberius is intensified in the phrase 'as equal to the star of your father and grandfather'. Julius Caesar and Augustus were formally declared to be divine at their deaths, but Valerius appears, remarkably, to identify also the living Tiberius as divine.[57]

Importantly, Valerius presents Tiberius' *providentia* in connection to the virtues and vices, which the emperor himself praises and punishes. Tiberius is 'an appropriate inspiration for Valerius because his virtues, supremely apparent, establish his divinity'.[58] As the successor to Augustus, Tiberius is perceived to have inherited the virtues through Augustus and his *domus*.[59] In Augustus' *Res Gestae*, he states, 'By the passage of new laws I restored many traditions of our ancestors (*exempla maiorum*) which were then falling into disuse, and I myself set precedents in many things for posterity to imitate' (8.5). Moreover, Wallace-Hadrill elucidates on the people's perception of the emperor and his virtues: 'For the mass of the population of the Empire the legal and constitutional position of their ruler was an irrelevance. What mattered was their belief that he was right for them and that they needed him. This belief centered on his possession of certain "virtues"'.[60] The virtues and vices that Valerius presents through his memorable deeds and sayings are to be seen, then, in the supreme exemplification of the emperor. Valerius'

---

[55] Mueller, *Roman Religion*, 11. See his pp. 69–107, for a treatment of Jupiter's importance in *Facta et dicta*.

[56] Wardle, *Valerius Maximus*, 70–1.

[57] Cf. Wardle, *Valerius Maximus*, 72; idem, '*Domus Augusta*', 489–92. See also idem, 'Sainted Julius', 323–45, for the divinity of Caesar and Augustus.

[58] Wardle, *Valerius Maximus*, 73.

[59] For further studies of the emperor and the imperial virtues, see Charlesworth, 'Virtues', 105–33; Wallace-Hadrill, 'Emperor', 298–323. For studies of the *domus Augusta* (Caesar, Augustus, and Tiberius), see Wardle, '*Domus Augusta*', 479–93; Millar, '*Domus Augustus*', 1–17.

[60] Wallace-Hadrill, 'Emperor', 299. Also the *senatus consultum de Pisone Patre*, declares that virtues were 'learned from its forebears and especially from the deified Augustus and Ti. Caesar Augustus its *principes*' (lines 91–92, trans. by Potter & Damon, '*Senatus consultum*', 29). Furthermore, Cooley, 'Moralizing Message', 209, remarks: 'The decision to publish this decree fulfils the aim of moral didacticism on a grand scale. By publishing it throughout the empire, the Senate encourages the right sort of behavior in present and future generations by presenting to the world the virtues of the *domus Augusta* and the vices of Cn. Piso'.

contemporary, Velleius Paterculus, articulates the same sentiment regarding the emperor's exemplification of morality: 'Right is now honoured, evil is punished...for the best of emperors teaches his citizens to do right by doing it, and though he is greatest among us in authority, he is still greater in the example which he sets' (2.126.2–4). Valerius portrays in his preface, then, the same high regard for Tiberius' role as the epitome of honouring what is right and punishing what is evil.

Having this knowledge, Valerius appropriately dedicates his work to Tiberius, the authoritative emperor and pinnacle of Roman virtues. By flattering the emperor, Valerius is able to accentuate the moral message in his compilation of memorable deeds and sayings that express the traditional ideals of Roman virtues. Claude Loutsch explains that by extolling Tiberius, 'Valère Maxime inscrit explicitement son ouvrage dans la politique de restauration morale dont il crédite Tibère'.[61] Furthermore, the emperor's encouragement of virtues and his punishment of vices establish the criteria for Roman virtues and vices. Yves Lehmann intimates how Valerius' dedication serves to empower his moral agenda, 'En plaçant son recueil de faits édifiants sous l'égide d'un Tibère protecteur des vertus et pourfendeur des vices, Valère Maxime se présente essentiellement comme un moraliste'.[62] By stressing the importance of encouraging virtues and censuring vices, Valerius accordingly supplies the reader with the appropriate criteria to interpret his moral message that all subsequent memorable deeds and sayings are to be considered and judged as worthy of praise or blame.[63]

In summary, Valerius has sought to provide a brief, convenient, and comprehensive book of memorable deeds and sayings that would be useful for a wide audience. By dedicating his work to Tiberius – the beholder and exemplar of Roman virtues – with flattering praise, Valerius generates authority for his message of morality. Thus, *Facta et dicta* can be viewed as a handbook encouraging virtues and condemning vices, which helps to delineate his understanding of the ideal Roman *persona* – which is modelled by the emperor.

---

[61] Loutsch, 'Procédés', 32.
[62] Lehmann, 'Revendications', 24 n. 20.
[63] Cf. Livy, *praef.* 10. Also, cf. Paul's exhortation in Rom 13.1–7; Phil 4.8–9.

3.4 The *Exempla* of the Ideal Roman *Persona*

Facta et dicta is essentially a compilation of *exempla* of memorable deeds or sayings. Usage of the *exempla* tradition was common in Graeco-Roman literature.[64] The earliest Roman definitions of the *exemplum* are found in the rhetorical handbook *Rhetorica ad Herennium* (4.62) and Cicero's *De inventione rhetorica* (1.49), both of which mention the rhetorical technique of using examples from the past. Elsewhere, Cicero describes the orator as one who:

...should also be acquainted with the history of the events of past ages, particularly, of course, of our state, but also of imperial nations and famous kings...To be ignorant of what occurred before you were born is to remain always a child. For what is the worth of human life, unless it is woven into the life of our ancestors by the records of history? Moreover, the mention of antiquity and the citation of examples (*exemplorumque*) give the speech authority and credibility as well as affording the highest pleasure to the audience.[65]

Cicero's words reflect the present value of past events, as conveyed by Mueller: 'Past conduct retains present validity (and, by extension, endless future validity as well)'.[66]

Additionally, the *exempla* were not only beneficial for rhetorical purposes, but also for the education of Roman morality. Richard Saller writes, 'The widespread use of *exempla* in oratory is one consequence of deeper Roman attitudes towards moral authority'.[67] In *Pro Archia* 14, Cicero defends the necessity of studying literature because all literature has been a source of moral lessons for his own life:

All literature, all philosophy, all history, abounds of examples (*exemplorum*) to noble action, incentives which would be buried in black darkness were the light of the written word not flashed upon them. How many pictures of high endeavor the great authors of Greece and Rome have drawn for our use, and bequeathed to us, not only for our contemplation, but for our emulation! These I have held ever before my vision throughout my public career, and have guided the workings of my brain and my soul by meditating upon patterns of excellence.

Cicero recognised that literary works contained an abundance of words and deeds worthy for emulation, by which the morality for his public and private life was shaped.[68] Also, the elder Cato aimed to teach his son zealousness in virtue (ἀρετή) by handwriting his *Origines* (a history of Rome) in large letters

---

[64] Cf. Bloomer, *New Nobility*, 18–19, for other ancient works using *exempla*.

[65] *Or. Brut.* 120. Cf. Cicero, *De or.* 2.51–2. See Rawson, 'Cicero', 33–45, for Cicero's understanding of antiquity and history; Cape, 'Persuasive', 212–28, for the rhetorical use of historiography.

[66] Mueller, *Roman Religion*, 176.

[67] Saller, 'Anecdotes', 72. See Litchfield, '*Exempla Virtvtis*', esp. 5–9, for discussion of *exempla virtutum* in Roman literature.

[68] See Wardle, *Valerius Maximus*, 13; Wiseman, *Clio's Cosmetics*, 37–40.

for his son to read and learn from the ancient traditions (Plutarch, *Cat. Mai.*
20.7). Accordingly, in the preface to the work Valerius indicates his research
task of finding appropriate *exempla* from the various literary sources that
portray and promote Roman morality, which has consequences for one's ideal
Roman *persona*.

Various studies have analysed the social function of *exempla*.[69] For
instance, Saller investigates the generation and transmission of historical
anecdotes and expresses that 'anecdotes can be valuable evidence for the
attitudes and ideologies of people' and that 'perhaps a thorough analysis of
uses of anecdotes will offer some insight into the complex issue of the
development of Roman social roles'.[70] Moreover, in a recent illuminating
article, Matthew Roller shows that 'the socioethical dynamics of exemplarity
are fundamental to Roman historical consciousness itself', and offers a helpful
understanding of the dynamic social function of the *exempla* material.[71] He
suggests a schema of four components:[72]

1. An *action* (i.e. a deed or saying) held to be consequential for the
   Roman community at large, and admitting of ethical categorisation.
2. A 'primary' *audience* of eyewitnesses who observe this action, place it
   in a suitable ethical category (e.g. *virtus*, *pietas* or *gratia*), and judge it
   'good' or 'bad' in that category.
3. *Commemoration* of the deed by means of a *monument* – that is, a
   device that calls the deed to memory. Monuments aim to make the
   deed more widely visible by constructing 'secondary' audiences –
   persons who were not eyewitnesses, but who learn of the deed through
   the monument.[73]
4. Finally, *imitation*: any spectator to such a deed, whether primary or
   secondary, is enjoined to strive to replicate or to surpass the deed
   oneself, to win similar renown and related social capital – or, for
   negative examples, to avoid replicating an infamous deed.

Roller consequently observes 'a cyclical dimension to exemplary discourse:
deeds generate other deeds, spawning ever more audiences and monuments,
in an endless loop of social reproduction'.[74]

Roller's schema is invaluable for appreciating Valerius' use of *exempla*.
The 'action' (#1) can be applied to Valerius' *exempla* (deeds or sayings). The
'audience' (#2) can be applied on two levels: the primary audience who

---

[69] See e.g. Lumpe, 'Exemplum', 1229–57; Maslakov, 'Roman Historiography', 436–96;
Loutsch, 'Procédés', 27–41.

[70] Saller, 'Anecdotes', quotation from p. 82.

[71] See Roller, 'Exemplarity', 1–9, quotation from p. 7.

[72] This is a summary of Roller, 'Exemplarity', 4–5.

[73] Cf. Maslakov, 'Roman Historiography', 441 n. 7; Wiseman, *Clio's Cosmetics*, 39.

[74] Roller, 'Exemplarity', 6.

witnessed the action and deemed it memorable, and also Valerius, who researched and deemed the action worthy for his compilation of *exempla*. The 'commemoration' (#3) is observed in two parts – the *Facta et dicta,* which 'monumentalises' and exhibits the action; and also, the action itself, which is set up in the mind of the readers (secondary audiences) as a monument for contemplation (cf. 5.4 *ext.* 1; Livy, *praef.* 10). Finally, 'imitation' (#4) is the goal and purpose of Valerius' work – to promote moral living and the traditional virtues of the ideal Roman *persona.*

In addition, Roller also gives some important insights into his proposed scheme that are relevant for Valerius' work. First, he identifies the wide populace of Rome, and not only the elite, as the individuals involved in this process: 'Exemplary discourse, then, encompasses all of Roman society, from the loftiest aristocrats to the humblest peasants, laborers, and slaves'.[75] Second, he comments on the powerful ideological effects of exemplary discourse on the Roman populace, especially in the social context where 'they often acted with a view toward being observed, evaluated, monumentalized, and imitated, and assumed that other people did likewise'.[76] Third, he explains the possible challenges to his schema. He specifically remarks on the difficulties involved in the production of *exempla*, whereby the communicator has 'to struggle constantly to establish or disestablish a particular interpretation of an action's value'.[77] In the case of Valerius, this present study suggests that with the multiple *exempla* he compiled in a given chapter, along with his prefaces and transitions, Valerius helpfully limits erroneous interpretations and, instead, directs the reader to his intended interpretation.

Furthermore, Valerius employed the commonplace *exempla* tradition to exhibit his perception of the ideal Roman *persona*, and to urge his readers to respond and live according to his message of morality. In fact, Valerius was so keen on its rhetorical and moral value that he expressed his preference for the use of *exempla* over words (4.4 *praef.*; 5.4 *ext.* 1). Skidmore explains, 'Because of their more concrete nature, examples possess more verisimilitude than words alone and are more plausible and persuasive; this need for verisimilitude is relevant to the way that Valerius refers to his examples as images (*imagines*) or personalities (*personae*)'.[78] Therefore, being conscious of the rhetorical and moral value of *exempla*, Valerius researched and compiled some one thousand memorable deeds and sayings to promote virtues and punish vices. Attention will now be given to the formative attributes of Valerius' promotion of the ideal Roman *persona*: the emulation

---

[75] Roller, 'Exemplarity', 6.
[76] Roller, 'Exemplarity', 6–7.
[77] Roller, 'Exemplarity', 7.
[78] Skidmore, *Practical Ethics*, 84.

of virtues, the avoidance of vices, the *Romano* distinctiveness, and the traditional ideals of the *mos maiorum*.

3.4.1 Virtues: The Positive Aspect of Roman Identity

In order to address the positive aspects of Roman morality, Valerius organises his *exempla* into various books and chapters. The surviving text of *Facta et dicta* is organised into nine books.[79] Although the materials are organised into books, it is quite difficult to comprehend any clear systematic plan of organisation, especially between the books.[80] The structural level of the chapter, however, is a more discernible component in *Facta et dicta*.[81] Each chapter is based on a certain theme, which bears upon a particular virtue or vice. By surveying the chapter titles,[82] the importance of morality can be observed. The historical examples chosen for these chapters all exemplify the ideal of the particular virtue (or vice) he discusses. Glancing over the various chapter headings alone can give a sense of the pressing themes for Valerius and his contemporary readers.[83] Valerius' concern with morality and social ethics can be seen in the chapters: 'Of bravery' (3.2); 'Of fortitude' (3.3); 'Of self-confidence' (3.7); 'Of moderation' (4.1); 'Of abstinence and continence' (4.3); 'Of modesty' (4.5); 'Of friendship' (4.7); 'Of humanity and mercy' (5.1); 'Of chastity' (6.1); 'Of justice' (6.5); 'Of good fortune' (7.1); 'On study and diligence' (8.7). Additionally, Valerius devotes most of Book 1 to themes of Roman religion, which stress the link between Roman piety and virtue.[84]

---

[79] Although there have been some speculations over a missing book or longer ending to the work, there is no considerable evidence warranting these speculations. See Wardle, *Valerius Maximus*, 6 n. 21.

[80] See the negative evaluation by Carter, 'Valerius Maximus', 27–8. However, Römer, 'Aufbau', 101, has suggested that the preface to the work is the framework for Valerius' material, whereby Books 3–8 present the virtues and are consistent with 'das System der stoischen Kardinaltugenden', while Book 9 presents the vices. See Wardle, *Valerius Maximus*, 7–8, for a critique of Römer's argument.

[81] Wardle, *Valerius Maximus*, 9, concludes that the unit of book was less of a priority for Valerius, than the unit of chapter.

[82] The chapter headings were likely not part of the original text, but were included later by copyists; cf. Wardle, *Valerius Maximus*, 6 n. 22. Nevertheless, from the content of the chapters, the theme of each chapter is easily obtainable and cohesive.

[83] See Skidmore, *Practical Ethics*, xii–v, for a breakdown of Valerius' work by book and chapter.

[84] For more on this important theme, see Lane, 'Sabazius', 35–8; Mueller, '*Vita*', 221–63; idem, *Roman Religion*; and Wardle, *Valerius Maximus*, whose commentary is only on Book 1. Wardle assesses: 'The prominence he gives to religion within his work, by its position as the first book and in its scale, shows the importance of religion within the overall scheme of virtues and vices which informs the whole; belief in the gods and their active involvement in human affairs provide the fundamental incentive to the morality advocated by Valerius' (25).

Valerius accentuates the importance of the themes for his overall purpose by prefacing his themes and chapters, whereby the preface helps the transition between one theme and the next. With the prefaces, Valerius not only presents the themes of virtue or vice, but he also offers the key to interpret the supporting *exempla*. Skidmore explains that the prefaces are 'devoted to elaborate praise of virtues or to condemnation of vices, and seek to convince the reader of the point made by the chapter's examples'.[85] In effect, Valerius is able to highlight and accentuate the moral issue at hand, since 'Valerius provided such a catalogue with the morals inescapably highlighted by the arrangement and by his own introductions and conclusions to the individual *exempla*'.[86] Another important element of the preface is the end result or reward of exercising virtue. In his discussion 'Of natural temper' (3.1), he begins by prefacing his purpose of underscoring the virtues: 'I am about to touch upon certain cradles and elements of valour and shall relate samplings given with sure trial of natural temper of a spirit destined in course of time to attain the highest pinnacles of glory' (3.1 *praef.*). Also, in 'Of majesty' (2.10), he describes majesty and its worthiness: 'It glides up to the hearts of men covered with the adornment of admiration and enters welcome and pleasing' (2.10 *praef.*).[87] As Valerius highlights the ambition for adornment and praise as the result of a virtuous life (cf. 4.1 *praef.*; 8.15 *praef.*), his reader would be motivated to heed and emulate the worthy deeds and sayings. The preface, then, not only serves the reader by introducing and helping to interpret the *exempla*, but also by giving proper motivation to imitate the *exempla*. Therefore, through his use of both chapters and prefaces, Valerius is able to promote the virtues that are the formative attributes of the ideal Roman *persona*.

3.4.2 Vices: The Negative Aspect of Roman Identity

Although *Facta et dicta* has been regarded as a practical handbook promoting virtue, it is equally important, a practical work demoting vices, which is consistent with Valerius' moral agenda of promoting virtues and punishing vices (1.1 *praef*). Even though most of his chapters are positive examples of Roman virtues, he does underline a significant number of vices, most of which are in Book 9, for example: 'Of luxury and lust' (9.1); 'Of cruelty' (9.2); 'Of anger or hatred' (9.3); 'Of avarice' (9.4); 'Of arrogance and

---

[85] Skidmore, *Practical Ethics*, 58. He further comments that the preface 'is important to condition the reader's attitude before he reads the examples lest he draw the wrong conclusion from them'.

[86] Wardle, *Valerius Maximus*, 13.

[87] Examples of other end results are comfort and peace (4.4.11), and relief from anxiety (6.9 *praef.*).

outrageousness' (9.5); 'Of treachery' (9.6); 'Of violence and sedition' (9.7); 'Of rashness' (9.8); 'Of error' (9.9); and 'Of revenge' (9.10). In addition, Valerius' prefaces also underscore the importance of the themes of vices. For example, in 'Of Leisure', he warns that leisure opposes diligence and study (8.8 *praef.*), and in 'Of luxury and lust', he introduces these themes not to promote honour, but to bring about repentance (9.1 *praef*).

While the chapters on virtues exhibited positive examples of past individuals performing deeds or makings statements, which would encourage the reader to live according to virtue, these chapters on vices, on the other hand, portray the deeds and sayings of individuals who performed a particular vice or failed at being virtuous. This presentation of vices functions to deter the reader from vice, and alternatively, encourage the reader to virtue. Skidmore explains: 'The glory individual exemplars have achieved encourages readers to imitate their noble deeds. Conversely, those historical characters whose actions brought them infamy are used to deter the reader from a given course of action...Valerius' ethical aims are the encouragement of virtue and the deterrence of vice'.[88] Valerius appropriately provides guidance for his readers to develop and maintain the ideal Roman identity by instilling in their minds the 'unworthy' deeds and sayings that should not be imitated. Therefore, the avoidance of what he considered inappropriate behaviour is also fundamental to Valerius' conception of the traditional and ideal Roman *persona*.

3.4.3 Romano-*centricity*

In the preface to his work, Valerius expresses his task of compiling not only Roman examples, but also foreign examples (1.1 *praef.*). The foreign *exempla* portray similar virtuous deeds and sayings as the Roman *exempla*, and as a result they provide Valerius' audience with further guidelines for what he considers to be appropriate living in Roman society.[89] Despite his appreciation of the exemplary value of the foreign *exempla*, Valerius undoubtedly favours the Roman deeds and sayings over the foreign ones. This is clearly observed in the amount of Roman *exempla* outweighing the amount of foreign *exempla* in *Facta et dicta*. This pro-Roman focus can also be noticed in chapters 7.5 and 7.7–8.6, where there are no foreign examples. This partiality shows that

---

[88] Skidmore, *Practical Ethics*, xvi. See also his pp. 79–81, for some further discussion. With the exception of Skidmore, it should be noted that scholars have not produced adequate studies of this negative aspect of Valerius' moral purpose.

[89] Skidmore, *Practical Ethics*, 89, indicates that Valerius' foreign *exemplum* has the same effective results as the 'unlikely example', whereby 'the more barbarous and unexpected', the more effective the example would motivate his readers to act accordingly. See also Noy, *Foreigners*, 31–52, for the attitudes toward foreigners in Rome.

Valerius is particularly concerned about the Roman state and its virtues (cf. Livy, *praef.* 1; Tacitus, *Ann.* 1.1.1).[90] For instance, after Valerius ends his discussion of the foreign *exempla* in 'Of military discipline', he concludes with a remark on the abundance of Roman examples: 'But it suffices to have just taken a look at alien material since we can boast examples of our own far more copious and fruitful' (2.7 *ext.* 2). Before he begins to consider the foreign *exempla* in another chapter, Valerius again asserts his Roman pride: 'But since foreign notabilities can be taken into account without derogation to the majesty of Rome, we shall pass thereto' (8.15 *ext.* 1). These references highlight the importance of the Roman state for Valerius. Thus, regardless of how great the deed or saying of a foreigner was, it could not compare to the glorious deed or saying of a Roman.

The concept of Roman patriotism is fundamental for the Roman moral life. In his *De officiis*, Cicero explicates the various duties and moral obligations, of which 'love of country' is singled out to be the highest order, even above family and fellow kinsmen (*Off.* 1.57–8; cf. 1.152–61).[91] Henry Litchfield conveys the importance of this Roman nationalism, which naturally derived from a country saturated with success in warfare: 'The influence of patriotism thrilled through every fibre of moral and intellectual life...Patriotism almost always occupied a prominence in the scale of duties...'[92] Valerius demonstrates the relevance of patriotism for his readers' life, as seen in his chapters 'Of devotion to country' (5.6) and 'Of public faith' (6.6). Book 2 also contains an introduction of themes relating to ancient and memorable institutions and customs, in which he expresses his motivation for giving these examples: 'For it behooves us to learn what were the origins of the happy life we lead under our best of leaders, so that a backward look at them may yield some profit to modern manners' (Book 2 *praef.*). Valerius is attempting, then, to guide his readers to live according to the same Roman virtues demonstrated throughout Roman history. Skidmore explains, 'The purpose of many of these apparently antiquarian anecdotes is to introduce and praise the virtues which the author regards as essential to the moral rectitude of the individual and to the stability of the state'.[93] Since being 'Roman' is essential for Valerius' conception of the ideal Roman *persona*, he appropriately presents the past memorable deeds and sayings to portray what the ideal *persona* of a virtuous Roman should be.

---

[90] Cf. Wardle, *Valerius Maximus*, 66.

[91] See Bloomer, *New Nobility*, 5, who suggests that Cicero is Valerius' influence for subordinating the foreign examples to Roman examples.

[92] Litchfield, '*Exempla Virtvtis*', 11. He also articulates: 'Patriotism and military honor were indissolubly connected in the Roman mind. They were the two sources of national enthusiasm, the chief ingredients of the national conception of greatness' (10).

[93] Skidmore, *Practical Ethics*, 61.

3.4.4 *The* Mos maiorum *('Custom of the Ancestors')*

The domestic memorable deeds and sayings chosen by Valerius are all from the past history of Rome. A survey of the history of Rome reveals some indications of a problematic past, yet Valerius occasionally depicts his own era as a serene age.[94] Being aware of the troubling contexts of some of his *exempla*, Valerius compiles and presents these *exempla* in a certain fashion that portrays a history of Rome founded and maintained by people of virtue.[95] Valerius is able to render the past as one that had its trouble, yet was saved by virtues, since 'he has to assimilate material that shows the Roman past as violent and turbulent, as well as one in which traditional *virtus* was recognized and rewarded'.[96]

In particular, Valerius counteracts the social immorality that plagues Roman society by exercising the *mos maiorum*.[97] The worthy deeds and sayings of the heroic past create a tradition that should be maintained by present and future individuals. Moreover, the *mos maiorum*, which 'includes everything the Romans considered worth preserving', maintains stability for Roman society and is 'the very quintessence of Roman moral conservatism'.[98] Levi Lind writes: 'The Roman feeling for national unity and their love of fatherland, the Roman obedience to magistrates and elders, Rome's consciousness of a noble past worthy of imitation embodied in the deeds, traits, and ways of ancient behavior were all bound up with *mos maiorum*'.[99] Similarly Ronald Mellor reflects on the educational value of the *mos maiorum*:

---

[94] E.g. the preface to 8.13: 'tranquillity of our epoch, than which there never was a happier'. See Maslakov, 'Roman Historiography', 451–5, who describes Valerius' era as troubled and unstable.

[95] See Bloomer, *New Nobility*, 53–4, who examines one of Valerius' toughest subjects: the Roman civil war and the cruelty involved. Bloomer argues that while Valerius discusses Sulla, a terrorising Roman general and dictator, Valerius detaches Sulla from recent Roman history, resulting in the Romans being innocent of cruelty. The agents of cruelty are, then, 'the foreign nations and individuals or aberrant individuals, like Sulla, animated by personal vice or enmity'.

[96] Maslakov, 'Roman Historiography', 454.

[97] Cf. Edwards, *Politics*, 4: 'Roman texts regularly contrast the alleged constancy of *mores maiorum* with cultural and moral change, which are thereby characterised as changed for the worse'; Wallace-Hadrill, '*Mutatio morum*', 12–14, for discussion of 'tradition' (*mos maiorum*) in light of the Roman cultural revolution. For further studies of the *mos maiorum*, see Lind, 'Tradition'; Hölkeskamp, '*Exempla*'; Bettini, '*Mos*'; Engels, 'Exempla-Reihe'.

[98] Lind, 'Tradition', quotations from pp. 51, 56, respectively. He also explains that the *mos maiorum* consisted of moral concepts, such as *gloria, magnitudo, animi, dignitas, grauitas, and auctoritas* (15), but the most all-embracing *mos* was *uirtus* (52).

[99] Lind, 'Tradition', 51. Cf. Mueller, *Roman Religion*, 9: 'Acceptable patterns of behavior, custom, *mos*, handed down by tradition, are a source of strength (*virtus*) for society'.

By linking the present with the past, history would illuminate the contemporary state of society and provide both moral and practical guidance. Thus a Roman was encouraged to imitate the personal and civic virtues of his ancestors at the family hearth, in the Forum, or on the battlefield. This closely intertwined code of public and private conduct was called the *mos maiorum* – 'the traditions of our ancestors' – and formed the core of moral and political education at Rome.[100]

Augustus himself recognised the imitative value of the *mos maiorum*, 'By the passage of new laws I restored many traditions of our ancestors (*exempla maiorum*) which were then falling into disuse, and I myself set precedents in many things for posterity to imitate' (*Res Gestae* 8.5).[101] Thus, the motif of the *mos maiorum* was valuable in communicating the ideals of Roman virtue and the conservatism of the Roman elite.

Accordingly, Valerius' compilation of some one thousand *exempla* should be appreciated as a work promoting the virtues of the *mos maiorum*, which establishes the traditional criteria of the ideal Roman *persona*. In his work, Valerius attempts to construct this ideal Roman identity by displaying the precedence of the past *exempla*, who display the heroic conventions of Rome's traditional past, and their function for sustaining Roman society. Skidmore comments, 'Valerius is keen to emphasize that the men of the past were able to found the Roman Empire only because of their high moral standards of qualities such as self-control, propriety and severity'.[102] This idea is evident in Valerius' chapter on devotion to one's country (5.6), where he concludes with a statement about the weightiness of the *exempla*: 'It is evident, therefore, how men of all orders and ages have arisen with abundant and unstinting piety towards country. A wealth of marvellous examples famous worldwide has corroborated the holiest laws of Nature' (*ext.* 5). Here Valerius accentuates the supreme value of his *exempla*, and his readers are expected to evaluate the examples' acts of loyalty to country as worthy of emulation. Upon imitating the virtuous deeds, Valerius' readers will develop the elite ideal of a Roman identity that perpetuates the heroic values of the *mos maiorum*. In other words, the same traditional values and elite ideals that strengthened the foundations of Rome are, consequently, the rudiments of the ideal Roman *persona* which he promotes through his work.

Therefore, with his *Romano*-centricity and his deep reverence for the *mos maiorum*, Valerius produced a work that aimed to restore the traditional and ideal notions of a 'Roman' *persona*. Marianne Coudry aptly concludes on Valerius' concern with Roman identity:

---

[100] Mellor, *Roman Historians*, 3–4.

[101] Ramage, *Nature*, 111: 'The *mos maiorum* is the starting point for most, if not all, of Augustus' actions'.

[102] Skidmore, *Practical Ethics*, 61.

Le recueil de Valère Maxime contribuait du même coup à perpétuer un type de relation au passé profondément ancré dans la culture romaine, fait d'une remémoration régulière de ses grands épisodes constamment réinterprétés en fonction des perspectives du moment, et qui assurait ainsi, par l'instrumentalisation de la mémoire collective, la préservation d'une identité.[103]

3.5 Conclusion

Valerius Maximus' critique of social *persona* was observed in his work, *Facta et dicta*. The social context of Valerius and his work indicated a perennial condition of individuals not living according to the traditional Roman virtues. In particular, Valerius and his audience's social world reflected the typical preoccupation with the superficial aspect of one's social identity, which spawned from the conventional outworking of *persona* in their day. Accordingly, Valerius criticised this conventional projection as a warped presentation of the ideal values of *persona*, which was seen in Chapter Two. Moreover, since the Roman populace had engaged in vices and abused the Roman virtues, Valerius reacted to this crisis of Roman identity by producing a handbook that aimed to restore the traditional and ideal values of being a Roman, and to guide individuals to live according to virtues and not vices. Valerius' themes of virtues and vices followed the pattern that he established at the outset of his work, where he sought authority by invoking the highest moral power, the emperor, 'by whose celestial providence the virtues of which I shall tell are most kindly fostered and the vices most sternly punished' (1.1 *praef.*). Moreover, Valerius communicated his moral message by presenting *exempla* of the past (memorable deeds and sayings), which function to interact not only with the past, but also to bring transformation to individuals in the present and future.

Therefore, Valerius reacted against what he considered to be the inappropriate behaviour of flaunting a shallow presentation of Roman identity, and he also inculcated his conception of an ideal Roman *persona*. An individual could display this ideal Roman *persona* by doing the actions of virtue, and by not doing the deeds of vice. If Valerius' readers abide by his criteria, they would then be preserving and perpetuating the traditional and heroic Roman virtues – the rudiments of Roman morality – that gave Rome its strength, stability, and elitism. His conception of the ideal Roman *persona* was confirmed by his *Romano*-centricity and also the *mos maiorum*, with the latter serving as an authority and model for the traditional ideals of Roman identity. In addition to these abstract ideals, the closest image of what this traditional and ideal Roman *persona* looks like in *Facta et dicta* was the

---

[103] Coudry, 'Conclusion', 192.

emperor Tiberius, whom Valerius regard as the authoritative source and ideal exemplar.

As a social critic, Valerius reacted to a superficial view of identity in his social world. Although his reaction should be regarded as a serious critique, he significantly did not indicate any negative attitudes toward the Roman social hierarchy of rank and status. In fact, he was quite concerned about using *exempla* of Roman individuals with high rank and status for his portrayal of memorable deeds and sayings. Moreover, Valerius affirmed the fact that although *persona* was important for the majority of the Roman populace, it was nonetheless an elite ideal. This is especially confirmed by his depiction of the emperor as the quintessence of the ideal Roman *persona*. Since Valerius appreciated and upheld the traditional values of Roman society (e.g. Roman social hierarchy) his point of contention was with the conventional obsession with the shallow features of *persona*, and also the notion that one's superficial presentation of certain ideals of Roman identity was enough for attaining virtue. Valerius, essentially, was not inculcating an innovative interpretation of *persona*, but an interpretation that viewed the concept of *persona* in its traditional and ideal form; that is, he was restoring the genuine values of 'Roman' *persona*. In fact, Valerius was not a strong critic of Roman *persona*, but one who was reaffirming the proper use of Roman social conventions for living a virtuous life. Thus, Valerius' critique helped to fill in the picture of what is truly an ideal 'Roman' *persona*, rather than the conventional picture that is a distortion and exploitation of this traditional and ideal concept.

Chapter 4

Epictetus and Identity in the Greek East

4.1 Introduction

Having examined Valerius Maximus and his critique of *persona*, specifically the conventionally projected *persona* in his day, this chapter will focus on the second figure of this study, Epictetus and his critique of *persona*. As was the case of Valerius, after searching for instances of the term πρόσωπον, Epictetus was perceived to have some notable uses of the word πρόσωπον in his work, *Dissertationes,* that were pertinent to this study's interest in social identity. Instead of merely examining these instances, Epictetus' work was read as a whole for more insights into his understanding of social identity. By reading through his work in light of his social setting and looking beyond the instances of the lexical term πρόσωπον for similar terms and expressions, more relevant details concerning the social concept of *persona* were found. As in the research on the terms *persona* and πρόσωπον, the social features of rank and status were used to discern which details counted as part of Epictetus' knowledge and critique of social identity. While organising the evidence, a preliminary view of the details revealed that Epictetus, like Valerius, had both a negative and a positive critique of social identity. In addition, a survey of the secondary literature on Epictetus and his work confirmed this possible two-fold critique of social identity.

In the previous chapter, Valerius provided a valuable social description of the city of Rome – particularly the Roman stress on *persona* in that social setting. In Chapter Two, it was mentioned that the concept of *persona* could have a general conception in the Graeco-Roman world, rather than only a Roman distinction. One would expect this to be the case in the Roman Greek East, which is the primary setting of Epictetus' work. Although Epictetus probably had a broad understanding of *persona*, the evidence from his work indicates the existence of a strong Roman emphasis on *persona* in his social environment. As will be seen, Epictetus often reflects on aspects of Roman society and, in particular, issues of Roman social identity. In fact, Epictetus spent a large portion of his life in Rome before relocating to Nicopolis in the Roman Greek East where he was a teacher of students who belonged to the Roman elite. Thus, an examination of Epictetus and his work will provide insights into social identity and the concept of *persona* in the social worlds of both Rome and the Roman Greek East. Before exploring Epictetus as a social critic of the Roman stress on *persona*, an introduction will be given to Epictetus, his audience, work, and philosophy.[1]

4.1.1 Epictetus

The introduction to Epictetus will focus on three major facets of his life: his experiences as a slave in Rome, a philosopher in Rome, and a moral teacher in Nicopolis. This survey of these three aspects will pay particular attention to his experiences in the Roman social milieu, which will be relevant for understanding his perception of social *persona* in the Graeco-Roman world, and in particular the Roman Greek East.

4.1.1.1 Slave

Little is known of the details of Epictetus' life, but from the few historical details there is enough information for a biographical sketch.[2] He was born in the mid-first century CE (ca. 55) in the Graeco-Roman city of Hierapolis in Asia Minor.[3] Although there is speculation to whether he was born into slavery,[4] it is clear that at some point Epictetus lived in Rome as a slave of Epaphroditus,[5] a famous freedman and administrative secretary of emperors

---

[1] This chapter has benefited from Long, *Epictetus*, which is an excellent introduction to Epictetus and his philosophy. For substantial studies prior to Long, see Colardeau, *Epictète*; Bonhöffer, *Die Stoa*; idem, *Ethik*. See also Hershbell, 'Stoicism', 2148–63, whose slightly dated, but still useful work provides a history of scholarship on Epictetus up to 1986. Also, it should be noted here that Epictetus has usually been studied for knowledge of ancient philosophy and has tended to be neglected by social historians. The few notable studies of Epictetus and his social context are Millar, 'Imperial Court', 141–8; Brunt, 'Epictetus', 19–48; Hock, 'By the Gods', 121–42; Yieh, *One Teacher*, 185–236.

[2] For a collection of external evidence and autobiographical allusions in *Dissertationes*, see Schenkl, *Dissertationes*, iii–xxxiii; Souilhé, *Entretiens*, I:i–x; Long, *Epictetus*, 34–5.

[3] For the dating of Epictetus' life, see Schenkl, *Dissertationes*, xv–xxxii; Millar, 'Imperial Court', 141–2; Dobbin, *Discourses*, xii–xiii. See also Gill, *Discourses*, xii–xv, who provides a timeline of Epictetus' life.

[4] For inscriptional data suggesting his servile origin, see Schenkl, *Dissertationes*, vii; Millar, 'Imperial Court', 141.

[5] Epictetus confirms his slavery in 1.9.29; cf. Gellius, *Noct. att.* 2.18.10. Scholars have probed Epictetus' self-description as 'a lame old man' (1.8.14; 1.16.20), but the source of his lameness is speculative. Christian sources (e.g. Origen, *Cels.* 1.7) relate his lameness to the cruelty of his master, Epaphroditus, as may be seen in 1.9.29–30. However, the *Suda*, a tenth-century Greek lexicon/encyclopaedia, suggests that the cause of his lameness was rheumatism. In addition, Epictetus does not depict his former master in harsh terms (1.1.20; 1.19.19; 1.26.11). For more discussion, see Schenkl, *Dissertationes*, vi–ix; Weaver, 'Epaphroditus', 475–9; Dobbin, *Discourses*, xi; Long, *Epictetus*, 10.

Nero and Domitian.[6] Even though Epictetus was a slave, it is significant that he was a slave to the powerful Epaphroditus, through whom Epictetus gained access into the social world of the elite at Rome. In fact, Epictetus' experiences in Rome were such an influential part of his life that in his discourses he occasionally gives details of Rome and life in Rome.[7] He mentions details such as scenes from the circus or theatre (1.11.27; 1.29.37), and places like the Aqua Marcia (2.16.30–1) and the Palatine (1.19.6).[8] For this study of Epictetus as a social critic of the Roman emphasis on *persona*, it is important that he had experiences at the imperial court, where individuals jostled as they vigorously sought patrons (e.g. the emperor) and other influential people (e.g. Epaphroditus) for status, favours, and privileges.[9] For instance, he exposes the Roman elite's ambitions to achieve higher rank and status: 'If you wish to be consul you must keep vigils, run around, kiss men's hands, rot away at other men's doors, say and do many slavish things, send presents to many persons, and guest-gifts to some people every day' (4.10.20–1: cf. 4.1.60; 4.1.148). Epictetus especially provides harsh criticisms of individuals who desire the status of 'friends of Caesar' (*amici Caesaris*), since they go to great lengths to achieve this distinguished status in relation to the emperor (4.1.6–13; 4.1.45–8; 4.1.95 cf. 2.14.18). Fergus Millar writes:

Since Rome and Roman political life loomed so large in the mind of Epictetus it is not surprising that when he came to discourse to his pupils on what men imagined to be good fortune or bad, freedom or slavery, he should frequently use as examples cases involving the favour or disfavour of the Emperor.[10]

In fact, the significance of Rome can be seen in Epictetus' statement, 'For there in Rome are found in truth the great resources, while the riches of Nicopolis look to them like mere child's-play' (1.26.10). In light of these details, it is important to be mindful that Epictetus' experience as a slave in Rome impacted his life and would have influenced his critique of certain aspects of Roman society.

---

[6] For more on Epaphroditus, see Millar, 'Imperial Court', 141; Weaver, 'Epaphroditus', esp. 475–9; cf. 1.1.20; 1.19.19–21; 1.26.11–12.

[7] Millar, 'Imperial Court', 142–3: 'one cannot but note how often Epictetus' mind turned to Rome and Roman life, which he had left some fifteen years before'.

[8] These details are from Millar, 'Imperial Court', 142–3.

[9] For more details, see Millar, 'Imperial Court', 143–7.

[10] Millar, 'Imperial Court', 143. He further remarks on how striking the political system was that the personal judgements and actions of the Emperor affected not only the members of the governing class in Rome, but a wide range of individuals in the provinces, especially in the Greek East (146). Also, he states that the status 'friend of Caesar' is 'the type of worldly success on which Epictetus pours most scorn' (144).

4.1.1.2 *Stoic Philosopher*

Epictetus is popularly known as a Stoic philosopher and teacher.[11] While Epictetus was a slave, he studied philosophy under the influence of the famous Stoic philosopher and teacher, Musonius Rufus (1.9.29),[12] and it was possibly during this period that he was manumitted by Epaphroditus. Epictetus' identity as a philosopher in Rome is confirmed by the fact that he and all other philosophers were banished from Rome by Domitian sometime around the year 95 (Gellius, *Noct. att.* 15.11.3–5; Simplicius, *In Ench.* 153B).[13] Epictetus often expresses his great esteem for philosophers and also identifies himself as one. For instance, he sarcastically remarks to a young rhetoric student from Corinth, 'But nevertheless, since somehow or other I have been condemned to wear a grey beard and a rough cloak, and you are coming to me as to a philosopher...' (3.1.24). Epictetus proudly portrays the image of a philosopher, since he fashions the philosopher's beard and even declares, elsewhere, that he would rather lose his neck than his beard (1.2.29). More precisely, Epictetus identifies himself as a Stoic, which is clearly seen in his challenge to an imperial bailiff to live his life according to his Epicurean philosophy, 'If not, you will be no better than we who bear the name of Stoics' (3.7.17).

Stoic philosophy was among the popular philosophies of the late Roman Republic and imperial periods.[14] Living within the Roman socio-political world, these Roman Stoics, in comparison to their Stoic predecessors, had a greater interest in practical ethics, rather than theory.[15] For example, Epictetus describes the practicality of his philosophy by equating the philosopher's classroom to a hospital, where 'you ought not to walk out of it in pleasure but in pain, for you are not well when you come' (3.23.30).[16] Another difference between Epictetus and the traditional Stoics is that the latter were more rigid and concerned about progress to the 'rational ideal', while the former was more concerned about the present moral life. Anthony Long writes, 'Rather

---

[11] For more on his identity as a philosopher, see Stanton, 'Sophists', 356–7; Yieh, *One Teacher*, 189–95. See also Sedley, 'Philosophical Allegiance', 97–119, who examines the philosopher's allegiance to a philosophical school.

[12] For references to Musonius, see 1.1.27; 1.9.29; 1.7.32; 3.15.14; 3.23.29. For more on him, see Laurenti, 'Musonio', 2105–46; Lutz, 'Musonius Rufus', 1–147; and also Horst, 'Musonius Rufus', 306–15, for a NT study.

[13] For the dating of the banishment, see Sherwin-White, 'Pliny's Praetorship', 126–30.

[14] See Long, 'Roman Philosophy', 184–210, for discussion of Roman philosophy; Gill, 'School', 33–58, for Stoicism in the imperial period; Griffin, 'Philosophy', 5–11, for the popularity of the different philosophical schools.

[15] See Long, *Epictetus*, 19; Schofield, 'Stoic Ethics', 253–6; Gill, 'School', 36–8.

[16] For Epictetus and ancient 'psychotherapy', see Gill, *Discourses*, xviii–xix; idem, 'Psychotherapy', esp. 320–3; e.g. 3.21.20; 3.23.27–32.

than constantly emphasizing long-term goals, he urges on his students the importance of what they can do to make progress *now*.[17] Epictetus expresses this concern in a statement about how he and his students are not able to achieve the ideal of moral perfection: 'Is it possible to be from fault altogether? No that cannot be achieved, but it *is* possible ever to be intent upon avoiding faults' (4.12.19). Interestingly, according to Long, Epictetus favours and adopts practical virtues (e.g. integrity, freedom, and courage) that relate well with the Roman values of *virtus, pietas, dignitas*, and *fides*, rather than the traditional terms for virtue (e.g. ἀρετή), since the traditional ones had strong associations with the ideal sage.[18]

In addition to the practical relevance of Epictetus' Stoicism, it is possible that his time spent with Musonius in their Roman social context would have amplified his practical ethics.[19] As was the case with his experiences with Epaphroditus, Epictetus would have had additional experiences with the socio-political environment of the Roman elite, since Musonius held the elite rank of a Roman equestrian. These experiences would have shaped and enhanced his philosophical outlook, especially towards Roman society. For instance, 'As Stoics, Musonius and Epictetus aligned themselves with the philosophy that elite citizens, or at least the few who had any time for it, found most in keeping with the traditional Roman virtues of rectitude in public and domestic life, material simplicity, and self-discipline'.[20] However, they observed social realities indicating that many elite citizens were actually not living according to the traditional Roman virtues, but were rather ambitiously looking to climb up the social ladder in order to achieve social prestige. Furthermore, although Musonius was a Roman elite, his Stoicism displeased the emperors, especially Nero, who exiled Musonius to a small Greek island, Gyara. Interestingly, this conflict could have loomed in Epictetus' mind since he occasionally uses Gyara as a catchword for exile (1.25.20; 2.6.22; 4.4.34).[21] Moreover, it was not only Musonius, but also the Stoics in general, who showed resistance to the emperors. Consequently, this tension would have further sharpened Epictetus' identity and outlook as a philosopher and social critic (cf. 1.1.18–32; 1.2.19–24; 1.25.22), and even 'account for the embattled nature of his philosophy'.[22]

---

[17] Long, *Epictetus*, 33 (italics his).

[18] Long, *Epictetus*, 33.

[19] Cf. Bonhöffer, *Die Stoa*, 3; Souilhé, *Entretiens*, I:vii; Dobbin, *Discourses*, xv.

[20] Long, *Epictetus*, 15.

[21] Long, *Epictetus*, 13–14.

[22] Dobbin, *Discourses*, xiii. For more on the negative relationship between the philosophers/Stoics and the emperors, see Starr, 'Tyrant', 20–9; Brunt, 'Principate', 7–39. However, see Rawson, 'Roman Rulers', 233–57, for their positive relationship.

Therefore, given Epictetus' formative experiences and their effects on his philosophy, Long appropriately writes, 'As a person who knew the indignity of slavery from direct experience and who had also lived under the tyrannical regime of Domitian, Epictetus' philosophy acquires an experiential dimension that removes from it any vestige of mere theorizing or posturing'.[23] As one reads Epictetus' discourses it is important to bear in mind that Epictetus' social experiences in Rome, not only as a slave, but also as a philosopher are pertinent for understanding his critique of particular social problems.

4.1.1.3 Moral Teacher

Although it is not possible to determine whether Epictetus could have begun teaching philosophy in Rome, it is clear that after the philosophers were banished from Rome he eventually settled and started a school in Nicopolis in the Roman Greek East. It is unknown whether Epictetus visited other areas, but it is probable that he lived in Nicopolis until his death sometime around the year 135.[24] Nicopolis was a city founded in 31 BCE by Augustus to commemorate his victory over Mark Antony near the bay of Actium, and was the major political, economic, and religious centre of the region. The school's location in this strategic coastal location would have attracted many visitors and prospective students. As will be seen below, the students he attracted were young men preparing for a career among the higher ranks of Roman society, as indicated by a student who said, 'I wish to sit where the senators do' (1.25.26).

As a Stoic teacher,[25] he taught them philosophical matters (e.g. 1.17, 'That the art of reasoning is indispensable'; 2.25, 'How is logic necessary?'), and also issues of moral ethics (e.g. 1.12, 'Of contentment'; 1.24, 'How should we struggle against difficulties?'). Moreover, as was seen above of his philosophy, his teachings demonstrate a similar interest in moral practicalities rather than abstract postulations:

What do I care, says Epictetus, whether all existing things are composed of atoms, or of indivisibles, or of fire and earth? Is it not enough to learn the true nature of the good and the evil, and the limits of the desires and aversions, and also of the choices and refusals, and, by

---

[23] Long, *Epictetus*, 11–12.

[24] Although there are no explicit indicators of Epictetus visiting other areas, he does exhibit a familiarity with surrounding areas, such as Corinth, Athens, and Olympia. Also, Simplicius, *In Ench.* 272C, remarks that later in life the celibate Epictetus adopted and raised a child, and possibly took a wife. For a discussion of the dating of his death, see Dobbin, *Discourses*, xii–xiii.

[25] See Gill, 'School', 36–8, for the status of a 'Stoic teacher'; Yieh, *One Teacher*, 185–236, who studies Epictetus as a moral teacher, and his particular roles as *Seelenführung* (soul-guide) and *Seelsorgen* (soul-tender).

employing these as rules, to order the affairs of our life, and dismiss the things that are beyond us?[26]

Epictetus' teaching objective was also directed at correcting his students' desire to acquire technical proficiency rather than to experience transformation of character and consciousness.[27] For example, his students were interested in studying Chrysippus for mastery of Stoic philosophy, rather than reading it for virtue and happiness (1.4.3–10). Joseph Souilhé writes, 'Epictète est essentiellement un éducateur. Il vise moins à faire des savants, des érudits, qu'à former des hommes. Philosopher ne consiste pas pour lui à construire un système de doctrine, mais "à se trouver prêts pour tous les événements"'.[28] Given this practical dimension, John Yieh correctly identifies Epictetus' social role as a 'moral teacher', since for Epictetus 'it is more important to teach "moral rules" to help pupils find freedom in the complexities of life'.[29] In light of his social role as a moral teacher and the practicality of his teachings, Epictetus can be regarded as a mentor and guide to life.[30]

With his slavish social makeup, it is remarkable that Epictetus gained popularity as a teacher and philosopher during his own day and thereafter. Long comments on Epictetus' distinctiveness:

Not a strikingly eventful life, but yet a memorable one, especially in the context of elite Roman society and its conventional members' jockeying for position over wealth, repute, and status. Former slaves, as the career of Epaphroditus shows, could rise well up the social ladder, but Epictetus without any of that achieved renown simply by being a dedicated teacher, impervious to all external marks of success.[31]

As will be seen below, he not only attracted students from high society, but he was also frequented by high-ranking visitors intrigued to hear him speak. Based on the frequency of individuals visiting Epictetus, Ronald Hock describes him as 'something of a tourist attraction in Nicopolis'.[32] This is illustrated in the sentiments of certain visitors coming to see him: 'We are passing, and while we are hiring our ship, we have a chance to take a look at Epictetus; let's see what in the world he has to say' (3.9.14).

---

[26] Stobaeus, *Ecl.* 2.1.31 = Fragment 1 in Oldfather, *Epictetus*, II:441–2. Cf. Yieh, *One Teacher*, 196–7.

[27] Long, *Epictetus*, 46. Another supporting evidence of the practicality of Epictetus' teachings is the consensus that his Greek is *koine*. For comments about Epictetus' Greek, see e.g. Browning, *Greek*, 23; Gill, *Discourses*, xvii; Dobbin, *Discourses*, xxi.

[28] Souilhé, *Entretiens*, I:xxxvi.

[29] Yieh, *One Teacher*, 197.

[30] Cf. the titles of two of Long's studies: *Epictetus: A Stoic and Socratic Guide to Life*; 'Epictetus as Socratic Mentor'.

[31] Long, *Epictetus*, 11.

[32] Hock, 'By the Gods', 135; cf. Brunt, 'Epictetus', 22.

There is also some later evidence that confirms Epictetus' popularity and influence.[33] For instance, Herodes Atticus, one of the richest and most influential freedmen and philosophers, puts to shame a young and arrogant student of philosophy – who only had the appearance of a philosopher – by reading a passage from Epictetus, the 'greatest of the Stoics' (Gellius, *Noct. att.* 1.2).[34] A later source also suggests that Emperor Hadrian made a visit to Epictetus (Scriptores Historiae Augustae, *Hadr.* 16.10). Furthermore, the Stoic emperor Marcus Aurelius indicates that he was influenced by the teachings of Epictetus (Marcus Aurelius, *Med.* 1.7).[35]

4.1.2 Epictetus' Audience

Attention will now be given to the social identity of his audience, who can be broadly categorised into students and visitors.[36] A description of his audience's social makeup will give the appropriate context for analysing Epictetus' discourses, especially those discourses that mention aspects of social identity.

4.1.2.1 Students

Although Epictetus' students were the individuals with whom he would have had the most intense and frequent interaction, they tend to be quite elusive to identify. The descriptors of Epictetus' students do not yield specific details of their identity; for example, they are often only identified with an indefinite pronoun, τις ('someone').[37] It is possible, nonetheless, to draw a broad profile of his students based on the vague details given in the work.

In one discourse, a father and son visit Epictetus' school and attend one of his lectures (2.14). Although it is not certain, the father in attendance is likely to be observing Epictetus as a prospective teacher for his son, which could indicate the young age of the typical student. Moreover, the students are often referred to as νέοι,[38] and are old enough possibly to have a wife and children

---

[33] For more details, see Schenkl, *Dissertationes*, vii–xi; Spanneut, 'Epiktet', 616–76; Long, *Epictetus*, 34–5. See also idem, *Epictetus*, 259–72, for his popularity throughout history in general.

[34] Cf. Gellius, *Noct. att.* 17.19, for Favorinus' use of a saying of Epictetus.

[35] See Stanton, 'Cosmopolitan Ideas', 183–95, who looks at Epictetus' influence on Marcus Aurelius' understanding of 'citizen of the universe'.

[36] A few studies have focused on the social relationships of Epictetus and the individuals mentioned in the work. See Millar, 'Imperial Court', 141–8; Brunt, 'Epictetus', 20–30; Hock, 'By the Gods', 121–42. This section has benefited from these studies and their collation of details. See also the recent treatment by Yieh, *One Teacher*, 206–14.

[37] E.g. 1.2.26, 30; 1.13.1; 1.14.1; 1.26.1; 2.25.1; 3.6.1, 8. See Hock, 'By the Gods', 127.

[38] 1.9.18–19; 1.29.34; 1.30.5; 2.8.15; 2.17.29; 3.21.8. Long, *Epictetus*, 43, suggests that they would be young males whose ages ranged from about 18 to 25.

(1.18.11; 2.22.4–5). It seems that the young students have left their families and homes, and travelled some distance to study at Epictetus' school.[39] Concerning Epictetus' teaching content and the age of his students, Long comments, 'The main content of Epictetus' lessons is so grown-up, demanding and tough that it comes as a shock to realise that he was largely addressing youths'.[40]

In addition to their age, there are details indicating that they are from upper-class families. These students were the sort of young men privileged to be raised by nurses and παιδαγωγοί (2.16.39; 3.19.4–5; 3.24.53), and were served by various other slaves (1.18.19; 2.21.11; 3.19.5; 3.26.21–2). Coming from this lifestyle, they desired the luxuries of elite culture. As a result, Epictetus constantly exhorts his students not to set their desires on wealth and reputation.[41] For example, Epictetus chides a student who has exchanged his modesty for shame by reading erotic writers and wearing fancy clothes and perfume (4.9.6–7). Throughout the work, the students are generally seen to be valuing and desiring external markers of prestige and also the pleasures and luxuries of elite culture. While attending Epictetus' school, their leisurely activities included reading books and writing their own compositions (1.4.22; 2.1.33–4; 2.17.34–6; 2.21.10–14), frequenting baths and gymnasia (2.16.29; 2.21.14), going to gladiatorial shows and circuses (3.16.14), and travelling and sightseeing places like Olympia (1.6.23). Furthermore, Epictetus' students also had certain expectations after leaving his school, since they 'were the sons of families in the upper echelons of society and expected to distinguish themselves as officials, soldiers and so forth'.[42] They were expected to return to family and friends (3.21.8), and to manage their properties (3.5.3; 4.10.19). They also aspired to hold high offices and engage in the affairs of their city,[43] and perhaps go to Rome to seek out the emperor as a patron for higher offices and honours.[44] One notable student of Epictetus who followed this career path is Arrian – the compiler of *Dissertationes* – who later became an individual of high rank and status. Therefore, with this profile of his students, it is no wonder that Epictetus characterises his students, 'you rich people!' (4.1.144).[45]

---

[39] 1.4.21; 3.5.1; 3.21.8; 3.23.32; 3.24.22, 78.

[40] Long, 'Socratic Mentor', 83.

[41] 1.1.14; 1.15.3; 2.9.15; 2.17.24; 2.19.32; 3.24.71; 3.26.34; 3.1.60, 87; 4.3.10; 4.4.33; esp. 3.26.21–4 and 4.7.37.

[42] Long, *Epictetus*, 243.

[43] 2.10.10; 2.14.24; 2.23.39; 3.24.36.

[44] 1.25.26; 2.6.20; 4.10.18–21.

[45] Cf. Brunt, 'Epictetus', 22, who comments that they were 'surely drawn from the better classes'.

4.1.2.2 Visitors

In contrast to the details of the students, the portrayal of Epictetus' visitors in the *Dissertationes* provides a sufficient amount of detail for a profile. Visitors are important characters within Epictetus' teachings, which is evident in the frequency of discourses involving various visitors. Since Nicopolis was an important coastal city, it was reasonable for visitors to stop by while awaiting a boat for transport to places like Italy (cf. 3.9.14). In addition to these random passers-by, Epictetus was visited by individuals who approached him with some specific purpose in mind. The following individuals are among the visitors who interacted with Epictetus in the *Dissertationes*: a rich and handsome orator who frequented Epictetus without being accepted as a pupil (2.24.1, 22–9); a public official visiting Epictetus from Rome (1.11.1, 32, 39); Naso, an influential Roman of equestrian rank who was known by Caesar and has wealthy friends (2.14); a young student of oratory from Corinth, who was possibly of curial rank (3.1); the procurator of Epirus, Cn. Cornelius Pulcher, who was a friend of Caesar (3.4); the wealthy *corrector* of the free cities of Greece, who was an Epicurean philosopher and had connections to Caesar (3.7); a man from Cnossus en route to Rome, whom Epictetus criticised for striving to achieve prestige (3.9); a man in exile at Nicopolis, who was once rich and powerful (1.9.27–34); a former exile now returning back to Rome, who eventually became *praefectus annonae* – the emperor's supervisor of the city's grain supply (1.10.1–6); and also a priest of Augustus at Nicopolis (1.19.26–9).

The visitors identified in Epictetus' discourses are valuable because of the particulars given of each individual, especially their high social position and their appreciation of status symbols that relate to the concept of *persona*. Therefore, with the profile of his students and visitors, it is clear that Epictetus chiefly interacted with members of the Roman elite. Brunt correctly states, 'Humble as his own origins were, it was certainly not to the poor and weak that he discoursed'.[46]

4.1.3 Epictetus' Work: Dissertationes

Epictetus could have been following the example of his teacher Musonius Rufus and the great Socrates by not publishing any written work. Epictetus' teachings are survived primarily in *Dissertationes*, which was compiled by one of his pupils, Lucius Flavianus Arrianus Xenophon (*c.* 86–160) from

---

[46] Brunt, 'Epictetus', 20. Cf. Hock, 'By the Gods', 134, who assesses that Epictetus' network noticeably shows little social diversity.

Nicomedia, a prosperous metropolis in Bithynia (Asia Minor).[47] Arrian had the typical background of Epictetus' students, coming from a wealthy and elite family. Subsequent to his training at Epictetus' school, Arrian achieved a highly distinguished career, which could be an indication of the direction of many of Epictetus' students. Lucian describes Arrian as 'the disciple of Epictetus, a Roman of the highest distinction, and a life-long devotee of letters' (*Alex.* 2). Under Hadrian's reign, Arrian acquired senatorial rank and a consulate, and later became a great military leader and governor of Cappadocia. He was also a prolific writer of several important works, including *Anabasis*, which is a history of Alexander the Great. In addition, with his philosophical background, Arrian presented himself as the 'Roman Xenophon'.[48]

Despite his notoriety as a Roman elite, Arrian is most regarded for his extensive compilation of *Dissertationes* and a handbook of excerpts of Epictetus' teachings, *Encheiridion* ('Manual').[49] The extant manuscripts include a prefacing letter to *Dissertationes*, which Arrian wrote to Lucius Gellius, whom some scholars have identified as L. Gellius Menander, a prominent Corinthian of the Hadrianic period.[50] Arrian writes in the letter:

> I have not composed the discourses (λόγους) of Epictetus in the way one might 'compose' such works, nor have I published them myself; for I do not claim to have composed them at all. Rather, I tried to write down whatever I heard him say, in his own words as far as possible, to keep notes (ὑπομνήματα) of his thoughts and frankness for my own future use...[I]n uttering them he was clearly aiming at nothing except to move the minds of his audience towards what is best. So if these discourses achieve that much, they would have just the effect, I think, that a philosopher's discourse ought to have. But if not, those who read them should realize that when Epictetus spoke them the hearer could not fail to experience just what Epictetus intended him to feel. And if the discourses on their own do not achieve this, I may be to blame, or perhaps it is unavoidable.[51]

This letter presents a few important details that have bearing on the character and purpose of the *Dissertationes*.[52] First, there is the issue of the work's authorship. It is clear that Arrian maintained λόγους ('discourses') and ὑπομνήματα ('notes') of Epictetus' lectures and compiled them into the extant work, *Dissertationes*.[53] Despite the clear recognition of Arrian's

---

[47] For more on Arrian, see Brunt, 'Epictetus', 30–48; Stadter, *Arrian*. For an inscription identifying Arrian, see Bowersock, 'New Inscription', 279–80.

[48] See Stadter, 'New Xenophon', 155–61.

[49] For more on the *Encheiridion*, see the introduction in Hadot, *Manuel*, 11–36.

[50] See Millar, 'Imperial Court', 142; Bowersock, 'New Inscription', 280.

[51] §§ 1–8. Translation from Long, *Epictetus*, 39–40.

[52] For more discussion of the character of the *Dissertationes*, see Spanneut, 'Epiktet', 600–3; Radt, '*Diatriben*', 364–8; Dobbin, *Discourses*, xx–xxiii; Long, *Epictetus*, 38–66.

[53] See Photius, *Bibliotheca* 58, who remarks that there are eight books to *Dissertationes*, but assuming that Photius is correct, only four of the eight books are survived today. Also for

authorship in this letter, scholars have debated over the historical reliability of Arrian's portrayal of 'the historical Epictetus'. Traditionally, scholars have held that Arrian recorded the *ipsissima verba* of Epictetus, but this view was challenged by Theo Wirth, who has proposed that the *Dissertationes* is not based on Epictetus' actual teachings but is Arrian's own depiction of Epictetus which is modelled after Xenophon's depiction of Socrates.[54] Robert Dobbin also proposed another extreme view that Epictetus was the actual author of *Dissertationes*.[55] Recently, however, Long has compiled evidence to affirm the traditional view that the gist of Arrian's account is authentic to Epictetus' own language and style.[56] Long summarises his main evidence: 'These include the distinct vocabulary, repetition of key points throughout, a strikingly urgent and vivid voice quite distinct from Arrian's authorial persona in his other works, and a focus on Socrates that is far more reminiscent of Plato's dialogues than designedly evocative of Xenophon'.[57] In addition, many scholars have appealed to the compelling argument that Arrian used *koine* Greek in recounting Epictetus' words in *Dissertationes*, while using Attic Greek for his own words in other writings.[58] Given all the evidence, Arrian's account should be regarded as authentic of Epictetus' actual discourses.

Secondly, Arrian in the letter expressed his devotion and appreciation of Epictetus' teachings.[59] Arrian, who was moved by his teacher's sayings, recognised the need to produce a compilation of Epictetus' teachings for his own future use (§ 2). Besides this large compilation, Arrian displayed his devotion to Epictetus by producing the condensed *Encheiridion* as a convenient handbook of Epictetus' teachings. Also, according to Simplicius in the preface to his commentary on *Encheiridion*, Arrian also wrote a work on the life and death of Epictetus.

Thirdly, Arrian articulated on the practical function of the *Dissertationes*. Arrian wrote down the words of Epictetus so that one could read and

---

the title of work, see Schenkl, *Dissertationes*, ii–xv, xxxiii–xxxv; Souilhé, *Entretiens*, I:xii–x; Long, *Epictetus*, 42–3, 48–9, 65. The oldest and archetypal text of *Dissertationes*, the Bodleian codex, has the term 'diatribes', which Schenkl has adopted for the title of the whole work. Long has reservations about describing Epictetus' works as 'diatribes', since the term is associated with Cynic discourses and has distracted attention to Epictetus' Socratic methodology. For more on the manuscript tradition and texts, see Dobbin, *Discourses*, xxiii–xiv.

[54] Wirth, 'Arrians Erinnerungen', 172, 216.

[55] Dobbin, *Discourses*, xxi–xxii.

[56] Long, *Epictetus*, 39–41.

[57] Long, *Epictetus*, 41.

[58] For more on the language and style of Epictetus, see Souilhé, *Entretiens*, I:lxvii–lxxi.

[59] Cf. Long, *Epictetus*, 41, who writes that it is important for readers to keep Arrian's devotion in mind.

'experience just what Epictetus intended him to feel', since Epictetus was 'clearly aiming at nothing except to move the minds of his audience towards what is best' (§§ 6–8). Thus, Epictetus' discourses have an invaluable practical use for his readers, as they did for Arrian, which is indicative of the practical and moral dimensions of Epictetus' philosophy.

4.1.4 Epictetus' Philosophy: Four Unifying Concepts

A final point of introduction is Epictetus' philosophy, which is pertinent for understanding his discourses and his critique of *persona*. Rather than exhaustively and systematically presenting Epictetus' philosophy, it will suffice for the purview of this study to introduce only the basic framework of his philosophy.[60] Fortunately, Long has recently provided a succinct description of the four unifying concepts of Epictetus' philosophy, which will be summarised here to present a broad outline of Epictetus' philosophy.[61]

Epictetus' philosophy can be perceived to have four unifying concepts: freedom, judgement, volition, and integrity. For Epictetus, 'freedom' can have two related meanings: a social and political freedom that Epictetus himself had experienced, and more importantly, a freedom from 'being constrained or impeded by any external circumstance or emotional reaction'.[62] The basis for the individual to achieve freedom is through the second concept, 'judgement'. Being consistent with Stoic philosophy, Epictetus holds that as rational beings, there are no actions in life that not conditioned by the individual's judgements, and that all emotions and actions are ultimately controlled by the judgements of the individual. This leads to the third concept of 'volition' (προαίρεσις),[63] which is a key element of Epictetus' philosophy. Long defines the προαίρεσις as 'what persons are in terms of their mental faculties, consciousness, character, judgements, goals, and desires: volition is the self, what each of us is, as abstracted from the body'.[64] Also, external

---

[60] The two most detailed studies of the Stoicism of Epictetus are Bonhöffer, *Die Stoa*; idem, *Ethik*. However, some scholars have pointed out that he overemphasises Epictetus' Stoic orthodoxy and overlooks Epictetus' style and methodology. E.g. Jagu, *Epictète*, 120–2; Long, *Epictetus*, 17, who comments that Epictetus used Stoicism 'selectively and creatively'. Accordingly, Long has drawn attention to Epictetus' predominate use of the Socratic dialectic (54–96). For the 'eclecticism' in Stoic philosophy of the imperial period, see Gill, 'School', 44–50.

[61] Long, *Epictetus*, 27–32.

[62] Long, *Epictetus*, 27.

[63] This study follows Long's translation of προαίρεσις as 'volition'. See Long, *Epictetus*, 218–20, for support of this translation. Other common translations are 'moral purpose', 'moral character', 'personne morale', and 'choice'. See discussion in Asmis, 'Choice', 386. See below for more discussion on this philosophical concept.

[64] Long, *Epictetus*, 28.

things, such as social status and social relationships, often impede the προαίρεσις. Consequently, the proper use of the volition is where one can make true judgements and find true freedom. Although the volition is the essential self of the individual, which can appear to be only self-interested, the next concept, 'integrity', importantly relates the volition to social ethics. 'Integrity is as much a part of Epictetus' normative self as a good volition; in fact, it is not distinct from a good volition but the way that that mental disposition is disposed in relation to other persons'.[65] The individual is thus able to fulfil the moral sense of the volition by honouring one's social relationships with others (e.g. family and social roles). It is this unified philosophy that Epictetus strives to impart to his students. Long aptly summarises:

Epictetus is concerned throughout with elucidating, justifying, and internalizing Stoicism as *the* philosophy, with training his students, advising them on how to apply Stoic teaching in their own lives, on what character they need to cultivate, on how they should deal with the persons and situations they encounter from day to day; he continually counsels and cajoles them to use the mental resources they have at their disposal for tackling contingencies that may be as trivial as a jealous brother or as serious as exile, threat of execution, or loss of family.[66]

In sum, this introduction to Epictetus, his audience, work, and philosophy, has provided insights that will be helpful in understanding his critique of the social problems associated with the Roman emphasis on *persona*. From Arrian's prefacing letter it was recognised that the *Dissertationes* has a practical function for its readers – to bring transformation of character through Epictetus' philosophy. This practical dimension of his philosophy is important for understanding his critique of certain social problems in the Graeco-Roman world. In particular, it is his social pilgrimage as a slave, philosopher, and moral teacher that gives his philosophical discourses their force for chiding what he considered to be the inappropriate behaviour and values of the Roman elite. Long appropriately advises the modern reader that Epictetus' life experiences as a slave and exile 'are experiences to keep in mind as one reads his often severe comments on the inability of more materially fortunate people to handle themselves with dignity and equanimity'.[67] Therefore, for this exploration of Epictetus' understanding and critique of social *persona*, it is important to bear in mind his robust philosophy and life experiences.

---

[65] Long, *Epictetus*, 30. He continues: 'Integrity bridges the gap for Epictetus between egoism and altruism; or, better, it closes the gap...Integrity is the concept in Epictetus that answers to moral sense'.

[66] Long, *Epictetus*, 47–8 (italics his).

[67] Long, *Epictetus*, 11.

4.2 The Preoccupation with the Superficial Aspect of *Persona*

Throughout Epictetus' discourses one is able to observe a social milieu where individuals were particularly preoccupied with the superficial features of *persona*. Long describes how the Roman elite, including Epictetus' students, 'were generally raised to be intensely ambitious and many of them were obsessed with the external accoutrements of rank and office'.[68] Moreover, this social description is consistent with the problem of the conventionally projected *persona* as seen in Chapter Two. This depiction of *persona* in Epictetus' time was a skewed depiction of the traditional values and ideals of *persona*, since it was an exaggeration and exploitation of certain surface elements of social identity, especially rank and status. Many individuals were preoccupied with the superficial features, since they believed that these external displays indicated their possession of the elite ideals and virtues of Roman identity. This section will examine Epictetus' approach to this distorted view of identity – that is, his critique of the Roman stress on *persona* and the pervasive preoccupation with shallow displays of social prestige.

In one of Epictetus' teachings he presents an imaginary dialogue between two individuals who emphasise and rely on their social identity, in order to outrank the other: '"I am superior to you, for my father has consular rank". Another says, "I have been tribune, and you have not"' (3.24.11–12). In another discourse, Epictetus exposes the desires of his students for the surface displays of wealth and prestige, which serve to project conspicuously their *persona*: 'It is your concern how to live in marble halls, and further, how slaves and freedmen are to serve you, how you are to wear conspicuous clothing, how to have many hunting dogs...' (4.7.37). In a different context, Epictetus indicates this desire for 'externals': 'We too experience something of the same kind. What do we admire? Externals (τὰ ἐκτός). What are we earnest about? About externals (τὰ ἐκτός)' (2.16.11). Moreover, in a discussion 'Of anxiety', Epictetus criticises that 'we are anxious about our wretched body, about our trifling estate, about what Caesar will think, but are anxious about none of the things that are within us' (2.13.11). These texts confirm that for Epictetus there was a crisis of identity in his social world – more specifically, a social problem of an intense longing for the superficial status symbols of *persona*.

This prevalent problem with the superficial projection of one's social standing can vividly be seen also in the discourse, 'To those who are vexed at being pitied' (4.6). Epictetus' interlocutor explains that people are pitying him for things that he deems inappropriate, which include poverty and not holding office (4.6.1–2). Epictetus responds by posing two options as to how his

---

[68] Long, *Epictetus*, 243.

interlocutor can respond to those pitying him: first, he can 'convince the multitude that none of these things is bad, but that it is possible for a poor man, and one who holds no office or position or honour, to be happy'; or secondly, he can be pretentious and show himself 'off to them as a rich man and official' (4.6.3). In fact, Epictetus rebukes the worthless person who takes the second option because that person has to take extreme measures to achieve that pretence:

> You will have to borrow some paltry slaves; and possess a few pieces of silver plate, and exhibit these same pieces conspicuously and frequently, if you can, and try not to let people know that they are the same; and possess contemptible bright clothes, and all other kinds of finery, and show yourself off as the one who is honoured by the most distinguished persons; and try to dine with them, or at least make people think that you dine with them; and retort to base arts in the treatment of your person, so as to appear more shapely and of gentler birth than you actually are. All these contrivances you must adopt, if you wish to take the way of the second alternative and avoid pity.[69]

This text reveals the social problem of people exaggerating and valuing certain displays of status so much that they have to live ostentatiously by portraying a *persona* that was fashionable in order to attain social acceptability. Epictetus explains to the interlocutor that the 'first alternative' is indeed the more tedious and ineffectual, but nonetheless it is something that Zeus himself is not able to accomplish – that is, to persuade all men of what things are good, and what things are bad (4.6.5). This last comment highlights the severity of the preoccupation with the shallow appearance of *persona*, since so many have simply opted to live according to the conventional values of the second option.

The few passages mentioned so far are only a sample of the many social descriptors in the *Dissertationes* of people's obsession with and exploitation of the distinctive social markers of *persona* (e.g. wealth, prestige, rank, and status). Epictetus even equates this intense longing for material possessions to an 'incurable fever' (4.9.1–5).[70] Moreover, from a cursory observation of the titles of his discourses, it is obvious that many important discourses are specifically addressing the problems of individuals parading and assessing the superficial aspect of *persona*. Some titles worth noting are: 'On the faculty of expressions' (2.23); 'Of personal adornment' (3.1); and, 'To those who read and discuss for the purpose of display' (3.23). Therefore, it is apparent that within Epictetus' social world there was a great preoccupation with the conventionally projected *persona*, which he criticised.

---

[69] 4.6.4–5.
[70] Cf. Long, *Epictetus*, 137–8.

4.2.1 Critical of or Indifferent to Roman Society?

One particular issue that is crucial for understanding Epictetus' critique of the Roman stress on *persona* is whether he was critical of or indifferent to Roman society. Scholars writing on social aspects of Epictetus have expressed mixed opinions on this matter. Millar views him as critical of the conventional values of Roman society: 'The slave of Epaphroditus exiled under Domitian would not be likely to view the values and aspirations of Roman society with much enthusiasm; and the philosopher on show for culturally-minded travellers at Nicopolis had a certain role to play as a critic of the world and its occupations'.[71] Millar further assesses that the *Dissertationes* are unique since 'no other work read and valued in Roman society dealt so harshly with the values of status and ambition on which that society was based'.[72] Hock also affirms Epictetus' negative disposition by expressing that 'Epictetus was expressing contempt (as διάνοια) for those networks of power and public life which had forced him into exile'.[73] Contrary to these views, Peter Brunt perceives Epictetus as having 'no objection to the hierarchic social order, which corresponds to that of the Universe'.[74] Similarly, Yieh writes of Epictetus' students and visitors' positive view to the status quo of the world: 'Epictetus did not object to their political aspirations...In his view, social status and career opportunities are matters of indifference...'[75] With the mixed review of Epictetus' reaction to the conventional values of the Roman social order, it is important to assess whether he was critical of or indifferent to them.

An example of Epictetus' harsh statements on Roman elite society is his discussion with Naso, an elite Roman citizen, who visited Epictetus' school with his son (2.14). In the dialogue, Epictetus acknowledges the distinguished *persona* of Naso, which lacks nothing according to the conventional estimation of Roman social identity – he is rich, has many slaves, Caesar knows him, and he has many friends in Rome (2.14.18).[76] Epictetus, however, rejects these social distinctions as having no true value. He criticises Naso of actually lacking the things that are most necessary for happiness, since he has only devoted his attention to everything that was inappropriate – superficial social markers (2.14.19). Epictetus even anticipates that Naso would not be able to handle the dialogue and will resort to leaving insulted (2.14.19–22).

---

[71] Millar, 'Imperial Court', 147.

[72] Millar, 'Imperial Court', 148.

[73] Hock, 'By the Gods', 138.

[74] Brunt, 'Epictetus', 24; cf. 30 (quoted below).

[75] Yieh, *One Teacher*, 213.

[76] For Naso's identification and elite rank, see Millar, 'Imperial Court', 144; Brunt, 'Epictetus', 20 n. 7.

Epictetus continues the discourse with an analogy of the animals in a fair, in which the animals are metaphorically compared to people in the 'fair of this world' (2.14.23–5).[77] He states that some people, like the cattle, are only interested in their 'fodder' (χόρτος) because they are only preoccupied 'with property and land and slaves and one office or another, all this is nothing but fodder!' (2.14.24). These blunt words are particularly against the Roman elite, and those desiring to be like the elite, who are only concerned about the 'fodder' of wealth, fame, and prestige.

Epictetus' negative critique is further observed in a confrontational dialogue with another visitor, Maximus, the Roman *corrector* of the free cities of Greece,[78] who was an Epicurean philosopher (3.7). After Epictetus discusses the things belonging inside or outside one's volition (προαίρεσις), the Roman official states that he is rich and lacks nothing (3.7.29). Epictetus responds by asking him why he is only pretending to be a philosopher. Additionally, in questioning how Maximus became a judge, Epictetus makes strong criticisms against him: 'Whose hands did you kiss – that of Symphorus or that of Numenius?[79] In front of whose door did you sleep? To whom did you send presents?' (3.7.29–31; cf. 4.10.20–1). This text reveals Epictetus' reaction against individuals seeking to achieve certain elite ideals of Roman social identity (e.g. social prestige) by taking great measures and performing degrading deeds. In fact, concerning the kissing of hands Epictetus chides, 'Or again, when for the sake of these mighty and dignified offices and honours you kiss the hands of other men's slaves, so as to be the slave of men who are not even free?' (4.1.148). Epictetus, again, is underlining the absurdity of the Roman social system. Similarly, Epictetus cautions against falling into a spiritual slavery:

Make an end, I adjure you by the gods, of admiring material things, make an end of turning yourselves into slaves, in the first place, of things, and then, in the second place, on their account, slaves also of the men who are able to secure or take away these things.[80]

Epictetus is elucidating that by seeking the artificial things of society, one ludicrously becomes a slave to those things and also to those who control them. Therefore, the evidence examined here conveys Epictetus as a severe

---

[77] For this popular comparison, which is attributed to Pythagoras, see Cicero, *Tusc.* 5.9; Diogenes Laertius 8.8.

[78] On this senatorial office, see Oldfather, *Epictetus*, II:49.

[79] These two individuals were possibly influential freedmen at the imperial court of Rome. See Millar, 'Imperial Court', 145.

[80] 3.20.8.

social critic of the Roman elite and their ambitions to possess and display the conventional projection of an elite *persona*.[81]

On the other hand, in some discourses there appears to be some indication of Epictetus being indifferent to the Roman social system. For example, he makes reference to the duties of slaves and their need to perform appropriately these slavish tasks (1.2.8–11).[82] Moreover, while referring to the process of freeing a slave, Epictetus does not object to a slave's worth of a five percent tax for manumission (2.1.26; cf. 4.1.33). Also, when he discusses a procurator of Epirus (3.4), who loathsomely sided with a tragic actor in the theatre, he does not make any criticisms of his rank and status, but only of the manner in which he should be an example to those below him. Examples as these have led Brunt to assess that Epictetus has 'no objection' to the Roman social order. Brunt elaborates:

Epictetus' assumption that in general men should carry out the tasks appropriate to their station and social relationships means in fact that in his view they should act in the ways in which it was accepted by the society of his day that they ought to act. Thus, although it is true that 'status and ambition' were vanities in his eyes, it would be wrong to infer that he sought to reform society except by effecting a spiritual change in the minds of men, or that men whose minds had been so changed would have taken actions different in objective content from those which ordinary, decent persons who had never heard a word of Stoic philosophy thought it proper to take.[83]

It is also important to bear in mind that Epictetus is not criticising Roman society as a whole or against the notion of being a Roman, which might be because of his status as a Roman freedman and his occupation as a teacher of young students who belonged to the Roman elite.

However, despite some indications of an indifference to the Roman social order, the majority of passages examined thus far in this chapter suggest that it is tenuous to regard Epictetus as having no objections to or criticisms of certain aspects of Roman society. It seems appropriate, then, to regard that while Epictetus' indifference is towards the static notions of the Roman hierarchical system, his critical remarks are primarily directed at exposing the dynamics of individuals' lives and conduct in the system. That is, it is not the attainment of rank and status that is the problem for Epictetus *per se*, but rather it is the intense longing ('incurable fever') for superficial displays of social prestige that is the problem, which happens to be the prevailing condition of Roman society. In fact, in 4.10 he points out the incompatibility

---

[81] Hock, 'By the Gods', 131, intimates that his relations with his visitors of high rank and status are 'rather strained, to say the least'.

[82] See Brunt, 'Epictetus', 23, who notes that Epictetus surprisingly does not make much references to slaves and freedmen.

[83] Brunt, 'Epictetus', 30. Cf. Yieh, *One Teacher*, 213–14.

of an individual living appropriately to God while pursuing social distinctions. For instance, Epictetus articulates:

You cannot be continually giving attention to both externals (τὰ ἐκτός) and your own governing principle. But if you want the former, let the latter go; otherwise you will have neither the latter nor the former, being drawn in both directions. If you want the latter, you must let the former go.[84]

Thus, despite some indications of indifference, Epictetus' discourses exhibit him as a strong critic who reacted against what he considered to be inappropriate behaviour in the Roman socio-political world, and, in particular, against the conventional and shallow outworking of *persona* in his day.

4.2.2 Epictetus' Social World of Philosophy and Sophistry

To further demonstrate the social problem with the widely projected *persona* in Epictetus' day, attention will now be given to the preoccupation with the superficial side of *persona* in his social world of philosophy and sophistry, which is similar to the problem seen in the discussion in Chapter Two of *persona* in the context of rhetoric/oratory/sophistry. With the popularity of rhetoric and oratory many individuals spent more energy on developing and enhancing their oratorical skills rather than on the training of philosophy. During Epictetus' era, popular orators, such as the Sophists, were using philosophy for superficial displays, and the crowds were attracted to these orators because of their eloquence, mannerisms, and visual appearance. As a result, philosophy had turned away from being a teaching of how to live life, and instead turned into a form of entertainment. More specifically, these popular orators projected certain superficial features of *persona* in order to receive honour and prestige, and accordingly the crowds assessed these orators chiefly based on their shallow displays.

Epictetus points out that there were 'philosophers' who were inappropriately inviting people to come and listen to them speak. In fact, Epictetus uses a comparison of these philosophers to the doctors in Rome who ridiculously advertise and invite patients to come and be healed (3.23.27–8). He explains to his students that a philosopher's discourse alone should be able to attract people because it should show the audience how wretched and miserable their lives are, and if the philosophical content fails to meet this objective, then the speaker and the speech should both be regarded as lifeless (3.23.28–9). Epictetus then recounts a saying of Musonius Rufus, 'If you have nothing better to do than praise me, I am speaking to no effect'. This discourse portrays Epictetus as incongruous with the popular orators of his day – such as the famous sophists, Dio Chrysostom and Favorinus – and as

---

[84] 4.10.26.

taking a strong stance on the proper training and use of philosophy.[85] Orators like Dio and Favorinus held their audience through their 'verbal pyrotechnics rather than through anything that was ethically creative or deeply thought out'.[86] Moreover, Epictetus' appreciation of traditional philosophy could explain why he was an appealing option for the Roman elite. Parents of prospective students sent their children, who would probably assume a political career in the future, to be trained in philosophical schools. Speculating on the popularity of Epictetus, Brunt postulates that one reason for Epictetus' attractiveness as a teacher may have been his 'reputation for eloquence', since the 'vigour of his discourses may well have appealed to connoisseurs of rhetoric whose taste have been jaded by the vapourings of sophists'.[87]

Like many social distinctions in Roman society, philosophers had a certain outward appearance that identified them as philosophers – a rough cloak, long hair, and a beard – which Epictetus proudly displayed (cf. 1.2.29). Epictetus' discourses show a concern with individuals being preoccupied with the outward appearance of the philosopher. An interesting discourse where Epictetus engages this matter is: 'To those who hastily assume the guise of the philosophers' (4.8). Epictetus criticises those individuals who pretentiously display themselves as philosophers. Accordingly, Epictetus teaches his students not to make judgements based on these externals (ἐκτός) (4.8.10). While comparing the various professions, such as a musician, Epictetus complains of how people do not look at the essence of a true philosopher and the content of the discourse, but only look at the philosophers' shallow looks. For example, he explains that if one puts on a cloak and grows a beard, he cannot simply claim himself to be a philosopher, just as one does not become a musician if one picks up an instrument. Consequently, he accentuates that the essential identifying component of an individual's *persona* is not the outward appearance, but appropriate conduct – whereby 'the guise is fitted to the art, and they get their name from the art, but not from the guise' (4.8.15–16). Epictetus underscores repeatedly that an authentic philosopher is not known by his superficial displays of the accoutrements of a philosopher, but only by his actions and philosophical teachings. He even points out that, indeed, the great Socrates was often not readily identified as a philosopher by

---

[85] See Stanton, 'Sophists', 356–7, for how Epictetus identifies himself as a philosopher, but distinguishes himself from the Sophists. Also, Long, 'Socratic Mentor', 94, suggests a distinction of a capital and lowercase 'P' for philosopher: 'Epictetus disclaims being a capitalised philosopher. He does not want to be taken for a popular lecturer or sophist, for a Favorinus or a Dio, someone who puts on epideictic displays of erudition'. See the discussion of Favorinus in Chapter Five.

[86] Long, *Epictetus*, 49.

[87] Brunt, 'Epictetus', 21.

his outward appearance (4.8.22–9). This leads Epictetus to question his students regarding the essence of a genuine philosopher: 'What is the function of a good and excellent man (καλοῦ καὶ ἀγαθοῦ).[88] To have many pupils? Not at all. Those who have set their hearts on it shall see to that' (4.8.24).

The discourse 'On personal adornment' (3.1) further illustrates the fixation with the superficial dimension of *persona* in philosophy and oratory. This discourse involves Epictetus and a young student of rhetoric from Corinth, who has extremely elaborate hair and attire (3.1.1).[89] This young male has taken drastic measures to project the look of a contemporary orator, such as plucking out his chest hairs. In fact, he made his appearance so elaborate that Epictetus questioned whether he was a man or woman (3.1.27; cf. 2.24.24–9). Epictetus, moreover, exposed that the young student's motivation for elaborately adorning his external self was for the attainment of high rank and status in the Roman social order (3.1.34–5). For many people in the Graeco-Roman world, this outward adornment and ostentatious use of superficial features were the means to achieve further prestige. Elsewhere, Epictetus reacted to this problem by warning against the pretentious use of philosophy: 'But if a man reads upon the subject and resorts to the philosophers merely because he wants to make a display at a banquet of his knowledge of hypothetical arguments, what else is he doing but trying to win the admiration of some senator sitting by his side?' (1.26.9).

In another discourse, Epictetus addresses 'those who read and discuss for the purpose of display' (3.23). In his discussion with an interlocutor, Epictetus points out the tendency of people doing certain deeds and actions for the sole purpose of receiving acclamations. To the interlocutor he raises:

The other day, when your audience gathered rather coolly, and did not shout applause, you walked out of the hall in low spirits. And again the other day, when you were received with applause, you walked around and asked everybody, 'What did you think of me?' 'How did I render that passage?'[90]

Continuing to expose his interlocutor's hypocrisy, Epictetus accuses him of outwardly praising other individuals and flattering a senator for selfish motives, while compromising his own internal disposition (3.23.13–14). Epictetus points out that people, like this senator, are only interested in and attracted to how a philosopher ought to deliver a speech, rather than the respectfulness and faithfulness of the philosopher (3.23.17). Consequently, Epictetus comments that his interlocutor, who is in such a sorry state for gaping at people's accolades, would have the following useless thoughts: '"Today I had a much larger audience". "Yes, indeed, there were great

---

[88] This important epithet will be discussed below.

[89] The young student from Corinth (3.1.34) will be discussed further in Chapter Five.

[90] 3.23.10–11.

numbers". "Five hundred, I fancy". "Nonsense, make it a thousand". "Dio never had so large an audience"' (3.23.19). Epictetus responds sarcastically by expressing that this pretentious philosopher is not concerned about doing good for men, but only concerned about attaining and receiving praises from people. This is also seen in 2.16.5–10, where an orator is prepared to give a fine speech, but is still anxious because he is not satisfied with the actual practice of oratory, and is only seeking the praise of the audience. Epictetus indicates that when he is praised, he leaves the stage 'puffed up' (φυσηθείς).[91]

Therefore, the preoccupation with the shallow features of *persona* is clearly seen in the behaviour of externally portraying the fashionable image of a philosopher in order to receive accolades. Long comments on Epictetus' teachings on these sorts of philosophers, 'Epictetus' dialogical lessons are packed with warnings against parading oneself as a philosopher, showing off one's logical skills, putting on finery to lecture, and so forth'.[92] In addition, 'Epictetus strongly distances himself from such displays, and he warns his students against mistaking rhetorical for philosophical success'.[93] More positively, Epictetus does offer examples of the true image of a philosopher: Socrates, who never bathed, yet people were attracted to him despite his lack of external appearances (4.11.19); and Diogenes, who was without a house or city, yet in exile he lived 'a life more tranquil and serene than that of all the noble and the rich' (4.11.23).

In summary, it is apparent that Epictetus identifies an ubiquitous problem in his social world, where one's identity was predominately expressed and validated by one's outward appearance. With society's preoccupation with the superficial aspect of *persona*, individuals often made great pursuits to project an image that was considered fashionable in Epictetus' day. This was also the case with philosophy, where the popular orators of the day were obsessed primarily with outward displays of oratory, rather than orations aimed at transforming their audience. Likewise, people evaluated philosophers and orators on the sole basis of their external appearance. Given this superficial view of identity in his social world, Epictetus reacted harshly against the conventional preoccupation with pretentious and exaggerated displays.

---

[91] Cf. Paul's accusation of the Corinthian Christians as being 'puffed up' in 1 Cor 4.6, 18–19; 5.2.

[92] Long, 'Socratic Mentor', 94.

[93] Long, *Epictetus*, 49–50.

4.3 'Freedom': The Rejection of the Superficial Side of *Persona*

Having observed the preoccupation with the superficial aspect of *persona* and indications of Epictetus' critique of it, this section will examine his denouncement of the conventionally presented *persona* as expressed through his theme of 'freedom'. Scholars have noted that no Stoic attaches more emphasis on freedom than Epictetus, which could be a result of his experiences as a slave.[94] A 'slave' in his teachings is one who is not living according to his volition, and instead living for external things, which are outside the volition. In *Dissertationes*, there is a lengthy discussion devoted to the theme, 'Of freedom' (4.1). The discourse begins with Epictetus' description of the free person: 'He is free (ἐλεύθερος) who lives as he wills, who is subject neither to compulsion, nor hindrance, nor force, whose choices are unhampered, whose desires attain their end, whose aversions do not fall into what they would avoid' (4.1.1–2). These powerful words describing freedom are the ideals that Epictetus urges his students to strive for, which happens to be antithetical to the prevailing conventional values of *persona*. According to Epictetus, these superficial status symbols do not necessarily portray one's character or virtue, and in fact these outward features often will hinder one's ability to live a life of freedom and virtue.

Epictetus continues the discussion with an elite person who has been consul twice. Epictetus bluntly accuses the man of being a slave (δοῦλος) and no better than a slave sold three times (4.1.6–8). The man abhorrently reacts by questioning how he could be a slave, since his father and mother were both free, and there is no deed of sale for him. He also points out that he has all the status indicators of the commonly projected social *persona* in Epictetus' day: a member of the senate, a 'friend of Caesar', a consul, and owns many slaves (4.1.8). Epictetus responds with the following sharp remarks:

> Now in the first place, most worthy senator, it is very likely that your father was the same kind of slave that you are, and your mother, and your grandfather, and all your ancestors from first to last. But even if they were free to the limit, what does that prove in your case? Why, what does it prove if they were noble, and you are mean-spirited? If they were brave, and you a coward? If they were self-controlled, and you unrestrained?[95]

Epictetus points out that this elite individual, like his ancestors, sought out and received social prestige, yet in reality they all have become slaves to something or someone (e.g. Caesar). In the senator's case, he has become a slave to his ambitions and behaviour.

The longing and quest for higher offices in Roman society involved the pursuit of measures that truly never result in freedom (cf. 4.10.18–21). To

---

[94] E.g. Brunt, 'Epictetus', 24.
[95] 4.1.9–10.

illustrate this point, Epictetus describes an individual who desires the privilege of wearing rings on his fingers, which would express the equestrian rank; but after receiving this privilege he only finds himself desiring more and more things (4.1.37–40). This is consistent with the intense longing for externals that Epictetus describes as an 'incurable fever' (cf. 4.9.1–5). Epictetus explains that when this individual attains social distinction and 'becomes a senator, then he becomes a slave (δοῦλος) as he enters the senate, then he serves in the *handsomest and sleekest slavery*' (4.1.40, italics mine). That is, even though he gains the outward appearance of nobility, he ironically becomes a well-dressed slave. According to Epictetus this sort of individual should ironically be called a 'slave in a *toga praetexta*' (4.1.58) – the *toga praetexta* being the robe reserved for Roman senators. Epictetus, elsewhere, exposes the absurdity of the pursuit of social prestige, 'Or again, when for the sake of these mighty and dignified offices and honours you kiss the hands of other men's slaves, so as to be the slave of men who are not even free?' (4.1.148). Those following this path of ambitiously climbing up the social ladder of Roman rank and status only find themselves, then, in slavery to: Caesar, others, their desires, and ultimately themselves.

In order to accentuate his teaching of freedom, Epictetus exhorts his listeners to abandon the things that are not their own:

If not, you will be a slave among slaves; even if you are consul ten thousand times, even if you go up to the Palace – a slave nonetheless...For you will learn by experience that what they [philosophers] say is true, and that none of these things which are admired and sought after are of any good to those who attain them; while those who have not yet attained them get an impression that, if once these things come to them, they will be possessed of all things good, and then, when they do come, the burning heat is just as bad, there is the same tossing about the sea, the same sense of surfeit, the same desire for what they do not have. For freedom is not acquired by satisfying yourself with what you desire, but by destroying your desire.[96]

With this exhortation, it is again clear that Epictetus has strong criticisms against the futile quest for rank and status in Roman society, which enslaves the ambitious person. His aim is to turn his listeners' ambitions from seeking the vain externals of the typically presented *persona* to seeking a life of freedom. Consequently, this experience of freedom has implications for what Epictetus considers one's authentic and genuine identity as a human being. Long explains, 'This freedom, Epictetus proposes, is available to all human beings who are willing to understand certain facts about nature and their own identity and cultivate a corresponding character and outlook'.[97] Thus, Epictetus deprecates the superficial dimension of the conventionally portrayed

---

[96] 4.1.173–6.
[97] Long, *Epictetus*, 27.

persona, since it truly does not display what he considers to be one's genuine identity.

4.4 The Genuine Aspect of One's Identity

In the above investigation of Epictetus' denouncement of the conventionally projected *persona*, there were some indications that Epictetus was interested in emphasising what he deemed to be the individual's true and genuine self. This authentic inner person can be seen in the discourse, 'On steadfastness' (1.29), where Epictetus mentions the situation of many tragic actors, who wear their buskins, masks, and long robes so frequently that after a while they begin to think of themselves as their characters. If, however, one of these tragic actors is stripped of his buskins and masks (προσωπεῖον) and placed on stage, the only way he can survive his character is to speak the part without the reliance of his external appearance (1.29.42–3). Epictetus uses this theatrical setting as an analogy for a situation in reality:

> And so it is in actual life. 'Take a governorship'. I take it and having done so, I show how an educated man behaves himself. 'Strip off the senatorial toga, put on the rags, and come forward in that πρόσωπον'. What then? Have I not been given a fine voice to display? 'How, then, do you appear on stage?'[98]

Here Epictetus is specifically dealing with an individual who has the Roman status of a governor. The status symbol of the senatorial toga (*latus clavus*) is stripped and he is left in rags, which identifies a person of low or no social status.[99] Similarly, in another discourse, Epictetus presents a scenario involving an interlocutor who is supposed to be the emperor:[100] 'He [the emperor] says to you, "Take off the senatorial toga". Look, I am wearing the equestrian toga. "Take that one off". Look, I am wearing an ordinary toga. "Take it off". Look, I am naked' (1.24.12–13).[101] As with the governor in the former text, Epictetus depicts here the stripping of the superficial accoutrements of one's social *persona* to expose the true and authentic

---

[98] 1.29.44–6, my translation.

[99] Long, *Epictetus*, 242 n. 10, identifies 'rags' as an allusion to the Cynic costume.

[100] Starr, 'Tyrant', 24, suggests that the emperor here is Domitian; *contra* Dobbin, *Discourses*, 203.

[101] My translation. Long, *Epictetus*, 194, writes that here Epictetus 'starkly contrasts the sham happiness of regal prosperity with the contentment and autonomy that are available in principle even to someone who lacks material goods'. Cf. Favorinus, *On His Exile* col. 18.17: 'Will you not put aside and take off these symbols and show yourself naked to us as you are – rather, not even naked, but clothed in poverty instead of purple, and crowned with freedom from office rather than with office and official insignia?' (quoted from Gleason, *Making Men*, 155).

person. With the stripping in this latter text each revealed layer is a specific toga representing the different hierarchical levels of the elite ranks in Roman society. Significantly, the individual is left 'naked', which is a symbolic condition that expresses the individual's true self – that is, a 'revelation of the original identity underneath'.[102]

Furthermore, in the former text, the governor, who is probably also naked, now must come forward in his revealed πρόσωπον – his authentic self – and use his 'fine voice' to portray who he really is without the reliance of any outward status symbols. Epictetus' point is that 'what reveals persons is not their appearance and the station in life they happen to occupy (their dramatic plot, as it were) but entirely how they perform and speak in these roles'.[103] In other words, Epictetus deprecates the commonly projected *persona* by showing that the genuine and authentic aspect of the individual's *persona* (πρόσωπον) is that which is beneath the superficial aspect of *persona*.[104]

Recognising that Epictetus rejects the conventionally projected *persona* as having any lasting value, attention will now be given to Epictetus' teachings regarding the contours and social implications of what he considers to be the genuine aspect of *persona*/πρόσωπον: appropriate social ethics, God's designation of one's *persona*, the προαίρεσις ('volition'), and the ideal of καλὸς καὶ ἀγαθός.

4.4.1 Appropriate Social Ethics

An important discourse that exhibits Epictetus' teaching of the genuine aspect of *persona* is 'How may a man preserve his proper πρόσωπον upon every occasion?' (1.2).[105] The seriousness of πρόσωπον for Epictetus could be noticed in the fact that this discourse is situated second in *Dissertationes*, after the first discourse, 'Of the things which are under our control' (1.1), which is essentially about 'a search for the self, for what we are'.[106] The second discourse, which is on the theme of πρόσωπον, should then be seen as

---

[102] Gleason, *Making Men*, 156. She elucidates: 'Like an athlete, one strips down to one's true self'.

[103] Long, *Epictetus*, 243.

[104] Cf. Stephens, 'Stoic Sage', 209–10, who comments on how Epictetus teaches that the Stoic sage's love for others is not external, but internal, because 'true happiness consists in inner goods, i.e. the virtues of character and mental freedom'.

[105] For Panaetius and Cicero's influence on Epictetus' philosophy of πρόσωπον here, see Gill, 'Personhood' 187–92. Although Epictetus does convey the philosophical concept of πρόσωπον, this study focuses more on how Epictetus uses that philosophical concept for his social context.

[106] Dobbin, *Discourses*, 68. He also comments that, significantly, the first discourse articulates some of Epictetus' most characteristic themes, is appropriately placed at the head of the corpus, and is abstracted in chapter one of *Encheiridion*.

attempting to fulfil that search for the self. In the discourse, Epictetus addresses the importance of education for understanding what is rational (εὔλογος) and irrational (ἄλογος): 'But for determining the rational and the irrational, we employ not only our estimates of what is the value of external things (ἐκτός), but also the criterion of that which is in keeping with one's own πρόσωπον' (1.2.7–8). He follows with a scenario of whether it is rational for one to carry the chamber-pot for others, which is a servile task, in order to avoid a beating.[107] Epictetus views that one should carry the pot, if it seems rational to his self-worth, but the interlocutor responds: 'Yes, but it would be unworthy of me' (1.2.11). Recognising the importance of self-worth, Epictetus adds another consideration to the question, 'For you are the one that knows yourself, how much you are worth in your own eyes and at what price you sell yourself. For different men sell themselves at different prices' (1.2.11; cf. 1.2.33). He is pointing out that one's πρόσωπον is a main criterion to determine one's appropriate social behaviour.[108] Long explains Epictetus' point:

His point, then, is that, in deciding what it is right or reasonable to do, we are never simply assessing material gains or losses; we are also, whether we acknowledge it or not, putting our individual characters on the line and implicating them in our judgements of reasonable behaviour. How people act, especially when critical choices have to be made, reveals their sense of values and thereby the value they assign to themselves.[109]

Thus, the idea of someone doing the task of a slave would be a reproach for his students from the elite class.[110]

In addition, there is a significant contrast between the genuine aspect of one's πρόσωπον, which is of great importance for Epictetus, and the external deeds and matters (ἐκτός), which seem to be of less importance. Epictetus warns his students not to be like those who stoop down to the level of calculating the value of externals (ἐκτός), which would result in forgetting one's own πρόσωπον (τοῦ ἰδίου προσώπου) (1.2.14–15). One's own πρόσωπον appears to have certain attributes and behaviour that would be proper and consistent with it. The need to have a proper perspective about externals in order to maintain one's πρόσωπον is seen in his discourse, 'What things should be exchanged for what things?' (4.3), in which Epictetus

---

[107] See further discussion of this text in Long, *Epictetus*, 238–40; Dobbin, *Discourses*, 82; Kamtekar, 'ΑΙΔΩΣ', 150–2. Also, cf. Plutarch, *Apoph. lac.* 234C, and Seneca, *Ep.* 77.14–15, who both use this scenario of the chamber-pot to show that death is preferred to such a demeaning role.

[108] Cf. Kamtekar, 'ΑΙΔΩΣ', 147–52.

[109] Long, *Epictetus*, 239. He further comments that 'Epictetus cannot tell anyone what a person is worth in their own eyes'. Cf. Kamtekar, 'ΑΙΔΩΣ', 151.

[110] Cf. Philo, *Det.* 34, where one of descriptors of the elite is that their 'hands have never known labour' (πόνον οὐκ εἰδότες).

maintains that if one loses some external thing, that person should weigh the payoff of the thing gained in return. He remarks, 'If you bear this in mind you will everywhere maintain your πρόσωπον as it ought to be' (4.3.3). Adolf Bonhöffer writes, 'Um vernünftig zu handeln, lehrt Epictet, darf man nicht bloss die äusseren Werte wägen, sondern muss auch τὸ κατὰ πρόσωπον, d. h. das Gebot der Ehre berücksichtigen'.[111]

Another important discourse for understanding Epictetus' views on the authentic dimension of πρόσωπον and its social implications is on the question, 'How is it possible to discover a man's duties from the designations (ὀνομάτων) which he bears?' (2.10), in which he begins by interjecting, 'Consider who you are' (2.10.1). As the title of the discourse indicates, it is a treatment on the various social roles a man might have in life, and the related duties entailed by each particular social identity. Although the term πρόσωπον has philosophical roots for Epictetus, he uses it here to denote one's authentic social identity. The social identities discussed are the status of man, citizen, father, son, brother, and various other roles (e.g. town councillor, a youth, and an elder).[112] Significantly, Epictetus explains that with each particular πρόσωπον there are outward duties that should appropriately express that identity. Thus, Long aptly writes, 'Epictetus treats family relationships, public office, and stages of life as *normative* identifications that specify the conduct appropriate to each designation'.[113]

From the above two discourses on πρόσωπον, it is clear that πρόσωπον (*persona*) was an important social concept for Epictetus and his social world. However, the conventional view of social identity by Roman society was so largely preoccupied with the superficial values of *persona* that the exterior features overshadowed what Epictetus considered to be one's genuine *persona*. Epictetus harshly criticised this preoccupation in order to draw attention to the true aspect of one's identity. Importantly, this identity that Epictetus inculcated is one that shapes and determines an individual's social values and ethics. Bonhöffer elaborates:

Epictets Prosopon aber bedeutet teils die äussere Lebensstellung des Menschen, die Rolle, die er auf der Bühne des Lebens zu spielen hat, teils die persönliche Würde und Ehre, die sittliche Selbstachtung, die freilich thatsächlich bei den Menschen sehr verschieden ist, aber bei allen gleich sein sollte, wie er denn auch der Ansicht ist, dass der Gebildete im stande sein muss, in jede äussere Lebensstellung sich zu finden, jede Rolle korrekt und mit Würde zu spielen.[114]

---

[111] Bonhöffer, *Ethik*, 34. Cf. Gill, 'Personhood', 188–91.

[112] In this discourse, Epictetus explicitly uses πρόσωπον to refer to some of the various social identities. E.g. 'Next bear in mind that you are a Son. What is the profession of this πρόσωπον?' (2.10.7); 'Next know that you are also a Brother. Upon this πρόσωπον also there is incumbent deference, obedience, kindly speech...' (2.10.8).

[113] Long, *Epictetus*, 236 (italics his).

[114] Bonhöffer, *Ethik*, 10–11.

4.4.2 God's Designation of the Individual's Persona

God (Zeus) has a foundational role in Stoic philosophy, including Epictetus' philosophy.[115] Epictetus teaches that the first lesson of philosophy is to recognise that there is a providential and omniscient God (2.14.11). In fact, Epictetus exhorts his students to live a life pleasing before God and not before human beings, 'When you come into the presence of some prominent man, remember that Another [God] looks from above on what is taking place, and that you must please Him rather than this man' (1.30.1). On several occasions, Epictetus even remarks about God living within the individual (1.14.11–14; 2.7.3; 2.8.11–14; 4.12.11–12.).[116]

In addition to these insights into the individual's relation to God, Epictetus accentuates an essential feature of one's authentic identity by explaining that God is the one who assigns an individual's proper *persona* in life. In *Encheiridion*, Epictetus uses a theatrical analogy to show how God assigns the different *personae*:

Remember that you are an actor in a play, the character of which is determined by the Playwright: if he wishes the play to be short, it is short; if long, it is long; if He wishes you to play the part of a beggar, remember to act even this role adroitly; and so if your role be that of a cripple, an official, or a layman. For this is your business, to play admirably the πρόσωπον assigned you.[117]

Since God is the one who determines one's *persona* (πρόσωπον) in life, all one has to do is to live it out admirably – that is, play the part well. In the text it is significant that God assigns different sorts of *personae*, which by conventional means, some would have a high status and others would have a low status. Nevertheless, Epictetus emphasises that whatever social identity a person has in life, he is to play the part well, like a good actor (cf. 4.7.12–15). Hence, social status is a matter of indifference for the genuine God-given πρόσωπον. For his elite students, then, there is no need to be ambitious and seek higher rank and status. In fact, elsewhere, Epictetus warns against assuming a πρόσωπον that is beyond one's power, since 'you both disgrace yourself in that one, and at the same time neglect the role which you might have filled with success' (*Ench.* 37). Thus, all one has to do is live according to the social identity God has assigned.[118]

---

[115] For Epictetus' conception of 'God', see Lagrange, 'Philosophie', 192–212; Jagu, *Epictète*, 112–33; Pohlenz, *Die Stoa*, I:93–110; Spanneut, 'Epiktet', 611–15; Long, *Epictetus*, 21–6, 142–94.

[116] For more on this idea, see Long, *Epictetus*, 163–8; Rist, *Stoic Philosophy*, 256–72.

[117] *Ench.* 17.

[118] Cf. Rom 12.3–7, where Paul exhorts the Christians not to think of themselves more highly than they ought to but consider themselves by the measure of faith that God has assigned, as seen in the various gifts God has given them.

As a practical teacher, Epictetus not only presents the philosophical truth of God assigning an individual's *persona*, but he appropriately provides encouragement on how to follow God in a world that is full of temptations.[119] He urges his listeners to weigh the values of their desires and to respond according to virtue and moral excellence:

> For it is no small matter that you are guarding, but self-respect, and fidelity, and constancy, a state of mind undisturbed by passion, pain, fear, or confusion – in a word, freedom. What are the things for which you are about to sell these things? Look, how valuable are they?...'I have a modest behaviour, he has a tribuneship; he has a praetorship, I have self-respect. But I do not shout where it is unseemly; I shall not stand up where I ought not; for I am a free man and a friend of God, so as to obey Him of my own free will. No other thing ought I to claim, not body, or property, or office, or reputation – nothing, in short; nor does He wish me to claim them. Had He so desired He would have made them good for me. But as it is, He has not so made them; therefore I cannot transgress any of His commands'.[120]

Here Epictetus appropriately joins the two themes of God and freedom. People are to understand their freedom from the endless ambitions of pursuing rank and status, and to live according to the true and authentic *persona* that God has given.

4.4.3 The Προαίρεσις and Persona

A key component of Epictetus' philosophy, which was briefly introduced above, is the προαίρεσις ('volition').[121] This philosophical feature will now be analysed for its social significance in Epictetus' teachings on the genuine aspect of one's identity. As defined above, the προαίρεσις is 'what persons are in terms of their mental faculties, consciousness, character, judgements, goals, and desires: volition is the self, what each of us is, as abstracted from the body'.[122] More importantly, the προαίρεσις is the individual's autonomous mental disposition that, if used correctly, helps the individual to make true judgements, which leads to freedom.[123] Having observed Epictetus' rejection of externals, and his emphasis on the genuine *persona* behind the superficialities, this study suggests that for Epictetus the προαίρεσις is tantamount to that authentic inner dimension of an individual's *persona*.

---

[119] See Long, *Epictetus*, 186, who states that Epictetus' favourite formula for the goal of human life is 'to follow the gods'; cf. 1.12.5; 1.30.4; 4.7.20.

[120] 4.3.7–10.

[121] In addition to the above discussion of this concept, see Long, *Epictetus*, 210–20; Dobbin, 'Προαίρεσις', 111–35; Asmis, 'Choice', 385–412. Scholars are in agreement that Epictetus' stress on the προαίρεσις is unique in comparison with earlier Stoics. See e.g. Pohlenz, *Die Stoa*, I:332–5; Dobbin, 'Προαίρεσις', 123.

[122] Long, *Epictetus*, 28.

[123] Cf. Asmis, 'Choice', 385: 'When perfected, choice [προαίρεσις] coincides with the goal of freedom'.

This correlation is seen in texts where Epictetus provides an antithesis of exterior-interior (i.e. externals–προαίρεσις).[124] For instance, in his discussion of the need of training and education for the 'good and excellent' person, Epictetus addresses the issue of those who are not living in accordance with their προαίρεσις, but are rather focused on others' opinions. In the dialogue, Epictetus questions his interlocutor:

Is it not evident that you set no value on your volition (προαίρεσιν), but look beyond to the things that lie outside the province of the volition (ἀπροαίρετα), namely, what So-and-so will say, and what impression you will make, whether men will think you a scholar, or that you have read Chrysippus or Antipater?[125]

This failure to recognise the προαίρεσις as one's true self is also observed in Epictetus' censure of the visiting student from Corinth who has spent his energy adorning his external appearance: 'For you are not flesh, nor hair, but προαίρεσις' (3.1.40). In fact, Epictetus tells the student that he has inappropriately spent his energy on his external appearance, rather than on his true self, his προαίρεσις (3.1.41–3).

Importantly, Epictetus teaches the practicality of the προαίρεσις by urging his students to focus not on the superficial matters that lie outside the sphere of one's προαίρεσις:

In the like manner, therefore, the principal task in life is this: distinguish matters and weigh them one against another, and say to yourself, 'Externals (τὰ ἔξω) are not under my control; προαίρεσις is under my control. Where am I to look for the good and the evil? Within me, in that which is my own'.[126]

The προαίρεσις here becomes the guiding principle for determining what external matters are appropriate and inappropriate for an individual. By relating it to the principal task in life, Epictetus is stressing the importance of the προαίρεσις for appropriate living.[127] Concerning the social implications of the προαίρεσις, Long explains that the basis of proper relationships 'should be entirely translated, like everything we deal with, into the domain of our volition and integrity'.[128]

---

[124] Cf. Asmis, 'Choice', 390: 'The dichotomy between the inner self and external things lies at the very root of the meaning of *prohairesis*'.

[125] 3.2.13.

[126] 2.5.5.

[127] Cf. 1.30.4, where Epictetus responds to the question of what is good: 'A proper προαίρεσις and use of impressions (φαντασιῶν)'. See Long, 'Representation', 264–85, for the philosophical term φαντασία and its important relationship to the προαίρεσις, especially for determining appropriate and inappropriate conduct.

[128] Long, *Epictetus*, 237, cf. 30. See 2.22.18–21, where the προαίρεσις establishes one's duties as a friend, son, and father (cf. 2.10).

Furthermore, Epictetus teaches that the individuals who are truly 'progressing' in life are those who live according to their προαίρεσις.[129] In answering the question, 'Where, then is progress?', he replies that it is the man who has withdrawn from external things (τῶν ἐκτός) and 'has turned his attention to the question of his own volition (προαίρεσιν), cultivating and perfecting it so as to make it finally harmonious with nature, elevated, free, unhindered, untrammelled, faithful, and honourable...' (1.4.18).[130] Through these sayings, Epictetus attempts to instil in his students the importance of the προαίρεσις for understanding and living out one's genuine *persona*. Therefore, the προαίρεσις is very significant for Epictetus' teachings of this identity, which is not established by external social markers, but is rather found in one's internal προαίρεσις.

4.4.4 Καλὸς καὶ Ἀγαθός

The final aspect to consider of Epictetus' understanding of the true aspect of one's identity is the ethical ideal of καλὸς καὶ ἀγαθός, which is usually translated 'good and excellent'. This phrase is a traditional expression used in Graeco-Roman literature and inscriptions to describe and praise people of honour and virtue.[131] More significantly, Epictetus uses the phrase to convey the ideal kind of *persona* (πρόσωπον) that a person can attain. In fact, in the discourse 'On the calling of a Cynic' (3.22), Epictetus noticeably uses καλὸς καὶ ἀγαθός to describe the πρόσωπον of the Cynic (τὸ τοῦ καλοῦ καὶ ἀγαθοῦ πρόσωπον) (3.22.69). Although this phrase καλὸς καὶ ἀγαθός is frequently used in the *Dissertationes*, scholars have paid little attention to this phrase.[132] It is worthwhile, then, to examine Epictetus' usage of the phrase and its social and moral implications for one's genuine *persona*.

---

[129] On 'progress', see Dobbin, *Discourses*, 88–90.

[130] On the epithets of the προαίρεσις (esp. 'free' and 'unhindered'), see 1.6.40; 1.17.21; 1.18.17. Cf. Long, 'Freedom', 190.

[131] See Ste Croix, 'KALOKAGATHIA', 371–6, who notes that the phrase has both a socio-political and a moral meaning; cf. Gomme, 'ΚΑΛΟΙ ΚΑΓΑΘΟΙ'; Donlan, 'καλὸς κἀγαθός', 365. For NT studies, see Clarke, 'Good', 134–7, and idem, *Leadership*, 163–5, who explains the term as a social distinction of the upper wealthy class; Winter, 'Public Honouring', 91, who explores the socio-political use of the phrase in public inscriptions as a praise for benefaction.

[132] 1.7.2; 1.12.7; 2.10.5; 2.11.25; 2.14.10; 3.2.1, 7; 3.3.1; 3.22.69, 87; 3.24.19, 50, 95, 110; 4.5.1, 6; 4.8.24. Long, *Epictetus*, 37: 'In order to put these references in perspective, one should note that our record of Epictetus runs to some 450 pages of Greek text'. See also idem, 'Socratic Mentor', 96, where he observes that Epictetus' 'preferred terms for male excellence are *kalos kagothos* or *agathos anēr*, or simply *anēr* or *anthropos* with the connotation "manly" or "properly human" respectively'.

In the same discourse (3.22), Epictetus converses with an acquaintance who is considering to take up the Cynic lifestyle.[133] Despite his admiration for the Cynics, Epictetus views that their ascetic and extreme lifestyle is not appropriate for just anyone to take up, but rather only for the few who have this rare and special calling.[134] Even Epictetus does not consider himself able to fulfil this calling, and urges his acquaintance to weigh carefully the costs of what it means to be a Cynic, whose lifestyle is one free of distractions. He presents the challenges that a Cynic encounters in fulfilling his duties, while attempting to maintain his *persona* of being καλὸς καὶ ἀγαθός (3.22.69).[135] That is, the Cynic's identity would be jeopardised if he were to fulfil certain distractions, such as obligations to his family. Conversely, the true Cynic must spend all his energy on fulfilling his volition, because there will be temptations – such as possessions, offices, and honours – which will rise up like a thief to his volition (3.22.100–6). Thus, the Cynic must be diligent in protecting his *persona* which reflects the ideal of καλὸς καὶ ἀγαθός.

In many of his teachings, Epictetus urges his students to achieve the genuine *persona* of καλὸς καὶ ἀγαθός, a goal that requires much learning and training.[136] For instance, Epictetus asserts, 'For our aim in every matter of inquiry is to learn how the good and excellent man (καλὸς καὶ ἀγαθός) may find the appropriate course through it and the appropriate way of conducting himself in it' (1.7.2–3). Besides highlighting the necessity of learning the subject matter of being καλὸς καὶ ἀγαθός (cf. 3.2.1, 7; 3.3.1–2), he further teaches about the social implications of one who is καλὸς καὶ ἀγαθός:

> Don't you know that a good and excellent man (καλὸς καὶ ἀγαθός) does nothing for the sake of appearances, but only for the sake of having acted right?...Does it seem to you so small and worthless a thing to be good, and excellent, and happy (καλὸν καὶ ἀγαθὸν καὶ εὐδαίμονα)?[137]

An individual who has this ethical ideal, then, acts out of moral rightness and not out of pretence, which would be a critical lesson for his students who live in a social world where there was a large preoccupation with artificial appearance.

One final aspect of καλὸς καὶ ἀγαθός to point out is the significance of Socrates as the ideal image of the genuine *persona* in *Dissertationes*, which is

---

[133] For a commentary on this discourse, Billerbeck, *Epiktet.*

[134] See Griffin, 'Cynicism', esp. 204, and Billerbeck, 'Ideal Cynic', esp. 207–8, for Roman attitudes towards Cynics, and how writers, like Epictetus, had to rework the image of the Cynic to present the Cynic as ideal.

[135] Cf. 3.22.87, where Epictetus explains that the Cynic should be able to use his body to prove to people that he is a 'good and excellent man (καλὸν καὶ ἀγαθόν)'.

[136] Cf. Bonhöffer, *Ethik*, 11, who indicates that 'ein Philosoph oder Kalokagathos kann und soll jeder werden'.

[137] 3.24.51–2.

clearly seen in Epictetus' description of him as being καλὸς καὶ ἀγαθός (e.g. 4.8.23–4).[138] It is noteworthy that Epictetus rarely refers to the ideal sage, and when he does, it is in a more traditional fashion (καλὸς καὶ ἀγαθός) than in an esoteric way (σοφός or φρόνιμος).[139] This presentation of Socrates as καλὸς καὶ ἀγαθός is also observed in Epictetus' identification of Socrates in 'the society of the good and excellent men (τῶν καλῶν καὶ ἀγαθῶν ἀνδρῶν)', with whom his students should compare themselves (2.18.21). Additionally, Epictetus accentuates Socrates as an *exemplum* (παράδειγμα) for one who strives to be καλὸς καὶ ἀγαθός (4.5.1; cf. 4.1.159–69).[140] Thus, in light of his teaching of the genuine aspect of *persona*, Epictetus appropriately exhibits Socrates 'as a model for public and private life and for exemplifying the practice of what he himself is trying to teach'.[141]

Therefore, with Epictetus' high regard for the Cynic and for Socrates, it is noteworthy that he used the traditional ideal of καλὸς καὶ ἀγαθός to describe them and to accentuate his teachings on an individual's true self. It was suggested above that Epictetus was an attractive choice as a teacher for the parents of prospective students because of his traditional views of philosophy. Long postulates:

> The parents who sent their sons to Nicopolis to study under Epictetus may have had a smattering of Stoic philosophy (who knows?), but what they were primarily looking for, I guess, and what they knew in advance to expect was that he would help turn their boys into men.[142]

However, to be more specific, given Epictetus' thoughts on the genuine πρόσωπον/*persona* and the important ideal of καλὸς καὶ ἀγαθός, Epictetus should be regarded as training his students how to have a genuine and proper *persona* of 'good and excellent' (τὸ τοῦ καλοῦ καὶ ἀγαθοῦ πρόσωπον).[143]

---

[138] For studies of the significance of Socrates in Epictetus' teachings, see Long, 'Socratic Mentor', 79–98; Döring, *Exemplum Socratis*, 43–79. For Socrates in Hellenistic philosophy, see Döring, *op. cit.*, and Long, 'Socrates', 150–71. It is also worth noting the importance of the idealised Cynic, Diogenes, for Epictetus; however, Diogenes is not as significant as Socrates in Epictetus' discourses. See Long, *Epictetus*, 58–61, for more on Epictetus' presentation of Diogenes.

[139] Long, *Epictetus*, 33.

[140] See Döring, *Exemplum Socratis*, esp. 43–79, for Socrates as an *exemplum*. See also Dobbin, *Discourses*, 74, who notes that the Stoics placed great value on moral *exempla* as 'personal role models'; cf. Seneca, *Ep.* 6.5. Interestingly, Valerius Maximus exhibits Socrates in his foreign *exempla*: e.g. 3.4 *ext.* 1; 3.8 *ext.* 3; 6.4 *ext.* 2; 7.2.1a–d; 8.7 *ext.* 8; 8.8 *ext.* 1.

[141] Long, 'Socratic Mentor', 85.

[142] Long, 'Socratic Mentor', 97.

[143] Another reason for Epictetus' attractiveness as a philosophical teacher is that he teaches his young students how to live appropriately to male virtue, which was an issue in Epictetus' day (e.g. 3.1.31). On this gender issue, see Gleason, *Making Men*, esp. 55–81; Richlin, 'Gender', 90–110.

Finally, this section on Epictetus' conception and inculcation of the genuine *persona* concludes with a text that harmonises several of the important themes discussed, and elucidates how an individual is to live in society in accordance with this identity:

For this reason the good and excellent man (καλὸς καὶ ἀγαθός), bearing in mind who he is, and whence he has come, and by whom he was created, centres his attention on this and this only, how he may fill his place in an orderly fashion, and with due obedience to God. 'Is it Thy will that I should still remain? I will remain as a free man, as a nobleman, as Thou didst wish it... Again as Thou didst wish it, as a free man, as Thy servant, as one who has perceived Thy commands and Thy prohibitions. But so long as I continue to live in Thy service, what manner of man wouldst Thou have me be? An official or private citizen, a senator or one of the common people, a soldier or a general, a teacher or the head of a household? Whatsoever station and post Thou assign me, I will die ten thousand times, as Socrates says, or ever I abandon it. And where would Thou have me be? In Rome, or in Athens, or in Thebes, or in Gyara? Only remember me there'.[144]

4.5 Conclusion

4.5.1 Epictetus' Critique of Persona and Identity

Epictetus' background as a slave, philosopher, and moral teacher would have influenced his role as a social critic of Roman society. Epictetus viewed that in Rome and Nicopolis there was a misconception of social identity. In particular, he observed a large preoccupation with the superficial aspect of *persona* which was widely projected in his day. Not surprisingly, in both of these social environments his philosophical teachings would have been regarded as sharp criticisms. He taught that unless one is called by God to be in a high social position, one should not pursue a life and career in the Roman socio-political system. The Roman elite lifestyle was full of temptations and desires for men to take great measures in order to attain social prestige; in fact, Epictetus described this intense longing for prestige as an 'incurable fever'. He accordingly reacted to the conventional outworking of social *persona* by denouncing the worth of the shallow features of *persona*, since these features hinder one's ability to live an ideal life of freedom and virtue. By doing so, Epictetus shifted the focus of the preoccupation from the superficial dimension of *persona* to the true inner dimension of *persona*. He elaborated on this genuine aspect of one's identity by elucidating: God as the one who assigns one's πρόσωπον in life; the true inner self being the προαίρεσις, which helps the individual discern how to live appropriately to the God-given πρόσωπον; and the goal of living to achieve the ethical ideal

---

[144] 3.24.95–100; cf. 4.5.1, 6–7.

of καλὸς καὶ ἀγαθός. This study consequently proposed that Epictetus trained his students to develop a virtuous *persona* of καλὸς καὶ ἀγαθός, and to live according to this true and authentic identity.

As a social critic of the Roman stress on *persona*, Epictetus sharply reacted to the conventionally presented *persona* in his day, and to what he considered to be inappropriate behaviour – the preoccupation with the shallow features of social identity. Although he shows some indications that the Roman social system was a matter of indifference for one's genuine *persona*, he does show sharp criticisms of how the system enslaved many who participate in it. Of chief importance to Epictetus was how one lived according to the identity that is God-given, and not according to society's pressures and the conventional criteria of *persona*. His counter-cultural stance is also observed in his appreciation and self-presentation of the visible image of the philosopher, who displayed a long beard, rough cloak, and staff. To emphasise this image, Epictetus portrayed the ideal images of the Cynic, Diogenes, and more significantly, Socrates, who achieved greatness not by his appearance but by his philosophy. These images he promoted would not have been esteemed by conventional standards, thus accentuating Epictetus' strong views as a social critic of the typically projected social *persona* in his day.

4.5.2 Comparison to Valerius' Critique

This chapter concludes by briefly comparing Epictetus' critique of *persona* to Valerius Maximus' critique. Valerius was observed to be reacting to the conventionally projected *persona* while still appreciating the Roman social order, which protected and promoted the traditional ideals of Roman identity and of Roman society. His reaction was primarily against what he considered to be inappropriate behaviour that exploited and skewed traditional Roman identity. In contrast, while Epictetus did criticise the commonly portrayed *persona*, he did not appreciate the values of the Roman social order but only viewed them as a matter of indifference at best. Rather than restoring the traditional values of an ideal 'Roman' *persona*, as Valerius did, Epictetus reconfigured the individual's worth as being found in the genuine aspect of *persona*, which follows more of his Stoic philosophy than an ideal Roman identity. In light of this, Epictetus' conception of the genuine aspect of *persona* could even be regarded as apathetic to the current conventional values. In addition, Valerius esteemed the emperor as the exemplar and ultimate embodiment of the ideal Roman *persona*, while Epictetus, like so many Stoic philosophers, negatively viewed the emperor, and instead presented Socrates as the exemplar of the genuine *persona*. Given this comparison, Valerius' critique is affirmed to be a milder reaction, while Epictetus' critique is assessed to be a stronger reaction to the Roman stress on *persona* and its popular presentation.

Chapter 5

Christian Identity in the Corinthian Church (Part I)

5.1 Introduction

Having examined the critiques of social identity and *persona* by Valerius Maximus and Epictetus, this chapter and the following chapter will consider the third and final figure of this study, the apostle Paul, and his critique. New Testament scholars have studied various social features (e.g. rank and status, leadership, honour/shame, patronage) to describe the social world of the Pauline churches, but have not given much attention to the related social feature of *persona*. These two chapters aim to explore Paul's perspective on this all-important social concept in 2 Corinthians. Although brief biographical introductions were provided for Valerius Maximus and Epictetus, given that this is a New Testament study, it is not necessary to provide a detailed introduction to the familiar figure of Paul.[1] The introductory matters that will be briefly discussed here are Paul's awareness of the social concept of *persona*, and a defence as to why 2 Corinthians is the primary focus of these two chapters.

5.1.1 Paul's Awareness of the Concept of Persona

This study has demonstrated that the majority of individuals living in the Roman empire would have been conscious of the concept of *persona* (and the Roman stress on it) and its consequences for life in the Roman socio-political world, regardless of whether their socio-economic status was rich/poor, free/slave, citizen/foreigner, elite/non-elite. The apostle Paul is no exception; he would have been mindful of the social implications of *persona*. Supporting evidence of his awareness can be seen in Will Deming's suggestion that Paul might have been acquainted with an early conception of Gaius' legal treatise 'law of *personae*' (*ius personarum*). Deming argues that Paul's experiences with legal matters in Corinth (e.g. 1 Cor 5.1–5; 6.1–11) led him to use the phrase ὁ νόμος κυριεύει τοῦ ἀνθρώπου in Rom 7.1.[2] As seen in Chapter Two, one's *persona* had a crucial role in determining the verdict of a legal

---

[1] For an introduction to Paul and his life, see e.g. Murphy-O'Connor, *Paul*.

[2] Deming, 'Paul, Gaius', 227–9. See Chapter Two for more discussion of Deming's study.

trial. According to Acts 18.11 Paul had spent 18 months in Corinth, which would have given him sufficient time to gain first-hand experience with issues involving the concept of *persona*. Regardless of whether Deming is correct in his interpretation of Rom 7.1, he is right in assuming that Paul would have been exposed to the social concept in the legal matters of the Corinthian church. In addition to Paul's awareness of the legal aspect of *persona* while living in Corinth, his own *persona* and missionary travels also testify to his consciousness of the social concept. Paul, who was born a Jew from Tarsus and studied under the notable Gamaliel (Acts 22.3), gives autobiographical details of the *cursus honorum* of his Jewish *persona*, as seen in Phil 3.5–6: 'circumcised on the eighth day, a member of the people of Israel, of the tribe of Benjamin, a Hebrew born of Hebrews; as to the law, a Pharisee; as to zeal, a persecutor of the church; as to righteousness under the law, blameless'.[3] Even more significant for his *persona* than the status of a noble Jew and citizen of Tarsus was the fact that he was born a Roman citizen, which granted him privilege and honours in the Roman world.[4] The social importance of this particular feature of his Roman *persona* can be gathered from Luke's account of Paul's missionary travels, where Paul used his legal privileges as a Roman-born citizen to avoid beatings and imprisonment (Acts 22.24–9; cf. 16.37–9) and to appeal to Caesar (25.10–12; 26.32).

Paul's awareness of the weightiness of *persona*, especially the Roman stress on *persona*, can further be seen in the large number of his associates who were ranked as Roman. In a recent article entitled, 'The Roman Base of Paul's Mission', E.A. Judge has provided a statistical analysis of the names of Paul's associates, with which he concluded: 1) one third of those around Paul bear Latin names, which remarkably is ten times more than one would expect; 2) these names suggest that most of these individuals would have been Roman citizens or possibly had the rank of Junian Latin; 3) since most Romans or Latins in the Roman East would have kept their Greek names, it is possible that more than half of Paul's associates were ranked as Roman.[5] Judge's study confirms Paul's awareness of the privileges associated with a Roman *persona* for his missionary travels, since Paul strategically associated with a large number of individuals who possessed Roman citizenship.

Paul's use of the term πρόσωπον is also evidence of his consciousness of the social feature of *persona*. Overall, New Testament scholars have not

---

[3] See Hellerman, *Reconstructing*, 121–7; Rapske, *Roman Custody*, 90–108.

[4] For Paul's Roman citizenship, see Sherwin-White, *Roman Law*, who discusses Paul's further experiences with Roman law; Rapske, *Roman Custody*, 71–90, who also discusses his dual citizenship. Some scholars, e.g. Stegemann, 'Römischer Bürger', 200–29, have challenged Paul's status as a Roman citizen; however, see Minnen, 'Roman Citizen', 43–53, for a strong argument for Paul's Roman citizenship.

[5] Judge, 'Roman Base', 103–17.

considered the significance of the term πρόσωπον as it relates to *persona* and social identity. Although scholars do occasionally use the term *persona*, it is almost always used in a generic sense to express the modern colloquial meaning of the word – that is, 'facade'.[6] In addition, there have been a few scholars who have used the term in a more technical sense, such as a 'rhetorical *persona*', but they have not given much attention to the social importance of the term in the first century CE.[7] For instance, in his study of Paul's Roman custody in Acts, Brian Rapske states that he aims, among other things, to draw together 'what is disclosed of the Pauline legal and social *persona* in Acts'.[8] Despite his appropriate assessment of Paul's legal and social status, Rapske does not consider the significance of the *persona* language in the Graeco-Roman world. It is also worth mentioning that Ben Witherington, in his socio-rhetorical commentary on Romans, makes a passing reference to the Roman conception of *persona*: 'The Roman persona, which included elements of assumed superiority in culture, race, and matters religious, is what Paul must deal with if he is to build bridges between Jewish and Gentile Christians in Rome'.[9]

One scholar who has given attention to the ancient conception of *persona* is Bruce Winter, although he primarily focuses on its legal aspect.[10] He has recognised that one's *persona* (legal *persona*) and its attached privileges are important features for interpreting Rom 12.3–21, where Paul urges the Roman Christians to understand the will of God over against conforming to this age – that is, the conventions of Roman society.[11] Elsewhere, Winter considers the socio-legal feature of *persona* in Gal 6.12, where Paul writes: 'It is those who want εὐπροσωπῆσαι in the flesh that try to compel you to be circumcised – only that they may not be persecuted for the cross of Christ'. The infinitive

---

[6] Although in this chapter and the following one there will be direct quotations from scholars that contain the word '*persona*', the term, unless noted otherwise, is only used by the scholar in a generic sense.

[7] See e.g. Selby, 'Seer', 351–73, who explains the concept of a 'rhetorical *persona*' and how Paul assumes a specific *persona* for persuasive purposes, but only discusses it in a rhetorical sense and not a social sense; Hester, 'Rhetoric', 83–105, who uses the term to interpret Paul as establishing his 'apostolic *persona*', but does not use ancient sources to draw out the significance of *persona* in the first-century social world.

[8] Rapske, *Roman Custody*, 4.

[9] Witherington, *Rom*, 333. Although this is a helpful description, he does not discuss the concept any further in his commentary.

[10] The only other NT scholar, to my knowledge, who has recognised the legal aspect of *persona* is Betz, *2 Cor*, 85–6, who suggests this meaning for the term πρόσωπον in 2 Cor 8.24 (εἰς αὐτοὺς ἐνδεικνύμενοι εἰς πρόσωπον τῶν ἐκκλησιῶν), in that the sent messengers are the legal and political representatives of the churches.

[11] Winter, 'Roman Law', 76–81. Note that there is no explicit language of πρόσωπον in this passage.

εὐπροσωπῆσαι here is often translated 'to make a good showing', but Winter suggests that there is a connotation of a Roman legal status behind the cognates of εὐπροσωπέω (i.e. πρόσωπον), and consequently translates the term as 'to secure a "good" status'.[12] He interprets that the Galatian Christians are tempted to be circumcised in order to gain a Jewish legal status, which would exempt them from imperial cult worship. This explanation of εὐπροσωπέω is consistent with the understanding of *persona*/πρόσωπον and the social consequences of one's *persona* in Roman society, even for Jews and Christians. Regardless of whether or not the conflict concerns imperial cult worship, Paul's use of this cognate of πρόσωπον here does portray a situation of individuals being compelled to do something externally that would give them a privileged social identity before others.

Including the instance of εὐπροσωπέω in Gal 6.12, Paul uses the term πρόσωπον 24 times in the Pauline corpus including the disputed letters. As seen in Chapter Two, the term has a wide semantic range, and Paul uses it similarly in this wide range. He uses it to denote the literal face (1 Cor 13.12; 2 Cor 3.7, 13, 18; 11.20), literal person (2 Cor 1.11), presence before (1 Cor 14.25; 2 Thes 1.9), physical presence (Col 2.1; 1 Thes 2.17; 3.10), and, as in Gal 6.12, there are instances where he seems to use it as equivalent to the Latin term *persona* (2 Cor 5.12; 10.7). There are, nonetheless, some instances where it is quite ambiguous as to whether it carries this *persona* connotation (2 Cor 2.10; 4.6; 8.24; 10.1; Gal 1.22; 2.6; 2.11). In these cases it is the context that determines whether or not the malleable term πρόσωπον is referring to one's social *persona*. For instance, in Gal 2.6 Paul uses the phrase λαμβάνειν πρόσωπον, which expresses the Hebrew phrase נשא פנים ('showing partiality'), to assert that he, like God, does not show partiality in regard to the conventional status of leaders. Given that the context is about Paul's devaluation of the status of certain leaders, this expression could have some bearing on recognising a preoccupation with the superficial aspect of *persona* in the Galatian church.

Therefore, Paul's experiences with the legal aspect of *persona* in Corinth, his own Roman *persona*, his missionary experiences, and his employment of the term πρόσωπον, all convey his awareness of this social concept of *persona*, which has been and remains generally overlooked by New Testament scholars. Also, it should be noted that this exploration of Paul's awareness of the concept of *persona* shows not only a broad conception of *persona* (e.g. his Jewish *persona*), but in particular the Roman stress on *persona*.

---

[12] Winter, 'Imperial Cult', esp. 73–5. *Contra* Witherington, *Gal*, 447–8.

5.1.2 *The Scope of the Study: 2 Corinthians*

Paul's correspondence to the Christians at Corinth is a valuable literary source to examine because, as noted above, Paul is reported to have lived there for 18 months (Acts 18.11), during which he was exposed to the function of *persona* in the church (e.g. 1 Cor 5–6). Within the Corinthian correspondence, however, the personal and emotional letter of 2 Corinthians is the more pertinent text for this study, since it contains 12 of the 24 instances of πρόσωπον in the Pauline letters, instances which could provide information on social identity in the Corinthian church. Some interpreters have noticed the frequent occurrence of the term in the letter, but have not considered the possible significance of its frequency[13] – with the exception of Timothy Savage who writes that the frequency indicates 'Paul's concern with the superficial perspective of the Corinthians'.[14] In light of Savage's observation, this present study seeks to investigate whether 2 Corinthians conveys the problem of a preoccupation with the superficial aspect of *persona* that was conventionally projected in the early imperial period, and whether Paul's frequent use of πρόσωπον in 2 Corinthians expresses a meaning of *persona*.

Not only is there a high concentration of occurrences of the term πρόσωπον in the letter, but there are also a few significant instances of the term that do convey aspects of social identity; and a cursory observation would indicate that the term has a meaning beyond the typical understanding of 'face'. For instance, in the key text of 2 Cor 5.12 Paul describes those who boast ἐν προσώπῳ and not in the heart (μὴ ἐν καρδίᾳ), which describes individuals preferentially boasting in 'outward appearance'.[15] As will be seen below, Paul in 2 Corinthians is making an *apologia* of his ministry, which has been criticised by his Corinthian rivals on the basis of his external appearance (cf. 10.10). Paul, then, is reacting to this boasting in outer appearance, which is possibly related to a preoccupation with the superficial aspect of *persona*. In addition to the frequency of πρόσωπον, it is also significant that 2 Corinthians (esp. chapters 10–13) contains numerous references to 'boasting', a social convention that would engender this preoccupation.[16] Therefore, in light of these details, it is appropriate to explore 2 Corinthians for Paul's understanding and critique of social identity and *persona*.

This chapter and the next will examine the concept of *persona* and social identity in 2 Corinthians, more precisely, in the literary units of chapters 1–7

---

[13] E.g. Collange, *Enigmes*, 75; Pickett, *Cross*, 127 n. 5.

[14] Savage, *Power*, 184 n. 11. Although he commendably observes the frequency of the term, he does not discuss the term any further.

[15] See Harris, *2 Cor*, 416, who explains 'πρόσωπον as a metonym for "what is outward", "externals", and καρδία as standing for "what is inward", the "character"'.

[16] The theme of boasting will be discussed below.

(specifically 2.14–7.4) and 10–13. Scholars have been able to explore adequately the social context of chapters 10–13 to show the social conventions used in the opponents' critique of Paul. In regard to the large section of 2 Cor 2.14–7.4, however, scholars have only considered the social context of a few specific texts, such as the Roman triumphal procession in 2.14–17, and the social importance of letters of recommendation in 3.1–3. Moreover, scholars have been primarily interested in probing specific portions of text that are theologically rich, such as Paul's theology of reconciliation in 5.18–21, physical and spiritual existence in 5.1–10, the identification of κύριος in 3.16–18, and most of all, Paul's hermeneutics and the letter–Spirit antithesis in chapters 3–4. Although these studies provide valuable insights into these specific texts, they tend not to give much attention to the wider context of 2 Cor 1–7.[17] A reason behind the lack of more thorough explorations of the larger context of 2 Corinthians is the complexity of the letter. Savage assesses the complexity of Paul's argument in 2 Corinthians 3:

> its argument is nearly impossible to follow, hindered at many points by mixed metaphors (writing on stones with ink, v. 3) and puzzling allusions (Moses' fading glory, vv. 7, 13). Most commentators tend to get bogged down in the perplexing details of the text and seldom focus on the broader contours of Paul's thought.[18]

Given Savage's observation, this study surmises that Paul was not chiefly concerned about presenting comprehensive treatises on his theology in this text.

Furthermore, this problem of being 'bogged down in the perplexing details of the text' also applies beyond 2 Corinthians 3. Although the literary unit of 2.14–7.4 contains several of Paul's important theological formulations, this study will not consider the theologically rich details of the literary unit in isolation or in a social vacuum for the sake of merely understanding Paul's theology. Rather, this study attempts to read the texts in light of their social setting in order to understand how Paul used the theologically rich language to construct his extended argument in 2 Corinthians. In fact, Peter Marshall advises that since Paul's theology is stated in social terms, which over time became theological notions in their own right, 'the social terms must be allowed their full social weight and reality if we are to understand Paul's theological perspectives'.[19] In light of Marshall's suggestion, it is critical to observe that Paul's argument probably involves the social concept of *persona*,

---

[17] A couple of exceptions worth noting are Wire, 'Reconciled', 263–75; Schröter, *Versöhner*.

[18] Savage, *Power*, 105. Cf. Hooker, 'Beyond', 296–7; Fitzgerald, *Cracks*, 68.

[19] See Marshall, 'Enigmatic', 153–6, quotation from p. 154. He also suggests, 'Paul's theological responses in Corinthians are more understandable and informative when seen as a response to social and moral problems' (156).

since the detail in 5.12 of those boasting ἐν προσώπῳ intimates a problem with social identity in the Corinthian church and Paul's reaction to the problem. This study, therefore, seeks to explore 2 Corinthians for the theme of social *persona*, and Paul's understanding and critique of it.

5.2 Roman Corinth and the Preoccupation with *Persona*

Donald Engels states that 'the problems Paul encountered at Corinth were a reflection of the nature of the city's people'.[20] Similarly, David deSilva writes, 'Many of the specific problems which Paul must address in both [Corinthian] letters radiate from the more basic issue of the believers' continued allegiance to their primary socialization'.[21] Thus, in order to grasp properly the Corinthian Christians' conception and application of *persona*, it is important to examine the social concept and its conventional outworking in the surrounding context of Roman Corinth. Having seen, in the previous chapters, the widely projected *persona* in the first-century Roman social milieu and the pervasive problem of a preoccupation with its superficial aspect, this section explores whether a similar conventional presentation and preoccupation existed in the context of Roman Corinth.

Fortunately, there have been copious studies that have explored the social context of Roman Corinth. Besides the many studies of Roman Corinth by ancient historians,[22] New Testament scholars have also highlighted the social setting of Corinth in the first century CE through numerous monographs and commentaries on Paul's letters to the Corinthians.[23] Given these studies of Roman Corinth, it is not necessary for this present study to reproduce all the details concerning the social context of Corinth. This study, rather, will glean from these previous studies and will highlight particularly those features relevant to the neglected social feature of *persona*. A further reason for not presenting a thorough study of Roman Corinth is that the previous chapters of

---

[20] Engels, *Roman Corinth*, 110.

[21] deSilva, 'Let the One', 73.

[22] E.g. Wiseman, 'Corinth I'; Engels, *Roman Corinth*; Gregory, *Corinthia*; Williams & Bookidis, *Centenary*; Schowalter & Friesen, *Urban Religion*; and the numerous journal articles in *Hesperia*. For a collection of primary sources and some archaeological essays concerning Corinth, see Murphy-O'Connor, *Corinth*. Many of these studies have benefited from the valuable collection of inscriptions from Corinth: West, *Corinth*; Kent, *Corinth*.

[23] E.g. the monographs by Chow, *Patronage*; Clarke, *Leadership*; Savage, *Power*; Horrell, *Social Ethos*; Winter, *Philo*; idem, *After Paul*; Ebel, *Attraktivität*; Dutch, *Educated Elite*. For commentaries, see Thiselton, *1 Cor*, 1–29; Witherington, *1–2 Cor*, 1–68. See also the recent survey by Adams & Horrell, 'Quest', 1–48. This present section has particularly benefited from Savage's depiction of Corinth's social milieu (35–53).

this present study have provided relevant details for the social world of Corinth. In particular, the information about the Roman stress on *persona* and an obsession with the superficial aspect of *persona* that was gained from the survey of Epictetus and the social milieu of Nicopolis is very relevant for Corinth. Since both cities are located in the Roman Greek East and are geographically close to each other, it is probable that there also would have been a similar Roman stress and a preoccupation in Corinth. In addition, it is reasonable to assume that the Roman emphasis on *persona* and the obsession with the superficialities of *persona* would have been more amplified in Corinth than in Nicopolis, given Corinth's status as a Roman colony. As will be seen, with this connection with Rome, Corinth would have had similar issues of social identity as those in Rome; hence, the details from the previous chapter on Valerius Maximus and social identity in Rome provide information on the social realities in Roman Corinth.

5.2.1 Roman Corinth

Following Julius Caesar's founding of Corinth as a new Roman colony in 44 BCE, the city probably served as the capital for the Roman province of Achaia.[24] As a Roman colony, Corinth would have had a distinct Roman cultural identity in the Greek East, and a strong resemblance to the city of Rome in almost every facet, including its architecture, laws, and social practices. Gellius states that Roman colonies, which he considers small copies and representations (*effigies parvae simulacraque*) of the city of Rome, 'do not come into citizenship from without, nor grow from roots of their own, but they are as it were transplanted from the State and have all the laws and institutions of the Roman people, not those of their own choice' (*Noct. att.* 16.13).[25] Corinth's Roman imprint can be observed in its official Latin name *Colonia Laus Julia Corinthiensis*, which significantly avoids 'the more common -*ius* or -*us* ethnic, which implies that the Italian colonists wished to distinguish themselves from the original Greek inhabitants of the city'.[26] The Romanness of the colony is also evinced by the fact that the official language was Latin up until the reign of Hadrian.[27]

---

[24] On Corinth's status as the capital, see Wiseman, 'Corinth I', 501–2; Acts 18.11–12; Apuleius, *Met.* 10.18.

[25] Cf. Stambaugh, *Roman City*, 244–7.

[26] Engels, *Roman Corinth*, 69.

[27] 101 of 104 pre-Hadrian extant inscriptions in Corinth were written in Latin. See Kent, *Corinth*, #181–9; Engels, *Roman Corinth*, 71. With Hadrian's reign, there was a revival in Greek culture; see ibid., 71–4. See also Adams, 'Romanitas', 184–205, who considers the relationship of the Latin language and *romanitas*.

In addition, the first colonial settlers were primarily Roman freedmen and veterans from Rome.[28] Antony Spawforth, after evaluating the extant epigraphic and numismatic remains of Roman Corinth, concludes that in the formative years of the colony it 'was dominated socially and politically by wealthy men of freedman stock and by Roman families with business interests in the east, some no doubt of freedmen stock themselves'.[29] He also states that 'an attraction of Caesar's colony may have been precisely the fact that it was a Roman, not a Greek, community – the colony's assertive *Romanitas* in the early Principate is one of its most striking features'.[30] One final piece of evidence of Corinth's *romanitas* is seen in its colonial grid layout and distinct buildings. For example, in a recent study of the identification of Paul's metaphor in 1 Cor 4.9, I have explored Corinth's amphitheatre, where the Roman death spectacles were exhibited, as an architectural symbol of Corinth's distinct Roman cultural identity.[31] The construction of an amphitheatre would have been important for the Corinthians, who needed to be conspicuously different and superior to their Hellenistic neighbours. Given all the evidence, this brief overview affirms the general consensus that the predominant culture in Corinth was Roman.[32] Therefore, although the concept of *persona* can be regarded as a general social feature in the Graeco-Roman world, there would have been a clear Roman stress on it in Roman Corinth.

Besides Corinth's status as a Roman colony, its resplendence as a city would also have been important for the Corinthians' *persona* and pride.[33] Corinth not only had a strategic location, but also a beautiful coastal location that amplified its visible splendour.[34] Pliny acclaimed that Corinth's location

---

[28] See Strabo 8.6.23; 17.3.15; Plutarch, *Caes.* 57; Pausanius 2.1.2; Appian, *Pun.* 8.20.136.

[29] Spawforth, 'Colonial Elite', 174.

[30] Spawforth, 'Colonial Elite', 175.

[31] Nguyen, 'Identification', 490–3; cf. Nguyen, 'Execution', 37. See Welch, 'Negotiating', 133–40, who convincingly dates the amphitheatre to the colonisation of Corinth; cf. Walbank, 'Foundation', 124–5. Welch also points out that Corinth's amphitheatre was a part of the Roman colony's grid-plan (137), which can be seen in the figures in Romano, 'City Planning', 279–301; cf. Walbank, 'Name', 251–64.

[32] There is debate as to whether there was such a clear break from Greek culture in Corinth's Roman colonisation. See e.g. Oster, 'Archaeological Evidence', 52–73, who is cautious about seeing such a distinction between Greek and Roman Corinth. For a recent summary of the debate, see Dutch, *Educated Elite*, 45–56. Dutch is right to conclude that although there is some level of Greek culture in Corinth, it is clear that the predominant culture is Roman. For those who convincingly demonstrate the Romanness of the colony, see Gill, 'Roman Colony', 259–64, and Winter, *After Paul*, esp. 7–22. Also, worth noting is Woolf, 'Becoming Roman', 116–43, whose study considers how Greeks adopted the Roman identity, while maintaining their Greek identity.

[33] On the importance of a city for the individual's identity, see Savage, *Power*, 24–5; Engels, *Roman Corinth*, 69.

[34] On Corinth's location, see Savage, *Power*, 42–3.

in the Peloponnese was 'inferior in celebrity to no region of the earth' (*Nat.* 4.9; cf. Horace, *Odes* 1.7.2). Moreover, it was during Corinth's formative decades that much of the city was built, which means that in Paul's time the city was flourishing.[35] Along with its architectural beauty, Corinth also had a reputation for its economic opulence, which is affirmed by Strabo: 'the city of Corinth, then, was always great and wealthy' (8.6.23; cf. Aristides, *Or.* 46.27; Alciphron, *Ep.* 3.24.3). Consequently, ancient writers considered it a great privilege to be able to visit Corinth and gaze at all its splendour. For instance, Horace conveys the proverbial saying that 'it is not the privilege of every man to visit Corinth' (*Epist.* 1.17.36), and Aristides remarks on all of Corinth's great features and sites, 'Not even the eyes of all men are sufficient to take it in' (*Or.* 46.25; cf. 46.28).[36]

5.2.2 The Corinthians

Corinth's buildings and layout were not the only grand spectacles at which individuals could marvel, for the Corinthians themselves were also a spectacle to behold. As with any other Roman society, the Corinthian people were preoccupied with the need to fashion and parade the surface features of their *persona* before others for validation of their status and honour. Moreover, literary sources inform that when Caesar founded the colony he settled it with freedmen and veterans from the city of Rome.[37] These individuals came to Corinth with the hopes of a more opportune environment for social advancement, and also brought with them their Roman social values and practices. With its rapid growth and development, Corinth provided an ideal social atmosphere that fostered great social mobility.[38] Concerning the freedmen, the extant epigraphical remains testify to the power and influence that were possessed by many of these freedmen or descendants of freedmen in Corinth.[39]

With homogeneity between Corinth and Rome, the Corinthians' social behaviour and practices would have resembled those in Rome. In fact, the Corinthians were similarly preoccupied with the superficial dimension of *persona*. Since the status and reputation of a city conferred status on the

---

[35] See Pausanius 2.2.6; Wiseman, 'Corinth I', 509–21.

[36] Cf. Alciphron, *Ep.* 3.24.3; Epictetus, *Diss.* 2.17.22; Lucian, *Herm.* 27, 29, 45.

[37] Also, Jews came to Corinth from Rome (Acts 18.1–16; Philo, *Leg.* 281–2), and also from Egypt (Acts 18.24; 1 Cor 1.12).

[38] See Stambaugh, 'Social Relations', 79, who points out that in comparison to Athens and their entrenched aristocracy, Corinth's hierarchy was much more fluid, which meant greater social mobility. Cf. Savage, *Power*, 35; Clarke, *Leadership*, 10.

[39] Some notable individuals in the first century CE were Gn. Babbius Philinus, C. Iulius Spartiaticus, and T. Claudius Dinippus. For a discussion of these three and other leading figures in Roman Corinth, see Clarke, *Leadership*, 9–39, 135–57.

individual, the Corinthians had a reputation for boasting in their Corinthian citizenship (Martial, *Epigr.* 10.65). With their boasting, it is no surprise that Dio Chrysostom, with his familiarity with Corinth, describes the Corinthians as being easily puffed up (*Or.* 9.21) and proud of their wealth (9.8; cf. Alciphron, *Ep.* 3.15.1). This mentality naturally fed into the Corinthians' passion to parade the surface features of their social identity before others. Savage assesses, 'In Corinth, perhaps more than anywhere else, social ascent was the goal, boasting and self-display the means, personal power and glory the reward'.[40] There are many examples from non-literary sources of Corinthians, particularly the freedmen, who conspicuously projected the prestigiousness of their *persona* by erecting public inscriptions and statues for people to gaze at in the city.[41] Besides these material remains, literary sources describe that the Corinthians fashioned themselves in such lavish appearance that they developed a reputation for their beauty. Lucian, for instance, describes Charaicles as 'a young man from Corinth who is not only handsome but shows some evidence of skillful use of the cosmetics' (*Am.* 9). Another Corinthian, Charmenion, is depicted as one who 'strolls about sleek with curled hair' (Martial, *Epigr.* 10.65).[42] Dio Chrysostom even explains that when Diogenes denounced the Corinthians' rashness in valuing one's physical appearance over intellect, his 'message fell on deaf ears' (*Or.* 9.15; cf. 8.7–8).[43] Thus, it can be asserted that the Corinthians 'were simply too enamoured with outward appearances', and they readily accepted those who fashioned these shallow appearances of beauty.[44]

5.2.3 *Sophistry and* Persona *in Roman Corinth*

As seen in the previous chapters, the superficial projections of prestige and beauty were especially important for orators and the presentation and assessment of their *persona*. Having demonstrated in the earlier chapters the influence of rhetoric, oratory, and sophistry in the Roman empire, it is important to underscore their importance also in Roman Corinth. George Kennedy remarks that 'Corinth was a prosperous and sophisticated Greek city; it is not surprising that eloquence should have an appeal there'.[45] Winter in his monograph, *Philo and Paul among the Sophists*, has shown the great

---

[40] Savage, *Power*, 41.

[41] See Clarke, *Leadership*, 9–21; Savage, *Power*, 41.

[42] Cf. Lucian, *Dial. D.* 20.13. See also Lucian, *Anach.* 36; Philostratus, *Vit. Apoll.* 4.25; Apuleius, *Met.* 10.29; Alciphron *Fr.* 5.

[43] See Dio Chrysostom, *Or.* 8.5, and Aristides, *Or.* 46.25, for the characterisation of the Corinthians as lacking intellect.

[44] Savage, *Power*, 47. See his pp. 48–9 for Nero and his particular love of Corinth, since the city satiated his cravings for fame (cf. Suetonius, *Nero* 53, 55).

[45] Kennedy, *New History*, 259.

influence of sophistic conventions in Corinth.[46] He has produced a compelling argument that the Second Sophistic, which is usually regarded as originating in the late first and early second century CE, can actually be seen earlier in the mid-first century CE with the Jewish-Christian 'sophists' who are depicted in Paul's letters.[47] Corinth was a place that clearly attracted many famous sophists, like Favorinus, Herodes Atticus, and Aelius Aristides. There were, additionally, other figures of rhetoric and philosophy who displayed a familiarity with Corinth and even offered some reactions to the sophistic movement – such as Epictetus, Plutarch, and possibly Dio Chrysostom.[48] The problem with the sophists in Corinth is seen in Dio Chrysostom's report that in nearby Isthmia the people would gather to hear 'crowds of wretched sophists around Poseidon's temple shouting and reviling one another' (*Or.* 8.9–10).

The sophistic influence in Corinth is important to this present investigation, since the earlier chapters have shown how sophistry relates to the preoccupation with the superficial aspect of *persona*. Audiences valued the physical features and showy gestures of the orator, and the orator fashioned such an eye-appealing image in order to receive accolades. Attention will now be given briefly to two Corinthian individuals who encapsulate the social problem of the conventionally projected *persona* in Corinth and its relation to oratory: first, a young student of oratory who visited Epictetus, and secondly, Favorinus.

In Epictetus' discourse 'On Personal Adornment' (Περὶ καλλωπισμοῦ, *Diss.* 3.1), he enters in a dialogue with a young student of rhetoric (ὁ νεανίσκος ῥητορικός) from Corinth.[49] The student comes to Epictetus with hair that was 'too elaborately dressed' and attire that was 'highly embellished' (3.1.1). The issue at hand is the conflict between the opposing views of Epictetus and the student on what is considered 'beautiful' (καλός). In the dialogue Epictetus poses to the student the question of what makes people truly 'beautiful', since some are naturally born ugly and others good looking; Epictetus declares that the answer is the excellence of one's presence (ἡ

---

[46] Winter, *Philo*, 109–239.

[47] See Winter, *Philo*, ix, for the foreword by G.W. Bowersock, a specialist in the Greek sophists, who praises Winter's study.

[48] See also Winter, *Philo*, 111–40, for analysis of these figures and also the Jewish-Christian sophists. Also, concerning Dio Chrysostom, some interpreters (e.g. ibid., *Philo*, 113–22) have regarded him as a critic of the sophists, but others have regarded him as a sophist, which was the case in Chapter Four.

[49] For more on this neglected discourse, see Winter, *Philo*, 113–18. It is possible that Epictetus had a reputation in Corinth, since Arrian, who was one of Epictetus' students and the compiler of the discourses, dedicates the work to L. Gellius Menander, who was an elite in Corinth; see Bowersock, 'New Inscription', 279–80.

ἀρετὴ ἡ ἀνθρώπου παροῦσα) (3.1.6–7). Epictetus then urges the young man that if he wants to be truly beautiful he needs to devote his attention and energy to this sort of excellence (cf. 3.1.40–1, προαίρεσις). In fact, Epictetus asserts, 'but so long as you neglect all this, you will be considered ugly, no matter if you employ every artifice to make yourself look beautiful' (3.1.9).

In the course of the discussion, it is evident that the student has gone to great lengths in beautifying his outward appearance in order to fashion himself like the popular orators of the day. The young man has plucked out all the hairs from his chest (3.1.27–8), which leads Epictetus to criticise him as being effeminate and even to question whether the student is a man or a woman (3.1.27–32). In fact, the student is in such a horrid and pathetic state that Epictetus lacks the boldness to call the student 'ugly'! (3.1.41). It is also worth noting that Epictetus lists the various ranks and offices (*cursus honorum*) in Corinth that many individuals, such as this student, aspired to hold (3.1.34).[50] This detail probably reveals the motive behind the Corinthians' preoccupation with the shallow displays of *persona*, and their cravings for prestige and power.

The other interesting figure to consider briefly is Favorinus of Arles (ca. 85–165 CE).[51] None of his philosophical works has survived and there are only few remains of his declamations.[52] There is, however, a declamation that is preserved by Dio Chrysostom, the 'Corinthian oration' (Κορινθιακός, *Or.* 37),[53] which offers insights into the problems in Corinth that are associated with social identity. Favorinus was a Gallo-Roman who held the elite rank of an equestrian (37.25). He had visited Corinth three times (37.1, 8, 9) and is said to be considered a 'cherished friend' by the Corinthians (37.8). In his earlier visits he impressed the Corinthian populace in such a way that they honoured him by erecting a bronze statue in a prominent place in the library, which served as stimulus for the youth to emulate (37.8).[54] Favorinus describes this placement of the statue in the library as being in 'a front row seat (προεδρία) as it were', which is significant because sitting in a προεδρία in any spectator building conspicuously projected the prestige of

---

[50] See Winter, *Philo*, 116–18.

[51] For more on Favorinus, see Barigazzi, *Favorino*; idem, 'Favorino', 556–81; Gleason, *Making Men*, 3–20, 131–58; Holford-Strevens, 'Favorinus', 188–217; König, 'Favorinus', 141–71; Winter, *Philo*, 129–34; idem, 'Toppling', 291–306.

[52] See Barigazzi, *Favorino*, 3–85, and also on pp. 87–135, where he presents ancient testimonies on Favorinus.

[53] Barigazzi, *Favorino*, 298–302. Favorinus was an eminent pupil of Dio Chrysostom; see Jones, *Roman World*, 78; Philostratus, *Vit. soph.* 492.

[54] It could be significant that the statue is in bronze, since Corinthian bronze was highly valued. On Corinthian bronze, see Murphy-O'Connor, *Corinth*, 200–18.

one's social standing. He also indicates that he was honoured as 'the noblest among the Greeks' (37.22).

Furthermore, his reputation was gained from his eloquence as an orator. Philostratus includes him in his biography of sophists (*Vit. soph.* 489–92) and remarks that he 'was proclaimed a sophist by the charm and beauty of his eloquence' (489). Philostratus also recounts that in Rome, even if Favorinus' audience did not know Greek they were still fascinated and enchanted 'by the tones of his voice, by his impressive glance and the rhythm of his speech' (491). This detail reveals not only the eloquent flair of Favorinus, but also the audience's primary interest in aesthetics rather than the content of the speech. In light of Favorinus' Corinthian oration, Duane Litfin describes the Corinthians as having similar tastes concerning rhetoric: 'They loved eloquence, lionized its practitioners, and were concerned that their own youth excel in it'.[55]

Most importantly, the issue that prompts Favorinus' oration is the fact that his statue has been toppled by some in Corinth (*Or.* 37.20–22).[56] Favorinus responds to the situation by making a defence to the people of Corinth ('gentlemen of the jury', 37.22), and putting them to shame for performing an unjust act of toppling his statue.[57] This is an urgent matter for Favorinus because the toppling of his statue has serious consequences for his *persona*; this act of *damnatio memoriae* seeks to shame him and even to eradicate his social existence.[58] Also, a statue of one's likeness was important because ancient people regarded the individual as being visible in the statue, which seems to be Favorinus' concern since he speaks words of comfort to his statue (37.46; cf. 37.28).[59]

Favorinus' oration gives two particular insights into the problem of the commonly projected *persona* that existed in Corinth. First, Favorinus is deeply concerned about his public *persona* and his visible expression of it. He has reinvented his *persona* into one that depicts himself as a Hellene *par excellence*, in that he has adopted 'not merely the language, but also the thought and manners and dress of the Greeks' (37.25). During Favorinus' time, there was a strong revival of Greek culture throughout the Roman empire, hence being a Hellenophile was en vogue and a highly valued status symbol.[60] Besides appealing to his *persona* as a Hellenophile, he claims that other cities have honoured him by setting up statues of him (37.37).

---

[55] Litfin, *Proclamation*, 144–5.

[56] Philostratus, *Vit. soph.* 490, explains that the Athenians also removed Favorinus' statues due to his conflict with an emperor.

[57] See Winter, 'Toppling', 296–300, on the defensive nature of this speech.

[58] See Chapter Two.

[59] Cf. Winter, 'Toppling', 291–2. See further discussion in Chapter Two.

[60] See Engels, *Roman Corinth*, 71–4, for the change in cultural identity.

Nevertheless, these honours that he has received are meaningless in Corinth, unless he is able to reverse the disgraceful toppling of his statue. That is, without the Corinthians' approval of his *persona*, he will not achieve the prestige that is due to his social identity. Secondly, the oration possibly informs of the Corinthians' fickleness in their assessment of orators.[61] Favorinus is perplexed at how quickly the Corinthians honoured and then shamed him – from regarding him as the 'noblest' (ἄριστος) to the 'worst' (πονρότατος) in such a brief span of time (37.22–3).

In summary, the Corinthians' obsession with the shallow features of *persona* is similar to the situation observed in the city of Rome and the rest of the Roman empire. With the emphasis on *persona* in the Roman colony of Corinth, the Corinthians would have been conscious of the superficial values of *persona*. They aspired to improve their social standing by visibly expressing their *persona* through their outward appearance. This preoccupation is clearly seen in the social realm of rhetoric/oratory/sophistry. Savage aptly states, 'Given their penchant for self-display it is hardly surprising that the Corinthians placed a premium on personal appearance and impressive speech, the most notable of human traits'; and also that, 'Of all the cities in the Graeco-Roman world, none engendered an atmosphere of self-centredness more striking than Corinth'.[62] Thus, there was a crisis of identity in Corinth that mirrors the crises seen in the previous chapters on Rome and Nicopolis.

5.3 The Corinthian Church and the Preoccupation with *Persona*

Having considered the preoccupation with the superficial aspect of *persona* in the context of the Roman colony of Corinth, attention will now be given to the conventional use of *persona* in the social setting of the church at Corinth. One might speculate that the concept of *persona*, and the Roman stress on it, would not have had any impact on a religious group such as the Corinthian Christians. However, it has been shown that this social concept affected the majority of the people living in the Roman empire, and especially in a Roman colony. Also, the conventional projection of an individual's social identity visibly communicated this concept throughout society. Moreover, scholars have demonstrated that 'minority' groups or foreigners, such as Diasporan Jews, who lived throughout the Roman empire were affected by the dominant Graeco-Roman culture, and inevitably would have assimilated, acculturated,

---

[61] See Winter, 'Toppling', 291–306, who compares Paul and Favorinus' experiences with the fickleness of the Corinthians.

[62] Savage, *Power*, 46, 78, respectively.

and accommodated, in various degrees, to many of the surrounding values and social practices.[63] Thus, the Christian communities, especially those in a Roman context, would have been susceptible to the conventional practices and values of Roman society, which would have included the preoccupation with the surface features of *persona*. Interestingly, in Jas 2.1–4 the Christians, who are a part of a church in the Diaspora, are showing favouritism (προσωπολημψία) to elite individuals, such as a wealthy person who comes in wearing fine clothes and a gold ring – the latter being a distinctive status symbol of the Roman equestrian rank.[64] More significantly, in the above survey of the Pauline occurrences of the term πρόσωπον there were indications that a preoccupation with the superficial side of *persona* existed in some of the Pauline communities (e.g. Corinth and Galatia).

This study proposes that the Corinthian Christians, who were in a Roman colony, also would have embraced the common outworking of *persona* and re-fabricated it for their conception of Christian identity. Even though their integration of *persona* in the church would not have been a strict application of the conventional *persona*, this *persona* would have been, nevertheless, a modified one that was used similarly to assess and grade individuals in the church. Moreover, this conventional outworking of social *persona* in the church was similarly a warped and distorted presentation of certain ideal notions of *persona* (e.g. status, privilege, eloquence). Consequently, it would be surprising if a similar preoccupation with the surface features of *persona* did not occur in the church at Corinth. In order to assess the adoption of the typically presented *persona* in the context of the Corinthian church, and also Paul's critique of it, this section will survey the issue of social stratification in the church and also the various ways in which the Corinthian Christians incorporated certain social conventions. After that, consideration will be given to some evidence in the Corinthian correspondence of their adoption of the commonly projected *persona*. As with the previous chapters of this study, certain social conventions (e.g. rank, social status, and patronage) will be used to identify the texts in the Corinthian correspondence that reveal evidence related to the concept of *persona*.

Before exploring the social concept of *persona* in the Corinthian church, there are four issues that need to be addressed. First, these two chapters on Paul observe the Roman stress on *persona* in the Corinthian church. As noted

---

[63] See e.g. Barclay, *Jews*, for an in-depth study into the various degrees of the Diasporan Jews' engagement with non-Jews, as seen in their assimilation (social integration), acculturation (language/education), and accommodation (use of acculturation); Gruen, *Diaspora*. See also Noy, *Foreigners*, who examines 'foreigners' who migrated and lived in Rome.

[64] Interestingly, Jas 2.6 indicates the problem of the rich taking the poor Christians to court, which is a problem that will be discussed below concerning the Corinthian church.

before, this study recognises that the concept of *persona* could be regarded as a general social feature in the Graeco-Roman world, and not solely a 'Roman' concept in a setting like the Roman Greek East. In fact, this study perceives that the Corinthian Christians have adopted and refashioned the concept of *persona* for their own use in the church. It is, nevertheless, possible to regard still the Roman emphasis on this social feature in the Corinthian church. As will be demonstrated, there are details of social identity in Paul's Corinthian correspondence that are similar to the details provided on the Roman emphasis on *persona* in Roman Corinth, and also in the Greek city of Nicopolis. Furthermore, since this social concept would have been important for the majority of people living in a Roman social setting – especially in a Roman colony – the Corinthian Christians would probably have been aware of it, and it would have played a part in their social relations in the church community.

Secondly, based on the limited evidence in the Pauline letters it is difficult to determine Paul's overall perception of *persona* (esp. the Roman stress on *persona*). Paul does not seem to promote nor reject this elite social concept, which possibly suggests that it was a matter of indifference to him. Moreover, Paul is not criticising the whole of Roman society or the idea of being 'Roman', especially since he is a Roman himself and, as seen above, he associated with many Romans and relied on his Roman *persona* during his missionary travels. In fact, in his letters, Paul often exhorts the Christians to fulfil their social obligations as benefactors and citizens of Roman society (e.g. Rom 13.1–7).[65] It is also interesting that Paul occasionally uses language which resonates with Graeco-Roman ideals and virtues. For instance in Phil 4.8–9, Paul provides a catalogue of distinct virtues (esp. ἀρετή) that were commonly used by moral philosophers of his day, such as the Stoics.[66] As will be seen, Paul's critique of *persona* is chiefly against the Corinthian Christians' adoption of the superficial and conventional values of *persona*, since these values conflicted with his understanding of Christian identity. That is, for Paul the problem is with what he considered to be inappropriate behaviour and conduct associated with the widely projected *persona*, especially the behaviour that disrupted the Corinthian church community.

Thirdly, this study does not aim to analyse Paul's comprehensive understanding of *persona*. This study is primarily interested in his perspective of and reaction to the particular problem with the conventionally projected *persona* as seen within the limited evidence in the Corinthian

---

[65] See Winter, *Seek*, for a valuable study of this.

[66] See Engberg-Pedersen, 'Virtues', 608–33, for a study of Paul's use of the ancient virtue system. For Phil 4.8–9, see Sevenster, *Paul*, 152–6; O'Brien, *Phil*, 501–7; Holloway, '*Bona Cogitare*', 89–96; cf. Cicero, *Tusc.* 5.23.67; Plutarch, *Mor.* 469A.

correspondence.[67] In other words, the Corinthian correspondence only conveys Paul's critique of certain elements of *persona*. In addition, it is difficult to determine the percentage of the Corinthians who were exhibiting the behaviour that Paul considered inappropriate. It is probably the case that not everyone in the church reflected the preoccupation with the superficial aspect of *persona*.

Finally, although the majority of interpreters consider that 1 and 2 Corinthians are dealing with different problems in the Corinthian church, the social description of the Corinthians in 1 Corinthians is, nonetheless, relevant and valuable for comprehending the social context of 2 Corinthians. Given that this study is interested in the underlying social realities of the Corinthian church as seen in 2 Corinthians, it is reasonable to assume that the social behaviour and values seen in 1 Corinthians would not have drastically changed within the approximate one year interval between the two letters. In other words, there are probably some consistent social behaviour and values that are at the root of the different social problems seen in both Corinthian epistles.[68] Moreover, the overview of 1 and 2 Corinthians in this section will further highlight similarities between the Corinthians' behaviour in both epistles. Therefore, this study of 2 Corinthians will consider the relevant social description given in 1 Corinthians for insights into the Corinthian Christians and their appreciation of the conventional values of social identity and *persona*.

5.3.1 Social Stratification and Social Conventions in the Corinthian Church

Scholars have been interested in Paul's correspondence with the Corinthian church, especially 1 Corinthians, because it contains valuable data that intimate the social configuration of the Pauline communities. Adolf Deissmann promoted the popular view that the Pauline communities consisted of people of the lowest classes.[69] However, this view has been seriously challenged by a 'new consensus', which is led by E.A. Judge, Gerd Theissen, and Wayne Meeks.[70] These scholars, especially Judge and Theissen, argue that the social makeup of the Corinthian church was a more diverse group that

---

[67] See Clarke, *Serve*, 170–2, who helpfully explains the nature of the New Testament evidence. Also, see Chapter Six for a section that briefly considers Paul's critique in his other letters (esp. Galatians).

[68] For an argument of the close link between 1 and 2 Corinthians, see Young & Ford, *Meaning*, 44–53; Murphy-O'Connor, *Theology*, 13 n. 15. See also deSilva, 'Let the One', 61–74, who commendably examines Paul's use of 'honour discourse' in both letters to counteract the social problems seen in both letters.

[69] Deissmann, *Paul*, 29–51.

[70] Judge, *Social Pattern*; idem, 'Social Identity', 210–17; Theissen, *Social Setting*; Meeks, *Urban*.

consisted of a minority group of elite individuals.[71] An important text that reveals this diversity and existence of an elite group is 1 Cor 1.26, where Paul writes: Βλέπετε γὰρ τὴν κλῆσιν ὑμῶν, ἀδελφοί, ὅτι οὐ πολλοὶ σοφοὶ κατὰ σάρκα, οὐ πολλοὶ δυνατοί, οὐ πολλοὶ εὐγενεῖς.[72] This triadic formula, which qualifies the 'status' (κλῆσιν) of the Corinthians (i.e. their *persona*), has been probed to show that the elements of wise, powerful, and well-born are social descriptors used to describe the ruling class of society.[73] Theissen has analysed those named individuals who are associated with the Corinthian church as having a higher social standing, due to factors such as title, property, and ability to travel.[74] He concludes that 'in all probability the most active and important members of the congregation belonged to the οὐ πολλοὶ σοφοί, δυνατοί, and εὐγενεῖς'.[75] Although it is uncertain that a significant proportion of the Christian leaders in the Pauline communities came from the ruling class of society, Andrew Clarke has recently demonstrated the similarities in *ethos* between the Christian leaders of the Pauline communities and the ruling elite.[76] With the elite practices of the Christian leaders, they probably would have adopted the elite concept of *persona* in order to establish their status in the church as 'Christian elite'. Thus, with the social makeup of elite and non-elite in the Corinthian church, the Corinthian Christians would have been aware and conscious of their

---

[71] Recently, Meggitt, *Poverty*, has challenged this consensus, by arguing that the Corinthian Christians were among the 99% of the population of the Roman empire who were poor. See the following series of articles concerning his thesis: Martin, 'Review'; Theissen, 'Social Structure'; a response by Meggitt, 'Response'; and further remarks by Theissen, 'Social Conflicts'. For other studies interacting with this issue, see Jongkind, 'Another Class', 139–48; the series of articles on poverty in the Pauline communities in *Journal for the Study of the New Testament* 26.3 (2004). Although Meggitt's study has attempted to challenge the 'new consensus', the majority of scholars still perceive a social mix for the Corinthian church.

[72] Wuellner, 'Sociological Implications', 666, comments on the importance of the verse: 'No other single verse of the entire New Testament was more influential in shaping popular opinion and exegetical judgement alike on the social origins of early Christianity than 1 Corinthians 1.26'. For more on this verse, see idem, 'Ursprung', 165–84; idem, 'Tradition', 557–62; Sänger, 'Die δυνατοί', 285–91; Clarke, *Leadership*, 41–5; Winter, *Philo*, 190–4.

[73] So Clarke, *Leadership*, 42–5; Winter, *Philo*, 190–2; Theissen, *Social Setting*, 71–3; Sänger, 'Die δυνατοί', 287; Malherbe, *Social Aspects*, 30; Horrell, *Social Ethos*, 117.

[74] Theissen, *Social Setting*, 73–99. One of the most intriguing named individual is Erastus, ὁ οἰκονόμος τῆς πόλεως (Rom 16.23), since there is epigraphical evidence of an Erastus who was an aedile in Corinth during Paul's time. For studies assessing the identity of the two Erasti, see Gill, 'Erastus', 293–301; Clarke, 'Another', 146–51; idem, *Leadership*, 46–56; Winter, *Seek*, 179–97; Meggitt, 'Erastus', 218–23.

[75] Theissen, *Social Setting*, 96.

[76] Clarke, *Serve*, esp. 145–208.

persona, since their *persona* was critical for social relations in the Graeco-Roman world.

Besides the social configuration of the church, the social behaviour and values of the church also reflected those of its surrounding society. It seems that the conventional behaviour and values of the elite Christians were behind many of the problems that prompted Paul's letters to the Corinthians. With the growing interest in the social context of the Corinthian correspondence, there have been many studies illuminating various conventional practices and values that have been adopted in the Corinthian church – such as those concerning leadership, patronage, education, politics, rhetoric, legal privilege, and wisdom.[77] It is not surprising that the Corinthian Christians were susceptible to these social practices, which were pervasive in their surrounding environment, since the Christians were still a part of that environment, and these values and behaviour still would have been ingrained in their minds. However, by integrating many of these elite conventional practices in the church setting, the members of the church would have created their own social hierarchy and assessed each other according to a set of criteria that was similar to the conventional criteria of the typically projected *persona* in their surrounding environment.

Unfortunately, space does not allow for an overview of these and other social features that reflect elitist behaviour in the Corinthian church. It is, nonetheless, sufficient to point out that these social aspects do mirror the picture portrayed in the earlier chapters of the conventional projection of *persona* in the early imperial period. For example, the social practice of patronage, which is critical for the superficial expression and validation of one's *persona*, would have been employed by elite Christians, and also the non-elite Christians, in order to maintain and enhance their social rating in the church, which generated greater power and privileges. Paul exposes this conduct as inappropriate and urges them 'not to boast in human leaders' (1 Cor 3.21) and not to 'be puffed up in favour of one against another' (4.6). In fact, the problems with patronage can be seen in the divisiveness in the church, which escalated in factions (1.10–13; 3.5, 21–3). Concerning these factions over various 'patrons' in the church community, Clarke states that 'by deferring in this way to their patronage, the Christian clients were adopting the same currency of honour and prestige which operated in the surrounding secular society'.[78] Clarke also remarks on the Corinthians' susceptibility to adopt social conventions: 'A group so strongly influenced by

---

[77] For leadership: Clarke, *Leadership*; idem, *Serve*. Patronage: Chow, *Patronage*. Education: Dutch, *Educated Elite*. Politics: Welborn, 'Discord'. Wisdom and rhetoric: Pogoloff, *Logos*; Litfin, *Proclamation*; Winter, *Philo*; Konradt, 'Weisheit'. See also Marshall, *Enmity*; Savage, *Power*.

[78] Clarke, *Serve*, 178.

the expectations of their surrounding society would feel bound by the conventions and obligations which were the norm'.[79] Therefore, the remainder of this chapter and the following one will highlight the pertinent social features (e.g. sophistry, leadership, legal privilege, wisdom, and boasting) that relate to the common projection of *persona* and the obsession with its superficial aspect in Corinth in Paul's time.

5.3.2 Sophistry and Persona in the Corinthian Church

Before shifting the focus to the texts of 1 and 2 Corinthians, the specific issues of oratory, rhetoric, and sophistry should be briefly discussed for their relevance also in the Corinthian church. In light of the discussion in previous chapters, and also above, of the superficial aspect of *persona* in the social context of rhetoric/oratory/sophistry, it is significant that there are details within the Corinthian correspondence indicating that issues of rhetoric and oratory were involved behind some of the problems.[80] More specifically, it seems that the church has assimilated sophistic conventions into their assessment of preaching and church leadership. As noted above, Winter has been able to trace the existence and influence of the sophistic movement in the mid-first century CE, by underscoring the sophistic conventions that are observed in the Corinthian correspondence.[81]

There are some notable texts that depict the sophistic environment of the Corinthian church. For instance, some interpreters have understood the triadic formula used in the important text of 1 Cor 1.26 to describe the elite Christians as having sophistic features, whereby these elements were the social markers that were highly regarded by them.[82] Also, in 1 Cor 2.1–5 Paul explains that in his initial 'entry' or 'coming' to Corinth, he did not come to the Corinthians with a sophistic method of parading his eloquence in speech and wisdom, but instead he came in weakness, fear, and trembling.[83] Since the Corinthians expected Paul to come to them like the other sophists in grandeur, they criticised his lack of eloquence.

There are also several texts that have sophistic connotations in 2 Corinthians, which will be examined in greater detail below. For example, in 5.12 Paul describes his Corinthian rivals as boasting in outward appearance (ἐν προσώπῳ), which could be describing the Corinthians' sophistic outlook. Importantly, in 2.17 Paul discusses his role as a minister of the new

---

[79] Clarke, *Leadership*, 93.

[80] See Pogoloff, *Logos*; Litfin, *Proclamation*.

[81] Winter, *Philo*, 141–239. See also Judge, 'Scholastic Community' 125–37, who examines Paul as a 'sophist'.

[82] So Munck, *Paul*, 162–3 n. 2; Clarke, *Leadership*, 42–5; Winter, *Philo*, 190–3.

[83] On the 'entry' of a sophist, see Winter, 'Entries', 55–74; idem, *Philo*, 143–64.

covenant and explains that he is not like 'the many' (οἱ πολλοί) who are peddling (καπηλεύοντες) the word of God. Scholars have demonstrated that Paul's description of his opponents here has allusions to philosophical and sophistic features. For instance, C.K. Barrett comments on the term καπηλεύοντες, 'Behind Paul's use of the word lies a long tradition of philosophical usage, in which the sophist is rebuked for selling his intellectual wares for cash'.[84] Interestingly, Dio Chrysostom depicts the sophists as οἱ πολλοί 'who call themselves philosophers, but who preach themselves' (*Or.* 13.11; cf. 12.13; 17.11), which could be contrasted with 2 Cor 4.5: Οὐ γὰρ ἑαυτοὺς κηρύσσομεν ἀλλὰ Ἰησοῦν Χριστὸν κύριον. Moreover, in 12.16 Paul responds to the Corinthians' accusation of craftiness (πανοῦργος) and deceit (δόλος), which were criticisms typically directed at the sophists in the first century CE.[85] Also, similar to the situation in 1 Cor 2.1–5, Paul is criticised for his lack of eloquence in his 'rhetorical delivery' in 2 Cor 10.10, which was a trademark of the sophists. In fact, Paul reacts by claiming that he is 'untrained in speech' (ἰδιώτης τῷ λόγῳ), but not in knowledge (11.6). In light of these texts, Clarke summarises the use of sophistic appearance in the Corinthian church:

> We have here, therefore, influential figures from Corinth who were exercising their sway according to the canons of the secular world. For these people the model of leadership by which they were assessing Paul was that of the sophists. In like manner, it was this pattern which they had adopted as appropriate in the church.[86]

Consequently, the sophistic influence in the Corinthian church would have influenced the Corinthians' use of the conventional values of *persona*.

5.3.3 1 Corinthians

For the examination of the conventional projection of social *persona* in 1 Corinthians, the cohesive literary unity of 1 Cor 1–4 will be primarily discussed here.[87] Within this pericope, which has been regarded as the foundation for the remaining of the epistle,[88] there is sufficient data that depict the social context of the Corinthian church. Paul begins by explaining that he

---

[84] Barrett, *2 Cor*, 103. Cf. Windisch, *2 Kor*, 100–1; Hafemann, *Suffering*, 100–26. See also Lucian, *Herm.* 59, which also has the synonym δολόω that is found in 2 Cor 4.2.

[85] Winter, *Philo*, 228–9. Although Paul's finance is an issue in this text, this matter will not be treated in this present study.

[86] Clarke, *Serve*, 189.

[87] See Nguyen, 'Execution', 33–6, for a similar presentation of 1 Cor 1–4.

[88] So Engberg-Pedersen, 'Social Practice', 562, who states that chs. 1–4 serve as 'an introduction to the principles that lie behind Paul's solutions to the specific problems of social practice that he discusses from chapter 5 onwards'; cf. Mitchell, *Reconciliation*, 1, who regards that the appeal for unity in 1.10 functions as the thesis statement for the entire epistle.

has heard reports of divisions (σχίσματα) and quarrels (ἔριδες) within the church, which has resulted in 'factions' over various apostolic figures (1.10–12; cf. 3.3–4).[89] Recently, a growing number of scholars have suggested that Paul's counteraction of divisions is primarily against Apollos, or a group of followers in Apollos' name, since Paul singles him out throughout the section (3.4–6; 4.6).[90] This behaviour of showing preference between the two figures is probable, since the Corinthians, with their high expectations in rhetoric and wisdom, would have been more attracted to Apollos who is an ἀνὴρ λόγιος and δυνατὸς ὢν ἐν ταῖς γραφαῖς (Acts 18.24), rather than Paul who came not with λόγος ἢ σοφία but in much weakness, fear, and trembling (1 Cor 2.1–5).[91] Given the numerous instances of σοφία/σοφός (also cf. γνῶσις in 8.1, 7, 10, 11) and λόγος in this section, the root of the problem involved the Corinthians' inappropriate use of worldly 'wisdom' instead of the wisdom of God. This prompts Paul's contrasts in 1 Cor 1–4 between σοφία λόγου/ 'wisdom of the world' and the λόγος τοῦ σταυροῦ/'foolishness of God'.

The Corinthians exploited this 'wisdom' as a status indicator, which resulted in a social hierarchy and behaviour in the church that resembled the conventional obsession with the shallow features of *persona*, which was pervasive in Roman Corinth.[92] This is confirmed by the use of the descriptor σοφοὶ κατὰ σάρκα as part of the triadic formula in 1.26, which describes the Christian elite in the church.[93] Moreover, this wisdom could have been used by the Corinthians to evaluate superficially their leaders according to their social standing. Throughout the section, Paul is reacting against their inappropriate wisdom and behaviour. He criticises these Corinthians as arrogant (πεφυσιωμένοι, 4.19), whose conduct is according to 'worldly' standards (σαρκικοί ἐστε...καὶ κατὰ ἄνθρωπον περιπατεῖτε, 3.3–4), since they boast in individuals (3.21; 4.6). In addition, Paul contrasts the elite status of the Corinthians with the lowly status of the apostles (4.8–10) in order to degrade the Corinthians' elite values that are based on the conventionally projected *persona*. For example, he presents himself and the other apostles as fools (μωροί) for Christ, weak (ἀσθενεῖς), and dishonoured (ἄτιμοι), while

---

[89] See Strüder, 'Preferences', 431–55, who perceives the problem as concerning 'personal preference' rather than 'parties'. However, it is speculative that factions, in one form or another, did not result from this behaviour of 'personal preference'.

[90] See e.g. Ker, 'Colleagues', 75–97; Smit, 'Apollos', 231–51; Konradt, 'Weisheit', 181–214, and his expanded list of supporters on p. 181 n. 3.

[91] Cf. Selby, 'Seer', 351–73, who regards Paul as assuming a 'rhetorical *persona*' of an apocalyptic visionary.

[92] See Konradt, 'Weisheit', esp. 186–92. He writes: 'Die Weisheit erscheint damit allem voran als ein soziales Phänomen, nämlich als gewichtige Säule gesellschaftlicher Anerkennung' (187).

[93] Cf. Konradt, 'Weisheit', 187.

he describes the Corinthians as wise (φρόνιμοι), strong (ἰσχυροί), and honoured (ἔνδοξοι) (4.10; cf. 4.8).[94]

In two recent studies, I have suggested that Paul's contrast reaches a climax with the spectacle of death metaphor in 4.9, where God is presented as exhibiting the apostles as condemned criminals on the arena stage who are awaiting a humiliating execution, while the Corinthians are honourably seated in their privileged seats and fine clothing in the *cavea* of the arena.[95] Consequently, Paul urges the Corinthians, who superficially displayed the accoutrements of an elite *persona*, to imitate his Christ-like behaviour and ignoble status (4.16; cf. 11.1). That is, according to the metaphor in 4.9, Paul would be inviting the Corinthians to join him on the arena stage in a degraded *persona* – one that would be similar to that of the crucified Christ. Therefore, Paul is attempting to subvert their conventional values of social identity, which in effect would invert their social hierarchy and denounce their factionalism.

As mentioned above, 1 Cor 1–4 serves as a foundation for Paul's treatment of specific problems in the remainder of the epistle. It is worth noting some of the problems observed in the remainder of the epistle that reflect the Corinthians' preoccupation with the commonly depicted *persona*. In 6.1–11, Paul deals with the problem of believers entering into civic litigation against one another over 'trivial cases' (κριτηρίων ἐλαχίστων, 6.2).[96] As seen in Chapter Two, an individual's *persona* was critical for the outcome of a case, and would often predetermine the verdict. Clarke writes, 'At the heart of the issue of legal privilege was the widespread Graeco-Roman preoccupation with personal standing and reputation'.[97] In fact, it was generally forbidden to those of lower social standing to enter into litigation against those with higher status.[98] It seems that the elite Christians – the wise, powerful, and well-born (1.26)[99] – were abusing this legal privilege for their own advantage by taking those less privileged to court. Moreover, if the elite were the patrons in the church, then their clients would have simply endured the legal abuse since

---

[94] Interestingly, Merklein, *1 Kor I*, 313–14, observes that the descriptors here are reversals of those in 1.26–8.

[95] See Nguyen, 'Identification', for my new identification of the metaphor, and idem, 'Execution', in which I assess the significance of the metaphor for Paul's argument in 1 Cor 1–4 by looking at the dynamics of the Roman arena.

[96] On this problem, see Winter, 'Civil Litigation', 559–72; Clarke, *Leadership*, 59–71; Mitchell, 'Rich', 562–86; Chow, *Patronage*, 123–30.

[97] Clarke, *Leadership*, 62.

[98] Cf. Garnsey, *Social Status*, 277: 'In general the unequal distribution of wealth, influence, and knowledge of the law prevented the lower orders from making full use of the legal system'.

[99] On the plaintiffs being among the 'not many wise, powerful, and well-born', see Chow, *Patronage*, 128; Horrell, *Social Ethos*, 111–12; Thiselton, *1 Cor*, 419.

they were bound to the social conventions of the patronage system. Also related to this issue is the similar situation of the incestuous man in 5.1–5, whom some interpreters have regarded, along with the woman, as belonging to the patronal classes.[100] If he was indeed a patron, this could then explain the clients' silence to this immoral act, 'because he is of such social status that he is beyond the reach of litigation for some in the community'.[101]

The Corinthians' preoccupation with the superficial side of *persona* also engendered the problem of splits (σχίσματα) and divisions (αἱρέσεις) occurring when they gathered together as an ἐκκλησία to share a meal and partake in the Lord's supper (11.17–34).[102] Paul informs of the two groups in conflict – those who have their own meals (ἴδιον δεῖπνον, 11.21) and the have-nots (μὴ ἔχοντας, 11.22) – which indicate that, again, the problem is over a difference in socio-economic status. Interpreters have shown that the Corinthians' behaviour in this Christian meal reflected the dining practice of Graeco-Roman society, in that the guests were socially stratified in accordance with their social standing. As seen in the discussion of private banquets in Chapter Two, the elite and wealthier individuals would receive privileged seats and finer quality and quantity of food, while those non-elite and poor individuals would receive unprivileged seats and lower quality and quantity of food, and possibly even no food at all.

This brief survey of 1 Corinthians has revealed that some of the social problems in the church certainly involved the Corinthians' adoption of the conventional values of *persona* in first-century Corinth – an adoption which spawned a distorted view of Christian identity in the church. Importantly, these insights from 1 Corinthians will help to accentuate the social behaviour and values of the Corinthians as seen in 2 Corinthians.

5.3.4 2 Corinthians

2 Corinthians is one of the most difficult letters in the Pauline corpus letters for modern interpreters, and it is not uncommon to find it described as 'notoriously difficult'. Jean-François Collange cites the following: 'La Deuxième aux Corinthiens est célèbre par ses obscurités. A chaque instant le lecteur est arrêté par des allusions, des sous-entendus, qui constituent de véritables énigmes'.[103] The difficulty can be seen in the vast number of studies on two notoriously difficult issues that have plagued scholarship of 2 Corinthians: the unity of the letter, and the identity of Paul's opponents. As

---

[100] See Clarke, *Leadership*, 73–88; Chow, *Patronage*, 130–41.

[101] Clarke, *Leadership*, 74.

[102] See Theissen, *Social Setting*, 145–74; Lampe, 'Herrenmahl', 183–213; Campbell, 'Acquiesce', 61–70; Horrell, *Social Ethos*, 150–5.

[103] Collange, *Enigmes*, 1.

will be explained, although both of these issues have bearing on the interpretation of 2 Corinthians, they are, in fact, moot for the purview of this present study. Since space does not allow for a thorough discussion of these two issues, they will not receive much attention in this study. In addition, Thomas Stegman has recently provided a sufficient and good overview on the history of research of these two issues, in which he devotes a whole chapter of his monograph to these two issues, hence alleviating the need to go in-depth here.[104] Nevertheless, since this present study examines a large part of the letter (specifically 2.14–7.4, chs. 10–13) and is interested in Paul's critique of his opponents, some brief comments regarding these two issues are necessary.

In challenging the literary integrity of 2 Corinthians, interpreters have presented several different partition theories, some of which are very complex. The most popular of the partition theories regards chapters 1–7, 8–9, 10–13 as three separate letters, of which the most prominent break occurs between chapters 9 and 10. There have also been studies looking at the chronology of the identified letter fragments to propose a particular sequence of them. For example, there are a number of scholars who interpret chapters 10–13 as preceding the other sections, thus equating it as the 'tearful letter' mentioned in 2.3–4.[105] Conversely, scholars have attempted to argue for the integrity and unity of the letter, especially with the use of rhetorical criticism,[106] which is a quickly growing interpretative approach for studies of 2 Corinthians.[107] Despite all these efforts there is no consensus regarding any of the partition theories. In his recent analysis, Stegman concludes that these theories are leading the quest to interpret 2 Corinthians into 'blind alleys', and 'that none of the partition theories is able to withstand critical scrutiny' and are 'found wanting'.[108] Given the untenability of these partition theories, this study will interpret the letter in its canonical form, while recognising that its literary integrity has not been conclusively proven. It should be noted, however, that the literary integrity of the letter is not necessary for the purview of this study, which focuses on the two unanimously regarded cohesive literary units of 2 Cor 2.14–7.4 and 10–13.[109] In this study, both of

---

[104] Stegman, *Character*, 5–42. See his study for a bibliography on these issues.

[105] E.g. Watson, 'Painful Letter', 324–46.

[106] E.g. Amador, 'Revisiting'; Hall, *Unity*; Long, *Ancient Rhetoric*. However, see Peterson, *Eloquence*, 53–7, who shows how rhetorical analysis can argue both ways regarding the letter's unity.

[107] See Stegman, *Character*, 43–73, for an overview on rhetorical analysis, and pp. 43–5 n. 122, for a lengthy list of recent studies of 2 Corinthians that employ this approach.

[108] Stegman, *Character*, 23–5.

[109] Scholars have recognised 2.14–7.4 as a cohesive literary unit, given that 7.5 (καὶ γὰρ ἐλθόντων ἡμῶν εἰς Μακεδονίαν) refers back to and continues from 2.13 (ἐξῆλθον εἰς Μακεδονίαν). This has resulted in much debate on whether 2.14–7.4 constitutes a separate letter, or whether it should be regarded as an extended digression. However, just because

these units generally will be treated as separate, yet related, and will be handled in a way that avoids the necessity to identify the unity or chronological sequence of the two.

The identification of Paul's opponents has also been a major issue in Pauline studies, and this is the case with 2 Corinthians.[110] In his recent commentary, Murray Harris lists almost 20 identifications that have been proposed in nearly the past two centuries, all of which can be reduced to four broad categories: Hellenistic Jewish propagandists, pneumatics, Gnostics, and Judaizers.[111] Interpreters have used various methods and criteria, such as mirror-reading, to ascertain the opponents' identity, but these approaches have limitations and dangers involved with their usage.[112] Another difficulty is the ambiguous distinction between the behaviour of the opponents and that of the Corinthians themselves, especially since the Corinthians have adopted some of the opponents' practices (cf. 11.4). With these and other difficulties, the identification of the opponents also remains disputed. Reimund Bieringer has aptly expressed, 'Wir wissen letzlich nur sehr wenig über die Gegner'.[113] Stegman also concludes that the efforts in identifying the opponents 'fail to impress' and have also 'led the quest to understand 2 Corinthians down blind alleys'.[114]

Although a case of agnosticism is being pleaded for here, there is a way around the issue of the opponents' identity for this study. The identity of the opponents is relevant for any study of the social situation of Corinth; however, this study does not seek to offer a detailed reconstruction of the *Sitz im Leben* of 2 Corinthians, since this study is only interested in the social behaviour of those in the Corinthian church – especially the behaviour that involved the common preoccupation with the superficial aspect of social identity. The study will look at the details objectively for information on the sort of opposition that Paul reacts against in the church.[115] This can especially be done in the texts that are clearly polemical in tone. Additionally, since this study is interested in looking at how the conventional values of *persona* have

---

there is a thematic and structural coherence in this section, there is no conclusive evidence to regard the letter as a separate letter.

[110] See the recent collection of essays in Porter, *Opponents*. For Paul's opponents in 2 Corinthians, see e.g. Georgi, *Opponents*; Sumney, *Identifying*; Bieringer, 'Gegner'; Kolenkow, 'Opponents'.

[111] Harris, *2 Cor*, 79–80.

[112] On the problems of mirror-reading, see Barclay, 'Mirror-Reading', 73–93.

[113] Bieringer, 'Gegner', 221. Cf. Hickling, 'Source', 287: 'It may be, then, that we must be content to remain largely in ignorance of the doctrinal position or tendencies of Paul's rivals'.

[114] Stegman, *Character*, 42, 41, respectively.

[115] Cf. Provence, 'Sufficient', 69: 'It is a far better policy to allow the context to speak for itself so that the identity of the opponents emerges from the text rather than assuming *a priori* that Paul intends to refute a certain sort of adversary'.

influenced the Corinthian church, the identity of the opponents is not an urgent matter, since the majority of individuals would have been aware of and affected by the social concept of *persona*. Therefore, this study will use the term 'opponents' and 'rivals' loosely to refer only to those who are in opposition to Paul, and who exhibit this behaviour in 2 Corinthians.

As indicated above, although the majority of interpreters do not hold that the conflicts in both 1 and 2 Corinthians are the same, the details in the two letters are closely related, especially the social behaviour and values of the Corinthians. For instance, in 1 Corinthians the source of the conflict seems to have been derived from the Corinthians themselves, while in 2 Corinthians it seems to be derived from a group outside the Corinthian church. It could be postulated that this particular group penetrated the church after the circumstances described in 1 Corinthians. Consequently, with their eloquence and rhetorical ability, these infiltrators would have been accepted by the Corinthians who were easily impressed and enamoured by these status symbols. This was the case in 1 Corinthians, where divisions occurred due to competing factions over leaders, which negatively affected Paul who lacked eloquence (1 Cor 2.1–5). Hans Betz, after discussing 1 Corinthians in his study of Paul and rhetoric, affirms a continuity by introducing his discussion of 2 Corinthians: 'The issues of eloquence and knowledge never left Paul throughout his later correspondence with the Corinthians'.[116] In 2 Corinthians, Paul again is negatively assessed and he reacts to the Corinthian opponents' behaviour, as seen in his criticisms over their peddling of God's word (2.17), letters of recommendation (3.1), boasting in 'outer appearance' (5.12), and criticisms over his lack of rhetorical presence and delivery (10.10).

Thus, Paul is constructing an *apologia* of the legitimacy of his apostleship – a defence that not only commends Paul as an apostle, but one that aims to correct the Corinthians' behaviour and values.[117] Two texts in 2 Corinthians will now be examined in part (and will be discussed further in Chapter Six) in order to demonstrate further the social problem related to the obsession with the shallow features of *persona* in the Corinthian church.

---

[116] Betz, 'Problem', 40.

[117] Stegman, *Character*, e.g. 41–2, suggests that studies in 2 Corinthians have incorrectly focused too much on the issue of opponents and have presented Paul as being negative in his reaction. He argues that Paul has positive overarching intentions of 'commending' his embodiment of the *ethos* of Jesus, and challenging the Corinthians also to embody the character of Jesus. Although Stegman convincingly argues for Paul's positive aim, he incorrectly denies the importance of Paul's defence in the letter. His view is only sustained if the text is interpreted in a social vacuum, which could be the case since Stegman does not discuss much of the social context of the letter. It is better, then, to regard Paul here as both making an *apologia* against his opponents and commending his embodiment of the *ethos* of Jesus. For a good treatment of Paul's *apologia* of the legitimacy of his apostleship, see Käsemann, 'Legitimität', 33–71.

5.3.4.1 2 Corinthians 5.12

In 2 Cor 5.12, Paul writes, Οὐ πάλιν ἑαυτοὺς συνιστάνομεν ὑμῖν ἀλλὰ ἀφορμὴν διδόντες ὑμῖν καυχήματος ὑπὲρ ἡμῶν, ἵνα ἔχητε πρὸς τοὺς ἐν προσώπῳ καυχωμένους καὶ μὴ ἐν καρδίᾳ. It can be seen from this text that boasting (καυχάομαι) is a problem in the Corinthian church.[118] Since his opponents are inappropriately boasting in 'outward appearance' (ἐν προσώπῳ), Paul not only responds by defending his ministry himself, but also by providing ammunition for the Corinthians to participate in the defence of his ministry.[119] As scholars have pointed out, the phrase ἐν προσώπῳ here is not concerned about the manner of boasting, but the content of the boasting.[120] Given the antithesis that Paul creates between ἐν προσώπῳ and ἐν καρδίᾳ in 5.12, which will be discussed in detail in Chapter Six, the majority of scholars have rightly understood the term πρόσωπον here as having the sense of 'external appearance' and what is visually observed on the surface – that is, as a metonym for 'what is outward' and 'externals'.[121]

In light of the evidence in 1 Corinthians that indicated an obsession with the conventional projection of *persona* in the church, this study suggests that Paul in 2 Cor 5.12 is specifically alluding to the similar preoccupation with the superficial aspect of *persona*, which appears to be also at the root of the issues in 2 Corinthians. Savage observes the concentration of Paul's use of πρόσωπον in 2 Corinthians and perceives it to be indicating 'Paul's concern with the superficial perspective of the Corinthians'.[122] Ralph Martin supports this visual preoccupation by regarding πρόσωπον, the opponents' place of pride, as similar in meaning to εἶδος in 5.7, which highlights the issue of things seen ('external things').[123] Besides εἶδος in 5.7, scholars have seen other phrases in the epistle that are used in a similar fashion to πρόσωπον in order to emphasise a concern for outward things, such as τὰ βλεπόμενα (4.18) and κατὰ σάρκα (5.16; 11.18).[124]

---

[118] See Collange, *Enigmes*, 247 n. 2, on the frequency of boasting in the epistle; cf. Martin, *2 Cor*, 125. Concerning Paul's opponents, Bultmann, *2 Kor*, 150, writes: 'Daß die καυχώμενοι die Konkurrenten des Paulus in Korinth sind, ist klar'. See below for more on boasting.

[119] Lambrecht, 'Reconcile', 173, that 5.11–13 is both apologetic and polemical; cf. Barnett, *2 Cor*, 282, that 5.12 'reflects the polemical environment implicit throughout 2 Corinthians'.

[120] See Harris, *2 Cor*, 416; Plummer, *2 Cor*, 171.

[121] Harris, *2 Cor*, 416.

[122] Cf. Savage, *Power*, 184 n. 11.

[123] Martin, *2 Cor*, 125. He also considers the things being boasted in as including the outward rhetorical appearance and delivery as seen in 2 Cor 10–11, which will be examined below.

[124] E.g. Bultmann, *2 Kor*, 150. This will be expanded in greater detail in Chapter Six.

In addition, 5.12 is reminiscent of the LXX's rendering of 1 Sam 16.7. God had rejected Saul as Israel's king and the text is about who will be recognised as God's anointed (χριστός) from among Jesse's sons. When Samuel beheld Eliab, Jesse's first-born son, he assumed that he was looking at the chosen χριστός (16.6). However, God told Samuel to look not at Eliab's outward appearance and the height of his stature because God has rejected Eliab, ὅτι ἄνθρωπος ὄψεται εἰς πρόσωπον ὁ δὲ θεὸς ὄψεται εἰς καρδίαν (16.7). Consequently, God chose the unexpected David, the youngest and smallest son. Regardless of whether or not 2 Cor 5.12 is an intentional echoing of 1 Sam 16.7, in both texts there is the problem of individuals evaluating only the superficial side of πρόσωπον. Paul, then, is directing the Corinthians not to evaluate others solely on outward appearance – a behaviour which resembles the typical estimation of social *persona* in first-century Corinth.

Although interpreters have not applied the understanding of *persona* to Paul's use of πρόσωπον, some have correctly aimed in this direction with their depiction of the opponents. In particular, a number of commentators provide helpful interpretations of 2 Cor 5.12 that can be used as a foundation for this present study of the preoccupation with the commonly projected *persona*. Alfred Plummer, for instance, explains that the opponents 'gloried in what was patent to the world, the superficial advantages which made an outward show',[125] the sort of behaviour that Maurice Carrez describes as 'tout de façade'.[126] According to Harris, the Corinthian opponents were those 'who were in the habit of priding themselves on position',[127] and Craig Keener suggests that it probably included 'worldly criteria like social status and rhetorical impressiveness'.[128] David Garland similarly comments that they were 'looking at such things as earthly status, worldly honor, and physical appearance'.[129]

Since the Corinthians have refashioned the conventional displays of *persona* for their own use in the church, it is worth indicating the status symbols of πρόσωπον that they would have boasted in and used to evaluate one another. In addition to the typical elements elevated in an individual's *persona* (e.g. rank, status, wealth, education, noble-birth), the Corinthian opponents seem to have included elements such as experiences of religious ecstasy, revelations, and visions (2 Cor 12.1–7; possibly 5.13),[130] and Jewish

---

[125] Plummer, *2 Cor*, 171.

[126] Carrez, *2 Cor*, 143.

[127] Harris, *2 Cor*, 415.

[128] Keener, *1–2 Cor*, 183, in relation to 2 Cor 10.10–12, 11.6.

[129] Garland, *2 Cor*, 274; cf. Lang, *Kor*, 294, who refers to their boasting as '"fleischliches" Verhalten'.

[130] Concerning 5.13, Hubbard, 'Mind', 39–64, argues that the verbs ἐξίστημι and σωφρονέω do not refer to religious ecstasy, but to rhetorical style, as they are found in the

ancestry (11.22).[131] Hafemann writes: 'Paul's opponents took pride in their professional rhetorical prowess, their letters of recommendation from other churches, the payment they received for their ministry, their ethnic and spiritual pedigree, and their ecstatic spiritual experiences. These are the things that "are seen" (5:12), that is they are on the surface (cf. 10:7)'.[132] Moreover, the Corinthians boasted in these status symbols, which they included in the criteria used to determine the image and style of an apostle. Jorge Sánchez Bosch, who interprets ἐν προσώπῳ as a boasting 'en cosas de *pura* fachada', elucidates: 'Así queda perfectamente retratada la "gloria" de los adversarios de Pablo – que andan buscando cartas de recomendación de acá para allá (3,1), que quieren desautorizar a Pablo por su presentación externa (10,1), que se mueven en la comparación odiosa como en su propio ambiente (10,12), etc...'[133]

Furthermore, as discussed above, one social factor that contributed to the high value placed on the shallow appearance of one's *persona* was the sophistic movement. Witherington has aptly described the sophistic features behind the opponents' boasting in 5.12:

Verse 12b seems to provide us with a reliable aside about Paul's opponents in Corinth...The false ones, Paul suggests, boast in matters of form or outward appearance and not matters of substance or matters of the heart that really count. This was in fact a typical complaint against the Sophists – they were all show and no substance. They paid special attention to their clothing, appearance, and delivery and to the sound of their voices.[134]

Therefore, this social description of the Corinthians' boasting in outward appearance strikingly resembles the conventional obsession with superficialities that expressed one's social *persona* in Corinth. Since all these visible expressions of πρόσωπον were 'superficial advantages which made

---

rhetorical handbooks. He paraphrases, 'If, as some of you complain, my speech was unpolished and excessive [on my first visit], credit that to God's account; if I am presently reasonable and lucid [in my writing], credit that to yours' (61).

[131] For additional elements of their boasting, see Gräßer, *2 Kor*, 210–11. Due to the inclusion of ecstatic displays and other features of piety and zeal, some scholars have translated πρόσωπον in the literal sense of 'face'. Cf. Collange, *Enigmes*, 248–9; Plummer, *2 Cor*, 171: 'They wear a look of apostolic virtue which they do not possess'; Thrall, *2 Cor*, 404–5: 'the transformation of their faces when they were seized by ecstasy' (404). Thrall dismisses the common interpretation of ἐν προσώπῳ as 'external advantages', on the basis that 'had Paul meant external attributes in general, he would have written something like ἐν σαρκὶ καὶ μὴ ἐν πνεύματι'. This suggestion, however, overlooks the wider use of πρόσωπον in the Roman social context.

[132] Hafemann, *2 Cor*, 238.

[133] Bosch, *Gloriarse*, 233.

[134] Witherington, *1–2 Cor*, 393–4. Cf. Windisch, *2 Kor*, 178, comments that 5.12 reflects the polemic between the sophists and philosophers.

an outward show',[135] Paul negatively characterises his Corinthian opponents as being preoccupied with the superficial aspect of *persona* since they boast ἐν προσώπῳ and not ἐν καρδίᾳ.

5.3.4.2 2 Corinthians 10–13

The social descriptions provided in 2 Cor 10–13 are indispensable for analysing how issues of social *persona* were involved in Paul's conflict with the Corinthians.[136] Scholars have clearly noticed that 'boasting' is a central theme in 2 Cor 10–13, which would have amplified a preoccupation with the status symbols associated with one's *persona*.[137] Having seen the preoccupation with the superficial aspect of *persona* in 2 Cor 5.12, it is significant that a number of scholars have pointed out a correlation between 5.12 and the section at hand, which suggests a similar preoccupation in both these texts.[138] In this section Paul responds to accusations against the legitimacy of his apostolic authority, since he is being criticised for not displaying the appropriate marks of an apostle.[139] In interpreting the language of these accusations, many scholars have identified the root problem behind the accusations to be the opponents' adoption of particular social conventions.[140]

A text that displays the adoption of social conventions relating to the concept of *persona* is 10.10 where Paul repeats the opponents' criticism: ὅτι αἱ ἐπιστολαὶ μέν, φησίν, βαρεῖαι καὶ ἰσχυραί, ἡ δὲ παρουσία τοῦ

---

[135] Plummer, *2 Cor*, 171. On the visuality of the objects of their boasting, see Lang, *Kor*, 294: 'Die Gegner stützen ihr Ansehen offenbar auf Vorgänge, die ins Auge fallen'; Gräßer, *2 Kor*, 211: 'Jedenfalls ist das Rühmen "im Angesicht" ein Insistieren auf "Vorzüge, die vor Augen liegen und von jedermann festgestellt werden können"'; Lambrecht, *2 Cor*, 93: 'Paul's opponents visibly boast of the wrong things'.

[136] In 2 Corinthians 10 there are a couple of significant uses of the term πρόσωπον that are relevant for Paul's thoughts on social identity (10.1, 7), which will be considered in detail in Chapter Six.

[137] For some of the many studies of boasting in Paul's letters (esp. 2 Cor 10–13), see e.g. Bosch, *Gloriarse*; idem, 'L'apologie'; Judge, 'Boasting'; Travis, 'Boasting'; Barrett, 'Boasting'; Forbes, 'Comparison'; Hafemann, 'Self-Commendation'; Lambrecht, 'Dangerous Boasting'.

[138] On a link between 5.12 and parts of chs. 10–13, see e.g. Bultmann, *2 Kor*, 189; Martin, *2 Cor*, 125; esp. Marshall, *Enmity*, 330; Lambrecht, 'Reconcile', 169; Hafemann, *2 Cor*, 238; Gräßer, *2 Kor*, 210–11; Keener, *1–2 Cor*, 183. Also, Thrall, *2 Cor*, 404, indicates that there is 'almost universal agreement' that those boasting ἐν προσώπῳ (5.12) are the opponents of chs. 10–13.

[139] See Käsemann, 'Legitimität', 33–71; Hafemann, 'Self-Commendation', 66–88. See also Fitzgerald, 'Epistolary Theorists', 190–200, who examines the mixed epistolary type of this section, which includes a strong element of a quasi-legal appeal.

[140] See e.g. Judge, 'Boasting'; Betz, *Paulus*; Forbes, 'Comparison'; Marshall, *Enmity*; Winter, *Philo*, 203–39.

σώματος ἀσθενὴς καὶ ὁ λόγος ἐξουθενημένος. This two-fold critique of Paul indicates that the opponents were superficially evaluating Paul as an apostle. First, the opponents assessed Paul as producing weighty and strong letters.[141] Winter shows that there was a long-standing debate among orators, especially among the Sophists, over written versus extempore oratory that certainly continued through the first century CE.[142] Given that oratory was generally valued over writing, the Corinthians were more concerned about Paul's lack of rhetorical delivery than his weighty letters. In fact, they probably saw a stark contrast between Paul's *persona* that was impressively depicted in his letters, and the *persona* that was unimpressively seen in his visible presence – hence, their second point of critique: ἡ παρουσία τοῦ σώματος ἀσθενὴς καὶ ὁ λόγος ἐξουθενημένος. Betz suggests that the criticisms against Paul's appearance have to do with the rhetorical rubric of σχῆμα, which is a Cynic tradition that is concerned with outward appearance and form.[143] Consequently, Winter argues that the evaluation of Paul's lack of bodily presence and eloquent speech is based on the conventional understanding of ὑπόκρισις ('rhetorical delivery'), which was of supreme importance in public declamations.[144] The orator's delivery 'included not only his verbal and elocutionary skills but also his bodily "presence", the impression made by his physical appearance, his dress, and his general demeanor'.[145] Given that orators were primarily evaluated for their external appearance in the Graeco-Roman world, this seems to be the case with the Corinthian church and their superficial assessment of Paul's 'public *persona*'.[146]

In light of this social atmosphere, Paul's unimpressive visual presence is considered to be weakness (ἀσθενής) in the eyes of the Corinthians. Marshall intimates that their reception of Paul was characterised by a willingness 'to listen to a "clear voiced orator" until his defects were demonstrated or he would simply appear as an utterly ridiculous person because of his warped

---

[141] Marshall, *Enmity*, 385–6, examines the terms as commendable virtues or qualities that an orator should possess.

[142] Winter, *Philo*, 205–6, and pp. 206–13 for Paul's letters. See also O'Sullivan, 'Written', 115–27; Aristotle, *Rhet.* 3.12.1; Dio Chrysostom, *Or.* 11.18; Quintilian, *Inst.* 7.5.

[143] Betz, *Paulus*, 44–57; idem, 'Problem', 41. See also Harrill, 'Invective', 189–213, who interprets the details in 10.10 as slave physiognomics, which were used rhetorically to attack opponents as having a slavish appearance.

[144] Winter, *Philo*, 213–28; idem, 'Philodemus', 333–42. See idem, *Philo*, 222 n. 67, for his critique of Betz's arguments. For more on ὑπόκρισις, see Russell, *Declamation*, 82.

[145] Harris, *2 Cor*, 700.

[146] Winter, *Philo*, 208. Cf. Savage, *Power*, 65, that the charge against Paul here results from the fact that 'people in antiquity placed a great premium on outward appearance'.

and deformed body'.[147] Paul's unimpressive bodily presence can possibly be determined from: the illnesses and physical injuries he suffered as depicted in his lists of afflictions (e.g. 2 Cor 1.5–10; 6.4–10; 11.23–33; cf. 1 Cor 4.9–13); the tradition in the apocryphal *Acts of Paul and Thecla* (ch. 3) that describes Paul as a man of short stature, bald, bowlegged, in good health, with eyebrows meeting, and a nose somewhat hooked, full of charm;[148] and the idea that Paul's trade was associated with weakness.[149] Also, Margaret Thrall rightly explains that the phrase ἡ παρουσία τοῦ σώματος 'is to be understood in a comprehensive sense, of the apostle's whole outward character and personality, not only his personal appearance in the narrower sense'.[150]

In addition, Paul's speech is criticised as contemptible (ὁ λόγος ἐξουθενημένος), because 'Paul's critics were affirming that his speaking ability in extempore speech, was wholly without merit'.[151] This concern about his rhetorical delivery is also reflected in Paul's self-description as a 'non-professional orator' (ἰδιώτης τῷ λόγῳ) (11.6), which is in contrast to his opponents who are described as 'super-apostles' (cf. 11.5). This phrase ἰδιώτης τῷ λόγῳ has been explained to be referring to an individual who does not skilfully display eloquent speeches and does not follow the received form of sophistic speakers.[152] Winter remarks on 10.10 and 11.6: 'While in the former a contrast is drawn between Paul's writing and his public face as a speaker, in the latter a dichotomy occurs between Paul's capacity as an orator and his knowledge of rhetoric'.[153] There is, then, a contrast between Paul and his opponents' visible projections of *persona*, whereby Paul portrays himself

---

[147] Marshall, *Enmity*, 334. See Epictetus, *Diss.* 3.22.86–9 on the importance of bodily appearance.

[148] See Malherbe, 'Physical Description', 170–5, and Malina & Neyrey, *Portraits*, 100–52, whose studies both use ancient physiognomy to understand that the description is 'not unflattering', and that Paul is presented as 'an ideal male'.

[149] On Paul's trade as weakness, see Hock, *Tentmaking*, 50–65; Furnish, *2 Cor*, 479; *contra* Thrall, *2 Cor*, 631–2.

[150] Thrall, *2 Cor*, 631; cf. Barrett, *2 Cor*, 260–1: 'what he is when he arrives in the body'.

[151] Harris, *2 Cor*, 700. Savage, *Power*, 71, suggests that Paul's demeanour and manner in speech are contemptible because 'his humble physical presence is affecting his speech'.

[152] See Winter, *Philo*, 224–8; Betz, *Paulus*, 57–69; Kennedy, *Interpretation*, 95, who writes that the phrase here 'basically denotes a private person, not a professional'. Also, some have recognised this text as reminiscent of 1 Cor 2.1–5; see Marshall, *Enmity*, 338, 389; Winter, *Philo*, 227–8; Savage, *Power*, 71–3.

[153] Winter, *Philo*, 227. Cf. Savage, *Power*, 71: 'his critics commend his λόγος in letters (τῷ λόγῳ δι' ἐπιστολῶν, 10:11), but repudiate his λόγος in person (ἰδιώτης τῷ λόγῳ, 11:6)'. On the correlation between the two verses, see also Furnish, *2 Cor*, 490; Wolff, *2 Kor*, 218.

as an amateur in contrast to his 'professional' opponents, since he does not participate in their sort of empty and self-vaunting oratory.[154]

In 10.12 Paul also indicates that he refuses to participate in classifying and comparing himself with those who are in the habit of commending themselves (ἐγκρῖναι ἢ συγκρῖναι ἑαυτούς τισιν τῶν ἑαυτοὺς συνιστανόντων), a problem that is reminiscent of those who boast ἐν προσώπῳ (5.12).[155] The opponents' behaviour here has been identified to be the rhetorical convention of σύγκρισις, which 'in Paul's day was an accepted convention in Greek education, in public dialogue, and in historiography'.[156] Marshall defines:

[σύγκρισις] was a method by which a person amplified his own virtues and achievements and depreciated those of his enemies. By comparing himself with people of outstanding character or deeds or a standard of excellence he attempted to display his superiority. The economiastic [*sic*] topics, which included everything that was commendable in Greek and Roman society, are numerous: virtues such as justice, courage, self-control, magnanimity, liberality, gentleness, practical and speculative wisdom; physical qualities such as beauty, stature, agility, might and health; social standing, which included a man's city, race, upbringing, pursuits, affairs and connections.[157]

This form of invective became commonplace in oratory in the Graeco-Roman world, and contributed to the necessity of praising, advertising, and boasting in the surface features of one's social identity.[158] With Paul's descriptor in 10.12, then, 'he is alluding to illegitimate self-praise that aims at impressing others by exalting one's self, one's pedigree, abilities, and achievements (cf. 11:13, 18, 21–23)'.[159]

Therefore, as in 5.12, the social description in 2 Cor 10–13 shows strong similarities to the preoccupation with the shallow displays of *persona* that was prevalent in Roman Corinth. Paul, then, is reacting to this social problem in

---

[154] Cf. Savage, *Power*, 71.

[155] See Furnish, *2 Cor*, 480, who also observes a link between the two verses. Also, see Harris, *2 Cor*, 705–6, and Thrall, *2 Cor*, 636–9, for discussions on textual variants of 10.12, and arguments for the longer reading.

[156] Harris, *2 Cor*, 707. For more on this, see Marshall, *Enmity*, 53–55, 348–53; Forbes, 'Comparison'; Betz, *Paulus*, 119–20. Plutarch's *Lives* is a literary work that exemplifies the importance of comparisons.

[157] Marshall, *Enmity*, 325–6.

[158] See *P. Oxy* 2190 lines 23–8, where the sophistic teachers are depicted as eagerly participating in σύγκρισις of one another in order to attract students or lure them away from rival teachers; cf. Lucian, *Rhet. praec.* 13.21. On the importance of self-praise, see Plutarch's dialogue 'On praising oneself inoffensively', and the commentary by Betz, 'De laude ipsius', 367–93.

[159] Harris, *2 Cor*, 707; cf. Forbes, 'Comparison', 8: 'It is clear that a major part of Paul's critique of his opponents is directed towards their (to him) extravagant self-praise, formulated in frequently invidious comparisons'; and on p. 16: 'Neither in appearance nor in eloquence does he [Paul] match the ideal'.

the Corinthian church, by characterising his opponents as 'pretentious and fraudulent',[160] since they only superficially compare themselves to each other, which he considers to be senseless (οὐ συνιᾶσιν).[161] More specifically, their shallow self-comparison and self-commendation were centred on themselves (10.12), and not on the Lord (cf. 10.17–18). In fact, Paul denounces their self-praising and boasting as going beyond an appropriate limit (10.13, 15) and as based on human standards (κατὰ σάρκα, 11.18). As with their boasting ἐν προσώπῳ (5.12), Paul is clearly criticising their fixation on status symbols associated with the superficialities of *persona*, especially since he himself is being appraised by these status symbols. In order to defend his apostleship, he even accuses his rival 'super-apostles' (11.5) of being 'false-apostles' (ψευδαπόστολοι) who are merely disguising and pretentiously displaying themselves as apostles of Christ (11.13–15). Thus, Paul considers his opponents' conduct within the church community to be shallow and deceptive.

5.4 Summary

This chapter has observed the concept of *persona* and the Roman stress on *persona* in the Roman colony of Corinth, and presented the similarities that are observed in the Corinthian church. Scholars have satisfactorily explained the social situation behind 1 and 2 Corinthians of how the Corinthian Christians have adopted the social conventions of their surrounding culture in Corinth. For instance, John Barclay compares the Pauline communities of Thessalonica and Corinth, and indicates the distinctiveness of the Corinthian church's lack of conflict and hostility with their surrounding society.[162] Also, Clarke concludes that with their adoption of social conventions 'the Corinthian Christians have carried with them into the church those aspects of the surrounding society which were normally accepted. In doing this, Paul accuses them of being thoroughly secular'.[163] However, although scholars have helpfully drawn attention to various social conventions, this study suggests that many of those social conventions are related to the social rubric of *persona*.

As noted above, Paul is not reacting against the idea of being a 'Roman' or the whole of Roman society, but specifically against the Corinthian Christians' exploitation of certain ideal aspects of *persona* (e.g. social status,

---

[160] Forbes, 'Comparison', 2.
[161] Cf. Barrett, *2 Cor*, 263.
[162] Barclay, 'Corinth', 57–60, on the 'social harmony in Corinth'.
[163] Clarke, *Leadership*, 107.

privilege, and eloquence). Since the church was situated in the social milieu of a Roman colony, it was *de rigueur* for the Corinthians to imbibe the conventional values of social identity, and to assimilate these values into their outworking of Christian identity. Their conventional use of *persona* engendered a preoccupation with the superficial dimension of *persona* and a misconception of Christian identity in the church. With their susceptibility to conventional practices, the Corinthians have assimilated and refashioned the commonly presented *persona* in first-century Roman Corinth. They accordingly paraded the typical status symbols and used them as the criteria to assess one another's *persona*. This superficial assessment was clearly seen in the Corinthians' evaluation of Paul's outward appearance as an apostle. Accordingly, Paul criticised their adoption and use of the conventional values of *persona*. Therefore, in the Corinthian correspondence – especially 2 Corinthians – Paul clearly criticised the Corinthians' shallow projection of *persona*, and their preoccupation with its superficial aspect.

Chapter 6

Christian Identity in the Corinthian Church (Part II)

6.1 Introduction

Having observed indications of a high premium being placed on the superficial aspect of *persona* in the contexts of Roman Corinth and the Corinthian church, this chapter will continue to explore Paul's conception of social identity and *persona* in 2 Corinthians. While researching for details relating to social identity in 2 Corinthians, it was observed that Paul, like Valerius Maximus and Epictetus, had both a negative and positive critique of social identity. The previous chapter presented, in part, Paul's negative reaction against a crisis of identity in the Corinthian church that arose from the Christians' adoption of the conventional values of *persona* in first-century Corinth, and their preoccupation with its superficial aspect. This chapter will not only continue to underscore Paul's negative critique, but will pay particular attention to the positive side of his critique and approach to Christian identity: his emphasis on the internal aspect of one's identity, his promotion and embodiment of a new visible Christ-like identity, and the subversive role of this Christ-like identity. In addition, this chapter will provide a brief analysis of Paul's uses of πρόσωπον in 2 Corinthians to see whether they have implications for Paul's approach to Christian identity, and whether they have a clear meaning of *persona*.

6.2 The Internal Aspect of Christian Identity

In Chapter Five, the key verse of 2 Cor 5.12 was examined for Paul's negative reaction to the preoccupation with the superficial aspect of *persona*. However, in this verse there is a positive side of his critique. Paul indicates that he gives the Corinthians a reason to boast against those who boast in the shallow features of *persona* and not in the heart (ἐν προσώπῳ καυχωμένους καὶ μὴ ἐν καρδίᾳ) – hence, an encouragement for boasting ἐν καρδίᾳ. Murray Harris helpfully explains 'πρόσωπον as a metonym for "what is outward", "externals", and καρδία as standing for "what is inward", the "character"'.[1] With this verse, then, Paul constructs an external–internal antithesis of boasting ἐν προσώπῳ and boasting ἐν καρδίᾳ.[2] Since the term καρδία occurs 11 times in the epistle, it is worthwhile to consider its significance for Paul. The concept of the heart has been explored in terms of Pauline anthropology and defined as the centre of man: 'As the inner man, heart is defined as the seat of feeling and will as well as the receptive center for knowledge and revelation'.[3] In regard to 5.12, Robert Jewett describes the term as having a 'substantial and polemical' use,[4] which helps to accentuate the significance of Paul's placement of it in juxtaposition to another substantial and polemical term, πρόσωπον.

The dichotomy seen in this antithesis of πρόσωπον–καρδία is critical for Paul's argument in the larger context of 2.14–7.4, whereby he gives greater weight to the interior rather than the exterior. In fact, as will be shown, Paul frequently employs this exteriority–interiority antithesis within 2 Cor 2.14–7.4.[5] In addition, within this section there are not only significant instances of the term πρόσωπον, which 'is closely associated with the external–internal antithesis',[6] but also of the πρόσωπον–καρδία interplay, which according to François Collange 'est partout présente'.[7] Besides the fact that Paul heavily uses the term πρόσωπον in 2 Corinthians, Collange has noted that with Paul's six uses of the term in 3.7–5.12 (3.7 [2x], 13, 18; 4.6; 5.12), it is remarkable that Paul uses the term καρδία five times roughly within the same space (3.2, 3, 15; 4.6; 5.12), which indicates the weightiness of the πρόσωπον–καρδία antithesis for Paul's argument in 2.14–7.4.

---

[1] Harris, *2 Cor*, 416. However, Lambrecht, 'Reconcile', 170, incorrectly regards the opposition as 'insincerity' and 'honesty'; Furnish, *2 Cor*, 308, as between appearance and 'reality'.

[2] Besides the possible allusion to 1 Sam 16.7 in this text, the πρόσωπον–καρδία contrast also occurs in 1 Thes 2.17 (προσώπῳ οὐ καρδίᾳ), where it has the sense of 'physical and not spiritual'.

[3] Jewett, *Anthropological*, 305. See his pp. 305–33, for the importance of the καρδία for Paul's anthropology and polemic. See also Schlier, 'Menschenherz', 184–200; Collange, *Enigmes*, 46–7 n. 4.

[4] Jewett, *Anthropological*, 329.

[5] Cf. Hubbard, *New Creation*, 151–3; Theissen, *Psychological Aspects*, 143, on Paul's reliance of his 'multiplication of interiorized conceptions', in reference to the heart.

[6] Hubbard, *New Creation*, 197. Also, it should be noted that there are two instances of πρόσωπον prior to this literary unit. First in 1.11 where it appears to be referring to physical persons. Secondly, in 2.10 Paul writes about forgiveness δι' ὑμᾶς ἐν προσώπῳ Χριστοῦ, which possibly has the sense of 'in the presence of Christ'. Scholars have noted that this phrase in the LXX (e.g. Prov 8.30, 4.3; 25.7) is used for לפני ('in his presence'). Thrall, *2 Cor*, 180–1, supports this meaning because Paul throughout the epistle shows his awareness that his activity is witnessed by God or Christ (2.17; 4.2; 5.11; 8.21).

[7] Collange, *Enigmes*, 75, in reference to the passage of 3.7–5.12.

Before looking at some important texts that highlight Paul's antithetical language, some brief comments should be made concerning the first subsection of 2.14–17, which is critical for understanding his more extended argument in 2.14–7.4. Some interpreters have identified 2.14–17 as a thematic statement for Paul's argument in 2.14–7.4.[8] Paul starts off this digression by presenting a metaphor of a Roman triumphal procession, in which God is portrayed as the victorious conqueror who leads (θριαμβεύοντι) the apostles as his captives.[9] Remarkably, Paul thanks God (τῷ δὲ θεῷ χάρις) for displaying him and the other apostles in this lowly position as captives who are doomed to death. This metaphor graphically depicts Paul's privileged identity and role as an apostle of God, which is presented throughout the Corinthian correspondence in terms of suffering and afflictions. Moreover, he continues the imagery by depicting the apostles as the odour (ὀσμή) and fragrance (εὐωδία) of Christ that are ascending to God and spreading everywhere (2.14–15). Through this imagery, Paul portrays the apostles as God's agents who diffuse the knowledge of Christ, that is, the gospel.

Consequently, Paul poses a pressing question: 'Who is sufficient (ἱκανός) for these things?' (2.16). It is possible that Paul expected a positive answer which would denote him as being the one qualified. This interpretation is consistent with his following contrast between 'the many' (οἱ πολλοί) who are deceitfully making an illegal profit and adulterating (καπηλεύοντες) the word of God, and Paul who acts out of pure motives in the sight of God, is sent from God, and speaks ἐν Χριστῷ (2.17). His defence in 3.1 that he is not commending himself again also confirms a positive answer.[10] In fact, Paul later asserts that his and the apostles' sufficiency (ἱκανοί) comes not from themselves, but from God, who has made them sufficient to be ministers of a new covenant (ἱκάνωσεν ἡμᾶς διακόνους καινῆς διαθήκης) (3.5–6).

Since 2.14–17 can be seen as a thematic statement for what follows, the negative portrayal of Paul's opponents (οἱ πολλοί) in 2.17 as inappropriately handling the word of God (cf. 4.2) is significant in providing the *Sitz im Leben* for the remainder of 2.14–7.4. As noted in Chapter Five, scholars have demonstrated that Paul's description of his opponents has allusions to rhetorical and sophistic conventions. This was seen in the earlier analysis of 2 Cor 10–13, where the Corinthians superficially evaluated Paul and were

---

[8] So Collange, *Enigmes*, 21–41, who concludes 'que 2:14–17 constitue le thème, l'intitulé de ce qui va être repris et développé jusqu'en 7:4' (318–19); Thrall, *2 Cor*, 189. Also, in Hafemann, *Suffering*, and idem, *Moses*, he has evolved both studies around the key theme of Paul's ἱκανός; cf. Savage, *Power*, 105.

[9] On this metaphor, see Marshall, 'Metaphor', 302–17; and Hafemann, *Suffering*, esp. 18–39, for his discussion of the term θριαμβεύω and the role of the conquered prisoners in the Roman triumph.

[10] Cf. Thrall, *2 Cor*, 209.

disconcerted by his lack of oratorical prowess and physical splendour, which his rivals themselves were able to display.[11] Moyer Hubbard writes:

On the surface, the Corinthians were embarrassed by the oratory and demeanor of their apostle – especially in comparison with the crowd pleasers they were accustomed to – and this became a running joke among some of them. But under the surface was the much larger issue of a superficial, status-conscious community who had yet to grasp the message of the cross and the power of a cruciform life.[12]

It is within the framework of Paul's *apologia* of his sufficiency as an apostle that the extended section of 2.14–7.4 will be analysed for his critique of social identity.[13] Since Paul is chiefly responding to harsh criticisms of his ministry, he defends himself by emphasising interiority over exteriority, which would have conflicted with the Corinthians' obsession with the shallow features of *persona*. Similarly, Linda Belleville looks at Paul's line of argument in 3.1–18 and proposes that the overarching theme is one of 'appropriate credentials for a gospel minister':

The thesis that Paul puts forward is that the proper criteria for ascertaining credibility are ones that focus on the inward, spiritual dimension as opposed to some outward, material dimension. Outward credibility is represented by his opponents, who are concerned about material profit (2.17) and letters of recommendation (3.1). Paul, on the other hand, argues for a credibility that is focused on inward, spiritual values, one motivated by sincerity (2.17) with commendatory letters written on the heart (3.2–3).[14]

Thus, 2.14–7.4 will now be examined for Paul's coherent argument in light of the external–internal (πρόσωπον–καρδία) interplay.

6.2.1 Letters of Commendation and the Letter–Spirit Contrast (3.1–6)

Having seen Paul's depiction of his privileged and qualified ministry as an apostle of God (2.14–17), Paul now anticipates possible charges of whether he is beginning to commend himself or needs letters of recommendation (3.1).[15] Paul's opponents, who had outstanding credentials, are accusing him of not having commendatory letters that would establish his apostolic credentials. Letters of commendation were important for social relations in the Graeco-

---

[11] Collange, *Enigmes*, 37–9, and Georgi, *Opponents*, 229–30, both identify these opponents in 2.14–17 to be the rival missionaries of chs. 10–13.

[12] Hubbard, *New Creation*, 161.

[13] See Belleville, *Reflections*, 104–35, who identifies the epistolary type of 2 Cor 1–7 as a type of Hellenistic commendation, or more specifically a sort of 'apologetic self-commendation'. She bases this on Paul's consistent pairing of expressions of commendation and the denial of worldly conduct.

[14] Belleville, *Reflections*, 145–6.

[15] See Hafemann, 'Self-Commendation', 66–88, who proposes 'self-commendation' as the central motif of 2 Corinthians.

Roman world, particularly for establishing one's *persona*.[16] As with the case of many other social markers in the Graeco-Roman social milieu, individuals would exploit and exaggerate the use of these letters for self-advertisement and the evaluation of others. However, Paul refuses to participate in any futile self-comparisons based on superficial features (cf. 10.12). Instead he redirects the Corinthians' attention towards the Corinthians themselves, who are his letter of recommendation that is to be known and read by all (3.2).[17] Paul, moreover, emphasises the non-external nature of this letter of Christ, by showing that it is written, not with ink, but with the Spirit of the living God on their *hearts* (καρδίαις) (3.2–3).[18]

Of significance are the two contrasts in 3.3. The first contrast is between the permanence and impermanence of the letters, that is, written not with ink (μέλανι) but with the Spirit of the living God (πνεύματι θεοῦ ζῶντος). This text is an allusion to Exod 31.18 (cf. Deut 9.10), which describes the two stone tablets that God gave to Moses as inscribed by the finger of God. Harris comments on Paul's contrast here: 'Human writers use ink that is perishable. The divine penman, Christ, writes his letters by means of the Spirit, whose person and work are imperishable'.[19] The second contrast is between the external and internal material types, that is, the tablets of stones (πλαξὶν λιθίναις) and tablets of hearts of flesh (πλαξὶν καρδίαις σαρκίναις). Here Paul alludes to Ezek 11.19 and 36.26–7, which have a similar contrast between human hearts and 'stony' hearts. Significantly, Ezekiel reveals God as removing the 'stony' hearts of his people and replacing them with other new hearts, in which he places his Spirit. As with the πρόσωπον–καρδία contrast in 2 Cor 5.12, Paul places more emphasis on the heart than on the externals, since the καρδία 'est ici le lieu privilégié de l'action de l'Esprit'.[20] Thus, through these allusions, Paul is clearly depreciating externals, such as

---

[16] For more on letters of recommendation, see: Cotton, *Letters*; Kim, *Letter*; Keyes, 'Letter'; Baird, 'Letters'. Also, Paul in 2 Cor 3.1–3 is not rejecting the use of letters of commendation, for in the Book of Acts and in his epistles he did have positive uses of them (e.g. Acts 9.2; 22.5; Rom 16.1–2; 1 Cor 16.10–11; 2 Cor 8.22–3).

[17] Cf. 1 Cor 9.2, where Paul depicts the Corinthians as a seal of his apostleship.

[18] The phrase 'written on hearts' is possibly an allusion to Jer 38.33 (LXX) in reference to the promise of the new covenant. Also, Harris, *2 Cor*, 263, and Thrall, *2 Cor*, 225, both convey that Christ is presented as the author of the letter in the Corinthians, and Paul as the amanuensis.

[19] Harris, *2 Cor*, 264.

[20] Collange, *Enigmes*, 46 n. 4: 'Comme nous le montrerons encore (cf. surtout *ad* 3:7) καρδία est ici le lieu privilégié de l'action de l'Esprit – promoteur de l'alliance nouvelle – que Paul oppose au "visage" – apparence dont se vantent ses adversaires et qui en fait, ne relève que de la "vieille alliance" (3:14)'. Cf. 2 Cor 1.22, where God puts his seal on the Corinthians and places the down-payment of the Spirit in their hearts (τὸν ἀρραβῶνα τοῦ πνεύματος ἐν ταῖς καρδίαις ἡμῶν), and similarly in 5.5.

commendatory letters, and is emphasising the interiority of the Spirit's work in the Christian.

In his discussion on letters of recommendation, Paul noticeably makes a shift in his imagery, in that his 'letter' is being contrasted not to the conventional letter of recommendation but to the 'stone tablets' of the old covenant. Although there are no explicit statements of the old or new covenants within 3.1–3, they are implied from Paul's allusions to Old Testament texts that deal with the new covenant, particularly the promise of it. Also, interpreters have pointed out that in 3.3 one would have expected the term papyrus or parchment, rather than 'tablets of stone', which recalls the story of Moses and the old covenant.[21] It is important, then, to recognise the contrast between the old and new covenants, which have been described respectively as stony and fleshy hearts. Paul significantly uses this contrast to commend his apostolic ministry.

In 3.6 Paul explains that God has made him a minister of the new covenant (διακόνους καινῆς διαθήκης), and that this covenant, in contrast to the old covenant, is not of letter but of Spirit, because the letter (γράμμα) kills while the Spirit gives life. In fact, Paul also contrasts these two ministries as death versus Spirit (3.7–8), and condemnation versus righteousness (3.9). Paul is exhibiting here the letter–Spirit (γράμμα–πνεῦμα) antithesis, which has been the subject of numerous studies of 2 Corinthians 3.[22] For this study, though, the main concern is that through this antithetical presentation, Paul emphasises again the interiority of the person. He diminishes the value of the visible γράμμα (like the letters of commendation) and maximises the value of the Spirit, which is written on hearts.[23] Moreover, Paul's ministry, which has 'la marque de l'Esprit et la rénovation des cœurs',[24] not only diminishes the value of external things, but also points to a depreciation of the Mosaic ministry. This is consistent with Paul's other uses of the γράμμα–πνεῦμα antithesis (Rom 2.29; 7.4–6), where both elements 'are contrasted as outward sign and inward reality'.[25] In fact, the resurrection is even explained to be accomplished through God's Spirit 'who dwells in you' (Rom 8.11) – hence, Paul's grand statement 'but the Spirit gives life' (2 Cor 3.6).

Therefore, in 2 Corinthians 3, Paul can be seen as constructing an argument that aims to counteract his Corinthian opponents' preoccupation

---

[21] So e.g. Provence, 'Sufficient', 60; Harris, *2 Cor*, 264.

[22] See e.g. the following studies and their bibliography for more references: Hofius, 'Gesetz'; Gleason, 'Covenantal Contrasts'; Grindheim, 'Law'.

[23] Cf. Lambrecht, 'Structure', 353; Hughes, *2 Cor*, 100, who describes the contrast in the antithesis as being 'between the law as *externally* written at Sinai on tablets of stone and the *same* law as written *internally* in the heart of the Christian believer' (italics his).

[24] Collange, *Enigmes*, 55.

[25] Thrall, *2 Cor*, 234. Cf. Harris, *2 Cor*, 274; Westerholm, 'Letter and Spirit', 229–48.

with outward displays of commendation. He diminishes the values of certain outward elements, which the Corinthians would have exploited and exaggerated (esp. letters of commendation), while highlighting the significance of particular internal features. C.K. Barrett writes:

[Paul] is contrasting the letters, written by men with pen and ink, which his rivals carried as their authorization, with the work of God the Spirit in the hearts of the Corinthian converts, which was the only authorization upon which he could depend. The contrast is thus between human opinion and performance, and the work of God by his Spirit.[26]

Also, as mentioned above, Belleville has recognised this external–internal interplay in the context of Paul's polemic against his opponents. She observes the shift in metaphor from letters of recommendation to stone tablets, which has to do with outward 'material accreditation':

He [Paul] appears to be contrasting written documents – which are able to impart an initial glory and credibility to the bearer, but because of their material nature had no lasting effects – with the permanent and lasting credibility that an inward change of the heart and the internal work of the Spirit impart to the bearer. So Paul introduces the old covenant and the figure of Moses to show that even the highest forms of documentary certification can only impart a limited credibility to the bearer because of their external character (γράμμα). In linking his opponents and Moses, Paul is stating that their competence is like the material ministry which they represent: one whose glory fades and whose credentials pass away.[27]

6.2.2　The Glory of God and the Heart (3.7–4.6)

Having observed Paul as a minister of the new covenant, 'whose hallmark is the inward work of God's life-giving Spirit',[28] it is important to see how Paul develops his contrast between the old and new covenant. Moreover, this contrast could reveal more insights into Paul's understanding of πρόσωπον, a term used five times in 3.7–4.6.[29] In this text, Paul continues his allusion to the stone tablets, but his focus shifts to Exod 34.29–35, which is the narrative account of Moses and the people of Israel after Moses had received the stone tablets on Mount Sinai for the second time.

Before looking at the text, there are some points that need to be addressed concerning this notoriously difficult section, which has been 'squeezed and prodded by generations of interpreters'.[30] One difficulty is sorting out the

---

[26] Barrett, *2 Cor*, 112.

[27] Belleville, *Reflections*, 148–9. On p. 148 she lists the material/spiritual contrasts that pervade 3.1–18; she also explains, 'The non-durable character of material documents is reflected in Paul's use of the terminology of μέλανι, λιθίναις, γράμμα, and καταργουμένην, as opposed to the durable nature of πνεῦμα, καρδία, and τὸ μένον' (149).

[28] Harris, *2 Cor*, 275–6.

[29] Cf. Collange, *Enigmes*, 74–5.

[30] Hays, *Echoes*, 123. Also, Unnik, 'Unveiled Face', 154, has expressed that in 3.7–18 'there is hardly a single point on which expositors agree', which is still the case today. He

details that Paul provides which are not explained in the LXX, for instance: Moses' motivation for veiling his face, the fading glory on his face, and the Israelites' inability to gaze on his face. Due to Paul's additional commentary on the Exodus narrative, scholars have probed this section of the Moses-*Doxa* tradition (esp. 3.1–18) in order to understand Paul's hermeneutical strategy in reading Scripture and whether he was innovative.[31] In recent scholarship, however, there has been a move away from regarding this passage as a source for understanding Pauline hermeneutics. Richard Hays, for instance, acknowledges that in 2 Corinthians 3, 'Paul is writing an *apologia* for his ministry, not an excursus on hermeneutical method'.[32] Hays' statement is significant since the interest of this study, as stated in Chapter Five, is to move beyond the reading of Paul in a social vacuum for the sake of merely analysing the texts for aspects of Pauline theology or hermeneutics. Rather, this study will examine how Paul uses his theologically rich language to interact with the particular social situation that has prompted him to write the letter.

In her form-critical analysis of 2 Cor 3.1–18, Belleville presents the various sources of this Moses-*Doxa* tradition and concludes that there is 'no real uniqueness' to Paul's presentation of it, and that, 'It is, rather, in the application of these traditions to the Mosaic covenant itself and to the apostle's contemporary situation that Paul's original contribution is made'.[33] Her statement suggests, again, the need to evaluate Paul's use of the Exodus narrative for his social situation in Corinth, particularly for the *apologia* of his ministry in the midst of the Corinthians' preoccupation with the superficialities that expressed one's identity.[34]

---

continues, 'Cataloguing them all would outlast the time at our disposal'. Cf. Hafemann, *Moses*, 255.

[31] See Hays, *Echoes*, 122–5, for a brief overview of these hermeneutical enquiries. Some scholars, have proposed various understandings of Paul's use of Exod 34, such as a midrash, pesher, midrash-pesher, or an allegory. Hays, however, aptly describes it as 'an allusive homily based on biblical incidents' (132).

[32] Hays, *Echoes*, 124–5. Cf. Westerholm, 'Letter and Spirit', 241, who concludes that 'the letter–spirit antithesis has nothing to do with Pauline hermeneutics', and is 'the key to Pauline ethics, not Pauline hermeneutics'. See Watson, *Hermeneutics*, esp. 281–98, whose study demonstrates that Paul uses a hermeneutical key of the exalted Christ in order to interpret scripture, and that in the case of 2 Corinthians 3 Paul is firmly grounded in the Exodus text. See also Hafemann, 'Paul's Argument', 277–303, who shows Paul's vast use of the OT and christology in 2 Cor 1–9.

[33] Belleville, *Reflections*, 78.

[34] Cf. Vanhoye, 'L'interprétation', 159–96. Savage, *Power*, 106, explains that Paul chose the Moses narrative because it would help his case to defend the integrity of his ministry by comparing it favourably with other ministries. He also shows that Moses would have been a suitable choice for Paul's Gentile audience since Moses was well known and highly respected in Graeco-Roman antiquity (106–9). Cf. Gager, *Moses*; Droge, *Homer*. See Duff, 'Glory',

In the text Paul contrasts the two covenants by referring to the glory (δόξα)[35] that came with the ministry of death and the surpassing glory of the ministry of the Spirit (3.7–8).[36] He states that the Israelites were not able to gaze (ἀτενίσαι) at the glory on the 'face' (πρόσωπον) of Moses, a glory that is, in fact, 'fading away' (τὴν καταργουμένην).[37] Important in this text are the details of the glory on Moses' πρόσωπον and the Israelites' inability to gaze on his πρόσωπον, and how the details contribute to Paul's exterior–interior contrast.

Although the term πρόσωπον here is normally understood as Moses' literal face, some scholars have attempted to interpret Moses' πρόσωπον as referring to something beyond his literal face. In particular, it has been suggested that Moses' features of a 'shining face' and veil (v. 13) should be understood in terms of a 'mask' that has a cultic function of visually representing a deity; in the case of Moses' πρόσωπον and its exhibition of God's glory, this 'mask' portrays his 'social authority' as a priest and lawgiver of God.[38] Interestingly, this understanding of 'mask' is consistent with the original meaning of 'mask' for *persona*/πρόσωπον (as seen in Chapter Two), which raises the possibility of understanding Paul's use of πρόσωπον here as having a nuance of 'social identity'. However, it is difficult to substantiate a clear reading of '*persona*' into Moses' πρόσωπον. It is, nevertheless, reasonable to regard Moses' πρόσωπον as relating to the outward material things that Paul presents as being of little worth. In other words, although πρόσωπον does not have a clear meaning of *persona* in this text, the details of πρόσωπον still contribute to Paul's reaction against the Corinthians' preoccupation with superficialities.

313–37, who submits that Paul is writing about the status of Gentiles before God, rather than a polemic about Torah-observant Judaism. See also Stanley, *Arguing*, esp. 97–113, who explores Paul's rhetorical use of scriptural quotations, and also analyses the different ways his readers would have understood Paul's use of scripture.

[35] Note the concentration of δοξα/δοξαζω, which occurs 15 times in 3.7–4.6. Cf. Young & Ford, *Meaning*, 12–13, 260.

[36] It has often been pointed out that in 3.7–11, Paul uses the *qal wahomer* (i.e. *a minore ad maius* or *a fortiori*) mode of argumentation, which shows how one of two similar elements is better or greater than the other one – here, it is the superiority of the glory of the new covenant over that of the old covenant.

[37] Note that in Exod 34.29–30 it is the 'skin of his face' that was glorified and radiant. Although Paul reveals that the glory is indeed fading, in the narrative the Israelites were not able to gaze because of its dazzling brightness; cf. Philo, *Moses* 2.70. Also, Belleville, *Reflections*, 77, points out that the idea of the Israelites being unable to gaze is a widely known tradition. On καταργέω, see Harris, *2 Cor*, 284–5, for this favourite Pauline word.

[38] See e.g. the intriguing study by Dozeman, 'Masking Moses', 21–45. Scholars have occasionally regarded Moses' veil as a mask, but Dozeman proposes that there are two masks: Moses' shining face and veil.

There are indications in the text that πρόσωπον ('face') has connotations of exteriority and visuality, which affirm the word's role in the external–internal interplay throughout the section. The Israelites, for instance, were intent on gazing at the glory of Moses' πρόσωπον, which Michael Theobald regards as a concern with 'der Kategorie des *Visuellen*'.[39] The notion of visuality is emphasised with Paul's use of the vivid verb ἀτενίζω, which denotes a prolonged and attentive observation: 'keep one's eyes fixed on', 'gaze intently at'.[40] Theobald, in his clarification of Paul's use of πρόσωπον as 'äußeren Erscheinung des Menschen', acknowledges the πρόσωπον–καρδία contrast and also the nexus between the term πρόσωπον and other terms used synonymously:

πρόσωπον bezeichnet nicht nur das Antlitz des Menschen, sondern steht darüber hinaus für seine nach außen gewandte, ihn offenbarende und verbergende Erscheinung überhaupt und ist so mit Begriffen wie ἔξω ἄνθρωπος (4,16), σῶμα (4,10) und θνήτη σάρξ (4,11) verwandt. Das Wort ist aus der Opposition zu καρδία, einem Zentralbegriff biblischer Anthropologie, zu begreifen, der bei Paulus *zunächst* die verborgene Mitte des Menschen, 'das Innere im Gegensatz zum Äußeren, das eigentliche Ich im Unterschied von der Erscheinung des Menschen' bezeichnet. Mit beiden Begriffen, πρόσωπον und καρδία, sind nicht 'Teile' des Menschen, sondern dieser als ganzer, nur jeweils in verschiedener Hinsicht gemeint.[41]

Furthermore, the visual sense of πρόσωπον is also grasped from the meaning of δόξα ('glory'), since the Hebrew equivalent כבד is often used in the Old Testament to refer to the 'visible manifestation of God's nature, presence, and power'.[42]

Paul additionally provides the detail that Moses' πρόσωπον was visibly projecting the glory of the 'ministry of death', which he describes as being engraved in letters on stone (3.7). This phrase 'engraved in letters on stone' recalls the contrast observed in 3.3 between tablets of stone and tablets of human hearts, and 'hints at the inferiority of the old covenant with its focus on externals'.[43] Although Paul asserts in 3.7 that the Israelites were unable to gaze on Moses' πρόσωπον because of the dazzling brightness of the glory, he explicitly disdains Moses' projected glory by qualifying that it is, in fact, 'fading away'.[44] Regardless of whether Paul knew of a source that viewed

---

[39] Theobald, *Gnade*, 184 (italics his). He also takes the visuality to be associated with Paul's maxim in 4.18: τὰ γὰρ βλεπόμενα πρόσκαιρα, τὰ δὲ μὴ βλεπόμενα αἰώνια.

[40] Harris, *2 Cor*, 283. Hafemann, *Moses*, 281–2, comments that Paul uses this 'vivid verb' ἀτενίζω to describe Israel's action, rather than 'the more common and neutral' εἶδον ("to see") found in the LXX (Exod. 34:30, 35)'; cf. Hofius, 'Gesetz', 92.

[41] Theobald, *Gnade*, 185 (italics his). He also connects the πρόσωπον language here to 5.12.

[42] Harris, *2 Cor*, 282.

[43] Harris, *2 Cor*, 282.

[44] Watson, *Hermeneutics*, 290, considers Paul's two references to the Israelites' inability to gaze on Moses' face (3.7, 13) as alluding to two different points of the Exodus narrative

Moses' glory as fading or temporary, it is clear that Paul is pointing out the inferiority of Moses' ministry, and the surpassing glory of his own ministry of the Spirit (cf. 3.9–11). Since the new covenant is described as the ministry of the Spirit, Paul's emphasis is on the *inward* work of the Spirit in the heart, rather than the *outward* fading glory of Moses' πρόσωπον. Moreover, Margaret Thrall suspects that in 3.7–8 there are some implicit allusions to criticisms of Paul that were current in Corinth, because the Corinthians 'were all too ready to judge by externals'.[45] Paul's argument here, then, would be directed at the Corinthians' preoccupation with superficialities.

Paul further relates the fading glory to Moses' veiling of his face, which hid the fading glory from the gaze of the Israelites (3.13). A matter of debate is Moses' motivation in veiling his face, since the Exodus narrative (34.33–5) does not give a reason for the veiling and unveiling. Paul explains that Moses veiled his face in order to keep the Israelites from gazing at the end of that which was indeed fading away (τὸ τέλος τοῦ καταργουμένου). Since the Exodus narrative does not explicitly mention this 'end of the fading glory', nor does Paul explicitly explain it, scholars have speculated and debated over the phrase τὸ τέλος τοῦ καταργουμένου.[46] However, regardless of Paul's precise meaning, this phrase clearly portrays the glory on Moses' face as transitory.[47] Through his depiction of Moses' veiling, Paul again diminishes

---

story. First, they were unable to gaze because of the dazzling glory, and secondly, because of the veil which concealed the fact that the glory was departing. Concerning the fading here in 3.7, he explains, 'The fact that the glory is temporary is something that Paul knows but the sons of Israel do not'.

[45] Thrall, *2 Cor*, 246.

[46] This phrase contains two points that are debated among scholars. The interpretation here follows the recent summary argument by Watson, *Hermeneutics*, 293–4 n. 42. First, does τέλος mean 'end' or does it mean 'aim'? Linked with τοῦ καταργουμένου, the sense of 'end' is more appropriate. In virtually all of the Pauline uses of καταργέω 'the reference is to a (potentially violent) bringing-to-an-end, and never to a brining-to-a-goal' (cf. 1 Cor 15.24). The second issue, is with τοῦ καταργουμένου which can be translated as 'that which is being put aside' as in 3.7, 11. Watson is right that: 'This over-literal rendering of a present passive particle cannot account satisfactorily for the contrast in v.11 between *to katargoumenon* and *to menon* (cf. the similar antithesis in 4.18 between *proskaira* and *aiōnia*). While it is true that *katargein* does not in itself mean "fade", a "passing" glory is also a "fading" glory. See also Schulz, 'Die Decke', 1–30, for more on Paul's understanding of the transiency of Moses' glory.

[47] There have been suggestions that the Exodus account does in fact imply that Moses' glory was fading or transient. Moses' transfiguration of glory resulted from his direct interaction with God in the Tent of Meeting (Exod 33.7–11) and on Mount Sinai (Exod 34), but its temporariness could be implied from the detail in Exod 40.35 that Moses was not able to enter the Tabernacle because God's presence was now in there. See Dozeman, 'Masking Moses', 21–45, who explains that the temporariness of Moses' visible representation of God's glory and presence developed from the redaction of Mosaic authority by the 'Priestly'

the value of the glory of Moses' πρόσωπον, which symbolises the temporary and visible characteristics of the old covenant.

Concerning Paul's social situation, in 3.12–13 Paul responds to criticisms that he has been deceitful, since he describes his ministry as being forthright and unlike Moses' intentional concealment of something.[48] Harris also regards this text as concerned about a preoccupation with externals:

with the repeated appearance of Moses before the people with a radiant face (Exod. 34:35), their initial fear would have turned to continual amazement, which may have prompted Moses to veil his face, lest they become preoccupied by his appearance as a divine 'reflector' as opposed to his words as a divine spokesman.[49]

His comment is consistent with this study's presentation of the Corinthian problem of a preoccupation with outward appearance. Thus, Paul is showing, as in the case of the Israelites' fixation with Moses' outward appearance, the futility of his opponents' preoccupation with shallow features, which were only temporary (cf. 4.16).

Paul further discusses the veil as being over the reading of the old covenant and those hearing it, even up to this day (3.14–15). The external veiling has now shifted and is an internal veiling of minds/hearts. Thrall suggests that Paul is accusing the Christian rivals 'of veiled hearts because they concentrate on the superficial aspects of the Mosaic experience, that is, on its radiance, *preoccupied as they themselves are with outward appearance*, and fail to understand that in the era of the new covenant it is the heart that is all-important'.[50] In light of the πρόσωπον–καρδία contrast, Collange paraphrases Paul's critique of his opponents: 'vous ne vous préoccupez que de l'apparence – qu'elle soit lumineuse ou voilée – n'ais vous ne comprenez pas que, dans l'alliance nouvelle, il s'agit du cœur. Or, si un voile est sur mon visage, le même est certainement sur vos cœurs!'[51] Paul then reveals that the remedy for this internal veiling over the heart occurs 'in Christ' (ἐν Χριστῷ)[52] when one turns to the Lord (3.14, 16),[53] which should be

---

tradition. On p. 44 n. 79, he even wonders whether Paul's depiction of his ministry was from this 'Priestly' interpretation, given his sacrificial imagery (2 Cor 2.14–17), Moses' fading glory (3.7–10), and the reference to tent/tabernacle (5.1–5).

[48] See Thrall, *2 Cor*, 254, and also p. 255, where she suggests that the covering of the face or head, was a sign of shame; cf. Unnik, 'Unveiled Face', 161–2.

[49] Harris, *2 Cor*, 299; cf. 297, 300. Also, Theobald, *Gnade*, 188, expresses that this preoccupation would lead to 'elitären Bewußtsein'.

[50] Thrall, *2 Cor*, 267 (italics mine).

[51] Collange, *Enigmes*, 100.

[52] See Dunn, *Theology*, 390–412, for a good overview of Paul's important motifs of 'in/with/into/through Christ' and 'Christ in me'.

[53] Although the subject of this turning to the Lord (ἡνίκα δὲ ἐὰν ἐπιστρέψῃ πρὸς κύριον, 3.16) is understood here to be anyone in general, it should be noted that some

understood in terms of Christian conversion – that is, a transformation of identity.[54] In contrast to Moses and the veiled Israelites' inability to see fully God's glory, Paul presents all Christians (ἡμεῖς πάντες)[55] as having unveiled faces (ἀνακεκαλυμμένῳ προσώπῳ) 'in Christ', who now see God's glory and are being transformed into that image (3.18). Significantly, this transformation ἐν Χριστῷ, which is the work of the Spirit, 'marks the decisive difference between the old and new covenant ministries of Moses and Paul'.[56]

In 4.6 Paul further emphasises the internal work of God – which establishes Christian identity – by conveying God as shining in the *hearts* (ἐν ταῖς καρδίαις) of believers to give the light of the knowledge of God's glory on the πρόσωπον of Jesus Christ (ἐν προσώπῳ ['Ιησοῦ][57] Χριστοῦ).[58] Paul's understanding of God's illumination of the believers' hearts can also be seen in Rom 5.5 where 'the love of God has been poured into our hearts (ἐν ταῖς καρδίαις) through the Holy Spirit that has been given to us', and also in Eph 1.18, where the 'eyes of the hearts' are enlightened. In regard to 2 Cor 4.6, Carol Stockhausen writes, 'It is entirely typical of the new covenant which Paul ministers...to be interior, to be in the heart'.[59] Also, in light of the πρόσωπον–καρδία contrast, Harris comments: 'Again, the glory is displayed not outwardly on the face but inwardly in the character'.[60]

---

interpreters have suggested 'heart' (3.15) as the subject (cf. 1 Sam 7.3). See the discussion in Thrall, 'Conversion', 205–8.

[54] Some have recognised the importance of Paul's conversion behind this passage, and that the removal of the veil is similar to Paul's scales falling away from his eyes (Acts 9.18). Also, in questioning why καρδία (2 Cor 3.15) has replaced νοῦς (3.14b), Thrall, 'Conversion', 203, explains that since Paul is talking of conversion he chose the 'most comprehensible term possible, and that for him *is* "heart" rather than "mind"' (italics her).

[55] Curiously, Belleville, *Reflections*, 276, has interpreted 'we all' as 'all true gospel ministers'. See the critique by Hafemann, *Moses*, 407–8 n. 407.

[56] Hafemann, *Moses*, 408. Concerning the relation of Paul and Moses, some (e.g. Jones, *Second Moses*), regard Paul as a 'second Moses', while others (e.g. Bammel, 'Paulus', 408) regard Paul as more than Moses; cf. Savage, *Power*, 110.

[57] On the textual variant, see Metzger, *Textual Commentary*, 510, who explains that the shorter reading Χριστοῦ has considerable support over 'Ιησοῦ Χριστοῦ, and that it is difficult to account for the missing 'Ιησοῦ.

[58] Especially with the plural in 4.6, the experience here is not only for Paul, but a paradigm for all Christians; so Theissen, *Psychological Aspects*, 123; Klauck, 'Erleuchtung', 294; Kim, *Origin*, 6; MacRae, 'Anti-Dualist', 423. Also, Paul's positive use of πρόσωπον here will be evaluated below.

[59] Stockhausen, *Moses' Veil*, 174. Cf. Wright, 'Reflected', 185: that 'Paul is dealing not merely with his own ministry but with the state of heart of his hearers'; Schlier, 'Menschenherz', 191.

[60] Harris, *2 Cor*, 318. Klauck, 'Erleuchtung', 271, recognises a connection between 4.6 and 5.12, and both their details of καρδία and πρόσωπον.

Therefore, Paul, once again, dramatically emphasises the significance of the heart – given that it is the place where God shines the light of his glory – while rejecting the Corinthians' preoccupation with and boasting in outward appearance.

6.2.3 Treasure in Earthen Vessels (4.7–12)

Paul's elaborate depiction of the depreciated exterior elements and the more valuable interior elements shifts from the theme of the new covenant to his present suffering and situation (4.7–15), which is a crucial part of the *apologia* of his apostolic ministry.[61] Although Paul has experienced the glory of God, the Corinthian rivals would have regarded his afflicted body as conspicuously lacking in glory. Ralph Martin comments that in regard to Paul's outward appearance (10.7, 10), 'he is just the opposite of an impressive, commanding, self-sufficient persona'.[62] However, Paul is able to reconcile this apparent paradox by giving prominence to the interior over the exterior. He claims that he has God's glory as an internal treasure (θησαυρός), which is in an earthen vessel (ἐν ὀστρακίνοις σκεύεσιν) (4.7).[63] This treasure is formulated by Paul in a highly condensed statement in 4.6 as the 'illumination of the heart',[64] which is probably referring to 'the ministry of the gospel of the glory of God'.[65]

This text, accordingly, should be read within the framework of Paul's external–internal contrast. Victor Furnish relates the imagery here to 4.16, where the outer man is wasting away, and writes: 'Because he contrasts these *earthen pots* with the *treasure* they contain, it seems clear that he has in mind the great value of the one and the trifling value of the other'.[66] Paul confidently explains that the purpose of his inglorious human condition is so that the surpassing power working in him is clearly seen to be from God and not from himself (4.8). Moreover, he maintains this dichotomy by describing his suffering in several antithetical statements (4.8–10), in which the first element illustrates weakness (outward), but the second accentuates divine power (internal).[67] This list reaches a climax with Paul's statement in 4.10

---

[61] See Lambrecht, 'Nekrōsis', 123; Thrall, *2 Cor*, 321; Martin, *2 Cor*, 84–5, writes that Paul 'quickly turns to the realities of the situation of his missionary labors – there is no nimbus of glory surrounding, the messenger of such a glorious Gospel'.

[62] Martin, *2 Cor*, 86.

[63] This metaphor is commonly used in the Graeco-Roman world for valuable treasures (e.g. coinage) being carried in ordinary containers, which connote cheapness and weakness. See Thrall, *2 Cor*, 322–4; Savage, *Power*, 165–6.

[64] Betz, 'Concept', 331.

[65] Savage, *Power*, 164.

[66] Furnish, *2 Cor*, 278 (italics his). Cf. Barrett, *2 Cor*, 137; Harris, *2 Cor*, 340.

[67] See Thrall, *2 Cor*, 329–31, for an excursus on the thought and significance of these

which further depicts the treasure as the 'dying and life of Jesus', which Paul is always carrying in the body (ἐν τῷ σώματι) (4.10–11). Therefore, in continuity with his denunciation of the preoccupation with the outward displays of identity, Paul detracts the Corinthians' attention from his inglorious outer body (earthen vessel) and shifts it to the glorious treasure that is inside him.

6.2.4 The Inner Person, Not the Outer Person (4.16)

In 4.16 Paul conveys more language that clearly affirms the antithesis of exteriority–interiority: 'Therefore we are not discouraged, even though our outer person (ὁ ἔξω ἄνθρωπος) is wasting away, our inner person (ὁ ἔσω [ἄνθρωπος]) is being renewed day by day'.[68] This text has been important for discussions of Paul's anthropology, especially in debates about whether he has notions of a dualism.[69] Regardless of how one understands Paul's anthropology, his essential point in this verse is clear: 'it is the fact of inward renewal, set over against outward degeneration, that is of importance'.[70] Also, this antithetical statement has implications for Paul's social situation in Corinth. Thrall comments, 'In the context, the ἔξω ἄνθρωπος is Paul's outward persona as it is seen by his Corinthian critics, who simply observe the lack of the superficial splendour they would expect from the agent of a new covenant superior to that of Moses'.[71] Here, Paul is again consistent in his counteraction of the Corinthians' obsession with superficialities of *persona*, whereby he devalues the external dimension of the person and advocates the inner spiritual dimension.[72] Given the πρόσωπον–καρδία antithesis, it is significant that Collange concludes, 'ὁ ἔσω ἄνθρωπος n'est qu'une autre désignation de ce que Paul a appelé jusqu'ici καρδία, lieu de l'œuvre de l'Esprit et de la conformation au Christ'.[73]

---

antitheses; cf. Betz, 'Antagonisms', 557–75. Also, on Paul's catalogues of affliction, see Kleinknecht, *Der leidende*, 242–304; Fitzgerald, *Cracks*; Hodgson, 'Tribulation', 59–80.

[68] Cf. 'the old man' (παλαιὸς ἄνθρωπος) in Rom 6.6.

[69] On the issue of dualism, see Jewett, *Anthropological*, 391–5; Betz, 'Concept', 315–41.

[70] Thrall, *2 Cor*, 351.

[71] Thrall, *2 Cor*, 351. Cf. Jewett, *Anthropological*, 396–9.

[72] See Betz, 'Concept', 329–35, who shows Paul's development of this verse from, at least, 2.14. Also, Furnish, *2 Cor*, 288, intimates that in 4.16–5.5, the overall theme is 'the contrast between what is of preliminary significance only and what is of absolute significance', which is seen in the various contrasts: '*outer/inner*, 4:16; *momentary/eternal*, 4:17; *trifling/abundance*, 4:17; *seen/not seen*, 4:18; *temporary/eternal*, 4:18; *earthly/heavenly*, 5:1–2; *tent-like house/building from God*, 5:1; *destroyed/eternal*, 5:1; *naked/clothed*, 5:2–4; *mortality/life*, 5:4' (italics his).

[73] Collange, *Enigmes*, 175. Cf. Jewett, *Anthropological*, 396–9, who also relates this antithetical statement to the one in 5.12, and remarks that 5.12 gives the clue to understanding the 'inner man'; Martin, *2 Cor*, 92.

6.2.5 Looking at Things Unseen, Not at Things Seen (4.18)

In 4.18 Paul conveys to his readers his application of and response to the knowledge of God's renewal and glorification of the inner person (4.16–17): μὴ σκοπούντων ἡμῶν τὰ βλεπόμενα ἀλλὰ τὰ μὴ βλεπόμενα, τὰ γὰρ βλεπόμενα πρόσκαιρα, τὰ δὲ μὴ βλεπόμενα αἰώνια. Interpreters have rightfully connected the previous details in 2 Corinthians as being included in Paul's contrast between things that are seen with their eyes and things that cannot be seen with their eyes. For instance, after associating Paul's θλῖψις (v. 17) with τὰ βλεπόμενα, Harris remarks:

> Probably also to be included within this category are the earthenware vessel, the dying of Jesus, the body, death on account of Jesus, the mortal flesh, and the outward self. Similarly τὰ μὴ βλεπόμενα probably incorporates God's power, the resurrection and presentation of believers, the inward self, and the eternal weight of glory.[74]

Like 4.16, this text is important for Paul's understanding of his suffering because his gaze was on inward realities that were 'eternal' and not 'temporary'. With this interiority-centred perspective Paul trivialises the preoccupation with evaluating others by sight,[75] which was a characteristic of the Corinthian Christians.[76] Collange, again, rightfully links the language here to Paul's overarching antithesis of external–internal, and more importantly, πρόσωπον–καρδία: 'Cette dernière possibilité s'appuie, bien sûr, sur l'antithèse du v. 16 ("homme intérieur – homme extérieur") et elle aurait l'intérêt de correspondre à la polémique cœur–apparence, si importante pour notre épître'.[77]

6.2.6 Living by Faith, Not by Outward Appearance (5.7)

In 5.1–10 Paul changes imageries again and transitions to a discussion of life after death, which is still within the framework of exteriority–interiority. Since the γάρ in 5.1 is looking back to 4.18, the earthly tent (οἰκία τοῦ σκήνους) should be identified as one of τὰ βλεπόμενα that is transient, and the future building from God (οἰκοδομὴν ἐκ θεοῦ) as one of τὰ μὴ βλεπόμενα that is eternal.[78] That is, Paul places less confidence in the body

---

[74] Harris, *2 Cor*, 365; cf. Barrett, *2 Cor*, 148.

[75] Cf. Thrall, *2 Cor*, 356, who comments that as in the case of ὁ ἔξω ἄνθρωπος of 4.16, 'This terminology [eternal and invisible] may be used to suggest the relative insignificance of outward phenomena in general'.

[76] Savage, *Power*, 184, who expresses that given the high incidence in 2.14–4.18 of words that have visual connotations, Paul doubtlessly chose them 'for their usefulness in correcting the display-conscious perspective of the Corinthian church'.

[77] Collange, *Enigmes*, 179. Cf. Gräßer, *2 Kor*, 179.

[78] Cf. Harris, *2 Cor*, 369; Martin, *2 Cor*, 102; Barrett, *2 Cor*, 150. Also, Furnish, *2 Cor*, 293, comments that the earthly dwelling is to be identified with the 'outer person' (4.16).

that he presently indwells and is 'clothed with', because it is in fact temporary; instead, he is confident of a future heavenly and eternal dwelling, with which he will be clothed (cf. σῶμα πνευματικόν, 1 Cor 15.44). Then in 2 Cor 5.7, Paul reverts again to his exterior–interior antithesis to explain his confidence: διὰ πίστεως γὰρ περιπατοῦμεν, οὐ διὰ εἴδους. As noted by many scholars, εἶδος should be translated here in the sense of 'visible form' or 'outward appearance', rather than 'sight'.[79] With this meaning, 'Paul may be responding to those who questioned his apostolic vocation because their attention was directed towards his own εἴδους, i.e., his outward appearance, and was not guided by faith'.[80] In addition, Paul stresses the seriousness of following this lifestyle of living διὰ πίστεως, by asserting that Christ will judge all Christians according to their earthly activities (5.10; cf. 1 Cor 4.5: 'God will reveal the purposes of the *heart*'). This understanding of 5.1–10, then, is consistent with Paul's deprecation of superficial social identity.

6.2.7 Boasting in the Heart (Καρδία), Not in Πρόσωπον (5.12)

This exploration of how Paul denounces the preoccupation with the external dimension of the person and promotes the internal dimension of the person now returns to 5.12. This verse explicitly communicates the antithesis of πρόσωπον–καρδία, which describes those who superficially boast ἐν προσώπῳ and not ἐν καρδίᾳ. The survey of Paul's *apologia* from 2.14, thus far, has demonstrated that for Paul the artificial matters of a person's identity are of little value, while the matters of the καρδία are of far greater worth. Although Paul uses different antithetical language to articulate the contrast of exteriority–interiority, there have been instances of πρόσωπον seen in the text up to this point (3.7, 13, 18; 4.6) that seem to play some part in his πρόσωπον–καρδία contrast. In 5.12 Paul continues the negative connotation of πρόσωπον by asserting the inappropriateness of boasting in such superficialities. Moreover, Paul significantly uses numerous words and phrases that have visual connotations – such as the vivid term πρόσωπον, which was used for Moses' face that temporarily displayed God's glory.[81] Due to Paul's concentrated usage of πρόσωπον in 3.7–5.12, Collange recognises

---

[79] See e.g. Thrall, *2 Cor*, 387–8; Furnish, *2 Cor*, 273; Collange, *Enigmes*, 232.

[80] Thrall, *2 Cor*, 388. Cf. Furnish, *2 Cor*, 302, and Harris, *2 Cor*, 397 n. 179, who both recognise 5.7 as depicting the Corinthians' criticisms of Paul as in 4.18. Also, Martin, *2 Cor*, 111, observes a connection between 5.7 and 5.12.

[81] Savage, *Power*, 184. Cf. Theobald, *Gnade*, 184, who points out that the gazing at Moses' πρόσωπον is associated with 'der Kategorie des *Visuellen*'; Thrall, *2 Cor*, 405, who associates the opponents' boasting ἐν προσώπῳ here as relating to a boasting in the glorified πρόσωπον of Moses in 2 Cor 3; Keener, *1–2 Cor*, 183, that 'it might be more than coincidence that Paul's term for "outward appearance," *prosōpon*, is "face", and Paul has just been contrasting the mere glory on Moses' face with the new covenant glory on the heart'.

the significance of the term, and even perceives that Paul's use of term culminates here in 5.12.[82]

This antithetical statement is significant in the context of Paul's *apologia*, since he returns to the theme of his ministry by conveying that he is open to God's scrutiny (5.11). In order to be transparent before God and others, Paul places his confidence in the heart, because to God 'superficial appearances count for nothing, the state of the heart is everything'.[83] This is consistent with the possible echo of 1 Sam 16.7 in 2 Cor 5.12, where God does not assess individuals as humans do, ὅτι ἄνθρωπος ὄψεται εἰς πρόσωπον ὁ δὲ θεὸς ὄψεται εἰς καρδίαν (cf. Gal 2.6: πρόσωπον [ὁ] θεὸς ἀνθρώπου οὐ λαμβάνει). Accordingly, in 2 Cor 5.12, Paul brings up again the important theme of commendation (συνίστημι) as seen in 3.1.[84] It is crucial to bear in mind that Paul in 5.12 is negatively characterising his Corinthian critics, for he 'is writing to a congregation which is being tempted to think that only externals are important for estimating a person's authority'.[85] They were evaluating his visible credentials, which Paul lacked (cf. 10.10). Thrall expresses that the problem was with the surface features of Paul's *persona*, because his own supporters in Corinth 'would have wished to be able to point to his outward religious *persona*...He would then be telling them, by implication, that this was the wrong thing to look for'.[86] Jewett fittingly explains Paul's antithetical point: 'They rest their case on the visibly transfigured face and Paul rests his on the invisibly transfigured heart'.[87]

Therefore, through his πρόσωπον–καρδία antithesis, Paul corrects his Corinthian critics' habit of boasting in superficial displays. He gives his Corinthian supporters a reason to boast of him in order to defend the glory of his ministry, which is ultimately the work of the Spirit in his and the Corinthians' hearts. Interestingly, the significance of the heart could have prompted him to express later that his heart is 'wide open' (6.11), which

---

[82] Collange, *Enigmes*, 74–5.

[83] Harris, *2 Cor*, 416; cf. Thrall, *2 Cor*, 400; Lang, *Kor*, 294: 'Was im Herzen ist, bleibt den Menschen verborgen, es ist aber entscheidend vor Gott, der ins Verborgene sieht. Die Gegner stützen ihr Ansehen offenbar auf Vorgänge, die ins Auge fallen'.

[84] Cf. Gräßer, *2 Kor*, 209, who notes the 'fast wörtliche Wiederholung' of 3.1 here; Furnish, *2 Cor*, 324, who relates this portrayal of the opponents to those soliciting and presenting letters of recommendation (3.1) and those peddling the word of God (2.17); Thrall, *2 Cor*, 405.

[85] Furnish, *2 Cor*, 324. Also, Jewett, *Anthropological*, 329, expresses that Paul's use of καρδία here 'is substantial and polemical'.

[86] Thrall, *2 Cor*, 407.

[87] Jewett, *Anthropological*, 329. He also writes that 'the polemic in II Cor. 5:12 is a repetition of the argument in II Cor 4:16ff. which implied that the invading missionaries were resting their case on the doubtful grounds of the "outer man" which cannot be anything but corrupt and mortal' (330).

would invite the Corinthians 'to look beyond his appearance and into his heart' because, 'Only then will they see him for who he truly is'.[88]

6.2.8 Κατὰ Πνεῦμα and Καινὴ Κτίσις, Not Κατὰ Σάρκα (5.16–17)

Finally, Paul's rejection of the superficial values of outward appearance is also seen in 5.16, where he states, 'From now on we regard nobody from a worldly perspective (κατὰ σάρκα), even though we once knew Christ from a worldly perspective (κατὰ σάρκα), we know him no longer in that way'. Paul's use of κατὰ σάρκα here probably refers to the shallow assessment of an individual's worth based on status symbols, such as wealth, status, and religious reputation.[89] Moreover, several interpreters have recognised the association of κατὰ σάρκα with the boasting ἐν προσώπῳ in 5.12.[90] Furnish, for instance, writes, 'It seems clear that Paul has been prompted to the statement in v. 16*a* by the fact that his readers are being tempted to judge him and his rivals *according to worldly standards* – that is, by *what is outward* rather than by *what is within* (v. 12*b*)'.[91]

Paul's statement of formerly knowing Christ κατὰ σάρκα is curious. One way of interpreting this difficult phrase is to regard it as an argument of an 'extreme case' – that is, since it is inappropriate to view Christ κατὰ σάρκα, then how much more would it be to view others in the same manner.[92] Also, given Paul's strong emphasis on the Spirit, especially the Spirit's work in the hearts of believers, scholars have viewed that Paul's contrast of living κατὰ σάρκα and κατὰ πνεῦμα (cf. Rom 8.4–5) is implicit here.[93] This text, then, discourages the inappropriate 'assessment of human beings on the human or worldly preoccupation with externals',[94] and instead encourages the need to live κατὰ πνεῦμα.

In the following verse Paul consequently presents his 'new creation' motif (2 Cor 5.17), which is significant since he uses it to highlight the Spirit's glorious work in the inner person.[95] Moyer Hubbard aptly remarks:

---

[88] Fitzgerald, *Cracks*, 201. Cf. 6.13 where they are exhorted also to be wide open.

[89] See Thrall, *2 Cor*, 412–14, who translates it adverbially: 'it is a matter of evaluating others by means of purely human criteria, worldly standards, and the like' (412).

[90] E.g. Gräßer, *2 Kor*, 218–19; Harris, *2 Cor*, 427; Thrall, *2 Cor*, 414.

[91] Furnish, *2 Cor*, 330 (italics his).

[92] Cf. Furnish, *2 Cor*, 330: 'His concern is to emphasize that for the Christian *no worldly standards* have any proper role in the evaluation of other persons (v. 16*a*), since they certainly play no role in one's evaluation of Christ (v. 16*b*)' (italics his); Thrall, *2 Cor*, 419; Harris, *2 Cor*, 428.

[93] For understanding κατὰ πνεῦμα in 5.16, see e.g. Plummer, *2 Cor*, 176; Collange, *Enigmes*, 259; Young & Ford, *Meaning*, 181; Wolff, *2 Kor*, 127–8.

[94] Harris, *2 Cor*, 429.

[95] See Hubbard, *New Creation*, esp. 133–87, for a thorough study of this motif, which he

...it is quite reasonable to suggest that Paul's κατὰ σάρκα–καινὴ κτίσις antithesis[96] should be added to that long list of internal–external antitheses noted earlier and seen as a further elaboration of Paul's New Covenant retrospective. As such, καινὴ κτίσις relates to the internal work of the Spirit and should be closely associated with the 'making anew of the inner person' (4.16).[97]

Furthermore, Paul emphasises the 'newness' of this new creation 'in Christ', by declaring that the 'old things have passed away, behold, the new has come' (5.17b). Accordingly, within the immediate context the 'old things' would be: boasting ἐν προσώπῳ (5.12), living for one's self (5.14–15), and regarding others κατὰ σάρκα (5.16).[98]

6.2.9 Summary

Paul's *apologia* of his ministry in the literary unit of 2.14–7.4 has been examined to show how Paul uses this theologically rich text to form a particular argument in light of his social situation and environment. Throughout this text Paul presents and maintains a consistent contrast between exteriority and interiority, which constructs his reaction to a particular social problem that is affecting the Corinthian church – a preoccupation with the artificial matters of identity. Paul's liberal use of language that has visual connotations, and more specifically, his recurrent use of πρόσωπον in 2 Corinthians, are 'indicative of Paul's concern with the superficial perspective of the Corinthians'.[99] The Corinthians' superficial perspective resulted in their superficial evaluation of Paul's identity as an apostle, which lacks the expected glory and splendour. Paul reacts to this conflict by diminishing the value of the exterior features of identity and placing all weight on the interior features of identity, the latter being the more authentic and genuine aspect of the person. It is significant that the details provided in this reaction show similarities to the conventional preoccupation with the superficial aspects of *persona* in Corinth.

---

understands to have an anthropological sense. He also associates the motif with the language of interior transformation in 3.18 and 4.4 (pp. 178, 182–3). Also cf. Stockhausen, *Moses' Veil*, 175, who expresses that the texts of 3.18; 4.16, 18; 5.12, 17 all 'bear witness to the interiority of the transformation of the Christian'.

[96] Hubbard, *New Creation*, 183–5, argues that the antithesis of κατὰ σάρκα (5.16) is actually καινὴ κτίσις, and not κατὰ πνεῦμα. However, it is better to regard Hubbard's pneumatological interpretation of καινὴ κτίσις as having the same antithetical force as κατὰ πνεῦμα, since the Spirit is strongly associated with the new creation motif.

[97] Hubbard, *New Creation*, 185. See his p. 152, for a list of Paul's antithetical statements in 2 Cor 2.14–5.21.

[98] Cf. Hubbard, *New Creation*, 183.

[99] Savage, *Power*, 184 n. 111. He also writes that they are 'words which doubtless were chosen for their usefulness in correcting the display-conscious perspective of the Corinthian church'.

In his castigation of the Corinthians' preoccupation with superficialities, Paul uses various antithetical language that reaches a climax with the antithetical rubric of πρόσωπον–καρδία, which depicts individuals boasting ἐν προσώπῳ and not ἐν καρδίᾳ (5.12). He rejects the obsession with features associated with the superficialities of πρόσωπον, such as: letters of recommendation (3.1); stone tablets written in ink (3.3); Moses' πρόσωπον (3.7, 13); Moses' veil (3.12–18); the earthen vessel (4.7); the outer man (4.16); the things seen (4.18); an earthly dwelling tent (5.1); living by appearance (εἴδους) (5.7); and regarding others κατὰ σάρκα (5.16). Conversely, he promotes the elements associated with the authentic and inward spiritual dimension of a Christian's identity (καρδία): letters written on hearts (3.2); tablets of human hearts written with the Spirit (3.3); the transformation into the image of Christ (3.18, 4.4); God's glory shining in hearts (4.6); the internal treasure (4.7); the inner man (4.16); the things unseen (4.18); living by faith (5.7); regarding others κατὰ πνεῦμα (5.16); and the new creation in Christ (5.17). Savage aptly remarks on Paul's language: 'By filling these terms with new meaning Paul hopes to teach his converts that the correct outlook, the perspective of faith, does not fix its gaze on what can be seen, the counterfeit glory of outward displays, but on what cannot be seen, the authentic glory of the heart'.[100]

Remarkably, Paul seems to disparage not only the exterior side of the person, but even the interior, if there is no work of the Spirit in it (3.14–15). For Paul it is not merely the heart that matters, but what kind of heart – one that is unveiled 'in Christ'. This understanding is consistent with the anthropological understanding of the heart, as conveyed by Jewett: 'A characteristic of the heart as the center of man is its inherent openness to outside impulses, its directionality, its propensity to give itself to a master and to live towards some desired goal'.[101] The reason for the heart being so paramount to Paul is that God has enlightened it with the light of his glory (4.6; cf. Rom 5.5). Jewett aptly writes, 'Although the heart is the place where man encounters God in obedience or disobedience, passages like II Cor. 4:6 and Rom. 5:5 show that it is not inherently connected or open to God, but instead is the center of the person where God chooses to reveal himself'.[102] Paul's life-giving gospel, then, involves 'la rénovation des cœurs', which Collange describes as 'une rénovation totale et radicale de l'homme'.[103] Accordingly, this inward spiritual transformation should be perceived as part of Paul's understanding of Christian identity.

---

[100] Savage, *Power*, 184. He also writes, 'They fail to see the splendour of the new life irrupting in the hearts of those formerly engulfed in darkness' (185).

[101] Jewett, *Anthropological*, 313.

[102] Jewett, *Anthropological*, 310.

[103] Collange, *Enigmes*, 66.

Finally, given the similarities of the details throughout 2 Cor 2.14–7.4 and the details of the concept of *persona* in Roman Corinth, it is probable that Paul is rejecting a conventional and habitual preoccupation with the shallow features of *persona* in the Corinthian church. Moreover, he is perceived to be inculcating, instead, a preoccupation with the internal work of the Spirit in the hearts of the Corinthian believers – a work that occurs 'in Christ' and can be perceived as marking a Christian's identity.[104]

6.3 The External Aspect of Christian Identity

The above section had focused on Paul's critique of the Corinthians' preoccupation with superficialities and outward appearance, whereby Paul diminished the value of surface features and emphasised the internal spiritual features. There are, however, some texts where Paul seems to be neutral or even positive about particular external elements – for instance, the Christian's transformation (μεταμορφόω) into an 'image' (εἰκών) (3.18), which is identified to be Christ, the εἰκὼν τοῦ θεοῦ (4.4). Interpreters have generally understood this transformation to be presently an internal one, and a physical one that occurs at Christ's *parousia*. Paul Barnett, for example, states, 'Our transformation is nothing else than a transformation into the moral and spiritual likeness of the now glorified Christ'.[105] David Garland similarly comments, 'Paul chose his words carefully ["the same image"] because he knew that it is not our physical appearance that is being changed but our inner being!'[106]

Despite the confidence of only an inward transformation by many scholars, Thrall questions whether this transformation is more than 'a purely inward transformation'.[107] Since Paul had articulated the inferiority of Moses' ministry, which was symbolised by the visible glory on Moses' face, she wonders whether Paul considers his more superior ministry as being symbolised also by a visible glory. She ponders, 'In the Christian order, there must be some "visible" equivalent as regards the medium through which

---

[104] Cf. Harris, *2 Cor*, 424, who argues that one of Paul's motives for Christian service is 'his preoccupation with God's glory and his converts' well being'. It is also striking that throughout the text the source of the glorious work in the lives of believers is identified to be from God, and more specifically ἐν Χριστῷ (2.17; 3.14; 5.17, 19). Beyond the ἐν Χριστῷ motif, see e.g. 2.14; 3.3–4, 5, 16–17, 18; 4.1, 2, 6, 7, 11–12, 14; 5.1, 5, 11, 14, 19–20; 6.4, 16.

[105] Barnett, *2 Cor*, 208.

[106] Garland, *2 Cor*, 200. Also cf. Murphy-O'Connor, *Theology*, 40: 'Paul did not intend to speak of physical transformation of believers'.

[107] See Thrall, *2 Cor*, 284–5. Also, idem, 'Conversion', 230, suspects that there must be a sense of visuality even though 'not in the same immediately obvious way'.

Christ's reflection of God's glory is perceived: Christ must become in some way visible'.[108] Another example that suggests a positive visuality is Paul's assertion that the Corinthians themselves are a 'letter of Christ' that is written on hearts to be 'known and read by all' (γινωσκομένη καὶ ἀναγινωσκομένη ὑπὸ πάντων ἀνθρώπων) (3.2–3; cf. 1 Thes 1.18). Since Paul expects the Corinthians to be known and read by all, Jerome Murphy-O'Connor remarks that 'καρδία cannot mean the interior dispositions of the Corinthians', but some sort of distinctive behaviour that is visibly displayed.[109]

In light of these inciting examples that suggest a visible aspect of the transformation, this section will explore this transformed image as part of Paul's conception of Christian identity and *persona*. This study suggests that Paul advocates this 'transformed' identity as the image which the Corinthian believers should visibly project, and that this image would be in contrast to the conventionally presented *persona* at the time. It is interesting that Paul's conception of this authentic outward dimension of Christian identity consists of some surface elements that Paul, as seen above, had denounced of their conventional value (e.g. the earthen vessel, 4.7). Paul, then, is not simply criticising the outer person and emphasising the inner person, but he is criticising outward appearance that reflects superficial values and commending, instead, outward appearance that is based on and reflects the spiritual transformation taking place in the inner person.

6.3.1 Transformation into the Image and Person of Christ (3.18–4.6)

Since this study is interested in the details of transformation, image, and the phrase ἐν προσώπῳ Χριστοῦ – a phrase that is often overlooked – the starting point of this enquiry will be the three interrelated texts of 2 Cor 3.18, 4.4, 4.6.[110] By 3.18, Paul had already elucidated that the glory of the old covenant which was visually observed on Moses' face was inferior to the surpassing glory of the new covenant (3.7, 13). In 3.18 Paul explains that by the work of the Spirit all Christians with an unveiled face, in contrast to the veiled Moses and Israelites, are beholding as in a mirror the glory of the Lord

---

[108] Thrall, *2 Cor*, 284.

[109] Murphy-O'Connor, 'Ministry', 124; though he does not recognise a physical transformation (as noted above), it is unclear how he perceives this visual display. See also Furnish, *2 Cor*, 194, who comments that 'it is unnecessary to worry about how a letter written on someone's heart, the most interior and secret dimension of one's being..., can at the same time be *known and read by everyone*' (italics his). Nevertheless, both of their comments do raise the need to understand this visual dimension.

[110] Cf. Collange, *Enigmes*, 141, for 'le triple parallélisme' of 3.18; 4.4; 4.6; Barnett, *2 Cor*, 205, who lists some common features found in all three verses; Lambrecht, *2 Cor*, 65–6; Hubbard, *New Creation*, 158.

(τὴν δόξαν κυρίου κατοπτριζόμενοι)[111] and are being transformed into the same image (τὴν αὐτὴν εἰκόνα μεταμορφούμεθα) progressively from one degree of glory to another (ἀπὸ δόξης εἰς δόξαν).[112]

6.3.1.1 A Visible Transformation (Μεταμορφόω)

It is crucial to analyse briefly the motif of transformation (μεταμορφόω) that is explicitly used in the text.[113] The verb μεταμορφόω is only used elsewhere by Paul in Rom 12.2, where he exhorts the Roman Christians to be transformed by the renewing of their minds (μεταμορφοῦσθε τῇ ἀνακαινώσει τοῦ νοός). With the detail of renewal here, it is worth considering Col 3.9–10 which is about removing the old man (παλαιὸν ἄνθρωπον) and being clothed in the new man (νέον [ἄνθρωπον]), the latter of which is being renewed (ἀνακαινούμενον) according to the 'image' of God (κατ' εἰκόνα τοῦ κτίσαντος αὐτόν). Although these two texts intimate an inward transformation and renewal, scholars have noted that the transformation and renewal cannot only be inward. Thrall, for instance, expresses that 'Paul's line of argument would be enfeebled if this were all', since there 'must be a "visible" element'.[114] This visible element can be grasped in Paul's use of imagery of clothing in Col 3.9–10.

Further support for comprehending μεταμορφόω as having a sense of visuality is evinced by the other two instances of μεταμορφόω in the New Testament – the parallel account of Jesus' transfiguration of his visible glory

---

[111] A debatable point is whether to translate κατοπτριζόμενοι as 'reflecting as a mirror' or 'beholding as in a mirror'. For those supporting the former view, see Belleville, Reflections, 278–82; Dupont, 'Le chrétien', 400; Unnik, 'Unveiled Face', 167; Allo, 2 Cor, 96–7; Héring, 2 Cor, 25–7; Carrez, 2 Cor, 101–2. For those supporting the latter view, which is taken here, see Hugedé, Le métaphore; Savage, Power, 146; Lietzmann, 1–2 Kor, 112–13; Collange, Enigmes, 116–18; Wolff, 2 Kor, 77–9. Within the context, it seems that Paul is probably using the latter sense, because it would have a parallel use with the verb ἀτενίζω (2 Cor 3.7, 13); cf. 1 Clem 36.2. This is also consistent with the sight of those with 'unveiled faces' (3.18), and also the blinding of unbelievers to see God's glory (4.4). Interestingly, 1 Cor 13.12 has the idea of 'looking (βλέπομεν) in a mirror' with the term πρόσωπον, which could have some bearing on beholding the πρόσωπον of Christ (3.18; 4.6). See also Weissenrieder, 'Blick', 313–43, for a recent study of viewing an 'image' on a mirror in antiquity, and the viewer's participation with the mirrored image, which results in the viewer's transformation.

[112] For the progressive sense of ἀπὸ δόξης εἰς δόξαν, see Allo, 2 Cor, 96; Barrett, 2 Cor, 125; Thrall, 'Conversion', 230–1; Harris, 2 Cor, 316–17.

[113] For more on this motif, see Koenig, 'Transformation'. It is worth pointing out that scholars have been interested in these texts for Paul's language that possibly reflects the language of religious conversion, mysticism, or apocalypticism (cf. 2 Cor 3.17–18, 4.4–6, 12.1–4). For more on Paul's mysticism, see the overview by Dunn, Theology, 390–6.

[114] Thrall, 2 Cor, 285.

in the presence of some of his disciples on a high mountain (Matt 17.2; Mark 9.2). Stephen Barton has investigated both of these transfiguration accounts and has shown that besides the obvious primary emphasis on the christology of the transfiguration, Matthew's transfiguration 'has an implicit theological anthropology at its heart', that is, 'the transfiguration is an event for the disciples as well as for Jesus'.[115] Since Christ's transfiguration was visible, it raises the possibility that the disciples' participation in the transfiguration would also be visible. It is also interesting that both Matthew (Matt 17.1–8) and Paul (2 Cor 3–4) are interested in showing Christ as greater than Moses,[116] which is very significant since Paul makes a sharp contrast between the *visible* transfigurations of Moses and Christ, as seen on their πρόσωπον (3.7, 13; 4.6).[117] While it is only plausible that Paul was aware of and used this Jesus tradition, it is quite clear that Paul uses the term μεταμορφόω in a similar fashion to convey the Christians' visible transformation into the glorious image of Christ.[118] Collange has also recognised this similarity with Matt 17.2 and explains Paul's use of μεταμορφόω:

Le verbe 'transformer' devrait donc être compris ici comme l'application aux disciples du Christ de la transfiguration de ce dernier, c'est-à-dire comme une expression de ce qui unit les disciples au Christ et characterise leur 'Nachfolge'. Cette transformation n'a donc pas qu'un aspect intérieur de renouvellement, mais aussi un *aspect extérieur* de conformation aux souffrances du Christ.[119]

6.3.1.2 Christ, the Εἰκών of God

Another striking detail in 3.18 is the phrase τὴν αὐτὴν εἰκόνα, which is the goal of the transformation.[120] From the context one would have expected Paul to use the phrase τὴν αὐτὴν δόξαν, which suggests that the phrase τὴν αὐτὴν εἰκόνα refers to the glory of God.[121] This glorious εἰκών is later explained in

---

[115] Barton, 'Transfiguration', 231–46, quotations are from pp. 244, 245, respectively. In his conclusion, Barton cites 2 Cor 3.18 for support of his argument (246).

[116] See Barton, 'Transfiguration', 240–1, for Matthew's redaction of Mark's account, which accentuates his 'greater-than-Moses' theme.

[117] Cf. Lambrecht, 'Transformation', 251. See Fossum, 'Metamorphosis', 71–94, for similarities of Jesus' ascent on a high mountain to Moses' ascent on Mount Sinai.

[118] Cf. Hafemann, *Moses*, 418 n. 261.

[119] Collange, *Enigmes*, 119–20 (emphasis mine). The conformation to the suffering of Christ will be discussed below.

[120] Cf. Klauck, 'Erleuchtung', 271; Belleville, *Reflections*, 289. Also, cf. Col. 3.9–10, where the goal of the renewal is the image of the Creator (κατ' εἰκόνα τοῦ κτίσαντος αὐτόν).

[121] So Savage, *Power*, 147; Lambrecht, 'Transformation', 244–6; Garland, *2 Cor*, 200; cf. Dupont, 'Le chrétien', 404; Hugedé, *Le métaphore*, 28; Feuillet, *Le Christ*, 145. For Paul's linking of εἰκών and δόξα, which suggests a synonymity, see Rom 1.23; 8.29–30; 1 Cor 11.7; 2 Cor 3.18; 4.4; Larsson, *Vorbild*, 185. It should also be noted that some have

4.4 to be Christ, who is the εἰκὼν τοῦ θεοῦ. It is this concept of Christ as the εἰκὼν τοῦ θεοῦ that is critical for understanding the nature of this transformation.[122]

On the significance of Paul's εἰκών language in 2 Cor 3.18–4.6, Seyoon Kim in *The Origin of Paul's Gospel* has convincingly argued that Paul's conception of Christ as the εἰκὼν τοῦ θεοῦ originated from his conversion experience following the Damascus Christophany and that this conception holds the central place in Paul's christology.[123] Kim claims, 'When that δόξα of God shone in the face of Christ, Christ appeared to Paul as the εἰκών of God'.[124] Paul's conversion experience, then, can be understood as both an internal and external experience, and his εἰκών language here accentuates the external aspect.[125] Concerning the term εἰκών itself, it is important to bear in mind that it 'implies neither imperfection or inferior quality as of a copy over against its prototype, nor *perfect* representation' and rather it 'is primarily a functional term for manifestation, representation and revelation, although sometimes it carries an implication of substantial participation in the original or prototype'.[126] In a later work, Kim provides a succinct summary of Paul's weighty use of the synonymous terms εἰκών and μορφή:[127]

in the New Testament only Paul uses the terms εἰκών and μορφή, and he uses them abundantly to designate Christ as the εἰκών or μορφή of God (2 Cor 4:4; Col 1:15; Phil 2:6), to refer to the εἰκών of Christ (Rom 8:29; 1 Cor 15:49; 2 Cor 3:18), and to speak of our being 'conformed' (συμμορφοῦσθαι) to or 'transformed' (μεταμορφοῦσθαι) into the εἰκών of Christ (Rom 8:29; 1 Cor 15:49; 2 Cor 3:18; Phil 3:21; cf. also 1 Cor 15:52; Gal 4:19; Phil 3:10; Col 3:9–10; Eph 4:24; Rom 12:2).[128]

---

understood the phrase τὴν αὐτήν as referring to 'group sameness'. So Belleville, *Reflections*, 290–1; Wright, 'Reflected', 188: 'Christians are changed into the same image as each other'.

[122] Cf. Rom 8.29–30; 1 Cor 15.49, where transformation/conformation is also associated with glory.

[123] See Kim, *Origin*, 137–268, for his treatment of this christological conception. He regards 2 Cor 3.1–4.6 as 'the most convincing evidence' for Paul's εἰκών motif being rooted in the Damascus Christophany (229). See 159–62, for his critique of the various suggestions for the origins of this concept, such as Paul's Adam-christology (see below) and Wisdom-christology (cf. Wisdom 7.26).

[124] Kim, *Origin*, 230.

[125] It is generally acknowledged that Luke's depiction of Paul's conversion in Acts chs. 9, 22, 26 places more emphasis on the external phenomena, while Paul in 2 Cor 3.18–4.6 is more concerned about the internal (see e.g. Harris, *2 Cor*, 336–7); however, Paul does intimate the external implications of his language here. Cf. Thrall, *2 Cor*, 317, who comments that Paul is referring 'not *only* to a purely interior experience of enlightenment even here'.

[126] Kim, *Origin*, 195 (italics his); cf. Kleinknecht, 'εἰκών', 389.

[127] For those who regard the terms as more or less synonymous, see e.g. Kim, *Origin*, 195–8; Eltester, *Eikon*, 133; Jervell, *Imago*, 204ff; Feuillet, *Le Christ*, 344ff. For more on μορφή, see Behm, 'μορφή'.

[128] Kim, *Second Thoughts*, 165–6. Lambrecht, 'Transformation', 244, explains that Paul

What is important from Kim's analysis of the two similar terms is that both do express a clear sense of visual appearance and external form, which suggests that Paul's understanding of Christ as the εἰκὼν τοῦ θεοῦ was a visible one. Kim espouses this argument by pointing out that the source of Paul's εἰκών-christology is found in the epiphanies and visions in the Old Testament and Judaism – most prominently in the chariot-throne theophany in Ezekiel 1 where God appears like a human being.[129] Paul, accordingly, uses this language to express similarly how in the Damascus Christophany he perceived Christ to be the visual image of the invisible God, an image which Christians are now beholding.[130]

Paul's significant communication of a transformation into the 'εἰκὼν of Christ' (4.4)[131] is further developed in the anticipated text of 4.6: 'For it is God who said, "Let light shine out of darkness," who has shone in our hearts to give the light of the knowledge of the glory of God in the "face" (πρόσωπον) of Christ'. The language Paul uses here is reminiscent of the Genesis creation account of humans being made in the εἰκών of God (Gen 1.26–8; 5.1–3; 9.6), which has bearing on the transformation in the εἰκὼν τοῦ θεοῦ in 2 Cor 3.18–4.6.[132] With Paul's experience of Christ as the visible εἰκών of God, Paul accordingly identifies Christ as that εἰκών of God in Genesis. Paul's Adam-christology explains that with humanity's image of God being lost through humanity's sin, Christ's designation as the genuine divine image, the Last Adam (1 Cor 15.42–9), has brought about restoration to humanity's image of God. In other words, Christ as the εἰκὼν τοῦ θεοῦ is also 'the Last Adam, who has recovered the divine image so that we may be transformed into his image (2Cor 3.18) and become a new creature (2Cor 4.6)'.[133] Consequently, this transformation of humanity into the image of Christ can be perceived as a mark of Christian identity.

---

uses the term both in a christological and anthropological sense. For a more thorough treatment of the term, see Larsson, *Vorbild*, 111–323; Kim, *Origin*, 195–205. Also note that in the gospels the term εἰκών only occurs in the synoptic parallel account of the εἰκών on the coin as a visible depiction of the emperor (Matt 22.20; Mk 12.16; Lk 20.24).

[129] Kim, *Origin*, 205–23.

[130] See Lambrecht, 'Transformation', 249, that Christians are beholding Christ as both 'mirror and image'.

[131] Although 'εἰκὼν of Christ' is not explicitly stated, this conceptual understanding is implied since the transformation is into an εἰκών, which is Christ, the εἰκὼν τοῦ θεοῦ.

[132] See Schüle, 'Image' 1–20, for a recent treatment of Gen 1–9 that examines humanity as the 'image of God' and representation of the presence of God on earth. Also, note the possible OT allusion to Gen 1.3 and/or Isa 9.1 (LXX). See Stockhausen, *Moses' Veil*, 162; Klauck, 'Erleuchtung', 289.

[133] Kim, *Origin*, 267. See Watson, 'Image', 277–304, who, in light of the Genesis creation account, considers Jesus and humans as 'in the image of God', and suggests that 'we learn from Jesus what it is to be human' (283).

C. Kavin Rowe has underscored the anthropological sense of Christ as the εἰκών of God (2 Cor 4.4): 'The shape, then, of God's image is in a very definite sense anthropological. That is to say, for Paul, Christ is always an ἄνθρωπος (cf. esp. Rom 5:15f.; Phil 2:7f.), and thus God's εἰκών is an image of a human...The εἰκών is the person [the Lord Jesus Christ] himself'.[134] It is also worth considering Col 1.15 where Christ is the image of the invisible God (εἰκών τοῦ θεοῦ τοῦ ἀοράτου; cf. 2.9). Christopher Rowland interprets Col 1.15 in light of Ezek 1.26:

Christ is then the image – even the features – of a God who cannot be seen. The stress on invisibility lends credence to the supposition that Christ is not simply to be regarded in general terms as the locus of revelation but the form or the features of God. He is the physical embodiment of divinity, who, unlike God himself, was visible.[135]

Rowe has also provided an insight into Col 1.15 that is helpful for understanding Paul's transformation motif in 2 Cor 3.18: 'Rather than a representation of the invisible God, Christ is the movement of the invisible God into visibility in the life of a human being, ἐν τῷ σώματι τῆς σαρκός (1:22)'.[136] Therefore, based on Paul's intentional disclosure of Christ – the visible εἰκών τοῦ θεοῦ – as the object of the transformation, this transformation not only has an internal dimension, but also an external one.[137] Thomas Stegman aptly states, 'Thus, the logic of 3:18 appears to depend on Paul's referring to *a present, ongoing transformation of human existence, a transformation that reflects more and more the prototype of humanity embodied by Jesus*, the εἰκών τοῦ θεοῦ'.[138]

6.3.1.3 Πρόσωπον of Christ

As with the case of Paul's unexpected use of εἰκών instead of δόξα in 3.18, in 4.6 it is also unexpected that Paul would use the term πρόσωπον instead of εἰκών (4.4) or δόξα (3.18). Stegman expresses that remarkably in 4.6, 'the apostle (literally!) puts a face onto the "glory" about which he has been writing about since 3:7 – namely the face of Jesus'.[139] Given this notable use of πρόσωπον, it is crucial to ascertain the meaning of the phrase ἐν προσώπῳ Χριστοῦ in 4.6. In addition to the interrelationship of 3.18, 4.4,

---

[134] Rowe, 'Iconography', 300.
[135] Rowland, 'Influence', 291f, as quoted in Kim, *Origin*, 226. Also, Jervell, *Imago*, 223, correlates 2.9 to the εἰκών concept in 1.15.
[136] Rowe, 'Iconography', 301–2.
[137] Cf. Lambrecht, 'Transformation', 253.
[138] Stegman, *Character*, 239 (italics his).
[139] Stegman, *Character*, 235.

and 4.6, it is significant that interpreters have noted the striking parallel between 4.4 and 4.6, which can be seen in their juxtaposition:[140]

4.4	4.6
ὁ θεός τοῦ αἰῶνος τούτου	ὁ θεός ὁ εἰπών· ἐκ σκότους φῶς λάμψει
ἐτύφλωσεν τὰ νοήματα τῶν ἀπίστων	ὃς ἔλαμψεν ἐν ταῖς καρδίαις ἡμῶν
εἰς τὸ μὴ αὐγάσαι τὸν φωτισμὸν	πρὸς φωτισμὸν
τοῦ εὐαγγελίου τῆς δόξης τοῦ Χριστοῦ	τῆς γνώσεως τῆς δόξης τοῦ θεοῦ
ὅς ἐστιν εἰκὼν τοῦ θεοῦ	ἐν προσώπῳ Χριστοῦ

With this parallel, the phrase τῆς δόξης τοῦ θεοῦ ἐν προσώπῳ Χριστοῦ (4.6) can be regarded as another way of expressing τῆς δόξης τοῦ Χριστοῦ, ὅς ἐστιν εἰκὼν τοῦ θεοῦ (4.4), which suggests that the concepts of 'πρόσωπον of Christ' and Christ, the 'εἰκών of God', are more or less synonymous here.[141] Betz intimates that since Paul probably had seen Christ's πρόσωπον, 'he interpreted Christ's πρόσωπον as the εἰκών of God'.[142] Therefore, as with δόξα and εἰκών in 3.18 and 4.4, Paul's use of πρόσωπον and εἰκών in 4.4, 6 should be regarded as synonymous, which indicates that the πρόσωπον of Christ is also depicting Christ as the visible image and representation of God.

Scholars generally have not given much attention to the magnitude of the phrase ἐν προσώπῳ Χριστοῦ in 4.6, which climactically concludes Paul's use of the Moses narrative and constitutes a high point for his πρόσωπον–καρδία contrast in 3.1–4.6.[143] In light of this study's interest in some of Paul's uses of the term πρόσωπον, this phrase – which is almost always translated as 'in the *face* of Christ' – will be investigated in order to grasp the significance of the term πρόσωπον in relation to Christ and also to the transformation into the image of Christ.

6.3.1.3.1 Person of Christ

Similar to εἰκὼν τοῦ θεοῦ, the term πρόσωπον in reference to God also has a rich Old Testament background. It occurs in the LXX over 850 times, is typically used to translate the Hebrew פָּנִים, and is often used in relation to

---

[140] Cf. Eltester, *Eikon*, 132; Klauck, 'Erleuchtung', 272; Savage, *Power*, 127; Hubbard, *New Creation*, 158.

[141] Cf. Kim, *Origin*, 230. Also, note use of δόξα in proximity to εἰκών and πρόσωπον in 3.18, 4.4, 6.

[142] Betz, 'Concept', 332.

[143] Hafemann, *Moses*, 416, articulates that 'Christ is not merely reflecting the glory of God as Moses did, he *is* the glory of God' (italics his).

God.[144] Importantly, it is used in reference to the countenance of God, the side he turns to man.[145] As God lifts and shines his πρόσωπον towards his people his presence and peace will be experienced (e.g. Num 6.25–6), and when he hides his πρόσωπον his grace is withdrawn (e.g. Deut 32.20; Mic 3.4). The term is also used in reference to people being able to behold or experience the πρόσωπον of God (e.g. Gen 32.30; Judg 6.22). Given Paul's interest in the Moses narrative, it is significant that Moses and the Israelites are warned of the consequence of beholding God's πρόσωπον (Exod 33.20). However, Moses does experience the presence of God from behind as God passes by him (33.23). Also important is the use of πρόσωπον in translating the Hebrew לפני to express the idea of being 'before the presence' of God. It is additionally significant to point out the numerous instances in the LXX where πρόσωπον is joined with κύριος (e.g. Gen 3.8; Judg 6.22; 1 Sam 1.22; 2 Kings 22.19; 2 Chron 33.12; Ps 114.7; Zech 8.21–2; Lam 4.16; Dan 9.13; Sir 35.4), which is critical for the linking of πρόσωπον and Χριστός in 2 Cor 4.6. As with the case of εἰκών, the usage of πρόσωπον in the Old Testament shows that Paul is using the phrase προσώπῳ Χριστοῦ in 4.6 to convey Christ as the visible representation of the invisible presence of God – the Christ whom Paul visibly encountered on the road to Damascus.[146]

Furthermore, studies of 2 Cor 3–4 have yet to engage with recent Old Testament studies on 'cultic representation', which have provided insights into understanding the Moses narrative. As mentioned above, since Moses' direct encounters with God in the Tent of Meeting and on Mount Sinai resulted in a transfiguration that visually displayed God's glory and presence, the objects of his πρόσωπον and veil could both be discerned as a cultic 'mask' that visually represents God and designates Moses' social authority as a lawgiver and priest.[147] Paul, however, negatively depicts the glory on Moses' πρόσωπον as temporary (3.7, 13), while accentuating Christ's πρόσωπον (and glory) as the permanent visible image of God (4.6). It is also worth noting that in Matthew's account of Jesus' transfiguration on a high mountain (17.2) he describes Jesus' πρόσωπον as shining, which might explain Paul's contrast in 2 Cor 3–4 between Moses' shining πρόσωπον on

---

[144] Lohse, 'πρόσωπον', 771–4, and see 774–5 for its usage in later Judaism.

[145] Lohse, 'πρόσωπον', 772–4, for references.

[146] See Kim, *Origin*, 229–30.

[147] See Dozeman, 'Masking Moses', 21–45. Interestingly, the Hebrew קרן in Exod 34:29–35 has a history of being translated as a verb deriving from the noun קֶרֶן ('horns'), which would regard Moses πρόσωπον as not 'shining' (קָרַן) but as 'emitting horns'; see e.g. the translation in the Vulgate. It is also interesting that since Moses was away, the Israelites requested that a 'god' be made in order to lead them, which resulted in their creation of the golden calf (Exod 32.1–6); this link between Moses and the calf could be indicative of Moses being perceived as a visible representation of God.

Mount Sinai and Christ's shining πρόσωπον on the mountain.[148] Thomas
Dozeman has explained that in regard to Moses' mask, 'a mask transforms the
wearer, bringing about metamorphosis or alteration of identity'.[149] Christ's
πρόσωπον, then, could be understood also as a 'mask' that serves to
establish his identity as the Christ who is the image and glory of God.
Therefore, with Paul's depiction of Moses' πρόσωπον as a temporary
expression of his identity as a visible presence of God, Christ's πρόσωπον
should be understood as the permanent expression of his identity as God's
visible presence; and like the εἰκὼν τοῦ θεοῦ, the latter of the two
πρόσωπα should be regarded as the appropriate goal for the Christians'
transformation of identity.

As noted above, the phrase ἐν προσώπῳ Χριστοῦ in 4.6 is almost always
translated as 'in the *face* of Christ'. Some interpreters, however, have grasped
πρόσωπον in 4.6 as not merely a reference to Christ's 'face', but to his
'person' (cf. 1.11).[150] Barrett, for instance, interprets the phrase as referring to
'the person of Christ', and that, 'As the image of God he is the place where
God himself, the invisible, is known'.[151] Also, Stegman intimates that the
phrase refers to the *entire person* of Jesus Christ.[152] In light of Paul's contrast
between Moses and Christ, Stegman additionally suggests a 'deeper
connotation' of the πρόσωπον of Christ here, and points out that since the
reference to Moses' πρόσωπον serves to evoke the story of Moses, so the
reference to Christ's πρόσωπον serves to evoke the story of Jesus.[153] In
addition, Rowe, after stating that God's εἰκών has a definite anthropological
shape (ἄνθρωπος), writes: 'In this way, πρόσωπον in II Cor 4:6 is probably
best rendered "person", rather than "face", so that the stress lies not so much
on the appearance – though this may certainly be implied – but on the totality
of the Lord Jesus Christ as the one who is the light of the knowledge of the
δόξα of God'.[154] Recognising that πρόσωπον does not simply mean 'face'
here, Paul's significant use of 'πρόσωπον of Christ' should be understood as

---

[148] See Collange, *Enigmes*, 119, who observes that the verb λάμπω occurs in both Matt
17.2 and 2 Cor 4.6. See also the above discussion of Paul and Matthew's similar interest in
presenting Christ as greater than Moses.

[149] Dozeman, 'Masking Moses', 26.

[150] Cf. 2 Cor 1.11, where πρόσωπον is referring to literal persons. Also note again that in
2.10 the same phrase ἐν προσώπῳ Χριστοῦ is used, but in a slightly different sense. With
the context here, interpreters have correctly understood the phrase as similar to the Hebrew
לפני 'in his presence'.

[151] Barrett, *2 Cor*, 135.

[152] Stegman, *Character*, 136, 238, 243.

[153] Cf. Stegman, *Character*, 237–8. He also explains that the πρόσωπον of Jesus Christ
'evokes the *whole* story and character of Jesus' (245).

[154] Rowe, 'Iconography', 300.

denoting the 'person of Christ', which has implications for the Christians' transformation 'into the person of Christ' (ἐν προσώπῳ Χριστοῦ).

As mentioned above, in the Exodus account Moses directly interacted with God in the Tent of Meeting and on Mount Sinai (Exod 33.7–11; 34), which resulted in the transfiguration of his face that exhibited the visible glory of God. It is significant that Christians' too, with unveiled πρόσωπον (3.16–18), are able to encounter God and be transformed into the εἰκών/πρόσωπον of Christ. Francis Watson intimates: 'Within the sanctuary, which is the dwelling place of the Lord who is the Spirit, the unveiled Moses signifies the reality of Christian worship (vv.16–18). There, participants behold the glory of the Lord with unveiled face and are thereby transfigured, just as Moses was'.[155]

Related to the possibility of viewing Moses' πρόσωπον as a cultic representation of God is the detail of the God-engraved stone tablets that are in Moses' hands as he appeared to the people from Mount Sinai. As mentioned earlier, it is interesting that as Paul transitions his discourse from the social problem of commendatory letters to the outward glory on Moses' face, he deliberately changes the imagery from letters to tablets, whereby he states that the Corinthians themselves are letters of Christ written on 'tablets' of hearts and not of stone. Although Paul negatively depicts the written Decalogue and clearly promotes the inward work of the Spirit, there is a visible dimension to the writing on the Corinthians, given that they are to be 'read and known by all' (3.2). Since Paul intentionally shifts from letters to stones, this recalls the significance of the tablets of the Decalogue that are specifically mentioned to be in Moses' hands as he came down Mount Sinai with his shining πρόσωπον. Interestingly, recent studies in iconography, have regarded the God-engraved tablets also as a visible cultic representation of God's presence.[156] Given these insights concerning a 'written presence of

---

[155] Watson, *Hermeneutics*, 297. His insight could explain, in part, the Christians' visible transformation that people could behold.

[156] Watson, *Hermeneutics*, 287 n. 32, has noted that recent interpreters have overlooked the relation between Moses' tablets and transfigured face. This observation is true, especially since most interpreters are too busy looking, rightfully so, at the allusions of fleshy and stony hearts in Jeremiah and Ezekiel. On the concept of a divine 'written presence', see the insightful study by Toorn, 'Iconic Book', 229–48. Concerning the text here, he points out that the most striking instance of the Torah being the material representation of the deity is the Deuteronomic reinterpretation of the ark, as seen in Deut 10.1–5 where Moses is commanded to put the tablets (Torah) in the ark (241–2). Moreover, with the centrality of the Torah for Judaism and the special care given to the Torah, this further suggests the possibility that the Torah (i.e. tablets) could have been regarded as a material representation of God. With Paul's details of writing and γράμμα here, it is worthwhile to consider whether Paul had this Deuteronomic understanding of the written presence of God. Given the lack of space and the purview of this study, this investigation will be pursued in a future study.

God' in the tablets, the Corinthians – as a letter of Christ written with the Spirit on tablets of flesh – should be regarded as having this 'written presence' that visibly displays Christ's image (εἰκών) and person (πρόσωπον). Accordingly, this detail in 3.1–3 anticipates the believers' transformation into the image and person of Christ in 3.18–4.6.

6.3.1.3.2 'Persona *of Christ'*

Having seen the significance of the phrase ἐν προσώπῳ Χριστοῦ as expressing more than the face of Christ, this study affirms the phrase's reference to 'the person of Christ'. Given this sense, it is important to assess briefly whether this use of the term πρόσωπον could have an explicit meaning of *persona*, as is the case in the next instance of the term (5.12). The πρόσωπον of Christ was identified to be synonymous to Christ as the image of God (3.18, 4.4), into which Christians are being transformed. Like the image of Christ, the πρόσωπον of Christ denotes his visible representation of God. With a Christian transformation into the image and person of Christ, the phrase ἐν προσώπῳ Χριστοῦ has strong implications for Christian identity. Given the complex meaning of πρόσωπον in 4.6, however, it is difficult to be certain whether Paul intended to convey a precise meaning of *persona*. Nevertheless, the phrase's reference to the person of Christ and its strong implications for Christian identity does allow for a *conceptual* understanding of *persona*. This study, therefore, will discuss the phrase 'person of Christ' as intimating the conceptual idea of the '*persona* of Christ' (or Christ-like *persona*).[157]

In light of the conceptual understanding of the *persona* of Christ, there is an important social dynamic of this phrase that is crucial for Paul's *apologia* to the Corinthian church, whose members were obsessed with the shallow features of *persona* and boasted ἐν προσώπῳ (5.12). While denouncing the conventionally projected *persona* in the Corinthian church, Paul does offer them a new visible *persona* to consider that not only criticises but also deepens their understanding of what a Christian's *persona* should be. This Christian identity not only has an inner dimension (the heart), but also a visible dimension (Christ's image and person) into which Paul and the Christians are being transformed. Thrall writes, 'In the case of the Christian, the thought must be that assimilation to Christ as the image of God produces a

---

[157] To clarify, although Paul does not explicitly communicate this '*persona* of Christ', the conceptual idea is at least implied in the text. This is similar to the idea of a Christ-like identity (i.e. Christian identity), which is not explicitly mentioned in the text, but is implied in the text. Thus, Paul's construction of a Christ-like identity is in essence a construction of a Christ-like *persona*.

visibly Christ-like character, so that the divine image becomes visible in the believer's manner of life'.[158]

With this intentional use of the term πρόσωπον, Paul conveys that God's glory, which used to be observed on the πρόσωπον of Moses as fading and veiled, is now seen more superiorly on two objects: first and foremost, the πρόσωπον of Christ, who is the εἰκών of God; secondly, on those with unveiled πρόσωπον, who are being transformed into that εἰκών/πρόσωπον of Christ.[159] Thus, with the transformation occurring within the sphere of Christ (ἐν Χριστῷ, cf. 3.14), Paul's visible transformation ἐν προσώπῳ Χριστοῦ should be regarded as one that is 'in Christ', which results in a new *persona* and identity 'in Christ' – that is, an embodiment of the *'persona* of Christ'.

6.3.2 The Contours of the Christ-Like Identity

Having grasped a visible dimension to Paul's motif of the transformation into the image and person of Christ, this leads to the question of what are the contours of this Christ-like identity.[160] Some scholars have recently identified an ecclesiological aspect of this 'image of God', into which all the Corinthian Christians are being transformed. Hays writes, 'Christ is the glory-bearing *eikōn* into which the community is being transformed, the paradigm for the prosopography of the new covenant'.[161] That is, as a result of the transformation the Corinthian ἐκκλησία can be perceived as the visible image

---

[158] Thrall, *2 Cor*, 285. Cf. Kim, *Origin*, 229, who comments about the πρόσωπον of Christ: 'If the heart stands for the entire being of man, the face represents his external form'.

[159] Cf. Gal 1.16: 'God revealing his son in me'; 4.19, 'Christ formed in you'. Although Unnik, 'Unveiled Face', 167, incorrectly translates κατοπτριζόμενοι (2 Cor 3.18) as 'reflecting', his following statement is relevant: 'The outward appearance of the Christians change; they now reflect the glory of God'. He also refers to the *Acts of Paul and Thecla* where Paul is described as sometimes looking like a man and other times having a face of an angel, and to Acts 6.5, 10, 15 where Stephen is a man full of the Spirit and had a face (πρόσωπον) like an angel.

[160] Bear in mind that Paul does not present the metaphysics of this visible transformation. It is also important to note that Paul regards this transformation as a 'realistic participation' with Christ. See Proudfoot, 'Realistic Participation', 140–60; cf. Lambrecht, *2 Cor*, 56: 'The expression "into the same image" warns us that Paul means real *trans*formation, more than *con*formation' (italics his). It is critical also to point out that Paul's transformation is not a 'mystical divination' of 'becoming' or being absorbed into the divine being (cf. Apuleius, *Met.* 11.23–4). In 3.18–4.6 Paul regards the transformation as a process (ἀπὸ δόξης εἰς δόξαν), and that the transformation is *into* the image of Christ, who is and remains the distinct object (cf. Rom 8.29). Proudfoot writes that Paul's transformation/participation expresses 'the sense of a real connection between believer and divinity in which there may be an actual sharing of experience, but not necessarily a merging of personalities' (140 n. 1). See below for more on Paul's *real* participation in Christ's suffering.

[161] Hays, *Echoes*, 153.

of God. In fact, Hays interprets 3.1–4.6 as Paul's support of his claim that the Corinthians are indeed 'a letter of Christ' (3.2–3). Following Hays' lead, Rowe explores Paul's use of εἰκών for whether a case can be made for New Testament iconography and suggests that with an absence of a Christian social and sacred space, which would be a prerequisite for the establishment of a Christian material culture, Paul can be understood as placing the εἰκών of God within the Christian ἐκκλησία. He writes, 'Instead of statues, altars, etc., Paul posits not different statues or statues remade but a human community, the ἐκκλησία'.[162] He further elucidates on the ἐκκλησία as the iconic representation of Christ:

> God's image is a human image, and thus a living image. Paul's iconism is not about a static image but a life-story, first of a particular human and then of the community that embodies the pattern which is the story of that human life: in Jesus Christ and the community of the ἐκκλησία God stands on the side of humanity and is known humanly. In this way the image of God is in fact God's humanity.[163]

It was also seen above that Watson also regards the visual transformation as manifested through Christian worship – that is, 'within the sanctuary' the Corinthians with 'unveiled face' are transfigured as they behold God's glory.[164]

While these ecclesiological interpretations are illuminating for understanding the nature of Paul's transformation motif, this study approaches the visible εἰκών/πρόσωπον of Christ from a different angle, which will provide insights that will complement these ecclesiological implications. In light of the concept of *persona*, this study focuses on Paul's own embodiment of Christ's image and person, an embodiment which is critical for the *apologia* of his apostolic identity.

Before proceeding it is worthwhile to draw attention to Stegman's recent monograph, *The Character of Jesus*, which is relevant for understanding this *persona* of Christ. In this valuable study, Stegman argues that the 'linchpin and heart' of Paul's presentation throughout 2 Corinthians is the character (*ethos*) of Jesus – the specific attitudes, virtues, values, behaviour, and self-emptying mode of existence that Paul extrapolates from Jesus, especially those manifested in Jesus' humanity, such as: πραΰτης (gentleness), ἐπιείκεια (forbearance), ὑπακοή (obedience), πίστις (faithfulness), ἀγάπη (love), μὴ γνῶναι ἁμαρτίαν (not knowing sin), χάρις (generosity),

---

[162] Rowe, 'Iconography', 309.

[163] Rowe, 'Iconography', 311.

[164] Watson, *Hermeneutics*, 296–7, see above for the quotation. Also, Thrall, *2 Cor*, 284–5, and Hafemann, *Moses*, 426, both intimate that 4.7–15 and the Lord's supper (1 Cor 11.23–6) are the two ways that Christ is made visible.

ἁπλότης (singleness of purpose), and ἀλήθεια (truth).[165] Stegman not only emphasises the importance of the 'story of Jesus' for Paul in 2 Corinthians, but also Paul's participation and identification with that story. He suggests that 2 Corinthians is essentially not about Paul's *self*-commendation of his own character, but Paul's self-*commendation* of his faithful embodiment of the *ethos* of Jesus, which is Paul's understanding of what an apostle should be like.[166] In addition to Paul's defence of his own embodiment, Stegman argues that Paul is concerned with exhorting the Corinthians to accept and appropriate his embodiment of Jesus' *ethos*.[167]

Stegman's study is helpful for this present study, given his understanding of Paul and the Corinthians' embodiment of Jesus' character. He rightfully associates Jesus' character with Paul's explicit language of a transformation into the image of Christ, by explaining that Paul brings 'the issues of commendation and competency to a climax in 3:18 by alluding to a Spirit-empowered transformation...whereby he and others are enabled by the Spirit to embody the character of Jesus'.[168] However, this present study continues to look at Paul's *apologia*[169] by exploring not only the 'character of Jesus', but also the more explicit details of the image and person of Christ. In fact, with the distinct language of μεταμορφόω, εἰκών, and πρόσωπον, the visible transformation is understood not merely as an ethical one, but one that depicts the visible presence of Christ, who was crucified and resurrected. These two facets of Christ's image – the dying and life of Jesus – are critical for Paul's presentation of the believers' transformation of identity in Christ, and are in fact the visible contours of the Christ-like *persona*.[170]

6.3.2.1 The Dying of Jesus

Since Paul conveyed a visible transformation into the glorious εἰκών/ πρόσωπον of Christ, the Corinthians would have expected Paul's outward appearance to be glorious. However, as already observed, according to the Corinthians' conventional criteria, Paul's life portrays an inglorious visible

---

[165] Stegman, *Character*, 18, for his thesis statement; pp. 2, 217, for his definition of the *ethos* of Jesus; p. 67, for a list of characteristics and attributes.

[166] Stegman, *Character*, 213–303.

[167] Stegman, *Character*, 304–67.

[168] Stegman, *Character*, 234.

[169] See Chapter Five for my critique of Stegman's denial of Paul's apologetic purpose in 2 Corinthians.

[170] See Schnelle, 'Transformation', 60, who has recently proposed: 'Die Kategorien der Transformation und der Partizipation bestimmen durchgängig das paulinische Denken; sie sind das einigende Band, aus dem alle anderen Vorstellungen abgeleitet werden können'. Schnelle, however, seems to stress more of the ethical nature of this transformation and participation.

image (cf. 2 Cor 4.7–15). For the Corinthians, who were keen on the superficial type of outward appearance and boasted ἐν προσώπῳ, this contemptible-looking *persona* would have been seen as inconsistent with his claims of sufficiency as an apostle of Christ. However, Paul does harmonise this paradox by depicting his inglorious appearance as indeed consistent with Christ's image and person.

In 2.14–17, which has been seen as a thematic statement for the rest of the epistle, Paul describes himself as a slave of Christ being led to death in a triumphal procession, and as an odour/fragrance of Christ's death that diffuses the knowledge of God (2.14–15). Barrett comments that Paul's self-description here expresses an 'identity between what is seen in Jesus, crucified and risen, and what is seen in Paul...'[171] Paul's visual proclamation of the death and life of Jesus can also be seen his statement in 4.5, κηρύσσομεν...Ἰησοῦν Χριστὸν κύριον, which some interpreters have considered to be parallel to his previous statement to the Corinthians: κηρύσσομεν Χριστὸν ἐσταυρωμένον (1 Cor 1.23).[172] This suggests that Paul's proclamation is essentially Christ as both Lord (κύριον) and crucified (ἐσταυρωμένον). Paul additionally states in 2 Cor 4.5 that 'we proclaim ourselves as your slaves (δούλους) for Jesus' sake'. This notion of being a slave is referring to Jesus' earthly ministry of becoming a slave and serving others (cf. 8.9; Phil 2.5–8). In 2 Cor 4.5, then, Paul embodies his message of the crucified Christ and Christ's ministry for others.[173] C. Merrill Proudfoot articulates that 'Paul's suffering is a sort of illustration of or commentary upon the preaching of the gospel', and has 'a function much like that of a sacrament when understood as the visible representation of the preached word'.[174]

It is significant that Paul's visual proclamation of the crucified Christ in 4.5 is sandwiched between 4.4, 6, which are two weighty texts for Paul's motif of a visible transformation into the εἰκών/πρόσωπον of Christ. Scholars have noted that within 3.18–4.6 Paul's transformation motif is innately linked with his theme of sharing in Christ's suffering. It is worth

---

[171] Barrett, *2 Cor*, 100. Cf. Savage, *Power*, 104; Barnett, *2 Cor*, 150. See also Hafemann, *Suffering*, esp. 51–4, 219–21.

[172] So Savage, *Power*, 153; Garland, *2 Cor*, 215; and perhaps Harris, *2 Cor*, 332. Wolff, 'Humility', 155, remarks that the use of the name 'Jesus' in the phrase διὰ Ἰησοῦν 'probably serves to recall particularly his self-offering on the cross'.

[173] Cf. Harris, *2 Cor*, 333: 'In this lowly service to others, Paul was following in the footsteps of his Lord, who himself had adopted the status and role of a δοῦλος'; Savage, *Power*, 152–4. See also Wolff, 'Humility', 155–6.

[174] Proudfoot, 'Realistic Participation', 155. Cf. Hafemann, *Moses*, 425: 'As the corollary to his preaching, Paul conceived of his experiences of suffering as the corresponding vehicle for the revelation of the glory of God in Christ'.

quoting again Collange's insight into Paul's use of μεταμορφόω: 'Cette transformation n'a donc pas qu'un aspect intérieur de renouvellement, mais aussi un aspect extérieur de conformation aux souffrances du Christ'.[175] Savage also remarks,

Paul seems to be drawing attention to the visible character, the salient image, of Jesus Christ. He is underscoring the fact that Christ, in his resolve to live for God's glory and not his own and in his act of consummate self-sacrifice on the cross, demonstrates not only what God is like but also, dramatically, what humans ought to be like. They ought to manifest the same self-emptying character which Christ displayed on the cross. They ought to be 'transformed into the same image'.[176]

Thus, regarding the Christians' transformation into the person (πρόσωπον) of Christ (4.6), it is important that what is seen 'is not shining faces, but a carrying of the dying of Jesus'.[177]

Paul's outward projection of a Christ-like appearance as his identification and participation with Christ's suffering is clearly evident in 4.7–15, which depicts 'Paul's inglorious life-style'.[178] Having reached a climax in 4.6 with his portrayal of God's glory shining on the πρόσωπον of Christ, Paul transitions seamlessly to his present suffering and afflictions (4.7–15), and indicates how he understands them in light of his Christ-like identity.[179] He elucidates that the purpose of this apparent weakness is to demonstrate visibly that the exceeding power in him 'belongs to God and not from us' (4.7).[180] Paul, then, is not merely making a contrast between his visible weakness and God's internal power, but is reinterpreting his inglorious body as the vehicle

---

[175] Collange, *Enigmes*, 120.

[176] Savage, *Power*, 151–2; cf. Proudfoot, 'Realistic Participation', 156, that 'to perceive most fully the δόξα in the face of the Lord, one must join the Lord in suffering'.

[177] Lacey, 'Image', 22.

[178] Thrall, *2 Cor*, 320, which is the heading for her commentary on 4.7–15.

[179] See Heath, 'Viewing', who employs an 'iconographic approach' to interpret 4.7–12 in continuity with 3.18–4.6, and to argue that Paul presents himself as an 'icon of Christ'. She points out that interpreters tend to treat 4.7–12 separately from 3.18–4.6, and rightly argues for a continuity. Cf. Schröter, *Versöhner*, 142: 'Nach der Darlegung der Größe seines Dienstes in 3,4–4,6, die in 4,6 in Schilderung der Erleuchtung durch Gott und der Weitergabe dieses Lichtes durch die Verkündigung gegipfelt hatte, geht es nun also um die *konkrete Gestalt*, in der sich diese Erleuchtung an ihrem Träger manifestiert' (italics his); and possibly Wright, 'Reflected', 190: 'In other words, the glory which is seen, as in a mirror, in Paul's ministry is the glory which shines through suffering'. See also Garrett, 'Affliction', 101–4, who commendably looks at the theme of Paul's afflictions in 4.1–12.

[180] Scholars have suggested that the verb ᾖ should be understood in the sense of visually displaying. E.g. Furnish, *2 Cor*, 254, that it should be seen in parallel to ἵνα...φανερωθῇ in 4.10–11; Savage, *Power*, 166, that Paul meant to write φανερωθῇ or φανῇ or εὑρεθῇ; Plummer, *2 Cor*, 127.

for the visible expression of God's glorious power.[181] Like his earthen vessel (4.7), Paul describes his outer person as 'wasting away' (4.16), not only to negate his body's external value in comparison to the inner person, but also to accentuate the weak outer man as, in fact, physically projecting Christ's suffering and death.[182]

Paul's embodiment of this Christ-like *persona* is further elucidated in his statement that he is always carrying in his body the 'dying of Jesus' (τὴν νέκρωσιν τοῦ 'Ἰησοῦ) so that the life of Jesus may be made visible (φανερωθῇ) in his body (4.10–11). There are two details in this text that elucidate how Paul understands his apostolic lifestyle and image. First, the term νέκρωσις is used, rather than the typical θάνατος, in reference to Jesus' death (2 Cor 1.9, 10; 2.16; 3.7; 4.11–12; 7.10; 11.23). With his employment of νέκρωσις Paul specifically refers to the process of dying, rather than the final state of death.[183] Secondly, Paul only uses the single name Jesus, which further suggests that he has in view the human life and ministry of Jesus. Given these two particulars, the phrase τὴν νέκρωσιν τοῦ 'Ἰησοῦ is alluding to Jesus' earthly ministry and dying on the cross,[184] which is what Paul claims he is always carrying about in his body for the world to see.[185] Stegman writes that 'the apostle makes clear that he understands his present and ongoing experience of suffering in light of – and *as a continuation of* – the story of Jesus'.[186] By claiming that he is carrying about the 'dying of Jesus' Paul recognises his own suffering as 'in some sense a public portrayal, a visual image, of the death of Jesus himself'.[187] In addition, Paul's embodiment of the

---

[181] Cf. Gräßer, *2 Kor*, 163: 'Gott macht schwache, hinfällige Menschen zu Gefäßen seiner Gnade, damit der Charakter seines Heilstuns erkennbar wird'; Savage, *Power*, 165; Dupont, *L'union*, 121–2; Allo, *2 Cor*, 113.

[182] Cf. Dunn, *Jesus*, 333.

[183] So e.g. Lambrecht, 'Nekrōsis', 120; Savage, *Power*, 172; Barrett, *2 Cor*, 139–40; Wolff, *2 Kor*, 92. For more on this, see Baumert, *Täglich*, 72–3.

[184] See Lambrecht, 'Nekrōsis', 124–5; Savage, *Power*, 172; Collange, *Enigmes*, 155.

[185] See Fitzgerald, *Cracks*, 163–4, who postulates that since Paul does use the term πάντοτε here, which was last used in 2.14, the two actions should be regarded as concomitant: 'God is always leading Paul about as a grateful captive in his victory procession, and Paul is always in that procession bearing around the *nekrōsis* of Jesus' (164); Duff, 'Apostolic Suffering', 158–65, who explains 4.7, 10 as metaphors of Graeco-Roman 'epiphany processions', in which the processions manifest the image of the deity for the spectators.

[186] Stegman, *Character*, 251 (emphasis his). Cf. Gorman, *Cruciformity*, 30: 'Paul wanted his life and ministry to tell a story, a story that corresponded to the "story of the cross", to his gospel'; Güttgemanns, *Der leidende*, e.g. 106–7, 117, whose thesis is that Paul's weakness is an 'epiphany' and presence of Christ's power.

[187] Thrall, *2 Cor*, 334, and that Paul possibly sees himself 'as presenting a replica or image of Christ's death'; cf. idem, 'Christ Crucified', 152. Furthermore, scholars are in general agreement that this text reflects Paul's participation in Christ's suffering and death; see e.g.

image and person of Christ depicts a *real* participation in Christ's suffering,[188] especially since he has physically experienced real suffering and afflictions as an apostle of Christ (2 Cor 6.4–10; cf. 1.8–11; 11.23–8; 12.10; 1 Cor 4.8– 13).[189] It is even striking that in his letter to the Galatians, Paul identifies himself as having been crucified with Christ (2.19), and regards his physical body as bearing the marks of the crucified Christ (τὰ στίγματα τοῦ Ἰησοῦ) (6.17).

Although Paul is specifically referring to his suffering and afflictions as an apostle, the participation in Christ's suffering is inherently applicable to all Christians, especially given that the transformation into the εἰκών/ πρόσωπον of Christ is intended for all Christians (ἡμεῖς πάντες, 2 Cor 3.18). Wolfgang Schrage writes on this theme, 'Der leidende Herr, die leidende Apostel und die leidende Christenschar gehören zusammen'.[190] Moreover, Paul's imitation (*mimēsis*) motif is relevant here, despite the fact that it is not explicitly stated in 2 Corinthians.[191] The Corinthians would have been familiar with this imitation motif, since Paul had employed it in 1 Corinthians, in which he explicated his *theologia crucis* (λόγος τοῦ σταυροῦ, 1.18–25). As mentioned in Chapter Five, I have argued elsewhere that in 1 Cor 4.9 Paul identifies himself with the crucified Christ and his shameful death.[192] It is significant that after Paul presents a list of afflictions (vv. 10–13), he exhorts the Corinthians to imitate him (μιμηταί μου γίνεσθε, v. 16), and later in 11.1, he repeats the call to imitation, but reveals Christ as his exemplar (μιμηταί μου γίνεσθε καθὼς κἀγὼ Χριστοῦ, 11.1). This imitation motif would then associate both Paul and the Corinthians with the

---

Savage, *Power*, 172–3; Collange, *Enigmes*, 154–5; Proudfoot, 'Realistic Participation', 155; Kamlah, 'Wie beurteilt?', 232; Lambrecht, 'Nekrōsis', 124–5, 137–8; Schrage, 'Leid', 168; Kleinknecht, *Der leidende*, 274.

[188] See Proudfoot, 'Realistic Participation', 140–60. Cf. Hughes, *2 Cor*, 142: 'But Paul is speaking of something more than example. Between Master and follower there is a certain unity of experience and destiny. There is an inclusiveness of the latter in the former'.

[189] Cf. Thrall, *2 Cor*, 335, that 'the apostle's real, visible sufferings are an objective representation of Christ's death'. See Harvey, *Renewal*, esp. 1–31, who argues that Paul's afflictions in Asia (2 Cor 1.8–11) was the impetus that shaped his positive understanding of his suffering as an essential part of his ministry. See also Sumney, 'Weakness', 71–91, who demonstrates that Paul's weakness was an integral part of his understanding of his apostleship much earlier than his conflict with the Corinthian opponents.

[190] Schrage, 'Leid', 158. He also writes, 'Christus und sein Kreuz sind Grund und Ursache des Leidens des Christens' (162).

[191] See Lambrecht, 'Nekrōsis', 138–40, who cautions that although the language is not explicit here, it should not be radically excluded; cf. Schrage, 'Leid', 162–3. For more on Paul's imitation, see Belleville, 'Imitate', 120–42; Clarke, 'Be Imitators', 329–60. Clarke points out that in 2 Corinthians, there is the key theme of servant leadership, which is 'primarily exemplified in Jesus' (348).

[192] Nguyen, 'Execution', esp. 44–5; cf. idem, 'Identification', esp. 501.

crucified Christ and his suffering (cf. 1 Thes 1.6). In 2 Cor 4.7–15 Paul implies this same notion with his list of afflictions (vv. 8–9) and his self-identification with Christ's suffering (vv. 10–11), which also would be an embodiment of the λόγος τοῦ σταυροῦ (1 Cor 1.18–25). This situation of carrying about the 'dying of Jesus' in 2 Cor 4.10–11 should be regarded, then, as pertinent for all Christians.[193] Jan Lambrecht writes: 'In an analogous way all Christians just like Paul carry the nekrōsis of Jesus in their bodies, so that there also the life of Jesus may be manifested'.[194]

6.3.2.2 The Life of Jesus

Lambrecht's statement indicates a flip-side of the visible projection of Paul's Christ-like identity/*persona* that is notable in 4.10–11, where Paul expresses that he carries around 'the dying of Jesus' (τὴν νέκρωσιν τοῦ 'Ιησοῦ) in order that 'the life of Jesus' (ἡ ζωὴ τοῦ 'Ιησοῦ) may also 'be made visible (φανερωθῇ) in our bodies'. Interpreters have argued that the 'life of Jesus' is linked with the 'power of God' (4.7) that brought about the resurrection of Christ, which suggests that the 'life of Jesus' is analogous to the exalted and glorified Christ.[195] If this concept of the 'life of Jesus' is applied to Paul's theme of transformation, the transformation into the image and person of Christ is visibly marked not only by Christ's suffering and death, but also by his resurrection power (cf. 4.14; 5.14–15).[196] Thrall expresses that 'Paul is not, here, concerned with the inward mortification of the old, unregenerate personality, but with external peril and divine rescue as a visual image of Christ's death and resurrection'.[197] Since only Christ's death has resulted in resurrection, Paul portrays the path of glorification as intrinsically linked to suffering, that is, 'to experience Christ's life through the experience of his death'.[198] In Rom 6.5 Paul states that 'if we have been united with the likeness of Christ's death, we will be united with the likeness of his resurrection' (cf. Phil. 3.10, 21). This future glorification (cf. Col 3.4) that takes place at the *eschaton* is, nonetheless, the consummation of the transformation into the

---

[193] So Lambrecht, 'Nekrōsis', 142–3, who asserts that 'we should not postulate an opposition between two kinds of suffering, apostolic and Christian' (142); Kamlah, 'Wie beurteilt?', 227, 231; Tannehill, *Dying*, 86–7.

[194] Lambrecht, 'Nekrōsis', 143.

[195] Cf. Tannehill, *Dying*, 95; Lambrecht, 'Nekrōsis', 125, that 'the expressions "the life of Jesus" in vv. 10b and 11b and (even more) "the Lord Jesus" in v. 14 indicate that for Paul the earthly Jesus is not separated from the glorified Christ'. For Paul's eschatological outlook in 4.7–15, see idem, 'Eschatological Outlook', 122–40; Baumert, *Täglich*, 36–48.

[196] For more on the motif of 'dying and rising with Christ', see Tannehill, *Dying*.

[197] Thrall, *2 Cor*, 337.

[198] Cf. Dunn, *Jesus*, 334.

image and person of Christ, which is when the Christian will be clothed in a new heavenly dwelling/body (2 Cor 5.1–5; cf. 1 Cor 15.42–9, 52).

Significantly, for Paul this 'life of Jesus' is not some future glorification that will occur at the resurrection after his present suffering, but is something that takes place *now* (cf. Col 3.4) – the very life of Jesus breaks through and manifests itself in the midst of his weakness and suffering.[199] Jacques Dupont writes, 'La vie de Jésus n'attend donc pas la résurrection pour se montrer dans notre "chair mortelle", et qu'elle laisse mortelle; sans la retirer de l'extrême limite de la mort, elle la soutient par une sorte de miracle continuel'.[200] Despite this 'already not yet' tension, Paul understands this Christ-like identity as a progressive transformation (ἀπὸ δόξης εἰς δόξαν, 2 Cor 3.18) that presently exhibits the image of the dying and life of Christ, and in the future will be fully completed into the image of the resurrected Christ. Lambrecht comments, 'The aim of the apostle's dying is the visible, bodily manifestation of Jesus' life'.[201] Paul accordingly describes his momentary afflictions as a preparation for a future eternal weight of glory (4.17–18). Furthermore, since power and glory are being manifested in the midst of visible weakness, Lambrecht rightly cautions against misunderstanding or radicalising the 'invisible' character of this transformative renewal: 'As for Paul, his apostolic life, with its work, suffering and persecution, even now manifests in a visible way in the midst of weakness and dying much victory, power and glory'.[202] Therefore, Paul conveys his present and stark human existence and reinterprets it as a situation in which Christ's glory is visibly manifested.

6.3.3 Summary

This section concentrated on the visible dimension of Paul's presentation of Christian identity. This identity is a result from the Christians' transformation into the image (εἰκών) and person (πρόσωπον) of Christ (3.18–4.6), which can conceptually be grasped as 'the *persona* of Christ'. Significantly, this Christ-like identity has been recognised as a visible projection of the 'dying and life of Jesus' (esp. 4.7–15), which is crucial for Paul's defence of his ministry, since the Corinthians have criticised him for his weak outward appearance. Concerning Paul's embodiment of this Christ-like identity, James

---

[199] On this tension, see Kim, *Origin*, 321–6.

[200] Dupont, *L'union*, 125. Cf. Lambrecht, 'Nekrōsis', 126; O'Collins, 'Power', 537: 'Christ's triumphant power is "effective" in the concrete circumstances of Paul's life, and hence it is visibly revealed'; Fitzgerald, *Cracks*, 176, creatively explains, 'The vessel is held together by the power of the divine adhesive, and the light that shines (4:5–6) through these cracks is none other than the light of the life of Jesus (4:10–11)'.

[201] Cf. Lambrecht, *2 Cor*, 73.

[202] Lambrecht, 'Nekrōsis', 131.

Dunn expresses that in the midst of suffering 'Paul sees the Spirit of Christ the Crucified and Risen, and he recognizes the image of this Christ taking shape in him'.[203] In Paul's estimation, then, the dying and life of Jesus are both characteristics of the power and glory of God that are manifested in the lives of Christians. It is also significant that Paul's 'new creation' motif (5.17) is placed in the context of Christ's death and resurrection (5.14–15). Scott Hafemann concludes 'that the transformation pictured in 3:18 is the evidence of and foundation for Paul's subsequent assertion in 5:14–17 that the eschatological "new creation" has indeed been inaugurated by the death and resurrection of Christ'.[204] Also, in light of the transformation into the 'dying and life of Jesus', it is interesting that towards the end of the large section of 2.14–7.4, Paul reminds the Corinthians 'for I said before that you are in our hearts (καρδίαις) to *die* together and to *live* together (εἰς τὸ συναποθανεῖν καὶ συζῆν)' (7.3).[205]

Therefore, Paul approaches identity by presenting both an internal and external aspect of Christian identity – an outward dimension that expresses the inward spiritual transformation, rather than superficial values. That is, Paul is not simply making an outward/inward distinction, but a distinction between outward expressions based on superficial values and outward expressions based on the inward spiritual transformation that is taking effect. There is, then, no hard line distinction between the outer and inner dimensions of Christian identity. Interestingly, although the text of 1 Sam 16.7, which is probably alluded to in 2 Cor 5.12 (cf. Gal 2.6), asserts that God considers the person's 'heart' rather than outward appearance, it is David's outward appearance that is described since it reflects his good inner character (1 Sam 16.8, 12). Thus, Christian transformation affects the whole person.

6.4 The Subversive Christ-Like Identity (2 Cor 10–13)

Having recognised the contours of Paul's Christ-like identity, which visibly portrays weakness and suffering, it is easy to perceive that his *persona* would have contradicted the Corinthians' conventional criteria of a reputable *persona* for an apostle. Attention will now be given again to Paul's *apologia* in 2 Cor 10–13, a text that was explored in Chapter Five for indications of the Corinthians' preoccupation with the conventionally projected *persona* in Paul's time, and also his reaction against it. Since this text contains social description of a misconception of Christian identity in the church – especially,

---

[203] Dunn, *Jesus*, 338. Cf. Kamlah, 'Wie beurteilt?', 232.
[204] Hafemann, *Moses*, 430. Cf. Thrall, *2 Cor*, 428.
[205] See Lambrecht, 'Together', 234–51.

the Corinthians' superficial assessment of Paul's *persona* – it will be revisited to examine more closely how Paul portrays and defends his Christ-like identity, and whether he subverts their conventional values of *persona*.

6.4.1 Paul's Πρόσωπον of Christ (10.1)

In 10.1, Paul emphatically begins the section with Αὐτὸς δὲ ἐγὼ Παῦλος, which is a conflation of two expressions that are used separately to accentuate his apostolic authority (αὐτὸς ἐγώ) and personal involvement (ἐγὼ Παῦλος).[206] He enhances the phrase with an appeal (παρακαλῶ) to the 'meekness and gentleness of Christ' (διὰ τῆς πραΰτητος καὶ ἐπιεικείας τοῦ Χριστοῦ), and also indicates a criticism levelled against him: he is timid when present, but bold when absent (ὃς κατὰ πρόσωπον μὲν ταπεινὸς ἐν ὑμῖν, ἀπὼν δὲ θαρρῶ εἰς ὑμᾶς). Paul's presence–absence antithesis, which is an important theme in chapters 10–13 (10.10–11; 13.2, 10; cf. 1 Cor 5.3), reveals that the problem was with the Corinthians' superficial assessment of Paul based primarily on his outward appearance. Paul is being charged here of inconsistently being bold when absent, yet weak when present (cf. 10.10).

Therefore, at the outset of 2 Cor 10–13 Paul states two things regarding his social identity: that he comes to the Corinthians in a particular *persona*, and that it was criticised by them. The issue at hand, then, is a conflict between Paul and the Corinthians' opposing views of his *persona*. The conflict arises because the social identity that Paul claims in 10.1 to have displayed to the Corinthians is, in fact, the image and person (πρόσωπον) of Christ.[207] In the opening verse Paul conveys that he appeals to the Corinthians by the 'meekness and gentleness of Christ' (πραΰτητος καὶ ἐπιεικείας τοῦ Χριστοῦ), and that according to his appearance (κατὰ πρόσωπον) he is ταπεινός ('humble' or 'servile') (10.1).[208] Concerning the significance of this appeal, Stegman submits that it 'functions to cover all of the various components in the following four chapters'.[209] It is critical that the phrase πραΰτητος καὶ ἐπιεικείας τοῦ Χριστοῦ highlights characteristics displayed by Christ, which are probably those of his earthly life and ministry.[210] This

---

[206] See Thrall, *2 Cor*, 599.

[207] Cf. Savage, *Power*, 103: 'On the one hand, the Corinthians imbibe the outlook of the world. On the other hand, he is conformed to Christ'.

[208] Cf. Dewey, 'Honor', 210, who explains that in 10.1 Paul's initial apologetical appeal is to link the rhetorical allusion of the *exemplum* of Christ to the way Paul has been characterised as ταπεινός.

[209] Stegman, *Character*, 121–9 (quotation from 125).

[210] For discussion of the phrase τῆς πραΰτητος καὶ ἐπιεικείας τοῦ Χριστοῦ, see Leivestad, 'Meekness', 156–64; Martin, *2 Cor*, 302–3; Thrall, *2 Cor*, 667–9; Lambrecht, 'Appeal', 411–14; Good, *Meek King*; Harris, *2 Cor*, 667–9; and esp. the two recent treatments by Stegman, *Character*, 121–9; Walker, *Leniency*. In Walker's thorough study of the phrase,

suggests that Paul embodies Christ's characteristics, especially for his social interaction with the Corinthians. Ragnar Leivestad recognises that by employing the keyword ταπεινός, which is a malicious characterisation of Paul, in relation to his appeal to the πραΰτητος καὶ ἐπιεικείας τοῦ Χριστοῦ, 'he [Paul] wants his readers to recognize a correspondence between the Lord and his apostle'.[211] Besides the association of Paul's ταπεινός and Christ's πραΰτης, there is also a relation between the charges made against Paul of being ταπεινός and ἀσθενής (10.1, 10), especially since Paul makes a virtue out of both of these negative accusations (i.e. his power-in-weakness motif).[212] Maurice Carrez writes, 'Paul veut que sa vie parmi eux soit significative et figure, reproduise et proclame l'abaissement du Christ' (cf. 8.9; 11.7).[213] Thus, Paul informs the Corinthians that he exhibited a Christ-like appearance among them, but they only observed it as 'weakness' because they expected something more 'powerful'.

Interestingly, in 10.1 Paul includes the phrase κατὰ πρόσωπον, which needs to be considered whether it has here any bearing on the concept of *persona*. The phrase κατὰ πρόσωπον is typically translated here as 'face to face' to denote 'presence', but interpreters have not given much support for this translation. In 1 Cor 13.12 the construction πρόσωπον πρὸς πρόσωπον would give precedence for a translation of 'face to face', but that is not the case with κατὰ πρόσωπον in 2 Cor 10.1. Also, many interpreters identify the phrase κατὰ πρόσωπον as functioning in opposition to ἀπὼν δὲ θαρρῶ; however, it is not entirely necessary to have κατὰ πρόσωπον functioning as merely the opposite of ἀπὼν since the antonym παρὼν is present in the following verse (10.2; cf. 10.11). In fact, the other instances of

---

he suggests the translation 'leniency and clemency of Christ', which Paul uses to innovatively appeal to Christ as the 'Good King'. It is also worth noting that most scholars recognise Paul as identifying himself with some characteristics of Christ, but there is debate whether they refer to those of Christ's earthly life (e.g. Matt 11.29) or his pre-existence (2 Cor 8.9; Phil 2.6–8). However, Martin, *2 Cor*, 302, and Barrett, *2 Cor*, 246, are both right that there seems to be no major difference between the two, since both are intimately related; cf. Stegman, *Character*, 120–1.

[211] Leivestad, 'Meekness', 161; cf. Kleinknecht, *Der leidende*, 285, who recognises the same connection. In addition, Dewey, 'Honor', 210, remarks that the linkage of ταπεινός and the virtues of Christ (πραΰτης and ἐπιείκεια) should not prevent one from noting that this term connotes the 'pejorative social sense of low estate or status'.

[212] Cf. Leivestad, 'Meekness', 162–3; Kleinknecht, *Der leidende*, 285; and Bultmann, *2 Kor*, 185, who paraphrases: 'denkt, wenn ihr mich als ταπεινός κατὰ πρόσωπον verachtet, an Christi Milde und Freundlichkeit, und denkt nicht, daß meine ταπεινότης eine Schwäche sei!'

[213] Carrez, *2 Cor*, 198. Lambrecht, 'Appeal', 398, writes 'that Christ is in one way or another an example for Paul's attitude and, equally, that the apostle is going to request from the Corinthians a moral conduct similar to Christ's example'.

ἄπειμι in the Corinthian correspondence (1 Cor 5.3; 2 Cor 10.11; 13.2, 10) all occur in close proximity to πάρειμι, and without πρόσωπον, to communicate the contrast of presence–absence. There is also a parallel between ἀπὼν θαρρῶ (2 Cor 10.1) and μὴ παρὼν θαρρῆσαι (10.2), which alleviates the need to regard κατὰ πρόσωπον as simply opposing ἀπὼν.

A few scholars have given some special attention to κατὰ πρόσωπον in 10.1. For instance, in his socio-historical study of 2 Corinthians, Arthur Dewey has interpreted the phrase as referring to 'Paul's public performance'.[214] Also, Jeffrey Crafton offers a 'dramatistic analysis' of 2 Cor 10–13 that identifies Paul in 10.1 as taking on an 'agent-*persona*' (an actor) who stands at centre stage for evaluation.[215] Although these studies offer some insights for understanding πρόσωπον here as expressing Paul's projected image, this present study considers Paul not as taking on a conventional or theatrical appearance, but as embodying the person (πρόσωπον) of Christ (cf. 4.6). Moreover, this proposed reading accentuates Paul's counteraction of his Corinthian opponents' preoccupation with the superficial aspect of *persona*. Significantly, in 10.2 Paul describes his opponents as τοὺς λογιζομένους (those 'considering' or 'examining', cf. 10.7, 11), which characterises the Corinthian opponents and their propensity to evaluate Paul's outward appearance according to conventional values.[216]

The phrase κατὰ πρόσωπον in 10.1, then, is regarded to be contributing to Paul's understanding of his Christ-like identity. The phrase helps to draw the Corinthians' attention to his display of the characteristics of the person of Christ, and the phrase also points to the Corinthians' superficial critique of Paul in 10.10. Many commentators suggest that the term refers to Paul's physical presence, but this study observes that the syntax does allow for a further meaning or implication. In fact, the context allows for the possibility of πρόσωπον having a sense of social *persona*, since Paul is highlighting his visible depiction of a Christ-like identity/*persona*. Therefore, Paul is explaining that his appearance (*persona*) is indeed humble and weak among them because it is a reflection of Christ's appearance and characteristics.

---

[214] Dewey, 'Honor', 210.

[215] Crafton, *Agency*, 104–6. He also recognises that πρόσωπον in 10.1, 7 indicates 'a supposed distinction between *superficial appearance* and hidden truth' (120, emphasis mine). See also, Walker, *Leniency*, who, in his treatment on chs. 10–13, often refers to Paul's 'persona' in a non-technical sense that seems to connote the idea of a rhetorical *persona*. However, in his monograph, which is centred on 10.1, Walker does not make any reference to the term πρόσωπον in 10.1 or 10.7. Also, Harris, *2 Cor*, 664: 'In this section [10.1–11] Paul is responding to an impression about him that had gained currency at Corinth, namely, that he had two radically different *personae* – "Paul the bold" and "Paul the timid"'.

[216] Interestingly, here the Corinthians are falsely accusing Paul ὡς κατὰ σάρκα περιπατοῦντας (10.3), which is similar to what Paul had accused the Corinthians of in 1 Cor 3.3: κατὰ ἄνθρωπον περιπατεῖτε. Paul explicates and refutes this charge in 2 Cor 10.3.

6.4.2 Τὰ Κατὰ Πρόσωπον Βλέπετε (10.7)

It is no surprise that the Corinthians would be quick to discredit Paul's projection of his Christ-like identity. They have been conditioned by the social conventions of *persona* and would naturally denounce Paul's public *persona* since it did not hold up to their standards and was the exact opposite of their expectations. Six verses later, after using metaphors of warfare to 'destroy strongholds' and 'take captive' (10.3–6),[217] Paul makes another important use of πρόσωπον, by expressing: Τὰ κατὰ πρόσωπον βλέπετε (10.7). Being positioned next to the term βλέπετε, the term πρόσωπον here is also associated with the idea of visuality. Dewey explains that with κατὰ πρόσωπον Paul moves from the symbolic realm of the previous verses to the public realm 'where the concern is manifestly that of social estimation'.[218]

There is, however, difficulty in translating this phrase, Τὰ κατὰ πρόσωπον βλέπετε, since it can be translated either as an indicative or an imperative statement.[219] If interpreted as an indicative Paul would be emphasising the Corinthians' inappropriate *modus operandi* of looking at things according to superficialities – that is, the preoccupation with external status symbols – which would be similar to his statement in 5.12 of those boasting in πρόσωπον. On the other hand, if translated as an imperative, Paul would be urging the Corinthians to look at things according to πρόσωπον, which would recall his Christ-like πρόσωπον that he described in 10.1.[220] The difficulty in choosing between the two options increases with the fact that the context allows for either of these two and possibly even assumes both of them. That is, if Paul is making a statement about their conventional behaviour, he would be aiming to correct their behaviour and to have them truly appreciate his Christ-like identity; conversely, if he is exhorting them to look at things according to his Christ-like identity, he is doing so because they inappropriately appraise the surface appearance of his

---

[217] On Paul's use of warfare imagery, see Gerber, 'Krieg', 105–13; Malherbe, 'Antisthenes', 143–73.

[218] Dewey, 'Honor', 212.

[219] The majority of scholars have been inclined to interpret the phrase as an imperative, so Windisch, *2 Kor*, 300; Allo, *2 Cor*, 246; Héring, *2 Cor*, 71; Lietzmann, *1–2 Kor*, 687; Barrett, *2 Cor*, 255–6; Furnish, *2 Cor*, 465; Martin, *2 Cor*, 307; Carrez, *2 Cor*, 201; Wolff, *2 Kor*, 200; Thrall, *2 Cor*, 618–19; Barnett, *2 Cor*, 470; Garland, *2 Cor*, 440; Lambrecht, *2 Cor*, 155; Harris, *2 Cor*, 687. Their main argument is that Paul always uses the verb form βλέπετε as an imperative. For those who interpret it as an indicative: Plummer, *2 Cor*, 279; Savage, *Power*, 184; Hubbard, *New Creation*, 161; and Bultmann, *2 Kor*, 189, who translates it as a question. Their main argument is that βλέπετε as an imperative is normally found in the initial position.

[220] For those who have made this connection of πρόσωπον in 10.1, 7, see Furnish, *2 Cor*, 465; Kleinknecht, *Der leidende*, 285; Martin, *2 Cor*, 307; esp. Wolff, *2 Kor*, 200; Garland, *2 Cor*, 440.

identity based on conventional standards. Regardless of which option is chosen, this dual understanding should be maintained for the context. Despite the difficulty, the slightly more preferable interpretation is the imperative option, given that the verb form βλέπετε is always used in the Pauline letters as an imperative.[221]

Since this verse contributes to Paul's approach to identity it is worth considering whether πρόσωπον here conveys the meaning of *persona*. Scholars who interpret 10.7 as an imperative have translated the verse in various ways, such as 'Face the obvious facts', 'Look at what is before your eyes', 'Look at what is staring you in the face'. However, with κατὰ πρόσωπον, Paul is probably recalling his other use of κατὰ πρόσωπον in 10.1, which describes his Christ-like appearance of humility and weakness, and points to the Corinthians' estimation of his outward appearance (10.10). Since it is possible for κατὰ πρόσωπον in 10.1 to communicate the sense of *persona*, the same phrase here can also be regarded as expressing the meaning of *persona*. Therefore, Paul is urging the Corinthians, 'Look at the facts according to appearance' – that is, Paul's Christ-like appearance (*persona*).

Since the Corinthians have criticised Paul's Christ-like identity (πραΰτης, ἐπιείκεια, and ταπεινός) and even considered it to be 'weakness' (ἡ παρουσία τοῦ σώματος ἀσθενὴς, 10.10), Paul in 10.7 urges them to consider his outward appearance as legitimate, though it appears to be the opposite of what they expected from an apostle.[222] In order for the Corinthians to approve his social identity, Paul must have them reinterpret his 'weak' and 'humble' Christ-like *persona* and recognise that he does in fact have authority (10.7). Thrall similarly suggests that Paul is bidding the Corinthians to look at him as 'Christ's person'.[223] While recognising Paul's portrayal of the 'ταπείνωσις und ἀσθένεια des Apostels', Karl Theodor Kleinknecht explains that Paul's confrontational manoeuvre is to prove his authority (ἐξουσία) as authentic, that is 'weshalb Paulus in 10,7 den Blick der Gemeinde förmlich auf diesen in ihren Augen als "Schwachstelle" erscheinenden Punkt seiner Existenz lenkt und in 10,10 die ihm von den

---

[221] Some scholars (e.g. Harris, *2 Cor*, 687; Windisch, *2 Kor*, 300) have explained the anomalous position of the verb here as Paul's emphasis on the stark reality of the evidence confronting the Corinthians. Also, Héring, *2 Cor*, 71, and Furnish, *2 Cor*, 465, have suggested that if Paul was contrasting the Corinthians' outlook (v. 7a) an adversative would have been expected in v. 7b.

[222] See Merritt, *Word and Deed*, 111–52, who considers the theme of 'word and deed' in 2 Cor 10–13, especially the charges against Paul's inconsistency (cf. 10.1, 10). See Paul's defence in 10.11 regarding his word (λόγῳ) and deed (ἔργῳ). Also note the importance of *facta et dicta* in Valerius Maximus' work.

[223] Thrall, *2 Cor*, 619. Cf. Garland, *2 Cor*, 440: 'He therefore demands that the Corinthians reconsider the evidence that will require them to admit his status as a man in Christ (10:7b)'.

Gegnern vorgeworfene ἀσθένεια anspricht'.[224] Hence, Wolff's suitable paraphrase: 'Angeblich bin ich bei euch immer klein und häßlich; aber bedenkt, wie die Dinge wirklich liegen!'[225]

6.4.3 Subversion of the Corinthians' Conventional Values

The rest of 10.7 further supports the legitimacy of Paul's Christ-like identity: 'If anyone is convinced in his own mind that he belongs to Christ (Χριστοῦ εἶναι), let him further consider himself that just as he is Christ's, so are we' (10.7b).[226] The issue at stake is both Paul and the Corinthians' claim to having the status 'of Christ' (Χριστοῦ εἶναι) – a phrase that could be a shorthand expression for ἀπόστολος Χριστοῦ or διάκονος Χριστοῦ, since his opponents have fashioned themselves as ἀποστόλοι Χριστοῦ and διάκονοι Χριστοῦ (11.13, 23).[227] Paul, then, intentionally draws attention to his 'weak' and 'humble' *persona* of Christ as a witness to his status of being a genuine apostle 'of Christ'. He urges the Corinthians to consider again (λογιζέσθω πάλιν, 10.7),[228] beyond their presumptuousness, the fact that he also has the right to make the same claim of status as Χριστοῦ εἶναι. Harris explains that while Paul does not endorse the truth of their claim, 'he uses it as a springboard to assert his own distinctive relation to Christ, presumably as a slave and apostle of Christ (cf. Rom. 1:1) and one who wields authority (note ἐξουσία in v. 8)'.[229] Eventually, Paul describes his opponents as false apostles (ψευδαπόστολοι) and servants of Satan, who are merely disguising themselves as apostles of Christ (11.13–15). Thus, in contrast to Paul's *bona fide* Christian identity (i.e. the image and person of Christ), his Corinthian opponents are only pretentiously displaying their own view of Christian identity, which reflects the conventional values of *persona* in first-century Corinth.

The subsequent texts reveal the reasons why the Corinthians have failed to understand properly the legitimacy of Paul's identity as an apostle of Christ. They grade his Christ-like *persona* by a conventional criteria, such as bodily presence, speech, and eloquence (10.10; 11.6), while boasting in their own

---

[224] Kleinknecht, *Der leidende*, 285.

[225] Wolff, *2 Kor*, 200.

[226] Cf. 10.8, which Heckel, *Kraft*, 14, regards as being concerned with Paul's 'Vollmacht als Apostel'. Also, some interpreters (e.g. Barrett, *2 Cor*, 256, 260–1) have suggested that the τις here refers to a particular person of this opposition group, while others (e.g. Furnish, *2 Cor*, 466) have understood the term in a general sense.

[227] Cf. Thrall, *2 Cor*, 621–3; Barrett, *2 Cor*, 256–8.

[228] Note the use of λογιζέσθω πάλιν here and τοὺς λογιζομένους (10.2), which could further indicate an allusion to Paul's *persona* in 10.1. Also cf. 3.5 where the term is used in the context of Paul's sufficiency as an apostle.

[229] Harris, *2 Cor*, 690–1.

displays of these status symbols. Paul, accordingly, points out and negates their social behaviour of self-comparison, self-commendation, and boasting κατὰ σάρκα and beyond a limit (10.12–15, 18; 11.18). Recognising the futility and shallowness of this behaviour, he reacts by placing his confidence in his identification with Christ. Paul expresses that he will legitimately boast only in the Lord (10.17), which is what he considers to be the only acceptable form of boasting, and will not commend himself since he will ultimately be approved and commended by God (10.18).[230] Despite the criticisms against his 'weak' and 'contemptible' depiction of Christ's image and person, Paul finds confidence in it, especially because this is the image into which he is being transformed (3.18; 4.4, 6).

Paul further reveals his motivation for embracing this Christ-like identity, which is marked by visible weakness.[231] Similar to 2 Cor 4.7–15, Paul understands that God's power is manifested through weakness. The critical term 'weakness', which is a key theme of this section, is used here not only in the sense of physical weakness (e.g. 12.5, 9, 10) but also in the sense of unimpressive appearance (10.10).[232] Martin suggests, 'Both those ideas – physical weakness and a "non-charismatic *persona*" – interlock, however'.[233] Martin also claims that this would fit into the understanding of ἀσθένεια as 'a sign of humanity in its earthiness and dependence on God' and 'as a christological aspect of Paul's apostolic life'.[234] With his preoccupation with God's power in his weakness, Paul continues the theme of boasting and makes his so-called 'Fool's Speech' (*Narrenrede*) (11.21b–12.12), whereby he joins in and plays their game of boasting.[235] In his foolish boasting Paul

---

[230] On Paul's boasting and 'self-commendation' of his apostolic authority and the nature of the divine commendation, see Hafemann, 'Self-Commendation', esp. 74–6, 80–4; Lambrecht, 'Dangerous Boasting', 325–46; Bosch, 'L'apologie', 43–63; and the other studies listed in Chapter Five.

[231] According to Harrill, 'Invective', 189–213, Paul is being criticised of having a slavish appearance. If this is the case, then Paul's visual image is tantamount to the image of Christ, who was also perceived as a slave.

[232] The ἀσθεν- word group occurs 14 times in 2 Corinthians, all of which are found in chs. 10–13.

[233] Martin, *2 Cor*, 382; cf. Thrall, *2 Cor*, 751. See also, Andrews, 'Too Weak', 263–76, who regards Paul's weaknesses as a matter of social status. He postulates that Paul succumbs to and is overcome by hardships in order to achieve a lowly status which results in shame. *Contra* Lambrecht, 'Strength', 285–90, who offers a good critique of Andrews to show that it is in the midst of Paul's weaknesses that God's power is made visible in Paul. However, Paul's weaknesses would have been associated with a lower social status in the Corinthians' evaluation of his social identity.

[234] Martin, *2 Cor*, 382, who refers to Black, *Paul*, 228–40.

[235] See Thrall, *2 Cor*, 799–800, who distinguishes Paul in 12.6 as not *being a* fool, but *playing the part* of the fool. She also notes that according to 12.6 'it appears to be Paul's general *persona* (rather than his specific activities) which primarily concern the Corinthians,

presents his own pedigree and his vision and revelation from God, all of which would give him honourable distinctions in relation to the Corinthians. However, as he continues in his speech, he seems to boast in favour of things that appear to be weaknesses, such as his afflictions as an apostle (11.23–7).[236] Paul takes pride in boasting in weakness (11.30; 12.5, 9) because it is through his weakness that Christ's power is visibly manifested (12.9).[237] This even leads him to express remarkably, 'Therefore I *delight* (εὐδοκῶ) in weaknesses, insults, hardships, persecutions, and calamities for the sake of Christ; for whenever I am weak, then I am strong (ὅταν γὰρ ἀσθενῶ, τότε δυνατός εἰμι)' (12.10). This last statement accentuates Paul's understanding that through his weaknesses 'Christ has the opportunity to bring his power into full operation'.[238]

Paul continues in 13.3–4 with his subversive power-in-weakness motif in his response to the Corinthians' demand for proof that he is an apostle of Christ (13.3a), since they only observe his visible weaknesses (10.1, 10). After affirming their experience of Christ's power (13.3b), Paul makes a climactic statement[239] that would have conflicted with the Corinthians' evaluation of Paul: 'Christ was crucified in weakness, but lives by the power of God' (13.4a).[240] Thrall aptly explains, 'The Christ of whose power in Paul his readers demand evidence has himself suffered weakness, but nevertheless is the recipient of divine power'.[241] Paul consequently uses this christological affirmation of 'weakness', to relate it to his own apostolic weakness: 'We are weak in him (ἐν αὐτῷ), but in dealing with you we will live with him (σὺν αὐτῷ) by the power of God' (13.4b). With this last statement Paul is clearly showing a parallel between his weakness with Christ's weakness (ἐν αὐτῷ–

---

together with his oratorical powers, or lack of them' (801–2). See also Holland, 'Speaking', 251, who explains that Paul's use of irony allows him 'to "speak like a fool" in his own defense, saying things that must be said but which he could not say *in proper persona*'; Lambrecht, 'Fool's Speech', 305–24.

[236] See Judge, 'Boasting', 47–50, who perceives that Paul's boasting is a 'parody of conventional norms'; cf. Heckel, *Kraft*, 194–5, 202–3. See also Phil 3.5–6, where Paul lists his Jewish *cursus honorum*, and considers it all 'rubbish' because of Christ (vv. 7–8); cf. Hellerman, *Reconstructing*, 121–7.

[237] Cf. Barrett, *2 Cor*, 302: 'Paul declares that he is weak, and that it is his weakness – his humble and humiliated behaviour, his poverty, his unimpressive appearance – that the power of Christ is made known'; O'Collins, 'Power', 537: 'Christ's triumphant power is "effective" in the concrete circumstances of Paul's life, and hence it is *visibly* revealed' (emphasis mine).

[238] Thrall, *2 Cor*, 830.

[239] So Stegman, *Character*, 205, who regards this as the climax of the entire epistle.

[240] See Heckel, *Kraft*, 130, who states that although Christ was crucified, the life here is his continual resurrection life. Also, see Stegman, *Character*, 206, on Paul's appeal here to the story and character of Jesus.

[241] Thrall, *2 Cor*, 882.

σὺν αὐτῷ), as explained by Harris: 'Both knew weakness, willingly accepted; both are "alive" because of God's power. But the correspondence was not superficial, for Paul's experience was a direct consequence of his union with Christ that is expressed by ἐν and σύν'.[242] Savage also conveys that Paul 'uses the language of incorporation to underscore that his suffering is uniquely and ultimately like Christ's'.[243] Thus, Paul is reinterpreting his weaknesses as indeed conforming to the pattern of Christ's power-in-weakness (i.e. the dying and life of Jesus), since the 'anticipative resurrection power is, of course, Paul's credential par excellence'.[244]

Therefore, in order to correct the distorted view of Christian identity in the church, Paul confounds the Corinthians and subverts their conventional values of social identity with his seemingly contemptible Christ-like identity – a subversive *persona* that is to be appraised as the authentic identity for an apostle.[245] The subversive force of Paul's Christ-like identity comes from the fact that his cruciform-shaped *persona* is an extension of the crucified Christ, and also an embodiment of his λόγος τοῦ σταυροῦ (1 Cor 1.18–25). Barton has aptly illuminated the social implications of Paul's understanding of the cross:

For Paul, the cross is a symbol of reversal...Such an idea [of a crucified Christ] constituted an inversion of the spiritual and moral ideas and institutions of Paul's days: it turned upside-down notions of honour and shame, both those of the Romans (based on the quest for personal prestige) and those of the Jews (based on Torah-observance). However, by constituting an inversion of, rather than a separation from the contemporary value system, Paul's ideology remained in contact (as its negation) and thus was able to build upon its power base. Further more, Paul capitalized upon this by presenting himself as the very embodiment of the negation...[246]

E.A. Judge similarly explains Paul's subversive strategy against particular social realities of the Graeco-Roman world:

The Corinthian letters show him [Paul] in a head-on confrontation with the mechanisms by which it imposed social power...His positive response to this collision was to build a remarkable new construction of social realities that both lay within the fabric of the old ranking system and yet transformed it by a revolution in social values.[247]

---

[242] Harris, *2 Cor*, 917. See his diagram of the three statements in vv. 3b–4 on p. 914, which highlights Paul and Christ's experiences; Heckel, *Kraft*, 139 for another diagram, and pp. 131–8 for the analogy between the Paul and Christ.

[243] Savage, *Power*, 174. Cf. Lambrecht, 'Philological', 262, who writes that Paul's 'weakness and strength are christologically conditioned'; Stegman, *Character*, 211.

[244] Lambrecht, 'Dangerous Boasting', 345.

[245] Cf. Martin, *2 Cor*, 476, who comments that Paul 'is asking them to consider that "weakness"...is the correct stance of a true apostle of Christ'.

[246] Barton, 'Cross', 15–16 (italics his).

[247] Judge, 'Conformity', 23. See also Marshall, 'Enigmatic', 161–6, who discusses how

Barton and Judge's insights are significant in relating how Paul uses the conventional 'power base' and 'mechanisms' of social *persona* and identity in order to present the Christ-like *persona* as an inversion and negation of the typically projected *persona* in first-century Corinth. Since this inversive practice is also seen in Paul's use of conventional boasting in order to boast legitimately in the Lord, it can be reckoned that Paul is counteracting the Corinthians' conventional boasting ἐν προσώπῳ (5.12), by promoting instead a boasting ἐν κυρίῳ (10.18) – that is, a boasting ἐν προσώπῳ Χριστοῦ (4.6).

6.5 An Analysis of Paul's Use of Πρόσωπον in 2 Corinthians

As explained in Chapter One, this study is a social concept study which looks beyond the language of *persona* and πρόσωπον for other terms and expressions in 2 Corinthians that communicate the concept of *persona*. This study has shown that there are terms and expressions that resemble the concept of *persona* throughout the letter. Nevertheless, this study did examine many instances of the term πρόσωπον in 2 Corinthians, since the term can convey a meaning of 'social identity' and occurs frequently in the letter. This section will briefly assess Paul's use of πρόσωπον in 2 Corinthians and evaluate whether any of the instances has a clear meaning of *persona* or implications for Paul's approach to identity.

There are 12 instances of the term πρόσωπον in 2 Corinthians. As seen in Chapter Two, the word has a wide semantic range; so it is not surprising that Paul employs the word in a variety of ways. In fact, some of the occurrences were not given much attention in this study (1.11; 2.10; 8.24; 11.20), since they did not seem to denote any meaning of *persona* or contribute to Paul's approach to identity. In these instances, Paul uses the term to convey: the prayers of many 'persons' (1.11), the forgiveness in the 'presence' of Christ (2.10), being open 'before' the churches (8.24), and being slapped in the 'face' (11.20).

More importantly, this study observed some instances of πρόσωπον that contributed to Paul's articulation of identity (3.7, 13, 18; 4.6; 5.12; 10.1, 7). The instance that shows the clearest equivalence to *persona* is 5.12, where Paul describes those who boast in 'outward appearance' and not in the heart. This key verse elucidates how individuals were obsessed with the superficial type of outward appearance. Although commentators have affirmed the term's meaning of 'outward appearance' here, this study advances a more nuanced

---

Paul uses the theme of 'dying and rising with Christ' to bring about a radical social change in the Corinthian church.

reading of social *persona*. This verse, moreover, is important because it clearly communicates Paul's external–internal antithesis in 2.14–7.4.

The other instances of πρόσωπον within this extended literary unit also contribute to Paul's external–internal interplay, whereby he rejects the values of the superficial type of externals and stresses instead the internal features that are related to Christian transformation. The references to Moses' πρόσωπον (3.7, 13) and the unveiled πρόσωπον of believers (3.18), while referring to the literal face, do contribute to this antithesis. In the case of Moses' πρόσωπον, it was shown that some Old Testament scholars have regarded Moses' πρόσωπον and veil as cultic masks, which is significant because *persona* and πρόσωπον were shown in Chapter Two to have an early meaning of 'mask' that influenced the terms' meaning of social identity. Here Moses' πρόσωπον contributes to Paul's external–internal antithesis, since it displays a fading glory and has to be veiled from the Israelites' gaze. However, the context suggests that the term does not explicate a meaning of *persona*, and is probably referring to Moses' literal face. In 3.18, with the transition from Moses' veiled face to the internal veiling of the Israelites, the detail of the unveiled πρόσωπον of Christians is likely to be also referring to the face; however, πρόσωπον is used here more figuratively, since the veiling is an internal veiling over the Israelites' hearts/minds (3.15).

The next use of πρόσωπον in this literary unit occurs in 4.6, where Paul explains that God shines his glory in the believers' hearts ἐν προσώπῳ Χριστοῦ. This text reaches a climax in the Moses narrative and provides a contrast between Moses' glory/πρόσωπον and Christ's. Although most interpreters translate the phrase as 'the face of Christ', the context suggests that a better translation should be 'person of Christ' – an interpretation which has been advanced by a few scholars. The shift of meaning from a literal face in 3.7, 13 to a more figurative face in 3.18 allows the term πρόσωπον in 4.6 to have a deeper sense than 'face'. More importantly, within the context of a transformation into the image (εἰκών) of Christ (3.18; 4.4), it is significant that Christ as the εἰκὼν τοῦ θεοῦ is closely parallel to the phrase ἐν προσώπῳ Χριστοῦ. Since this phrase can be regarded as part of Paul's transformation motif – that is, a transformation into the 'person of Christ' – this study grasps the term πρόσωπον here as having implications for Paul's treatment of identity. Although it is difficult to discern whether Paul intended a precise meaning of *persona*, the term can be understood as *conceptually* expressing the social feature of *persona*. Paul, then, would be promoting the '*persona* of Christ' (or Christ-like *persona*) as an essential component of Christian transformation and identity. After this important instance of πρόσωπον, the term is used again in Paul's castigation of the Corinthians' boasting in the superficial type of outward appearance and not in the internal features of one's identity (5.12).

In 2 Cor 10–13 there are two significant uses of πρόσωπον. Paul begins the section by appealing to the Corinthians by the gentleness and meekness of Christ, that when he is with them he is humble, but when away, he is bold (10.1). The phrase κατὰ πρόσωπον in 10.1 is usually understood as communicating a presence–absence contrast. However, the context suggests that the phrase is not merely denoting Paul's physical presence, but more specifically his outward appearance and characteristics. It is possible that Paul is communicating a precise meaning of *persona* with κατὰ πρόσωπον, since the phrase seems to be pointing to his embodiment of Christ's characteristics (gentleness, meekness, and humility) and to the charges made against his outward appearance of weakness in 10.10. Similarly, 2 Cor 10.7 has the phrase κατὰ πρόσωπον, which seems to be also indicating aspects of visuality. Since 10.7 should be translated as an imperative, Paul is understood to be urging the Corinthians to consider things according to his outward appearance, which he described in 10.1 as a Christ-like appearance. As in 10.1, it is possible that πρόσωπον here has a sense of *persona*, since the term is used to point to an aspect of Paul's Christian identity.

In sum, a number of Paul's uses of πρόσωπον in 2 Corinthians do contribute to his approach to Christian identity, and a few of them do express, to some degree, a meaning of *persona*. Of these occurrences, 5.12 seems to have the clearest meaning of social *persona*, and the instances in 10.1, 7 seem close to expressing a precise meaning of *persona*. The use of πρόσωπον in 4.6 is difficult to discern, but it seems to have at least a conceptual understanding of *persona*. The instances in 3.7, 13, 18 do not appear to have a precise meaning of *persona,* and are most likely to be referring to a literal face. Furthermore, it is important to point out that in the instances of πρόσωπον that have strong implications of *persona*, Paul uses the word both negatively to refer to the superficial type of outward appearance (5.12), and positively to refer to the sort of outward appearance that is based on and reflects the inner spiritual transformation (4.6; 10.1, 7).

6.6 Supporting Evidence in Paul's Other Letters

Before concluding this chapter on Paul's presentation of Christian identity in 2 Corinthians, it is worthwhile to consider briefly how Paul similarly approaches identity in his other letters. Throughout this chapter there were various texts from his other letters used to support certain facets of Paul's critique of the superficial displays of identity and his promotion of a new Christ-like identity. For instance, in the discussion of Paul's external–internal interplay, his understanding of God's illumination of the believer's heart was seen in texts like Rom 5.5 and Eph 1.18. Also, texts from his other letters highlighted themes such as Paul's transformation motif (e.g. Rom 12.2; Col 3.9–10), his εἰκών motif (e.g. Col 1.15), and his understanding of Christian identity as depicting the dying and life of Jesus (e.g. Rom 6.5). Although these various texts confirmed only certain elements of Paul's approach to identity, Paul's letter to the Galatians exhibits many similarities to his larger presentation of identity in 2 Corinthians, whereby Paul castigates a preoccupation with superficial matters and promotes a Christian identity that reflects a spiritual transformation. In fact, scholars have recently explored Paul's interest in constructing Christian identity in Galatians.[248] Attention will now be given to Galatians for a brief look at Paul's similar approach to Christian identity in the Galatian church.

Paul writes to the Galatians in order to refute the message of certain Jewish Christians who were urging the Galatians to observe the works of the law, especially circumcision. In his argument, it is noticeable that Paul shows some reaction against the Galatians' adoption of certain conventional social practices – such as boasting in social status, and estimating leaders based on external matters. Moreover, this problem in the church is similar to the wider problem of a preoccupation with outward *persona*. Like his argument in 2 Corinthians, Paul denounces the Galatians' inappropriate behaviour by showing the futility of evaluating leaders according to conventional values (e.g. social status), and by ridiculing those who boast in such superficial status markers.

This study had looked at two texts in Galatians that reveal an obsession with outward status symbols (see Chapter Five). Interestingly, these two texts were examined for how the term πρόσωπον (2.6) and its cognate εὐπροσωπέω (6.12) have connotations of the concept of *persona*. In 2.6 Paul denies the value of his opponents' status and position, and then asserts his reasoning: πρόσωπον [ὁ] θεὸς ἀνθρώπου οὐ λαμβάνει (cf. Rom 2.11). Paul, here, is deprecating the conventional estimation of leaders based on outward appearance.[249] Also, in 6.12 the opponents are described as those who want 'to make a good showing (εὐπροσωπῆσαι)'[250] in the flesh in order to avoid persecution for the cross of Christ. That is, by being circumcised and projecting this particular marker of Jewish identity, they will gain the

---

[248] E.g. Witherington, *Gal*, 41, observes that 'this document, perhaps more than any other in the Pauline corpus, raises questions about how one gets in, how one stays, and how one goes on in the Christian community'. For a recent study, see e.g. Longenecker, *Triumph*; also, for studies using the modern 'social identity theory', see e.g. Esler, *Galatians*; Asano, *Community-Identity*.

[249] See Hubbard, *New Creation*, 197–8, who considers this text as similar to 2 Cor 5.12, since they both express Paul's external–internal interplay and πρόσωπον motif.

[250] In Chapter Five, it was mentioned that Winter, 'Imperial Cult', esp. 73–5, translates the term as 'to secure a "good" status'.

privilege of not being persecuted for their Christian identity. Paul additionally describes these leaders as those who are self-deceived because they think of themselves as more important than they really are (6.3). The Galatians, then, have probably adopted the conventional values of *persona* into the church.[251] Accordingly, these Jewish Christian leaders are boasting in their Jewish *persona*, and are stressing the privilege of being circumcised.

As in 2 Corinthians, while denouncing the boasting in the superficialities of one's identity, Paul accentuates a more appropriate form of identity in which the Galatians should boast. Some scholars have recognised that Paul communicates in the letter his important theme of a transformation in Christ (1.15–16; 2.20; 3.3; 4.19), that is, a new creation (καινὴ κτίσις) in Christ (6.15).[252] The inner dimension of this Christian identity is observed in the transformative work of the Spirit (3.3, 14, 21–2; 4.6, 29; 5.16, 18, 25). Significantly, Paul promotes this new creation as the essence of Christian identity, rather than status symbols like circumcision: 'For neither circumcision nor uncircumcision is anything; but a new creation is everything!' (6.15). Furthermore, as in 2 Corinthians, there is a visible dimension to Paul's transformation and new creation motifs, which is an outward reflection of the inward work of the Spirit.[253] Paul describes this visible dimension as an embodiment of the crucified Christ. Paul affirms his own cruciform identity by stating that he has been crucified with Christ (2.19), and even regards his physical body as bearing the marks of the crucified Christ (τὰ στίγματα τοῦ Ἰησοῦ) (6.17). This embodiment of Christ, consequently, subverts the Galatians' conventional values of boasting. Paul states accordingly, 'May I never boast of anything except the cross of our Lord Jesus Christ, by which the world has been crucified to me, and I to the world' (6.14).

In sum, this brief survey of Paul's approach to a crisis of Christian identity in Galatians shows similarities to his approach in 2 Corinthians, thus supporting this study's findings of Paul's interest and critique of Christian identity in 2 Corinthians. The evidence from Galatians additionally supports this study's understanding of the concept of *persona* in 2 Corinthians, since

---

[251] Since Galatia is part of the Roman empire, there would have been some level of a Roman stress on *persona*, although probably not as strong as in the Roman colony of Corinth. This Roman stress could be confirmed if 6.15 communicates a need to achieve a legal *persona* that has the privilege of avoiding a form of Roman persecution. See Winter, 'Imperial Cult', esp. 73–5.

[252] Dunn, *Theology of Galatians*, 188–20; Longenecker, *Triumph*; Hubbard, *New Creation*, 229.

[253] Longenecker, *Triumph*, 69: 'Paul expects Christian moral identity to be exhibited in patterns of life that evidence the working of the Spirit'. See his chapter on 'Eschatological Transformation Embodied' (147–72).

there are some texts in Galatians that have connotations of *persona*. Therefore, this section affirms and strengthens this study's reading of Paul's critique of identity and *persona* in 2 Corinthians, since his critique can similarly be observed elsewhere in his letters.

6.7 Conclusions

6.7.1 *Paul's Critique of* Persona *and Identity*

This chapter and the previous one have investigated Paul's approach to Christian identity in 2 Corinthians – specifically, his critique of social identity and *persona*. The Christians had adopted and refashioned the typical outworking of social *persona* in first-century Corinth, and the conventional *modus operandi* of valuing individuals based on the superficial features of that *persona* – such as rank, status, wealth, eloquence, wisdom, and beauty. From the social problems observed in the Corinthian correspondence, the church was seen to be preoccupied with these shallow features that express a person's social identity, a preoccupation which mirrored the one in Roman Corinth. This preoccupation was clearly seen in 2 Corinthians, in which Paul responded to the Corinthian Christians' superficial assessment of his public *persona*, since he lacked eloquence in his preaching and displayed marks of suffering. According to their conventional criteria, Paul's contemptible appearance did not meet their expectations of the *persona* which an apostle should have.

In the extended literary unit of 2 Cor 2.14–7.4, Paul reacted at length to their inappropriate appraisal of superficial features by deprecating certain outward elements, and placing the emphasis rather on the inner person, which was ultimately seen in the internal work of the Spirit in the believers' hearts. In addition to this spiritual transformation, Paul positively conveyed a new and different identity that is 'in Christ' – the '*persona* of Christ' – which resulted from the Christians' transformation into the image (εἰκών) and person (πρόσωπον) of Christ (3.18; 4.4, 6). Importantly, Paul does not make a clear distinction between the internal and external aspects of Christian identity, for the outward dimension of the person expresses the transformative effects in the inner person. Paul, then, is specifically castigating the preoccupation with outward appearance that expresses superficial values, and commending, instead, the outward appearance that reflects an inward spiritual transformation. Moreover, this visible transformation into a Christ-like image was understood to be manifested not only in the shape of the Christian ἐκκλησία, but more specifically, in the Christians' visible embodiment of the 'dying and life of Jesus Christ', as exemplified by Paul's apostolic lifestyle.

This crisis of Christian identity in the Corinthian church was also clearly seen in 2 Corinthians 10–13, where there was a conflict with Paul and the Corinthians' opposing views on *persona*, specifically Paul's *persona*. Paul projected a Christ-like identity, which subverted the Corinthians' conventional estimation of social identity. That is, Paul used the 'power base' and 'mechanisms' of the conventional values of *persona*, and inverted its economy with his reconstructed *persona* 'in Christ', which depicted 'weakness' rather than the shallow displays of power and prestige. While the Corinthians had perceived his contemptible appearance as inglorious, he recognised his Christ-like *persona* as essentially 'power-in-weakness'. Savage has explained Paul's ability to perceive this cruciformed *persona* as divine power:

> In the cross of Christ he discovered not only that divine power had been manifested in human weakness, but also that it took eyes of humility, eyes of faith, to detect that power. It required an outlook which itself had been moulded by the cross – a cross-shaped faith which focused on the unseen, not the seen.[254]

Throughout the letter Paul urged the Corinthians to reinterpret his Christ-like appearance as appropriate for an apostle, and also to embody it themselves.

In contrast to the widely projected *persona* in the early imperial period, as seen in Chapter Two, Paul can be assessed to be a strong critic of it, since he clearly disparaged its shallow features, and emphasised the inner person. More significantly, he inverted the values of the typically presented *persona* by modelling and inculcating a lifestyle which reflected the image and person of the crucified Christ, who died a humiliating and shameful death. In addition to Paul's lowly display of weakness and his lack of eloquence, the status symbols associated with this Christ-like identity also would have been an inversion of the conventional values of social identity, since Paul's 'rank and status' were: an apostle of Christ Jesus (1.1), a slave of God (2.14–17), a minister of the new covenant (3.6), an ambassador of Christ (5.20), God's co-worker (6.1), and God's servant (6.4). Therefore, Paul's conception of an individual's authentic *persona* 'in Christ' (i.e. Christian identity) was a reconfiguration and inversion of the conventionally depicted *persona* – one that was not an ego-centric *persona*, but a theo- and christo-centric *persona*.

---

[254] Savage, *Power*, 185. Cf. Jewett, *Anthropological*, 396, who writes that 'it is a transformation [into the image of the crucified Christ] seen only by faith since the life of Christ is visible only in the aspect of the death of Christ'.

6.7.2 *Comparison to Valerius Maximus and Epictetus' Critiques*

Having compared Paul's critique of social *persona*, his critique will now be heuristically compared to those of Valerius Maximus and Epictetus. As noted in Chapter One, there have been a small number of studies that have compared these two individuals to the New Testament; however, none of these studies has explored any related concept of social identity. Although there are many points of comparison between Paul and the other two individuals, this comparison will concentrate only on the general contours of their critiques of *persona*, and will not provide an exhaustive or systematic comparison between Paul and the other two figures.

In regard to Valerius, both he and Paul had negative reactions to the Roman stress on *persona* in the early imperial period, since there was an exaggeration and exploitation of the traditional values and virtues of *persona*. In Chapter Three, it was determined that although Valerius' critique was a serious one, he still showed appreciation for the Roman social hierarchy and aimed to restore the traditional values of an ideal Roman *persona*. His reaction was particularly against the obsession with and exploitation of the status symbols of Roman identity. In contrast, although Paul also reacted to a preoccupation with the shallow features of *persona*, his critique was more severe than Valerius'. Despite Paul's reaction against the Corinthian Christians' exploitation of *persona*, his criticisms were not against the idea of being a Roman or against the whole of Roman society. As a Roman, he would have some appreciation for certain Roman ideals and virtues, especially those that resonated with what he considered to be appropriate Christian ideals and virtues; however, Paul's concern was not with the restoration of Roman ideals *per se*, but with the restoration of God's ideal of humanity as the image of God. Moreover, Paul's sharper criticism was also seen in his promotion of a Christ-like identity, which would have inverted many of the conventional values of *persona*. The main difference between the two figures was that Valerius understood one's identity as still rooted in the Roman socio-political world, while Paul understood it to be primarily rooted in a Christian context. It is also interesting that Valerius presented the emperor as the supreme embodiment of a traditional and ideal Roman *persona*. Paul, on the other hand, promoted his positive conception of the Christian *persona*, which he himself embodied, as rooted in the image and person of Jesus Christ.[255]

---

[255] See Oakes, 'Re-mapping', 301–22, who examines how Paul in Philippians and 1 Thessalonians 're-maps the universe', by de-centring the emperor and depicting Christ as occupying the centre of the universe. This has implications for 2 Corinthians; e.g. Paul presents in 2 Cor 2.14–17 the image of Christ's triumph, which would conflict with the emperor's triumphal position in the universe.

Overall, Valerius' critique of *persona* was a milder critique, while Paul's was a stronger critique.

In comparison to Epictetus, Paul's sharp criticism is similar to Epictetus', since both were not primarily interested in restoring the traditional values and virtues of an ideal Roman *persona*. The remainder of this comparison will focus not only on the similarities of their critiques but also the differences. Also, besides their similar reactions, there are additional benefits in comparing these two figures: both have considerable uses of the term πρόσωπον, both of their works reflect the social world in the Roman Greek East, and both are situated in a 'teaching' environment.[256] Moreover, some scholars have suspected the possibility of Epictetus' awareness of and familiarity with Christianity (cf. *Diss.* 2.9.21; 4.7.6), especially since the New Testament indicates that there were Christians in Hierapolis (Col 4.13), Rome (Rom 16), and Nicopolis (Tit 3.12) – places where Epictetus had lived.[257] Some have even proposed a relationship or interdependency between Paul and Epictetus. However, although there are parallels between the two, the consensus is that there is no clear evidence of a direct relationship or interdependency.

Concerning Epictetus and Paul's critiques, both conveyed the futility of parading the accoutrements of a fashionable *persona* in order to receive accolades, and also the futility of assessing one another according to these visible displays. They both placed the true value of an individual, instead, on the inner person. The main difference between their critiques is that although both acknowledged one's *persona* as not primarily rooted in the Roman socio-political world, Epictetus conceived it as rooted in a philosophical (Stoic) understanding, while Paul viewed it as rooted in a religious (Christian) understanding. Epictetus, who perceived the intense longing for status symbols as an 'incurable fever' (*Diss.* 4.9.1–5), viewed the προαίρεσις ('volition') as the genuine centre of the person, since it determines how an individual can live unhindered as a rational being. In addition, he valued the inner person because 'God' dwells within the individual (1.14.11–14; 2.7.3; 2.8.11–14; 4.12.11–12). Epictetus clearly expressed this exterior–interior antithesis: 'Externals (τὰ ἔξω) are not under my control; προαίρεσις is under

---

[256] See Stowers, 'Social Status', 69, who considers that Paul's role as a teacher in the Corinthian house church is parallel to Epictetus' role as a Stoic teacher in his philosophical school; cf. Alexander, 'Hellenistic Schools', 60–83.

[257] See the brief discussion in Yieh, *One Teacher*, 187–8. It should also be noted here that recently some scholars have been interested in comparing Paul with the Stoics, and even identifying him as a Stoic. See e.g. the important work by Engberg-Pedersen, *Stoics*. See the critique by Esler, 'Stoicism', and a response by Engberg-Pedersen, 'Relationship'. Given that this study is a heuristic comparison, it is not necessary to identify Paul's relationship with Stoicism.

my control' (2.5.5; cf. 1.4.18). In the case of Paul, he regarded the authentic aspect of the person to be the καρδία, where the Spirit is at work (2 Cor 3–4). Similarly, Paul explicated that God dwells in the Christian (6.16). He also articulated the exterior–interior (πρόσωπον–καρδία) contrast using various terms and expressions throughout 2 Corinthians, which was clearly seen in the key text of 5.12, where he exposed those who boast in shallow appearance (ἐν προσώπῳ) and not in the heart (ἐν καρδίᾳ).

Although both Epictetus and Paul denounced the conventional estimation of *persona*, they both presented a positive and modified conceptualisation of one's authentic and genuine *persona*. Epictetus expressed this positive value of πρόσωπον, 'But for determining the rational and the irrational, we employ not only our estimates of what is the value of external things (ἐκτός), but also the criterion of that which is in keeping with one's own πρόσωπον' (*Diss.* 1.2.7–8). Additionally, he conveyed various aspects of an individual's true πρόσωπον (cf. 2.10). For instance, he explained that God assigns each individual a particular social identity (πρόσωπον), and the individual should live out that assigned role well, regardless of the determined social position (*Ench.* 17). According to Paul, the positive value of one's identity is ultimately seen in God's work of unveiling the Christian's πρόσωπον and transforming the individual into the image (εἰκών) and person (πρόσωπον) of Christ (2 Cor 3.16–4.6). Both also warned that one should not live beyond this God-given identity. Epictetus states that one should not assume a πρόσωπον that is beyond one's power, since 'you both disgrace yourself in that one, and at the same time neglect the role which you might have filled with success' (*Ench.* 37). Similarly, Paul reacts against those who boast beyond a certain limit (2 Cor 10.12–15, 18), and elsewhere exhorts Christians not to think of themselves more highly than they ought to but to consider themselves by the measure of faith that God has assigned, as seen in the various gifts God has given them (Rom 12.3–7).

One further point of comparison is the visible image of the genuine *persona* that Paul and Epictetus each promoted. Epictetus did not seem to convey to any great extent a positive visible dimension of his concept of one's true identity, since he was primarily concerned with encouraging individuals to live out their God-given social role (πρόσωπον) – which according to Epictetus would be achieving the ideal of καλὸς καὶ ἀγαθός (cf. *Diss.* 1.7.2–3; 3.24.95–100). Nevertheless, as a Stoic philosopher, Epictetus proudly fashioned the image and visible indicators of a philosopher (long beard, cloak, and staff), as seen in his assertion that he would rather lose his neck than his beard (1.2.28–9). In his discourses Epictetus often identified the exemplar of an ideal philosopher to be Socrates, whom Epictetus qualified as καλὸς καὶ ἀγαθός (cf. 2.18.21; 4.5.1; 4.8.23–4). Interestingly, he also idealised the identity of a Cynic (τὸ τοῦ καλοῦ καὶ ἀγαθοῦ πρόσωπον, 3.22.69, 87), and the Cynic's projection of a plain and simplistic bodily appearance (3.22.9–12, 86–9).[258] However, given the ascetic and extreme lifestyle of a Cynic, Epictetus considered the Cynic's lifestyle as only appropriate for the few who have this special calling. In contrast, Paul articulated the visible image and person of Christ, and also the Christian's transformation into that Christ-like identity, which is essentially an embodiment of the dying and life of Jesus (2 Cor 3.18–4.15). Moreover, Paul pointed out that this visible transformation into the '*persona* of Christ' – which is patterned after Christ's suffering – is expected of all Christians (3.18).

Finally, since suffering was an important aspect of Paul's visible *persona*, it should be highlighted that there is a difference between Epictetus and Paul's understanding of human suffering. Both recognised God's involvement in human suffering, but Epictetus promoted the Stoic view that an individual, as a rational being, should endure and find happiness in the midst of the irrational matter of suffering (*Diss.* 1.9.16–17; 2.19.24). Even though Paul advocated the need to persevere in suffering (cf. 2 Cor 4.8–9), he did not promote the goal of happiness, but instead the understanding that God's power works in and through his weakness (12.9; cf. 4.7–15). The contrast in their views can be seen by comparing Epictetus' statement, 'It is difficulties that show what men are' (*Diss.* 1.24.1), with Paul's statement in 2 Cor 4.7, 'But we have this treasure in earthen vessels, so that it may be made clear that this extraordinary power *belongs to God and does not come from us*' (cf. 4.8–9). This shows that Epictetus regarded the realities of suffering as centred on the individual's ability to overcome them – a focus more on the self; in contrast, Paul regarded the Christian's suffering as being an extension of Christ's suffering, and as the condition in which God chooses to manifest his resurrection power – thus, a focus more on God/Christ.

---

[258] See Downing, *Cynics*, who suggests the influence of the Cynic traditions on Paul.

Chapter 7

Conclusions

7.1 Summary

This study has explored Paul's approach to the social conflicts involving Christian identity in 2 Corinthians. In order to grasp the dynamics of 'social identity' in the world of the New Testament, this study examined the concept of *persona* (esp. the Roman stress on *persona*), which denoted a person's identity in the Graeco-Roman social world in the first century CE. In addition, this study examined Paul's critique of social identity in light of two other figures – Epictetus and Valerius Maximus – and their critiques. All three social critics reacted against a conventional (or popular) view of *persona*, which is a preoccupation with its superficial features.

In Chapter One, the background and rationale for this study were explained. This study was explained to be interested in 'social identity' – that is, people's understanding of who they and others are, and how that understanding was projected and evaluated – in the social world of the New Testament. In order to grasp the dynamics of social identity in the Graeco-Roman world, this study focused on the ancient social concept of *persona*, which expressed aspects of social identity. Introductory matters were also addressed about the significance and need of this study. For instance, there has been no significant study of the social feature of *persona,* and New Testament scholars have not considered its relevance for the New Testament and Christian identity. In addition, this study's method was explained to be a combined method of a social concept study, social history, and a heuristic comparison.

With no substantial treatment of the concept of *persona* available, in Chapter Two the concept of *persona* was explained to be a key social factor for determining an individual's place and role in Graeco-Roman society. This critical feature of social identity affected the majority of individuals in the Roman empire, regardless of his or her socio-economic status. It was demonstrated that within the development of the Latin term *persona* and the Greek equivalent πρόσωπον, there existed a meaning that referred to 'social identity'. Although the concept of *persona* was seen to have somewhat of a broad understanding in Graeco-Roman society, this study focused on the

Roman stress on *persona*, since the dominant social, cultural, and political force throughout the Roman empire was Roman. In a Roman context, one's social identity was formulated by the Roman social hierarchy and Roman law, and had a critical function in his or her social relations. Importantly, it was emphasised that although the concept of *persona* had an effect on individuals from both ends of the social spectrum, this social concept was chiefly a traditional and elite ideal, which served to portray and protect the honour, virtues, and privileges of the elite members of society.

With the impetus to know one's place on the social ladder and the possibility of achieving social mobility, individuals were compelled to express visibly the status symbols associated with one's social identity in order to advertise one's possession of an ideal and reputable *persona*. Given the recognised value in these visible expressions, it only took a glance for individuals to assess one another. Since many of these visible status symbols became the determining factors of one's social standing and privileges, individuals exploited and exaggerated many of these status symbols. Furthermore, this conventional outworking of *persona* in the early imperial period spawned a social problem of individuals being preoccupied with its shallow features – as was seen in the specific problems of conspicuous consumption and social usurpation. Thus, the conventionally projected *persona* was a distortion of the ideal and traditional notions of an honourable *persona*.

This study then considered three figures who offered reactions to the large preoccupation with the superficial dimension of this widely depicted *persona* – a preoccupation which engendered a crisis of identity in their social worlds. In Chapter Three, the first figure, Valerius Maximus, was examined for his critique of social identity in the context of the city of Rome, in which there was clearly a strong Roman emphasis on *persona*. Valerius was observed to be reacting against a preoccupation with the superficial side of *persona*, since he considered it to be deviant behaviour that corrupted the traditional and ideal values of Roman identity. His work, *Facta et dicta*, was shown to be a practical handbook that aimed to restore the traditional notions and values of an ideal Roman *persona*, which was chiefly based on *Romano-centricity* and the *mos maiorum*. He inculcated this ideal Roman identity by presenting copious memorable deeds and sayings of virtues and vices that individuals had positively and negatively exemplified. This was ultimately seen in the prime *exemplum* of emperor Tiberius, to whom the work was dedicated, and who was lauded as promoting virtues and punishing vices.

In Chapter Four, the second figure, Epictetus, was investigated for his perception and critique of *persona*. Epictetus' experiences as a slave and philosopher in Rome and moral teacher in Nicopolis were observed to be influential for his perception of Graeco-Roman society. From the details in his discourses, it was shown that in his social contexts in Rome and Nicopolis there was indeed a Roman stress on *persona* and a preoccupation with the shallow features of *persona*. Epictetus reacted to this obsession, which he described as an 'incurable fever', by ridiculing the superficial status symbols and teaching that the genuine aspect of an individual's identity (πρόσωπον) is the person's inner 'volition' (προαίρεσις). He further showed that God has determined the individual's authentic identity and that the individual should live it out well, whether the God-determined social position was elite/non-elite, wealthy/poor, or free/slave. Consequently, in living such a moral and virtuous life, one could achieve the ideal epithet of καλὸς καὶ ἀγαθός. Interestingly, Epictetus was observed, to some extent, to be promoting the visible image of a philosopher (long beard, long hair, cloak), which was exemplified by the great Socrates. Furthermore, Epictetus' reaction was assessed to be a sharp reaction to the preoccupation with *persona*, and more negative than that of Valerius, since Epictetus did not strive to restore the traditional values of *persona*.

The third and final figure, Paul, was considered in Chapters Five and Six for his understanding and critique of *persona*. Paul's own life intimated an awareness of the social importance of *persona*, as seen in his use of his Roman citizenship in the Book of Acts, the large percentage of Romans that he associated with for his missionary work, and some of his uses of πρόσωπον to express the concept of *persona*. Also, the scope of the study was explained to be 2 Corinthians, since this letter has social data reflecting issues of social identity, and has the most occurrences of πρόσωπον in the Pauline corpus – some of which do convey the sense of *persona*.

After looking at the existence of a Roman stress on *persona* and a preoccupation with *persona* in the Roman colony of Corinth, attention was given to the Corinthian church. The investigation of the Corinthian correspondence revealed evidence that the Corinthian Christians adopted into the church the conventional outworking of *persona* which was pervasive in Corinth; they integrated the conventional values of *persona* into their outworking of Christian identity, and superficially assessed one another by these values. Their conventional use of *persona* resulted in many social conflicts and a crisis of Christian identity in the church. Thus, Paul was seen to be reacting to their preoccupation with the superficial values of *persona*.

In Chapter Six, particular attention was given to Paul's approach to Christian identity in 2 Corinthians. Throughout 2 Corinthians, the Corinthians are seen to be imbibing the *modus operandi* of boasting in outward appearance (ἐν προσώπῳ) and not in the heart (ἐν καρδίᾳ) (5.12), and assessing Paul based on superficial status markers. The Corinthians expected Paul to be an apostle who had a public image that was similar to the fashionable *persona* of contemporary orators; Paul's projected *persona*, however, lacked eloquence and contradictorily displayed 'weakness'. Paul, then, reacted to the Corinthians' preoccupation with the superficial aspect of social identity. Throughout the extended literary unit of 2.14–7.4, Paul denounced this social problem with an exteriority–interiority (πρόσωπον–καρδία) antithesis, whereby he devalued the superficial type of outward appearance, and valued, instead, the inner person – especially the heart (καρδία), where the Spirit is at work. In addition to this internal dimension of Christian identity, Paul promoted an external dimension of Christian identity, which is based on and reflects the inward work of the Spirit, rather than superficial values. This Christ-like identity was understood to be a result of a visible transformation into the image (εἰκών) and person (πρόσωπον) of Christ – that is, an embodiment of the 'dying and life of Jesus'. With the theme of power-in-weakness, Paul reinterpreted his own suffering as visibly projecting this Christ-like *persona*. In addition to defending his Christ-like identity, he subverted the Corinthians' conventional values of *persona* and also urged them to reconsider his Christ-like *persona* as indeed legitimate for an apostle.

Paul's critique of *persona* was assessed to be a sharp reaction against the conventional perception of social identity. His understanding of Christian identity inverted the conventional values of *persona*, since it was an embodiment of the image and person of the crucified Christ, who died a humiliating death on the cross. Paul was also heuristically compared to Valerius and Epictetus, in which all three were shown to be offering reactions to the conventional projection of *persona* in the early imperial period. Although all three reacted to a preoccupation with the superficial side of *persona*, they promoted their own understanding of what they considered to be an acceptable social *persona* for their audience. Valerius conceived it still within the Roman social structures, while Epictetus conceived it primarily in a philosophical (Stoic) understanding, and Paul conceived it in a religious (Christian) understanding.

7.2 Significance and Implications

In addition to the conclusions that are raised in the above summary, there are seven further points of implication and significance drawn from this study, which are presented in no specific order:

1) This study has filled in a lacuna of Roman social history, by demonstrating the important social feature of *persona* and the Roman stress on *persona*, which have been neglected by classicists and New Testament scholars. Although scholars have looked at other related social features, such

as honour/shame, and rank and status, this study has shown how these features are associated with the social rubric of *persona*.

2) This study has applied the understanding of *persona* to Paul's second epistle to the Corinthian church. This has resulted in a fresh reading of 2 Corinthians, in which the social feature of *persona* was seen as a major factor of the problems in the Corinthian church. This study also provided a more nuanced interpretation of some of the instances of the term πρόσωπον in 2 Corinthians, and has shown how Paul uses synonymous expressions and concepts to denote aspects of social identity.

3) Since this study has filled in a lacuna in the understanding of πρόσωπον, this study has shed light on the limitations and dangers involved in lexical studies. It is worth repeating again John Lee's intimation that reading through texts of the post-classical period 'you will sooner or later come across something poorly dealt with, or not covered at all, by LSJ and any other available tool';[1] this study has demonstrated that this is the case with πρόσωπον. Since the lexical information is inadequate, this study took on a more robust approach in looking at not only other instances of the term, but also other synonymous terms (e.g. the Latin term *persona*), expressions, and conceptualisations in ancient literary and non-literary sources. In addition, this study examined Valerius, Epictetus, and Paul by considering their social context and their works as a whole in order to gain valuable insights into their conception of social identity and *persona* that would have been otherwise missed. In doing so, this study has filled in a similar lacuna in Pauline studies by providing a different or refined interpretation of some of Paul's uses of πρόσωπον.

4) This study of 'social identity' has contributed to the research interest in Christian identity. In particular, this study has shown Paul's approach to Christian identity in 2 Corinthians. Paul reacts to the Corinthians' use of conventional values of identity in the church community, and promotes a robust Christ-like identity that is based on the inward work of the Spirit and reflects the image and person of Christ.

5) This socio-historical enquiry of 2 Corinthians has contributed to the growing numbers of studies that employ this interpretative approach to the Corinthian correspondence. More specifically, it is a contribution to socio-historical studies of 2 Corinthians, which has been overshadowed by the numerous studies of 1 Corinthians. This study has demonstrated that beyond the complexities of 2 Corinthians and Paul's theologically rich language in the letter, there are valuable social descriptions that reflect the social life of the Corinthian Christians.

---

[1] Lee, 'Present State', 72.

6) By providing an introduction to and an analysis of Valerius and Epictetus, New Testament scholars now have further information on and exposure to two figures that are a part of the same social world in which the New Testament writings are situated. In addition, the chapters on Valerius and Epictetus have contributed fresh studies to scholarship on Valerius and Epictetus, both of whom have generally been neglected not only in New Testament studies, but also in classical studies.

7) Finally, this study on social *persona* has not only contributed to the concern of *Antike und Christentum*, and the profitable use of ancient sources by New Testament scholars, but has also contributed to the converse concern of *Christentum und Antike*, and the use of the early Christian sources (e.g. 1 and 2 Corinthians) by classicists for supplemental information and new insights into ancient history.[2]

7.3 Further Study

There are four points of further research that are raised from this study:

1) The scope of this study of Paul's approach to identity was 2 Corinthians, and this study primarily focused on 2 Cor 1–7 and 10–13. However, the literary unit of 2 Cor 8–9 could also be examined. Moreover, 1 Corinthians, which was discussed in part, and 1 Clement are two other texts that could be explored for further insights into the dynamics of social identity and *persona* in the Corinthian church. In addition, the other letters in the Pauline corpus could also be explored for Paul's depiction of Christian identity. For instance, Galatians was seen to have some significant instances of πρόσωπον (Gal 2.6; 6.12) that expressed the concept of *persona* and social identity. The letter was briefly surveyed to see how social identity was involved behind the conflict in the Galatian church; however, a more in-depth study of the letter could be done. Also, the New Testament writings outside of the Pauline corpus could also be studied, such as James (cf. 2.1–4), 1 and 2 Peter, the Book of Acts, and the Gospels. All these texts could reveal insights into the concept of *persona*, since the setting of the whole New Testament is within the Roman empire, where this social feature affected the majority of individuals. Furthermore, it could be worth considering that an absence of parallels of the term/concept in the New Testament writings is just as significant as its existence.[3]

2) The description of the concept of *persona* in Chapter Two sufficiently demonstrated the social concept within the New Testament era, however, a

---

[2] See Winter, '*Christentum*', 121–30.
[3] Cf. Horst, 'Corpus', 1160.

whole separate study could examine the social concept in greater detail and its further developments in Roman history. In addition, this study examined the works of Paul, Epictetus, and Valerius, but further exploration could be made into other figures of the period and their perceptions of social *persona*. Some that might prove to be useful are Seneca, Plutarch, Petronius, and Dio Chrysostom. Seneca and Plutarch, for example, are moral philosophers who would be against the behaviour associated with the conventional values of *persona*. Petronius, also, offers a satirical account into the lives of some fictional Roman freedmen who foolishly portray themselves as aristocrats. Also, Dio Chrysostom could provide more insights into the problems of sophistry and oratory in the Greek East as they relate to *persona*.

3) The investigation into Valerius and Epictetus focused on their perceptions of social identity and *persona*, but they could be further analysed for insights into the social world of the New Testament. As noted in Chapter One, some scholars have considered Epictetus' discourses for pertinent information relating to the New Testament, but there remains more information to be discovered. Even more so, Valerius and his work remains largely an uncharted territory for exploration. For instance, Valerius' work could prove to be useful for considering the social context of Paul's letter to the Romans, since Valerius' work was written in Rome during the reign of Tiberius. Also, as already noted in the study, a future study that I plan to undertake is how Valerius' work of 'memorable deeds and sayings' can shed light on the preface of Luke-Acts, since Luke in Acts 1.1 asserts that he has dealt with all that Jesus began 'to do and teach' (ποιεῖν καὶ διδάσκειν).

4) Further socio-historical enquiries could be done in 2 Corinthians. This study has demonstrated only one social aspect of 2 Corinthians, but there remains a wealth of valuable information for future studies. In addition to socio-historical enquiries, 2 Corinthians can still be probed using other approaches to understand other themes in the letter. For instance, as also noted in this study, I intend to pursue in the near future an exegetical enquiry into Paul's presentation of divine presence in 2 Corinthians.

Bibliography

1. Ancient Sources

Alciphron. *The Letters of Alciphron, Aelian and Philostratus*. Translated by A.R. Benner et al. Loeb Classical Library. London: Heinemann; Cambridge: Harvard University Press, 1949.

Appian. *Roman History*. Translated by H. White. 4 vols. Loeb Classical Library. London: Heinemann, 1912–13.

Apuleius. *Metamorphoses*. Translated by J.A. Hanson. 2 vols. Loeb Classical Library. Cambridge: Harvard University Press, 1989.

Aristides, Aelius. *The Complete Works. Volume II: Orations XVII–LIII*. Translated by C.A. Behr. Leiden: Brill, 1981.

Aristotle. Translated by H.P. Cooke et al. 23 vols. Loeb Classical Library. London: Heinemann; Cambridge: Harvard University Press, 1938–60.

[Augustus]. *Res gestae divi Augusti*. Translated by F.W. Shipley. Loeb Classical Library. London: Heinemann, 1924.

Aurelius, Marcus. Translated by C.R. Haines. Loeb Classical Library. London: Heinemann, 1916.

Boethius. Translated by H.F. Stewart et al. Loeb Classical Library. London: Heinemann; Cambridge: Harvard University Press, 1973.

Cassius, Dio. *Roman History*. Translated by E. Cary. 9 vols. Loeb Classical Library. London: Heinemann, 1914–27.

Chrysostom, Dio. *Discourses*. Translated by J.W. Cohoon and H. Lamar Crosby. 5 vols. Loeb Classical Library. London: Heinemann; Cambridge: Harvard University Press, 1932–51.

Cicero. Translated by G.L. Hendrickson et al. 28 vols. Loeb Classical Library. London: Heinemann; Cambridge: Harvard University Press, 1912–72.

Diogenes Laertius. *Lives of Eminent Philosophers*. Translated by R.D. Hicks. 2 vols. Loeb Classical Library. London: Heinemann, 1925.

Epictetus. Translated by W.A. Oldfather. 2 vols. Loeb Classical Library. London: Heinemann, 1925–8.

Frontinus. *The Stratagems and the Aqueducts of Rome*. Translated by C.E. Bennett et al. Loeb Classical Library. London: Heinemann, 1925.

Gellius, Aulus. *The Attic Nights*. Translated by J.C. Rolfe. 3 vols. Loeb Classical Library. London: Heinemann, 1927–.

Herodotus. Translated by A.D. Godley. 4 vols. Loeb Classical Library. London: Heinemann; Cambridge, 1921–4.

Homer. *Odyssey*. Translated by A.J. Murray. Revised by G.E. Dimock. 2 vols. Loeb Classical Library. Cambridge: Harvard University Press, 1995.

Horace. Translated by N. Rudd and H.R. Fairclough. 2 vols. Loeb Classical Library. London: Heinemann; Cambridge: Harvard University Press, 1968–.

Josephus. Translated by H.St.J. Thackeray et al. 10 vols. Loeb Classical Library. London: Heinemann; Cambridge: Harvard University Press, 1926–.

Juvenal. Translated by G.G. Ramsay, Loeb Classical Library. London: Heinemann, 1969.

Livy. *History of Rome*. Translated by B.O. Foster et al. 14 vols. Loeb Classical Library. London: Heinemann; Cambridge: Harvard University Press, 1913–59.

Lucian. Translated by A.D. Harmon et al. 8 vols. Loeb Classical Library. London: Heinemann; Cambridge: Harvard University Press, 1967–.

Martial. *Epigrams*. Translated by W.C.A. Ker. 2 vols. Loeb Classical Library. London: Heinemann, 1919, 1920.

Ovid. *The Art of Love and Other Poems*. Translated by J.H. Mozley. Revised by G.P. Goold. Loeb Classical Library. London: Heinemann; Cambridge: Harvard University Press, 1979.

Pausanius. *Description of Greece*. Translated by W.H.S. Jones et al. 5 vols. Loeb Classical Library. London: Heinemann; Cambridge: Harvard University Press, 1918–35.

Petronius. *Satyricon*. Translated by M. Heseltine. Loeb Classical Library. London: Heinemann, 1913.

Philo. Translated by F.H. Colson et al. 12 vols. Loeb Classical Library. London: Heinemann; Cambridge: Harvard University Press, 1929–62.

Philostratus. *Life of Apollonius of Tyana*. Translated by F.C. Conybeare. 2 vols. Loeb Classical Library. London: Heinemann, 1912.

_____. *Lives of the Sophists*. Translated by W.C. Wright. Loeb Classical Library. London: Heinemann, 1922.

Pliny the Elder. *Natural History*. Translated by H. Rackham et al. 10 vols. Loeb Classical Library. London: Heinemann; Cambridge: Harvard University Press, 1938–62.

Pliny the Younger. *Letters*. Translated by B. Radice. 2 vols. Loeb Classical Library. London: Heinemann; Cambridge: Harvard University Press, 1969.

Plutarch. *Lives*. Translated by B. Perrin. 11 vols. Loeb Classical Library. London: Heinemann, 1914–26.

_____. *Moralia*. Translated by F.C. Babbit et al. 16 vols. Loeb Classical Library. London: Heinemann; Cambridge: Harvard University Press, 1927–2004.

Quintilian. Translated by H.E. Butler. 4 vols. Loeb Classical Library. London: Heinemann; Cambridge: Harvard University Press, 1921–61.

Sallust. Translated by J.C. Rolfe. Loeb Classical Library. London: Heinemann, 1921.

Scriptores Historiae Augustae. Translated by D. Magie. 3 vols. Loeb Classical Library. London: Heinemann, 1922–32.

Seneca. *Epistles*. Translated by R.M. Gummere. 3 vols. Loeb Classical Library. London: Heinemann, 1918–25.

Seneca the Elder. *Controversiae*. Translated by M. Winterbottom. 2 vols. Loeb Classical Library. London: Heinemann; Cambridge: Harvard University Press, 1974.

Strabo. *Geography*. Translated by H.L. Jones. 8 vols. Loeb Classical Library. London: Heinemann, 1917–32.

Suetonius. *The Lives of the Caesars*. Translated by J.C. Rolfe. 2 vols. Loeb Classical Library. London: Heinemann, 1913, 1914.

Tacitus. *The Annals*. Translated by W. Peterson et al. 5 vols. Loeb Classical Library. London: Heinemann; Cambridge: Harvard University Press, 1914–37.

Tertullian. Translated by T.R. Glover and G.H. Rendall. Loeb Classical Library. London: Heinemann, 1931.

Thucydides. Translated by C.F. Smith. 4 vols. Loeb Classical Library. London: Heinemann; Cambridge: Harvard University Press, 1919–23.

Valerius Maximus. *Memorable Doings and Sayings*. Translated by D.R.S. Bailey. 2 vols. Loeb Classical Library. Cambridge: Harvard University Press, 2000.

Velleius Paterculus. Translated by F.W. Shipley. Loeb Classical Library. London: Heinemann, 1924.

Vitruvius. *On Architecture*. Translated by F. Granger. 2 vols. Loeb Classical Library. London: Heinemann, 1931, 1934.

2. Modern Sources

Adams, E., and D.G. Horrell. 'The Scholarly Quest for Paul's Church at Corinth: A Critical Survey'. In idem, eds., *Christianity at Corinth: The Quest for the Pauline Church*, 1–48. Louisville: Westminster John Knox Press, 2004.

Adams, J.N. '"*Romanitas*" and the Latin Language'. *Classical Quarterly* 53 (2003): 184–205.

Alexander, L. *The Preface to Luke's Gospel: Literary Convention and Social Context in Luke 1.1–4 and Acts 1.1*. Society for New Testament Studies Monograph Series 78. Cambridge: Cambridge University Press, 1993.

_____. 'Paul and the Hellenistic Schools: The Evidence of Galen'. In T. Engberg-Pedersen, ed., *Paul in His Hellenistic Context*, 60–83. Studies of the New Testament and Its World. Edinburgh: T. & T. Clark, 1994.

Alexander, P.S. 'The Qumran *Songs of the Sabbath Sacrifice* and the *Celestial Hierarchy* of Dionysius the Areopagite: A Comparative Approach'. *Revue de Qumran* 22 (2006): 349–72.

Allo, E.B. *Saint Paul: Seconde Epître aux Corinthiens*. Etudes bibliques. 2nd ed. Paris: Gabalda, 1956.

Altheim, F. 'Persona'. *Archiv für Religionswissenschaft* 27 (1929): 35–52.

Amador, J.D.H. 'Revisiting 2 Corinthians: Rhetoric and the Case for Unity'. *New Testament Studies* 46 (2000): 92–111.

Andrews, S.B. 'Too Weak Not to Lead: The Form and Function of 2 Cor 11.23b–33'. *New Testament Studies* 41 (1995): 263–76.

Asano, A. *Community-Identity Construction in Galatians: Exegetical, Social-Anthropological and Socio-Historical Studies*. Journal for the Study of the New Testament Supplement Series 285. London: T. & T. Clark, 2005.

Asmis, E. 'Choice in Epictetus' Philosophy'. In A.Y. Collins, and M.M. Mitchell, eds., *Antiquity and Humanity: Essays on Ancient Religion and Philosophy. Presented to Hans Dieter Betz on His 70th Birthday*, 385–412. Tübingen: Mohr Siebeck, 2001.

Aubert, J.-J., and B. Sirks, eds. *Speculum Iuris: Roman Law as a Reflection of Social and Economic Life*. Ann Arbor: University of Michigan Press, 2002.

Bailey, D.R.S. *Valerius Maximus: Memorable Doings and Sayings*. 2 vols. Loeb Classical Library. Cambridge: Harvard University Press, 2000.

Baird, W.R. 'Letters of Recommendation: A Study of II Cor 3:1–3'. *Journal of Biblical Literature* 80 (1961): 166–72.

Bammel, E. 'Paulus, der Moses des Neuen Bundes'. *Theologia* 54 (1983): 399–408.

Barclay, J.M.G. 'Mirror-Reading a Polemical Letter: Galatians as a Test Case'. *Journal for the Study of the New Testament* 31 (1987): 73–93.

_____. 'Thessalonica and Corinth: Social Contrasts in Pauline Christianity'. *Journal for the Study of the New Testament* 47 (1992): 49–74.

_____. *Jews in the Mediterranean Diaspora: From Alexander to Trajan (323 BCE–117 CE)*. Edinburgh: T. & T. Clark, 1996.

Barigazzi, A. *Favorino di Arelate. Opere: Introduzione, testo critico e commento*. Firenze: Monnier, 1966.

_____. 'Favorino di Arelate'. In W. Haase, ed., *Aufstieg und Niedergang der römischen Welt* II.34.1, 556–81. Berlin: de Gruyter, 1993.

Barnett, P. *The Second Epistle to the Corinthians*. The New International Commentary on the New Testament. Grand Rapids: Eerdmans, 1997.

Barrett, C.K. *The Second Epistle to the Corinthians*. Black's New Testament Commentaries. London: A & C Black, 1973.

_____. 'Boasting (καυχᾶσθαι, κτλ.) in the Pauline Epistles'. In A. Vanhoye, ed., *L'Apôtre Paul: Personnalité, style et conception du ministère*, 363–8. Bibliotheca ephemeridum theologicarum lovaniensium 73. Leuven: Leuven University Press, 1986.

Barton, C.A. *Roman Honor: The Fire in the Bones*. Berkeley: University of California, 2001.

Barton, S.C. 'Paul and the Cross: A Sociological Approach'. *Theology* 85 (1982): 13–19.

_____. 'The Transfiguration of Christ according to Mark and Matthew: Christology and Anthropology'. In F. Avemarie, and H. Lichtenberger, eds., *Auferstehung – Resurrection. The Fourth Durham-Tübingen Research Symposium*, 231–46. Wissenschaftliche Untersuchungen zum Neuen Testament 135. Tübingen: Mohr Siebeck, 2001.

Bauer, W., and F.W. Danker, eds. *A Greek-English Lexicon of the New Testament and Other Early Christian Literature*. 3rd ed. Chicago: University of Chicago Press, 2000.

Baumert, N. *Täglich sterben und auferstehen: Der Literalsinn von 2 Kor 4,12–5,10*. Studien zum Alten und Neuen Testament 34. München: Kösel, 1973.

Behm, J. 'μορφή, κτλ.' In G. Kittel and G. Friedrich, eds., *Theological Dictionary of the New Testament*, 4:742–59. Grand Rapids: Eerdmans, 1967.

Bellemore, J. 'When Did Valerius Maximus Write the *Dicta et Facta Memorabilia*?' *Antichthon* 23 (1989): 67–80.

Belleville, L.L. *Reflections of Glory: Paul's Polemical Use of the Moses-Doxa Tradition in 2 Corinthians 3.1–18*. Journal for the Study of the New Testament Supplement Series 52. Sheffield: Sheffield Academic Press, 1991.

_____. '"Imitate Me, Just as I Imitate Christ": Discipleship in the Corinthian Correspondence'. In R.N. Longenecker, ed., *Patterns of Discipleship in the New Testament*, 120–42. Grand Rapids: Eerdmans, 1996.

Bergmann, B. 'Introduction: The Ancient Art of Spectacle'. In B. Bergmann, and C. Kondoleon, eds., *The Art of Ancient Spectacle*, 9–35. Studies in the History of Art 56. New Haven: Yale University Press, 1999.

Bergmann, B., and C. Kondoleon, eds. *The Art of Ancient Spectacle*. Studies in the History of Art 56. New Haven: Yale University Press, 1999.

Bettini, M. '*Mos, mores* und *mos maiorum*: die Erfindung der "Sittlichkeit" in der römischen Kultur'. In M. Braun, A. Haltenhoff, and F. Mutschler, eds., *Moribus antiquis res stat Romana: römische Werte und römische Literatur im 3. und 2. Jh. v. Chr*, 303–52. Beiträge zur Altertumskunde. München: K.G. Saur, 2000.

Betz, H.D. *Der Apostel Paulus und die sokratische Tradition: Eine exegetische Untersuchung zu seiner 'Apologie' 2 Korinther 10–13*. Beiträge zur historischen Theologie 45. Tübingen: Mohr, 1972.

_____. 'De laude ipsius (Moralia 539A–547F)'. In *Plutarch's Ethical Writings and Early Christian Literature*, 367–93. Studia ad corpus hellenisticum novi testamenti 4. Leiden: Brill, 1978.

_____. *2 Corinthians 8 and 9: A Commentary on Two Administrative Letters of the Apostle Paul*. Hermeneia. Philadelphia: Fortress Press, 1985.

_____. 'The Problem of Rhetoric and Theology According to the Apostle Paul'. In A. Vanhoye, ed., *L'Apôtre Paul: Personnalité, style et conception du ministère*, 16–48. Bibliotheca ephemeridum theologicarum lovaniensium 73. Leuven: Leuven University Press, 1986.

_____. 'The Concept of the "Inner Human Being" (ὁ ἔσω ἄνθρωπος) in the Anthropology of Paul'. *New Testament Studies* 46 (2000): 315–41.

_____. 'The Human Being in the Antagonisms of Life according to the Apostle Paul'. *Journal of Religion* 80 (2000): 557–75.

Bieringer, R. 'Die Gegner des Paulus im 2 Korintherbrief'. In R. Bieringer, and J. Lambrecht, eds., *Studies on 2 Corinthians*, 181–221. Bibliotheca ephemeridum theologicarum lovaniensium 112. Leuven: Leuven University Press, 1994.

Billerbeck, M. *Epiktet. vom Kynismus*. Leiden: Brill, 1978.

_____. 'The Ideal Cynic from Epictetus to Julian'. In R.B. Branham, and M.-O. Goulet-Cazé, eds., *The Cynics: The Cynic Movement in Antiquity and Its Legacy*, 205–21. Berkeley: University of California Press, 1996.

Black, D.A. *Paul, Apostle of Weakness*. New York: Peter Lang, 1984.

Bloomer, W.M. *Valerius Maximus and the Rhetoric of the New Nobility*. Chapel Hill: University of North Carolina Press, 1992.

Bodel, J. 'Punishing Piso'. *American Journal of Philology* 120 (1999): 43–63.

_____. 'Death on Display: Looking at Roman Funerals'. In B. Bergmann, and C. Kondoleon, eds., *The Art of Ancient Spectacle*, 259–81. Studies in the History of Art 56. New Haven: Yale University Press, 1999.

Bonhöffer, A. *Epictet und die Stoa. Untersuchungen zur stoischen Philosophie*. Stuttgart: Enke, 1890.

_____. *Die Ethik des Stoikers Epictet*. Stuttgart: Enke, 1894.

_____. *Epiktet und das Neue Testament*. Religionsgeschichtliche Versuche und Vorarbeiten 10. Gießen: Töpelmann, 1911.

_____. 'Epiktet und das Neue Testament'. *Zeitschrift für die neutestamentliche Wissenschaft* 13 (1912): 281–92.

Bonner, S.F. *Roman Declamation in the Late Republic and Early Empire*. Liverpool: Liverpool University Press, 1949.

_____. *Education in Ancient Rome: From the Elder Cato to the Younger Pliny*. Berkeley: University of California Press, 1977.

Bosch, J.S. *'Gloriarse' segun San Pablo, Sentido y teología de καυχάομαι*. Analecta Biblica 40. Rome: Biblical Institute Press, 1970.

_____. 'L'apologie apostolique – 2 Cor 10–11 comme réponse de Paul à ses adversaires'. In E. Lohse, ed., *Verteidigung und Begründung des apostolischen Amtes (2 Kor 10–13)*, 43–63. Benedictina 11. Rome: Benedictina, 1992.

Bowersock, G.W. 'A New Inscription of Arrian'. *Greek, Roman, and Byzantine Studies* 8 (1967): 279–80.

_____. *Greek Sophists in the Roman Empire*. Oxford: Clarendon Press, 1969.

_____, ed. *Approaches to the Second Sophistic*. University Park, PA: American Philological Association, 1974.

_____. 'Philosophy in the Second Sophistic'. In G. Clark, and T. Rajak, eds., *Philosophy and Power in the Graeco-Roman World: Essays in Honour of Miriam Griffin*, 157–70. Oxford: Oxford University Press, 2002.

Braun, H. 'Die Indifferenz gegenüber der Welt bei Paulus und bei Epiktet'. In *Gesammelte Studien zum Neuen Testament und seiner Umwelt*, 159–67. Tübingen: Mohr, 1967.

Briscoe, J. 'Some Notes on Valerius Maximus'. *Sileno* 19 (1993): 395–408.

Browning, R. *Medieval and Modern Greek*. 2nd ed. Cambridge: Cambridge University Press, 1983.

Brunt, P.A. 'Stoicism and the Principate'. *Papers of the British School at Rome* 43 (1975): 7–39.

_____. 'From Epictetus to Arrian'. *Athenaeum* 55 (1977): 19–48.

Buell, D.K. *Why This New Race? Ethnic Reasoning in Early Christianity*. New York: Columbia University Press, 2005.

Bultmann, R. 'Das religiöse Moment in der ethischen Unterweisung des Epiktet und das Neue Testament'. *Zeitschrift für die neutestamentliche Wissenschaft* 13 (1912): 97–110, 177–91.

_____. *Der zweite Brief an die Korinther*. Kritisch-exegetischer Kommentar über das Neue Testament. Göttingen: Vandenhoeck & Ruprecht, 1976.

Calboli, G., and W.J. Dominik. 'Introduction: The Roman *Suada*'. In W.J. Dominik, ed., *Roman Eloquence: Rhetoric in Society and Literature*, 3–12. London: Routledge, 1997.

Campbell, R.A. 'Does Paul Acquiesce in Divisions at the Lord's Supper?'. *New Testament Studies* 33 (1991): 61–70.

Cape, R.W. Jr. 'Persuasive History: Roman Rhetoric and Historiography'. In W.J. Dominik, ed., *Roman Eloquence: Rhetoric in Society and Literature*, 212–28. London: Routledge, 1997.

Carrez, M. *La deuxième épître de Saint Paul aux Corinthiens*. Commentaire du Nouveau Testament 2nd. ser. 8. Genève: Labor et Fides, 1986.

Carrithers, M. 'An Alternative Social History of the Self'. In M. Carrithers, S. Collins, and S. Lukes, eds., *The Category of the Person: Anthropology, Philosophy, History*, 234–56. Cambridge: Cambridge University Press, 1985.

Carrithers, M., S. Collins, and S. Lukes, eds. *The Category of the Person: Anthropology, Philosophy, History*. Cambridge: Cambridge University Press, 1985.

Carter, C.J. 'Valerius Maximus'. In T.A. Dorey, ed., *Empire and Aftermath: Silver Latin II*, 26–56. London: Routledge & Kegan Paul, 1975.

Chadwick, J., ed. *Lexicographica Graeca: Contributions to the Lexicography of Ancient Greek*. Oxford: Clarendon Press, 1996.

Charlesworth, M.P. 'Providentia and Aeternitas'. *Harvard Theological Review* 29 (1936): 107–32.

_____. 'The Virtues of a Roman Emperor: Propaganda and the Creation of Belief'. *Proceedings of the British Academy* 23 (1937): 105–33.

Chow, J.K. *Patronage and Power: A Study of Social Networks in Corinth*. Journal for the Study of the New Testament Supplement Series 75. Sheffield: Sheffield Academic Press, 1992.

Clarke, A.D. 'The Good and the Just in the City and Romans 5:7'. *Tyndale Bulletin* 41 (1990): 128–42.

_____. 'Another Corinthian Erastus Inscription'. *Tyndale Bulletin* 42 (1991): 146–51.

_____. *Secular and Christian Leadership in Corinth: A Socio-Historical and Exegetical Study of 1 Corinthians 1–6*. Arbeiten zur Geschichte des antiken Judentums und des Urchristentums 18. Leiden: Brill, 1993.

_____. '"Be Imitators of Me": Paul's Model of Leadership'. *Tyndale Bulletin* 49 (1998): 329–60.

_____. *Serve the Community of the Church: Christians as Leaders and Ministers*. First-Century Christians in the Graeco-Roman World. Grand Rapids: Eerdmans, 2000.

Clarke, J.R. *Art in the Lives of Ordinary Romans: Visual Representation and Non-Elite Viewers in Italy, 100 B.C.–A.D. 315*. Berkeley: University of California Press, 2003.

Cloud, D. 'The Pompeiian Tablets and Some Literary Texts'. In P. McKechnie, ed., *Thinking Like a Lawyer: Essays on Legal History and General History for John Crook on His Eightieth Birthday*, 231–46. Mnemosyne Supplement 231. Leiden: Brill, 2002.

Colardeau, T. *Etude sur Epictète*. Paris: Fontemoing, 1903.

Collange, J.-F. *Enigmes de la deuxième épître de Paul aux Corinthiens: Etude exégétique de 2 Cor. 2:14–7:4*. Society for New Testament Studies Monograph Series 18. Cambridge: Cambridge University Press, 1972.

Connors, C. 'Field and Forum: Culture and Agriculture in Roman Rhetoric'. In W.J. Dominik, ed., *Roman Eloquence: Rhetoric in Society and Literature*, 71–89. London: Routledge, 1997.

Cooley, A. 'The Moralizing Message of the "Senatus Consultum de Cn. Pisone Patre"'. *Greece & Rome, 2nd ser.* 45 (1998): 199–212.

Cotton, H. *Documentary Letters of Recommendation in Latin from the Roman Empire*. Beiträge zur klassischen Philologie 132. Königstein: Hain, 1981.

Coudry, M. 'Conclusion générale: Valère Maxime au cœur de la vie politique des débuts de l'Empire'. In J.-M. David, ed., *Valeurs et mémoire à Rome: Valère Maxime ou la vertu recomposeé*, 183–92. Paris: de Boccard, 1998.

Crafton, J.A. *The Agency of the Apostle: A Dramatistic Analysis of Paul's Responses to Conflict in 2 Corinthians*. Journal for the Study of the New Testament Supplement Series 51. Sheffield: Sheffield Academic Press, 1991.

Crook, J.A. *Law and Life of Rome*. Aspects of Greek and Roman Life. London: Thames and Hudson, 1967.

_____. 'Working Notes on Some of the New Pompeii Tablets'. *Zeitschrift für Papyrologie und Epigraphik* 29 (1978): 229–39.

_____. 'Legal History and General History'. *Bulletin of the Institute of Classical Studies* 41 (1996): 31–6.

Curchin, L.A. *The Romanization of Central Spain: Complexity, Diversity and Change in a Provincial Hinterland*. London: Routledge, 2004.

Dalby, A. *Empire of Pleasure: Luxury and Indulgence in the Roman World*. London: Routledge, 2000.

David, J.-M., ed. *Valeurs et mémoire à Rome: Valère Maxime ou la vertu recomposeé*. Paris: de Boccard, 1998.

Deissmann, A. *Paul: A Study in Social and Religious History*. Translated by W.E. Wilson. 2nd ed. New York: Harper, 1926.

Deming, W. 'Paul, Gaius, and the "Law of Persons": The Conceptualization of Roman Law in the Early Classical Period'. *Classical Quarterly* 51 (2001): 218–30.

deSilva, D.A. '"Let the One Who Claims Honor Establish That Claim in the Lord": Honor Discourse in the Corinthian Correspondence'. *Biblical Theology Bulletin* 28 (1998): 61–74.

Dewey, A.J. 'A Matter of Honor: A Social-Historical Analysis of 2 Corinthians 10'. *Harvard Theological Review* 78 (1985): 209–17.

Dobbin, R.F. 'Προαίρεσις in Epictetus'. *Ancient Philosophy* 11 (1991): 111–35.

_____. *Epictetus. Discourses Book 1: Translated with an Introduction and Commentary*. Clarendon Later Ancient Philosophers. Oxford: Clarendon Press, 1998.

Dominik, W.J., ed. *Roman Eloquence: Rhetoric in Society and Literature*. London: Routledge, 1997.

Donlan, W. 'The Origin of καλὸς κἀγαθός'. *American Journal of Philology* 94 (1973): 365–74.

Döring, K. *Exemplum Socratis: Studien zur Sokratesnachwirkung in der kynisch-stoischen Popularphilosophie der frühen Kaiserzeit und im Christentum*. Hermes Einzelschriften 42. Wiesbaden: Franz Steiner, 1979.

Downing, F.G. *Cynics, Paul and the Pauline Churches: Cynics and Christian Origins II*. London: Routledge, 1998.

Dozeman, T.B. 'Masking Moses and Mosaic Authority in Torah'. *Journal of Biblical Literature* 119 (2000): 21–45.

Droge, A.J. *Homer or Moses? Early Christian Interpretations of the History of Culture*. Hermeneutische Untersuchungen zur Theologie 26. Tübingen: Mohr, 1989.

Duff, A.M. *Freedmen in the Early Roman Empire*. Oxford: Clarendon Press, 1928.

Duff, P.W. *Personality in Roman Private Law*. Cambridge: Cambridge University Press, 1938.

Duff, P.B. 'Apostolic Suffering and the Language of Processions in 2 Corinthians 4:7–10'. *Biblical Theology Bulletin* 21 (1991): 158–65.

_____. 'Glory in the Ministry of Death: Gentile Condemnation and Letters of Recommendation in 2 Cor. 3:6–8'. *Novum Testamentum* 46 (2004): 313–37.

Dunn, J.D.G. *Jesus and the Spirit: A Study of the Religious and Charismatic Experience of Jesus and the First Christians as Reflected in the New Testament*. London: SCM Press, 1975.

_____. *The Theology of the Paul's Letter to the Galatians*. New Testament Theology. Cambridge: Cambridge University Press, 1993.

_____. *The Theology of Paul the Apostle*. Grand Rapids: Eerdmans, 1998.

Dupont, J. 'Le chrétien, miroir de la gloire divine, d'après II Cor III, 18'. *Revue biblique* 56 (1949): 392–411.

_____. *ΣΥΝ ΧΡΙΣΤΩΙ: L'union avec le Christ suivant saint Paul*. Bruges: Editions de l'Abbaye de Saint-Andre, 1952.

Dutch, R.S. *The Educated Elite in 1 Corinthians: Education and Community Conflict in Graeco-Roman Context*. Journal for the Study of the New Testament Supplement Series 271. London: T. & T. Clark, 2005.

Dyck, A.R. *A Commentary on Cicero, De Officiis*. Ann Arbor: University of Michigan Press, 1996.

Ebel, E. *Die Attraktivität früher christlicher Gemeinden: Die Gemeinde von Korinth im Spiegel griechisch-römischer Vereine*. Wissenschaftliche Untersuchungen zum Neuen Testament 2/178. Tübingen: Mohr Siebeck, 2004.

Eck, W. 'Senatorial Self-Representation: Developments in the Augustan Period'. In F. Millar, and E. Segal, eds., *Caesar Augustus: Seven Aspects*, 129–67. Oxford: Clarendon Press, 1984.

Edmondson, J.C. 'Dynamic Arenas: Gladiatorial Presentations in the City of Rome and the Construction of Roman Society during the Early Empire'. In W.J. Slater, ed., *Roman Theater and Society*, 69–112. E. Togo Salmon Papers I. Ann Arbor: University of Michigan Press, 1996.

Edwards, C. *The Politics of Immorality in Ancient Rome*. Cambridge: Cambridge University Press, 1993.

Elsner, J. *Roman Eyes: Visuality and Subjectivity in Art and Text*. Princeton: Princeton University Press, 2007.

Eltester, F.-W. *Eikon im Neuen Testament*. Beihefte zur Zeitschrift für die neutestamentliche Wissenschaft 23. Berlin: de Gruyter, 1958.

Emmet, D. *Rules, Roles, and Relations*. London: Macmillan; New York: St Martin's Press, 1966.

Engberg-Pedersen, T. 'The Gospel and Social Practice According to 1 Corinthians'. *New Testament Studies* 33 (1987): 557–84.

_____. 'Stoic Philosophy and the Concept of the Person'. In C. Gill, ed., *The Person and the Human Mind: Issues in Ancient and Modern Philosophy*, 109–35. Oxford: Clarendon Press, 1990.

_____. *Paul and the Stoics*. Edinburgh: T. & T. Clark, 2000.

_____. 'Paul, Virtues, and Vices'. In J.P. Sampley, ed., *Paul in the Greco-Roman World: A Handbook*, 608–33. Harrisburg: Trinity Press International, 2003.

_____. 'The Relationship with Others: Similarities and Differences Between Paul and Stoicism'. *Zeitschrift für die neutestamentliche Wissenschaft* 96 (2005): 35–60.

_____. 'Self-Sufficiency and Power: Divine and Human Agency in Epictetus and Paul'. In J.M.G. Barclay, and S.G. Gathercole, eds., *Divine and Human Agency in Paul and his Cultural Environment*, 117–39. Library of New Testament Studies 335. London: T. & T. Clark, 2006.

Engels, D. *Roman Corinth: An Alternative Model for the Classical City*. Chicago: University of Chicago Press, 1990.

Engels, J. 'Die Exempla-Reihe *De iure triumphandi* – römisch-republikanische Werte und Institutionen im frühkaiserzeitlichen Spiegel der *Facta et dicta memorabilia* des Valerius Maximus'. In A. Barzanò, C. Bearzot, F. Landucci, L. Prandi, and G. Zecchini, eds., *Identità e valori: fattori di aggregazione e fattori di crisi nell'esperienza politica antica*, 139–69. Centro ricerche e documentazione sull'antichità classica 21. Roma: L'erma di Bretschneider, 2001.

Esler, P.F. *Galatians*. New Testament Readings. London: Routledge, 1998.

_____. *Conflict and Identity in Romans: The Social Setting of Paul's Letter*. Minneapolis: Fortress Press, 2003.

_____. 'Paul and Stoicism: Romans 12 as a Test Case'. *New Testament Studies* 50 (2004): 106–24.

Feuillet, A. *Le Christ sagesse de Dieu d'après les épîtres pauliniennes*. Etudes bibliques. Paris: Gabalda, 1966.

Fitzgerald, J.T. *Cracks in an Earthen Vessel: An Examination of the Catalogues of Hardships in the Corinthian Correspondence*. Society of Biblical Literature Dissertation Series 99. Atlanta: Scholars Press, 1988.

_____. 'Paul, the Ancient Epistolary Theorists, and 2 Corinthians 10–13'. In D.L. Balch, ed., *Greeks, Romans, and Christians: Essays in Honor of Abraham J. Malherbe*, 190–200. Minneapolis: Fortress Press, 1990.

Fitzgerald, J.T., T.H. Olbricht, and L.M. White, eds. *Early Christianity and Classical Culture: Comparative Studies in Honor of Abraham J. Malherbe*. Supplements to Novum Testamentum 110. Leiden: Brill, 2003.

Flower, H.I. *The Art of Forgetting: Disgrace and Oblivion in Roman Political Culture*. Studies in the History of Greece and Rome. Chapell Hill: University of North Carolina Press, 2006.

Forbes, C. 'Comparison, Self-Praise and Irony: Paul's Boasting and the Conventions of Hellenistic Rhetoric'. *New Testament Studies* 32 (1986): 1–30.

Fossum, J.E. 'Ascensio, Metamorphosis: The "Transfiguration" of Jesus in the Synoptic Gospels'. In *The Image of the Invisible God: Essays on the Influence of Jewish Mysticism on Early Christology*, 71–94. Novum Testamentum et Orbis Antiquus 30. Göttingen: Vandenhoeck & Ruprecht, 1995.

Furnish, V.P. *II Corinthians*. The Anchor Bible 32A. New York: Doubleday, 1984.

Gager, J.G. *Moses in Greco-Roman Paganism*. Society of Biblical Literature Monograph Series 16. Nashville: Abingdon Press, 1972.

Gardner, J.F. 'Proofs of Status in the Roman World'. *Bulletin of the Institute of Classical Studies* 33 (1986): 1–14.

Garland, D.E. *2 Corinthians*. New American Commentary 29. Nashville: Broadman & Holman, 1999.

Garnsey, P. *Social Status and Legal Privilege in the Roman Empire*. London: Clarendon Press, 1970.

_____. 'Legal Privilege in the Roman Empire'. In M.I. Finley, ed., *Studies in Ancient Society*, 141–65. Past & Present Series. London: Routledge & Kegan Paul, 1974.

Garnsey, P., and R. Saller. *The Roman Empire: Economy, Society and Culture*. Berkeley: University of California Press, 1987.

Garrett, S.R. 'The God of this World and the Affliction of Paul: 2 Cor 4:1–12'. In D.L. Balch, E. Ferguson, and W.A. Meeks, eds., *Greeks, Romans, and Christians: Essays in Honor of Abraham J. Malherbe*, 99–117. Minneapolis: Fortress Press, 1990.

Georgi, D. *The Opponents of Paul in Second Corinthians*. Translated by H. Attridge et al. Philadelphia: Fortress Press, 1986.

Gerber, C. 'Krieg und Hochzeit in Korinth'. *Zeitschrift für die neutestamentliche Wissenschaft* 96 (2005): 99–125.

Gill, C. 'Ancient Psychotherapy'. *Journal of the History of Ideas* 46 (1985): 307–25.

_____. 'Personhood and Personality: The Four-*Personae* Theory in Cicero, *De Officiis* I'. *Oxford Studies in Ancient Philosophy* 6 (1988): 169–99.

_____. 'Introduction'. In idem, ed., *The Person and the Human Mind: Issues in Ancient and Modern Philosophy*, 1–17. Oxford: Clarendon Press, 1990.

_____. 'The Human Being as an Ethical Norm'. In idem, ed., *The Person and the Human Mind: Issues in Ancient and Modern Philosophy*, 137–61. Oxford: Clarendon Press, 1990.

_____. *The Discourses of Epictetus*. Everyman. London: J. M. Dent, 1995.

_____. 'The School in the Roman Imperial Period'. In B. Inwood, ed., *The Cambridge Companion to the Stoics*, 33–58. Cambridge: Cambridge University Press, 2003.

Gill, D.W.J. 'Erastus the Aedile'. *Tyndale Bulletin* 40 (1989): 293–301.

_____. 'Corinth: A Roman Colony of Achaea'. *Biblische Zeitschrift* 37 (1993): 259–64.

Glare, P.G.W., ed. *Oxford Latin Dictionary*. Oxford: Oxford University Press, 1982.

Gleason, M. *Making Men: Sophists and Self-Presentation in Ancient Rome*. Princeton: Princeton University Press, 1995.

Gleason, R.C. 'Paul's Covenantal Contrasts in 2 Corinthians 3:1–11'. *Bibliotheca sacra* 154 (1997): 61–79.

Gomme, A.W. 'The Interpretation of ΚΑΛΟΙ ΚΑΓΑΘΟΙ in Thucydides 4.40.2'. *Classical Quarterly* 3 (1953): 65–8.

Good, D.J. *Jesus the Meek King*. Harrisburg: Trinity Press International, 1999.

Gordon, W.M., and O.F. Robinson. *The Institutes of Gaius: Translated with an Introduction*. Texts in Roman Law. London: Duckworth, 1988.

Gorman, M.J. *Cruciformity: Paul's Narrative Spirituality of the Cross*. Grand Rapids: Eerdmans, 2001.

Gotoff, H.C. 'Oratory: The Art of Illusion'. *Harvard Studies in Classical Philology* 95 (1993): 289–313.

Graf, F. 'Gestures and Conventions: The Gestures of Roman Actors and Orators'. In J. Bremmer, and H. Roodenburg, eds., *A Cultural History of Gesture from Antiquity to the Present Day*, 36–58. London: Polity Press, 1991.

Gräßer, E. *Der zweite Brief an die Korinther. Kapitel 1,1–7,16*. Ökumenischer Taschenbuchkommentar zum Neuen Testament. Gütersloh: Gütersloher Verlaghaus Gerd Mohn; Würzburg: Echter, 2002.

Gregory, T.E., ed. *The Corinthia in the Roman Period: Including the Papers Given at a Symposium Held at Ohio State University on 7–9 March 1991*. Journal of Roman Archaeology Supplementary Series 8. Ann Arbor: Journal of Roman Archaeology, 1993.

Griffin, M. 'Philosophy, Politics, and Politicians at Rome'. In M. Griffin, and J. Barnes, eds., *Philosophia Togata: Essays on Philosophy and Roman Society*, 1–37. Oxford: Clarendon Press, 1989.

_____. 'Cynicism and the Romans: Attraction and Repulsion'. In R.B. Branham, and M.-O. Goulet-Cazé, eds., *The Cynics: The Cynic Movement in Antiquity and Its Legacy*, 190–204. Berkeley: University of California Press, 1996.

Grindheim, S. 'The Law Kills but the Gospel Gives Life: The Letter–Spirit Dualism in 2 Corinthians 3.5–18'. *Journal for the Study of the New Testament* 84 (2001): 97–115.

Gruen, E.S. *Diaspora: Jews Amidst Greeks and Romans*. Cambridge: Harvard University Press, 2002.

Gunderson, E. *Declamation, Paternity, and Roman Identity: Authority and the Rhetorical Self*. Cambridge: Cambridge University Press, 2003.

Güttgemanns, E. *Der leidende Apostel und sein Herr: Studien zur paulinischen Christologie*. Forschungen zur Religion und Literatur des Alten und Neuen Testaments 90. Göttingen: Vandenhoeck & Ruprecht, 1966.

Hadot, P. *Arrien. Manuel d'Épictète*. Paris: Livre de Poche, 2000.

Hafemann, S.J. *Suffering and Spirit: An Exegetical Study of II Cor. 2:14–3:3 within the Context of the Corinthian Correspondence*. Wissenschaftliche Untersuchungen zum Neuen Testament 2/19. Tübingen: Mohr, 1986.

_____. '"Self-Commendation" and Apostolic Legitimacy in 2 Corinthians: A Pauline Dialectic?'. *New Testament Studies* 36 (1990): 66–88.

_____. *Paul, Moses, and the History of Israel: The Letter/Spirit Contrast and the Argument from Scripture in 2 Corinthians 3*. Wissenschaftliche Untersuchungen zum Neuen Testament 81. Tübingen: Mohr, 1995.

_____. 'Paul's Argument from the Old Testament and Christology in 2 Cor 1–9'. In R. Bieringer, ed., *The Corinthian Correspondence*, 277–303. Bibliotheca ephemeridum theologicarum lovaniensium 125. Leuven: Leuven University Press, 1996.

_____. *2 Corinthians*. NIV Application Commentary. Grand Rapids: Zondervan, 2000.

Hall, D.R. *The Unity of the Corinthian Correspondence*. Journal for the Study of the New Testament Supplement Series 251. London: T. & T. Clark, 2003.

Hall, J. 'Cicero and Quintilian on the Oratorical Use of Hand Gestures'. *Classical Quarterly* 54 (2004): 143–60.

Harrill, J.A. 'Invective against Paul (2 Cor 10:10), the Physiognomics of the Ancient Slave Body, and the Greco-Roman Rhetoric of Manhood'. In A.Y. Collins, and M.M. Mitchell, eds., *Antiquity and Humanity: Essays on Ancient Religion and Philosophy. Presented to Hans Dieter Betz on His 70th Birthday*, 189–213. Tübingen: Mohr Siebeck, 2001.

Harris, M.J. *The Second Epistle to the Corinthians*. New International Greek Testament Commentary. Grand Rapids: Eerdmans, 2005.

Harvey, A.E. *Renewal through Suffering: A Study of 2 Corinthians*. Studies of the New Testament and Its World. Edinburgh: T. & T. Clark, 1996.

Hays, R.B. *Echoes of Scripture in the Letters of Paul*. New Haven: Yale University Press, 1989.

Heath, J. '2 Cor 4:7–12: Viewing Paul as an Icon of Christ'. In R. Hirsch–Luipold, H. Görgemanns, and M. von Albrecht. *Religiöse Philosophie und philosophische Religion der frühen Kaiserzeit. Literaturgeschichtliche Perspektiven. Ratio Religionis Studien I*. Tübingen: Mohr Siebeck, forthcoming.

Heckel, U. *Kraft in Schwachheit: Untersuchungen zu 2. Kor 10–13*. Wissenschaftliche Untersuchungen zum Neuen Testament 2/56. Tübingen: Mohr, 1993.

Hellerman, J.H. *Reconstructing Honor in Roman Philippi: Carmen Christi as Cursus Pudorum*. Society for New Testament Studies Monograph Series 132. Cambridge: Cambridge University Press, 2005.

Helm, R. 'Valerius Maximus'. In A. Pauly, G. Wissova and W. Kroll, eds., *Real-Encyclopädie der klassischen Altertumswissenschaft*, 8A:90–116. Stuttgart: Metzlersche Verlagsbuchhandlung, 1955.

Héring, J. *The Second Epistle of Saint Paul to the Corinthians*. London: Epworth, 1967.

Hershbell, J. 'The Stoicism of Epictetus: Twentieth Century Perspectives'. In W. Haase, ed., *Aufstieg und Niedergang der römischen Welt* II.36.3, 2148–63. Berlin: de Gruyter, 1989.

234 *Bibliography*

Hester, J.D. 'The Rhetoric of *Persona* in Romans: Re-reading Romans 1:1–12'. In S.E. McGinn, ed., *Celebrating Romans: Template for Pauline Theology. Essays in Honor of Robert Jewett*, 83–105. Grand Rapids: Eerdmans, 2004.

Hickling, C.J.A. 'Is the Second Epistle to the Corinthians a Source for Early Church History?'. *Zeitschrift für die neutestamentliche Wissenschaft* 66 (1975): 284–7.

Hock, R.F. *The Social Context of Paul's Ministry: Tentmaking and Apostleship*. Philadelphia: Fortress Press, 1980.

_____. '"By the Gods, It's My One Desire to See an Actual Stoic": Epictetus' Relations with Students and Visitors in His Personal Network'. *Semeia* 56 (1992): 121–42.

Hodgson, R. Jr. 'Paul the Apostle and First Century Tribulation Lists'. *Zeitschrift für die neutestamentliche Wissenschaft* 74 (1983): 59–80.

_____. 'Valerius Maximus and Gospel Criticism'. *Catholic Biblical Quarterly* 51 (1989): 502–10.

_____. 'Valerius Maximus and the Social World of the New Testament'. *Catholic Biblical Quarterly* 51 (1989): 683–93.

Hofius, O. 'Gesetz und Evangelium nach 2. Korinther 3'. In *Paulusstudien*, 75–120. Wissenschaftliche Untersuchungen zum Neuen Testament 51. Tübingen: Mohr, 1989.

Holford-Strevens, L. 'Favorinus: The Man of Paradoxes'. In J. Barnes, and M. Griffin, eds., *Philosophia Togata II: Plato and Aristotle at Rome*, 188–217. Oxford: Clarendon Press, 1997.

Hölkeskamp, K.-J. '*Exempla* und *mos maiorum*: Überlegungen zum kollektiven Gedächtnis der Nobilität'. In H.-J. Gehrke, and A. Möller, eds., *Vergangenheit und Lebenswelt: Soziale Kommunikation, Traditionsbildung und historisches Bewußtsein*, 301–38. ScriptOralia 90. Tübingen: Gunter Narr Verlag, 1996.

Holland, G. 'Speaking Like a Fool: Irony in 2 Corinthians 10–13'. In S.E. Porter, and T.H. Olbricht, eds., *Rhetoric and the New Testament: Essays from the 1992 Heidelberg Conference*, 250–64. Journal for the Study of the New Testament Supplement Series 90. Sheffield: Sheffield Academic Press, 1993.

Hollis, M. 'Of Masks and Men'. In M. Carrithers, S. Collins, and S. Lukes, eds., *The Category of the Person: Anthropology, Philosophy, History*, 217–33. Cambridge: Cambridge University Press, 1985.

Holloway, P.A. '*Bona Cogitare*: An Epicurean Consolation in Phil 4:8–9'. *Harvard Theological Review* 91 (1998): 89–96.

Hooker, M.D. 'Beyond the Things that are Written? St Paul's Use of Scripture'. *New Testament Studies* 27 (1981): 295–309.

Hopwood, K. 'Aspects of Violent Crime in Roman Empire'. In P. McKechnie, ed., *Thinking Like a Lawyer: Essays on Legal History and General History for John Crook on His Eightieth Birthday*, 63–80. Mnemosyne Supplement 231. Leiden: Brill, 2002.

Horrell, D.G. *The Social Ethos of Pauline Christianity: Interests and Ideology in the Corinthian Correspondence from 1 Corinthians to 1 Clement*. Studies of the New Testament and Its World. Edinburgh: T. & T. Clark, 1996.

_____. *Solidarity and Difference: A Contemporary Reading of Paul's Ethics*. London: T. & T. Clark, 2005.

Horst, P.W. van der. 'Musonius Rufus and the New Testament'. *Novum Testamentum* 16 (1974): 306–15.

_____. 'Corpus Hellenisticum Novi Testamenti'. In D.N. Freedman, ed., *Anchor Bible Dictionary*, I:1157–61. New York: Doubleday, 1992.

Hubbard, M.V. 'Was Paul Out of His Mind? Re-Reading 2 Corinthians 5.13'. *Journal for the Study of the New Testament* 70 (1998): 39–64.

_____. *New Creation in Paul's Letters and Thoughts*. Society for New Testament Studies Monograph Series 119. Cambridge: Cambridge University Press, 2002.

Hugedé, N. *Le métaphore du miroir dans les épîtres de Saint Paul aux Corinthiens*. Neuchâtel: Delachaux et Niestlé, 1957.

Hughes, P.E. *Paul's Second Epistle to the Corinthians*. New International Commentary on the New Testament. Grand Rapids: Eerdmans, 1962.

Huskinson, J., ed. *Experiencing Rome: Culture, Identity and Power in the Roman Empire*. London: Routledge, 2000.

Jagu, A. *Epictète et Platon: Essai sur les rélations du stoicisme et du platonisme à propos de la morale des entretiens*. Paris: Vrin, 1946.

_____. 'La Morale d'Epictète et le christianisme'. In W. Haase, ed., *Aufstieg und Niedergang der römischen Welt* II.36.3, 2164–99. Berlin: de Gruyter, 1989.

Jenkins, R. *Social Identity*. London: Routledge, 1996.

Jervell, J. *Imago Dei: Gen 1,26f im Spätjudentum, in der Gnosis und in den paulinischen Briefen*. Forschungen zur Religion und Literatur des Alten und Neuen Testaments 76. Göttingen: Vandenhoeck & Ruprecht, 1960.

Jewett, R. *Paul's Anthropological Terms: A Study of Their Use in Conflict Settings*. Arbeiten zur Geschichte des antiken Judentums und des Urchristentums 10. Leiden: Brill, 1971.

Johnson, W.A. 'Greek Electronic Resources and the Lexicographical Function'. In B.A. Taylor, J.A.L. Lee, P.R. Burton, and R.E. Whitaker, eds., *Biblical Greek Language and Lexicography: Essays in Honor of Frederick W. Danker*, 75–84. Grand Rapids: Eerdmans, 2004.

Johnston, D. *Roman Law in Context*. Key Themes in Ancient History. Cambridge: Cambridge University Press, 1999.

Jones, C.P. *The Roman World of Dio Chrysostom*. Loeb Classical Monographs. Harvard: Harvard University Press, 1978.

_____. '*Stigma*: Tattooing and Branding in Graeco-Roman Antiquity'. *Journal of Roman Studies* 77 (1987): 139–55.

Jones, P.R. *The Apostle Paul: A Second Moses according to II Corinthians 2:14–4:7*. Ann Arbor: University Microfilms, 1981.

Jongkind, D. 'Corinth in the First Century AD: The Search for Another Class'. *Tyndale Bulletin* 52 (2001): 139–48.

Joshel, S.R. *Work, Identity, and Legal Status at Rome: A Study of the Occupational Inscriptions*. Oklahoma Series in Classical Culture. Norman, OK: University of Oklahoma Press, 1992.

Judge, E.A. *The Social Pattern of Christian Groups in the First Century*. London: Tyndale Press, 1960.

_____. 'The Early Christians as a Scholastic Community: Part II'. *Journal of Religious History* 1 (1961): 125–37.

_____. 'Paul's Boasting in Relation to Contemporary Professional Practice'. *Australian Biblical Review* 16 (1968): 37–50.

_____. '"Antike und Christentum": Towards a Definition of the Field. A Bibliographical Survey'. In W. Haase, ed., *Aufstieg und Niedergang der römischen Welt* II.23.1, 3–58. Berlin: de Gruyter, 1979.

_____. 'The Social Identity of the First Christians: A Question of Method in Religious History'. *Journal of Religious History* 11 (1980): 210–17.

_____. *Rank and Status in the World of the Caesars and St. Paul*. Christchurch, New Zealand: University of Canterbury Publications, 1982.

_____. 'Cultural Conformity and Innovation in Paul: Some Clues from Contemporary Documents'. *Tyndale Bulletin* 35 (1984): 3–24.

_____. 'The Roman Base of Paul's Mission'. *Tyndale Bulletin* 56 (2005): 103–17.

Kamlah, E. 'Wie beurteilt Paulus sein Leiden? Ein Beitrag zur Untersuchung seiner Denkstruktur'. *Zeitschrift für die neutestamentliche Wissenschaft* 54 (1963): 217–32.

Kamtekar, R. 'ΑΙΔΩΣ in Epictetus'. *Classical Philology* 93 (1998): 136–60.

Käsemann, E. 'Die Legitimität des Apostels: Eine Untersuchung zu II Korinther 10–13'. *Zeitschrift für die neutestamentliche Wissenschaft* 41 (1942): 33–71.

Keener, C.S. *1–2 Corinthians*. New Cambridge Bible Commentary. Cambridge: Cambridge University Press, 2005.

Kennedy, G.A. *The Art of Rhetoric in the Roman World: 300 B.C.–A.D. 300*. Princeton: Princeton University Press, 1972.

_____. *New Testament Interpretation through Rhetorical Criticism*. Studies in Religion. Chapel Hill: University of North Carolina Press, 1984.

_____. *A New History of Classical Rhetoric*. Princeton: Princeton University Press, 1994.

Kent, J.H. *Corinth – Inscriptions, 1926–1950*. Corinth: Results 8.3. Princeton: American School of Classical Studies at Athens, 1966.

Ker, D.P. 'Paul and Apollos – Colleagues or Rivals?'. *Journal for the Study of the New Testament* 77 (2000): 75–97.

Keyes, C.W. 'The Greek Letter of Introduction'. *American Journal of Philology* 56 (1935): 28–48.

Kim, C.-H. *Form and Structure of the Familiar Letter of Recommendation*. Society of Biblical Literature Dissertation Series 4. Missoula: Scholars Press, 1972.

Kim, S. *The Origin of Paul's Gospel*. Wissenschaftliche Untersuchungen zum Neuen Testament 2/4. Tübingen: Mohr, 1981.

_____. *Paul and the New Perspective: Second Thoughts on the Origin of Paul's Gospel*. Wissenschaftliche Untersuchungen zum Neuen Testament 140. Tübingen: Mohr Siebeck, 2002.

Klauck, H.-J. 'Erleuchtung und Verkündigung. Auslegungsskizze zu 2 Kor 4,1–6'. In L. de Lorenzi, ed., *Paolo Ministro del Nuovo Testamento (2 Co 2,14–4,6)*, 267–316. Benedictina 9. Roma: Abbazia di S. Paolo, 1987.

_____. 'Dankbar leben, dankbar sterben: Εὐχαριστεῖν bei Epiktet'. In *Gemeinde, Amt, Sakrament: Neutestamentliche Perspektiven*, 373–90. Würzburg: Echter, 1989.

Kleinknecht, H. 'εἰκών'. In G. Kittel, ed., *Theological Dictionary of the New Testament*, 2:388–90. Grand Rapids: Eerdmans, 1964.

Kleinknecht, K.T. *Der leidende Gerechtfertigte: Die alttestamentlich-jüdische Tradition vom 'leidenden Gerechten' und ihre Rezeption bei Paulus*. Wissenschaftliche Untersuchungen zum Neuen Testament 2/13. Tübingen: Mohr, 1984.

Koenig, J.T. 'The Motif of Transformation in the Pauline Epistles: A History-of-Religions/ Exegetical Study'. Ph.D diss., Union Theological Seminary, 1971.

Kolenkow, A.B. 'Paul and His Opponents in 2 Cor 10–13: THEIOI ANDRES and Spiritual Guides'. In L. Borman, K. Del Tredici, and A. Standhardtinger, eds., *Religious Propaganda and Missionary Competition in the New Testament World: Essays Honoring Dieter Georgi*, 351–74. Supplements to Novum Testamentum 74. Leiden: Brill, 1994.

König, J. 'Favorinus' Corinthian Oration in its Corinthian Context'. *Proceedings of the Cambridge Philological Society* 47 (2001): 141–71.

Konradt, M. 'Die korinthische Weisheit und das Wort vom Kreuz. Erwägungen zur korinthischen Problemkonstellation und paulinischen Intention in 1 Kor 1–4'. *Zeitschrift für die neutestamentliche Wissenschaft* 94 (2003): 181–214.

Lacey, D.R. de. 'Image and Incarnation in Pauline Christology – A Search for Origins'. *Tyndale Bulletin* 30 (1979): 3–28.

Lagrange, L.M. 'La philosophie religieuse d'Epictète'. *Revue biblique* 9 (1912): 192–212.

Lambrecht, J. 'To Die Together and to Live Together: A Study of 2 Corinthians 7,3'. *Bijdragen* 37 (1976): 234–51.

_____. 'Structure and Line of Thought in 2 Cor 2,14–4,6'. *Biblica* 64 (1983): 344–80.

_____. 'Transformation in 2 Corinthians 3,18'. *Biblica* 64 (1983): 243–54.

_____. 'Philological and Exegetical Notes on 2 Corinthians 13,4'. *Bijdragen* 46 (1985): 261–9.

_____. 'The Nekrōsis of Jesus: Ministry and Suffering in 2 Cor 4,7–15'. *Bibliotheca ephemeridum theologicarum lovaniensium* 73 (1986): 120–43.

_____. '"Reconcile Yourselves ...": A Reading of 2 Cor 5,11–21'. In L. de Lorenzi, ed., *The Diakonia of the Spirit (2 Co 4:7–7.4)*, 161–209. Benedictina 10. Rome: St Paul's Abbey, 1989.

_____. 'The Eschatological Outlook in 2 Corinthians 4,7–15'. In T.E. Schmidt, and M. Silva, eds., *To Tell the Mystery: Essays on New Testament Eschatology in Honor of Robert H. Gundry*, 122–40. Journal for the Study of the New Testament Supplement Series 100. Sheffield: Sheffield Academic Press, 1994.

_____. 'Paul's Appeal and the Obedience to Christ: The Line of Thought in 2 Corinthians 10,1–6'. *Biblica* 77 (1996): 398–416.

_____. 'Dangerous Boasting. Paul's Self Commendation in 2 Corinthians 10–13'. In R. Bieringer, ed., *The Corinthian Correspondence*, 325–46. Bibliotheca ephemeridum theologicarum lovaniensium 125. Leuven: Leuven University Press, 1996.

_____. 'Strength in Weakness: A Reply to Scott B. Andrews' Exegesis of 2 Cor 11.23b–33'. *New Testament Studies* 43 (1997): 285–90.

_____. *Second Corinthians*. Sacra Pagina 8. Collegeville: Liturgical Press, 1999.

_____. 'The Fool's Speech and Its Context: Paul's Particular Way of Arguing in 2 Cor 10–13'. *Biblica* 82 (2001): 305–24.

Lampe, P. 'Das korinthische Herrenmahl im Schnittpunkt hellenistisch-römischer Mahlpraxis und paulinischer Theologia Crucis (1 Kor 11,17–34)'. *Zeitschrift für die neutestamentliche Wissenschaft* 82 (1991): 183–213.

Lane, E.N. 'Sabazius and the Jews in Valerius Maximus: A Re-Examination'. *Journal of Roman Studies* 69 (1979): 35–8.

Lang, F. *Die Briefe an die Korinther*. Das Neue Testament Deutsch 7. Göttingen/Zürich: Vandenhoeck & Ruprecht, 1986.

Larsson, E. *Christus als Vorbild: Eine Untersuchung zu den paulinischen Tauf- und Eikontexten*. Acta seminarii neotestamentici upsaliensis 23. Uppsala: Almqvist and Wiksells, 1962.

Laurence, R., and J. Berry, eds. *Cultural Identity in the Roman Empire*. London: Routledge, 1998.

Laurenti, R. 'Musonio, maestro di Epitetto'. In W. Haase, ed., *Aufstieg und Niedergang der römischen Welt* II.36.3, 2105–46. Berlin: de Gruyter, 1989.

Lee, J.A.L. *A History of New Testament Lexicography*. Studies in Biblical Greek 8. New York: Peter Lang, 2003.

_____. 'The Present State of Lexicography of Ancient Greek'. In B.A. Taylor, J.A.L. Lee, P.R. Burton, and R.E. Whitaker, eds., *Biblical Greek Language and Lexicography: Essays in Honor of Frederick W. Danker*, 66–74. Grand Rapids: Eerdmans, 2004.

Lehmann, Y. 'Les revendications morales et politiques de Valère Maxime'. In J.-M. David, ed., *Valeurs et mémoire à Rome: Valère Maxime ou la vertu recomposée*, 19–26. Paris: de Boccard, 1998.

Leivestad, R. '"The Meekness and Gentleness of Christ" II Cor. X.1'. *New Testament Studies* 12 (1965–66): 156–64.

Lendon, J.E. *Empire of Honour: The Art of Government in the Roman World.* Oxford: Oxford University Press, 1997.

Lewis, C.T., and C. Short, eds. *A Latin Dictionary.* Oxford: Oxford University Press, 1963.

Liddell, H.G., R. Scott, and H.S. Jones, eds. *A Greek-English Lexicon.* 9th ed. Oxford: Clarendon Press, 1985.

Lietzmann, H. *An die Korinther I, II.* Handbuch zum Neuen Testament 9. 5th ed. Tübingen: Mohr, 1969.

Lieu, J.M. *Neither Greek nor Jew? Constructing Early Christianity.* Studies of the New Testament and Its World. Edinburgh: T. & T. Clark, 2002.

_____. *Christian Identity in the Jewish and Graeco-Roman World.* Oxford: Oxford University Press, 2004.

Lind, L.R. 'The Tradition of Roman Moral Conservatism'. In C. Deroux, ed., *Studies in Latin Literature and Roman History*, I:7–58. Collection Latomus 164. Bruxelles: Latomus, 1979.

Lintott, A. 'Freedmen and Slaves in the Light of Legal Documents from First-Century A.D. Campania'. *Classical Quarterly* 52 (2002): 555–65.

Litchfield, H.W. 'National *Exempla Virtvtis* in Roman Literature'. *Harvard Studies in Classical Philology* 25 (1914): 1–71.

Litfin, D. *St. Paul's Theology of Proclamation: 1 Corinthians 1–4 and Greco-Roman Rhetoric.* Society for New Testament Studies Monograph Series 79. Cambridge: Cambridge University Press, 1994.

Lohse, E. 'πρόσωπον, κτλ.' In G. Kittel, ed., *Theological Dictionary of the New Testament*, 7:768–80. Grand Rapids: Eerdmans, 1968.

Long, A.A. 'Freedom and Determinism in the Stoic Theory of Human Action'. In idem, ed., *Problems in Stoicism*, 173–99. London: Athlone Press, 1971.

_____. 'Socrates in Hellenistic Philosophy'. *Classical Quarterly* 38 (1988): 150–71.

_____. 'Stoic Philosophers on Persons, Property-Ownership and Community'. In R. Sorabji, ed., *Aristotle and After*, 13–31. Bulletin of the Institute of Classical Studies Supplement 68. London: Institute of Classical Studies, 1997.

_____. 'Epictetus as Socratic Mentor'. *Proceedings of the Cambridge Philological Society* 46 (2000): 79–98.

_____. 'Representation and the Self in Stoicism'. In *Stoic Studies*, 264–85. Berkeley: University of California Press, 2001.

_____. *Epictetus: A Stoic and Socratic Guide to Life.* Oxford: Oxford University Press, 2002.

_____. 'Roman Philosophy'. In D. Sedley, ed., *The Cambridge Companion to Greek and Roman Philosophy*, 184–210. Cambridge: Cambridge University Press, 2003.

Long, F.J. *Ancient Rhetoric and Paul's Apology: The Compositional Unity of 2 Corinthians.* Society for New Testament Studies Monograph Series 131. Cambridge: Cambridge University Press, 2005.

Longenecker, B.W. *The Triumph of Abraham's God: The Transformation of Identity in Galatians.* Edinburgh: T. & T. Clark, 1998.

Loutsch, C. 'Procédés rhétoriaues de la légitimation des examples chez Valère Maxime'. In J.-M. David, ed., *Valeurs et mémoire à Rome: Valère Maxime ou la vertu recomposeé*, 27–41. Paris: de Boccard, 1998.

Louw, J.P., and E.A. Nida, eds. *Greek-English Lexicon of the New Testament: Based on Semantic Domains.* New York: United Bible Societies, 1988.

Lumpe, A. 'Exemplum'. In T. Klauser, ed., *Reallexikon für Antike und Christentum*, VI:1229–57. Stuttgart: Anton Hiersemann, 1966.

Lutz, C.E. 'Musonius Rufus: "The Roman Socrates"'. *Yale Classical Studies* 10 (1947): 1–147.

MacMullen, R. *Roman Social Relations: 50 B.C. to A.D. 284*. New Haven: Yale University Press, 1974.

MacRae, G.W. 'Anti-Dualist Polemic in 2 Cor. 4,6?'. In F.L. Cross, ed., *Studia Evangelica IV/1: The New Testament Scriptures*, 420–31. Texte und Untersuchungen 102. Berlin: Akademie, 1968.

Malherbe, A.J. *Social Aspects of Early Christianity*. 2nd ed. Philadelphia: Fortress Press, 1983.

_____. 'Antisthenes and Odysseus, and Paul at War'. *Harvard Theological Review* 76 (1983): 143–73.

_____. 'A Physical Description of Paul'. *Harvard Theological Review* 79 (1986): 170–5.

_____. 'Hellenistic Moralists and the New Testament'. In W. Haase, ed., *Aufstieg und Niedergang der römischen Welt* II.26.1, 267–333. Berlin: de Gruyter, 1992.

Malina, B.J. *The New Testament World: Insights from Cultural Anthropology*. 3rd ed. Louisville: Westminster John Knox Press, 2001.

Malina, B.J., and J.H. Neyrey. *Portraits of Paul: An Archaeology of Ancient Personality*. Louisville: Westminster John Knox Press, 1996.

Marshall, P.J. 'A Metaphor of Social Shame: θριαμβεύεις in 2 Cor. 2:14'. *Novum Testamentum* 25 (1983): 302–17.

_____. *Enmity in Corinth: Social Conventions in Paul's Relations with the Corinthians*. Wissenschaftliche Untersuchungen zum Neuen Testament 2/23. Tübingen: Mohr, 1987.

_____. 'The Enigmatic Apostle: Paul and Social Change. Did Paul Seek to Transform Graeco-Roman Society?'. In T.W. Hillard, R.A. Kearsley, C.E.V. Nixon, and A.M. Nobbs, eds., *Ancient History in a Modern University*, II:153–74. Grand Rapids: Eerdmans, 1998.

Martin, D.B. 'Review Essay: Justin J. Meggitt, Paul, Poverty and Survival'. *Journal for the Study of the New Testament* 84 (2001): 51–64.

Martin, R.P. *2 Corinthians*. Word Biblical Commentary 40. Waco: Word, 1986.

Maslakov, G. 'Valerius Maximus and Roman Historiography. A Study of the *exempla* Tradition'. In W. Haase, ed., *Aufstieg und Niedergang der römischen Welt* II.32.1, 436–96. Berlin: de Gruyter, 1984.

Mauss, M. 'Une catégorie de l'esprit humain: La notion de personne, celle de "moi"'. *Journal of the Royal Anthropological Institute* 68 (1938): 263–81.

McKechnie, P., ed. *Thinking Like a Lawyer: Essays on Legal History and General History for John Crook on His Eightieth Birthday*. Mnemosyne Supplement 231. Leiden: Brill, 2002.

Meeks, W.A. *The First Urban Christians: The Social World of the Apostle Paul*. New Haven: Yale University Press, 1983.

Meggitt, J.J. 'The Social Status of Erastus (Rom. 16:23)'. *Novum Testamentum* 38 (1996): 218–23.

_____. *Paul, Poverty and Survival*. Studies of the New Testament and Its World. Edinburgh: T. & T. Clark, 1998.

_____. 'Response to Martin and Theissen'. *Journal for the Study of the New Testament* 84 (2001): 85–94.

Mellor, R. *The Roman Historians*. London: Routledge, 1999.

Merklein, H. *Der erste Brief an die Korinther*. Ökumenischer Taschenbuchkommentar zum Neuen Testament 7/1. Gütersloh: Gütersloher Verlaghaus Gerd Mohn; Würzburg: Echter, 1992.

Merritt, H.W. *In Word and Deed: Moral Integrity in Paul*. Emory Studies in Early Christianity 1. New York: Peter Lang, 1993.

Metzger, B.M. *A Textual Commentary on the Greek New Testament*. 2nd ed. New York: United Bible Societies, 1994.

Meyer, E.A. *Legitimacy and Law in the Roman World:* Tabulae *in Roman Belief and Practice*. Cambridge: Cambridge University Press, 2004.

Millar, F. 'Epictetus and the Imperial Court'. *Journal of Roman Studies* 55 (1965): 141–8.

_____. 'Ovid and the *Domus Augustus*: Rome Seen from Tomoi'. *Journal of Roman Studies* 83 (1993): 1–17.

Minnen, P. van. 'Paul the Roman Citizen'. *Journal for the Study of the New Testament* 56 (1994): 43–53.

Mitchell, A.C. 'Rich and Poor in the Courts of Corinth: Litigiousness and Status in 1 Corinthians 6.1–11'. *New Testament Studies* 39 (1993): 562–86.

Mitchell, M.M. *Paul and the Rhetoric of Reconciliation: An Exegetical Investigation of the Language and Composition of 1 Corinthians*. Hermeneutische Untersuchungen zur Theologie 28. Tübingen: Mohr, 1991.

Mueller, H.-F. '*Vita, Pudicitia, Libertas*: Juno, Gender, and Religious Politics in Valerius Maximus'. *Transactions of the American Philological Association* 128 (1998): 221–63.

_____. *Roman Religion in Valerius Maximus*. London: Routledge, 2002.

Munck, J. *Paul and the Salvation of Mankind*. Translated by F. Clarke. London: SCM Press, 1959.

Murphy-O'Connor, J. 'A Ministry Beyond the Letter (2 Cor 3:1–6)'. In L. de Lorenzi, ed., *Paolo Ministro del Nuovo Testamento (2 Co 2,14–4,6)*, 105–57. Benedictina 9. Roma: Abbazia di S. Paolo, 1987.

_____. 'Faith and Resurrection in 2 Cor 4:13–14'. *Revue biblique* 95 (1988): 543–50.

_____. *The Theology of the Second Letter to the Corinthians*. New Testament Theology. Cambridge: Cambridge University Press, 1991.

_____. *Paul: A Critical Life*. Oxford: Oxford University Press, 1996.

_____. *St. Paul's Corinth: Texts and Archaeology*. 3rd ed. Collegeville: Liturgical Press, 2002.

Nédoncelle, M. 'Prosopon et Persona dans l'antiquité classique'. *Revue des sciences religieuses* 22 (1948): 277–99.

Newby, Z., and R.E. Leader-Newby, eds. *Art and Inscriptions in the Ancient World*. Cambridge: Cambridge University Press, 2006.

Nguyen, V.H.T. 'The Identification of Paul's Spectacle of Death Metaphor in 1 Corinthians 4.9'. *New Testament Studies* 53 (2007) 489–501.

_____. 'God's Execution of His Condemned Apostles. Paul's Imagery of the Roman Arena in 1 Cor 4,9'. *Zeitschrift für die neutestamentliche Wissenschaft* 99 (2008) 33–48.

Nicolet, C. 'Augustus, Government, and the Propertied Class'. In F. Millar, and E. Segal, eds., *Caesar Augustus: Seven Aspects*, 89–128. Oxford: Clarendon Press, 1984.

Noy, D. *Foreigners at Rome: Citizens and Strangers*. London: Duckworth, 2000.

O'Brien, P.T. *The Epistle to the Philippians*. New International Greek Testament Commentary. Grand Rapids: Eerdmans, 1991.

O'Collins, G.G. 'Power Made Perfect in Weakness: 2 Cor 12:9–10'. *Catholic Biblical Quarterly* 33 (1971): 528–37.

O'Sullivan, N. 'Written and Spoken in the First Sophistic'. In I. Worthington, ed., *Voice into Text: Orality and Literacy in Ancient Greece*, 115–27. Mnemosyne Supplement 157. Leiden: Brill, 1996.

Oakes, P. 'Epictetus (and the New Testament)'. *Vox Evangelica* 23 (1993): 39–56.

_____. *Philippians: From People to Letter*. Society for New Testament Studies Monograph Series 110. Cambridge: Cambridge University Press, 2001.

_____. 'Re-mapping the Universe: Paul and the Emperor in 1 Thessalonians and Philippians'. *Journal for the Study of the New Testament* 27 (2005): 301–22.

Oldfather, W.A. *Epictetus*. 2 vols. Loeb Classical Library. Cambridge: Harvard University Press, 1925–8.

Oster, R.E. 'Use, Misuse and Neglect of Archaeological Evidence in Some Modern Works on 1 Corinthians'. *Zeitschrift für die neutestamentliche Wissenschaft* 83 (1992): 52–73.

Parker, H.N. 'The Observed of All Observers: Spectacle, Applause, and Cultural Poetics in the Roman Theater Audience'. In B. Bergmann, and C. Kondoleon, eds., *The Art of Ancient Spectacle*, 163–79. Studies in the History of Art 56. New Haven: Yale University Press, 1999.

Petersen, L.H. *The Freedman in Roman Art and Art History*. Cambridge: Cambridge University Press, 2006.

Peterson, B.K. *Eloquence and the Proclamation of the Gospel in Corinth*. Society of Biblical Literature Dissertation Series 163. Atlanta: Scholars Press, 1998.

Pickett, R. *The Cross in Corinth: The Social Significance of the Death of Jesus*. Journal for the Study of the New Testament Supplement Series 143. Sheffield: Sheffield Academic Press, 1997.

Plummer, A. *A Critical and Exegetical Commentary on the Second Epistle of St Paul to the Corinthians*. International Critical Commentary. Edinburgh: T. & T. Clark, 1915.

Pogoloff, S.M. *Logos and Sophia: The Rhetorical Situation of 1 Corinthians*. Society of Biblical Literature Dissertation Series 134. Atlanta: Scholars Press, 1992.

Pohlenz, M. *Die Stoa: Geschichte einer geistigen Bewegung*. 2 vols. Göttingen: Vandenhoeck & Ruprecht, 1948–49.

Porter, S.E., ed. *Paul and His Opponents*. Pauline Studies 2. Leiden: Brill, 2005.

Potter, D.S. and C. Damon. 'The *Senatus consultum de Cn. Pisone Patre*'. *American Journal of Philology* 120 (1999): 13–42.

Proudfoot, C.M. 'Imitation or Realistic Participation? A Study of Paul's Concept of "Suffering with Christ"'. *Interpretation* 17 (1963): 140–60.

Provence, T.E. '"Who is Sufficient for These Things?" An Exegesis of 2 Corinthians ii 15–iii 18'. *Novum Testamentum* 24 (1982): 54–81.

Radt, S.L. 'Zu Epiktets *Diatriben*'. *Mnemosyne* 43 (1990): 364–73.

Ramage, E.S. *The Nature and Purpose of Augustus' 'Res Gestae'*. Historia Einzelschriften 44. Stuttgart: F. Steiner, 1987.

Rapske, B. *The Book of Acts and Paul in Roman Custody*. The Book of Acts in its First Century Setting 3. Grand Rapids: Eerdmans, 1994.

Rawson, E. 'Cicero the Historian and Cicero the Antiquarian'. *Journal of Roman Studies* 62 (1972): 33–45.

_____. '*Discrimina Ordinum*: The *Lex Julia Theatralis*'. *Papers of the British School at Rome* 55 (1987): 83–114.

_____. 'Roman Rulers and the Philosophic Adviser'. In M. Griffin, and J. Barnes, eds., *Philosophia Togata: Essays on Philosophy and Roman Society*, 233–57. Oxford: Clarendon Press, 1989.

Reinhold, M. 'Usurpation of Status and Status Symbols in the Roman Empire'. *Historia* 20 (1971): 275–302.

Richlin, A. 'Gender and Rhetoric: Producing Manhood in the Schools'. In W.J. Dominik, ed., *Roman Eloquence: Rhetoric in Society and Literature*, 90–110. London: Routledge, 1997.

Ricoeur, P. *Interpretation Theory: Discourse and the Surplus of Meaning*. Fort Worth: Texas Christian University Press, 1976.

Rist, J.M. *Stoic Philosophy*. Cambridge: Cambridge University Press, 1969.

Robinson, W.P., ed. *Social Group and Identities: Developing the Legacy of Henri Tajfel.* Oxford: Butterworth-Heinemann, 1996.

Roller, M.B. 'Exemplarity in Roman Culture: The Cases of Horatius Cocles and Cloelia'. *Classical Philology* 99 (2004): 1–56.

Romano, D.G. 'City Planning, Centuriation, and Land Division in Roman Corinth: *Colonia Laus Iulia Corinthiensis* & *Colonia Iulia Flavia Augusta Corinthiensis*'. In C.K. Williams, and N. Bookidis, eds., *Corinth: The Centenary, 1896–1996*, 279–301. Corinth Vol. XX. Princeton: American School of Classical Studies at Athens, 2003.

Römer, F. 'Zum Aufbau der Exemplasammlung des Valerius Maximus'. *Wiener Studien* 103 (1990): 99–107.

Rorty, A.O. 'Persons and *Personae*'. In C. Gill, ed., *The Person and the Human Mind: Issues in Ancient and Modern Philosophy*, 21–38. Oxford: Clarendon Press, 1990.

Rowe, C.K. 'New Testament Iconography? Situating Paul in the Absence of Material Evidence'. In A. Weissenrieder, F. Wendt, and P. von Gemünden, eds., *Picturing the New Testament: Studies in Ancient Visual Images*, 289–312. Wissenschaftliche Untersuchungen zum Neuen Testament 2/193. Tübingen: Mohr Siebeck, 2005.

Rowland, C.C. 'The Influence of the First Chapter of Ezekiel on Judaism and Early Christianity'. Ph.D diss., Cambridge University, 1974.

Russell, D.A. *Greek Declamation.* Cambridge: Cambridge University Press, 1983.

Saller, R.P. 'Anecdotes as Historical Evidence for the Principate'. *Greece & Rome, 2nd ser.* 27 (1980): 69–83.

_____. 'Status and Patronage'. In A.K. Bowman, P. Garnsey, and D. Rathbone, eds., *The Cambridge Ancient History, XI: The High Empire, A.D. 70–192*, 817–54. Cambridge: Cambridge University Press, 2000.

Sandmel, S. 'Parallelomania'. *Journal of Biblical Literature* 81 (1962): 1–13.

Sänger, D. 'Die δυνατοί in 1 Kor 1,26'. *Zeitschrift für die neutestamentliche Wissenschaft* 76 (1985): 285–91.

Savage, T.B. *Power Through Weakness: Paul's Understanding of the Christian Ministry in 2 Corinthians.* Society for New Testament Studies Monograph Series 86. Cambridge: Cambridge University Press, 1996.

Schenkl, H. *Epicteti Dissertationes ab Arriano Digestae.* Bibliotheca scriptorum graecorum et romanorum teubneriana. 2nd ed. Leipzig: Teubner, 1916.

Schlier, H. 'Das Menschenherz nach dem Apostel Paulus'. In *Das Ende der Zeit. Exegetische Aufsätze und Vorträge III*, 184–200. Freiburg: Herder, 1971.

Schlossmann, S. *Persona und ΠΡΟΣΩΠΟΝ im Recht und im christlichen Dogma.* Kiliae: Lipsius & Tischer, 1906.

Schnelle, U. 'Transformation und Partizipation als Grundgedanken paulinischer Theologie'. *New Testament Studies* 47 (2001): 58–75.

Schofield, M. 'Stoic Ethics'. In B. Inwood, ed., *The Cambridge Companion to the Stoics*, 233–56. Cambridge: Cambridge University Press, 2003.

Schowalter, D.N., and S.J. Friesen, eds. *Urban Religion in Roman Corinth: Interdisciplinary Approaches.* Harvard Theological Studies 53. Cambridge: Harvard University Press, 2005.

Schrage, W. 'Die Stellung zur Welt bei Paulus, Epiktet und in der Apokalyptik: Ein Beitrag zu 1Kor 7,29–31'. *Zeitschrift für Theologie und Kirche* 61 (1964): 125–54.

_____. 'Leid, Kreuz, und Eschaton. Die Peristasenkataloge als Merkmale paulinischer theologia crucis und Eschatologie'. *Evangelische Theologie* 34 (1974): 141–75.

Schröter, J. *Der versöhnte Versöhner: Paulus als unentbehrlicher Mittler im Heilsvorgang zwischen Gott und Gemeinde nach 2 Kor 2,14–7,4.* Texte und Arbeiten zum neutestamentlichen Zeitalter 10. Tübingen: Francke, 1993.

Schüle, A. 'Made in the "Image of God": The Concepts of Divine Images in Gen 1–3'. *Zeitschrift für die alttestamentliche Wissenschaft* 117 (2005): 1–20.

Schulz, S. 'Die Decke des Moses. Untersuchungen zu einer vorpaulinischen Überlieferung in II Cor. 3.7–18'. *Zeitschrift für die neutestamentliche Wissenschaft* 49 (1958): 1–30.

Sedley, D. 'Philosophical Allegiance in the Greco-Roman World'. In M. Griffin, and J. Barnes, eds., *Philosophia Togata: Essays on Philosophy and Roman Society*, 97–119. Oxford: Clarendon Press, 1989.

Selby, G.S. 'Paul, the Seer: The Rhetorical Persona in 1 Corinthians 2.1–16'. In S.E. Porter, and T.H. Olbricht, eds., *The Rhetorical Analysis of Scripture: Essays from the 1995 London Conference*, 351–73. Journal for the Study of the New Testament Supplement Series 146. Sheffield: Sheffield Academic Press, 1997.

Sevenster, J.N. *Paul and Seneca*. Supplements to Novum Testamentum 4. Leiden: Brill, 1961.

_____. 'Education or Conversion: Epictetus and the Gospels'. *Novum Testamentum* 8 (1966): 247–62.

Sharp, D.S. *Epictetus and the New Testament*. London: Charles H. Kelly, 1914.

Sherwin-White, A.N. 'Pliny's Praetorship Again'. *Journal of Roman Studies* 47 (1957): 126–30.

_____. *Roman Society and Roman Law in the New Testament*. Oxford: Clarendon Press, 1963.

_____. *The Roman Citizenship*. 2nd ed. Oxford: Clarendon Press, 1973.

Sinclair, B.W. 'Declamatory *Sententiae* in Valerius Maximus'. *Prometheus* 10 (1984): 141–6.

Skidmore, C. *Practical Ethics for Roman Gentlemen*. Exeter: University of Exeter Press, 1996.

Smit, J.F.M. '"What is Apollos? What is Paul?" In Search for the Coherence of First Corinthians 1:10–4:21'. *Novum Testamentum* 44 (2002): 231–51.

Smith, R.R.R. 'Cultural Choice and Political Identity in Honorific Portrait Statues in the Greek East in the Second Century A.D.' *Journal of Roman Studies* 88 (1998): 56–93.

Souilhé, J. *Epictète: Entretiens*. 4 vols. Budé. Paris: Les Belles Lettres, 1948–65.

Spanneut, M. 'Epiktet'. In T. Klauser, ed., *Reallexicon für Antike und Christentum*, 5:599–681. Stuttgart: Anton Hiersemann, 1962.

Spawforth, A.J.S. 'Roman Corinth: The Formation of a Colonial Elite'. In A.D. Rizakis, ed., *Roman Onomastics in the Greek East: Social and Political Aspects*, 167–82. Meletemata 21. Athens: Kentron Hellenikes kai Romaikes Archaiotetos, 1996.

Stadter, P.A. 'Flavius Arrianus, the New Xenophon'. *Greek, Roman, and Byzantine Studies* 8 (1967): 155–61.

_____. *Arrian of Nicomedia*. Chapel Hill: University of North Carolina Press, 1980.

Stambaugh, J.E. 'Social Relations in the City of the Early Principate: State of Research'. In P.J. Achtemeier, ed., *Seminar Papers: Society of Biblical Literature*, 75–99. Chico: Scholars Press, 1980.

_____. *The Ancient Roman City*. Baltimore: John Hopkins University Press, 1988.

Stanley, C.D. *Arguing with Scripture: The Rhetoric of Quotations in the Letters of Paul*. London: T. & T. Clark, 2004.

Stanton, G.R. 'The Cosmopolitan Ideas of Epictetus and Marcus Aurelius'. *Phronesis* 13 (1968): 183–95.

_____. 'Sophists and Philosophers: Problems of Classification'. *American Journal of Philology* 94 (1973): 350–64.

Starr, C.G. Jr. 'Epictetus and the Tyrant'. *Classical Philology* 44 (1949): 20–9.

Ste Croix, G.E.M. de 'Additional note on KALOS, KALOKAGATHIA'. In *The Origins of the Peleponnesian War*, 371–6. London: Duckworth, 1972.

Steel, C. *Roman Oratory*. Greece & Rome. New Surveys in the Classics 36. Cambridge: Cambridge University Press, 2006.

Stegemann, W. 'War der Apostel Paulus ein römischer Bürger?'. *Zeitschrift für die neutestamentliche Wissenschaft* 78 (1987): 200–29.

Stegman, T. *The Character of Jesus: The Linchpin to Paul's Argument in 2 Corinthians*. Analecta Biblica 158. Roma: Editrice Pontifico Instituto Biblico, 2005.

Steiner, D. *Images in Mind: Statues in Archaic and Classical Greek Literature and Thought*. Princeton: Princeton University Press, 2001.

Stephens, W.O. 'Epictetus on How the Stoic Sage Loves'. *Oxford Studies in Ancient Philosophy* 14 (1996): 193–210.

Stewart, P. *Statues in Roman Society: Representation and Response*. Oxford Studies in Ancient Culture and Representation. Oxford: Oxford University Press, 2003.

Stockhausen, C.K. *Moses' Veil and the Glory of the New Covenant*. Analecta Biblica 116. Rome: Pontifical Biblical Institute, 1989.

Stowers, S.K. 'Social Status, Public Speaking and Private Teaching: The Circumstances of Paul's Preaching Activity'. *Novum Testamentum* 26 (1984): 59–82.

Strüder, C.W. 'Preferences Not Parties: The Background of 1 Cor 1,12'. *Ephemerides theologicae lovanienses* 79 (2003): 431–55.

Sumney, J.L. *Identifying Paul's Opponents: The Question of Method in 2 Corinthians*. Journal for the Study of the New Testament Supplement Series 40. Sheffield: Sheffield Academic Press, 1990.

_____. 'Paul's "Weakness": An Integral Part of His Conception of Apostleship'. *Journal for the Study of the New Testament* 52 (1993): 71–91.

Tajfel, H. *Human Groups and Social Categories: Studies in Social Psychology*. Cambridge: Cambridge University Press, 1981.

Tannehill, R.C. *Dying and Rising with Christ: A Study in Pauline Theology*. Beihefte zur Zeitschrift für die neutestamentliche Wissenschaft 32. Berlin: Topelmann, 1967.

Taylor, B.A., J.A.L. Lee, P.R. Burton, and R.E. Whitaker, eds. *Biblical Greek Language and Lexicography: Essays in Honor of Frederick W. Danker*. Grand Rapids: Eerdmans, 2004.

Theissen, G. *The Social Setting of Pauline Christianity: Essays on Corinth*. Translated by J.H. Schutz. Edinburgh: T. & T. Clark, 1982.

_____. *Psychological Aspects of Pauline Theology*. Translated by J.P. Golvin. Edinburgh: T. & T. Clark, 1987.

_____. 'The Social Structure of Pauline Communities: Some Critical Remarks on J.J. Meggitt, *Paul, Poverty and Survival*'. *Journal for the Study of the New Testament* 84 (2001): 65–84.

_____. 'Social Conflicts in the Corinthian Correspondence: Further Remarks on J.J. Meggitt, *Paul, Poverty and Survival*'. *Journal for the Study of the New Testament* 25 (2003): 371–91.

Theobald, M. *Die überströmende Gnade: Studien zu einem paulinischen Motivfeld*. Forschung zur Bibel 22. Würzburg: Echter, 1982.

Thiselton, A.C. *The First Epistle to the Corinthians*. New International Greek Testament Commentary. Grand Rapids: Eerdmans, 2000.

Thrall, M.E. 'Christ Crucified or Second Adam? A Christological Debate Between Paul and the Corinthians'. In B. Lindars, and S.S. Smalley, eds., *Christ and Spirit in the New Testament. In Honour of Charles Francis Digby Moule*, 143–56. Cambridge: Cambridge University Press, 1973.

_____. 'Conversion to the Lord: The Interpretation of Exodus 34 in II Cor. 3:14b–18'. In L. de Lorenzi, ed., *Paolo Ministro del Nuovo Testamento (2 Co 2,14–4,6)*, 197–265. Benedictina 9. Roma: Abbazia di S. Paolo, 1987.

_____. *A Critical and Exegetical Commentary on the Second Epistle to the Corinthians*. 2 vols. International Critical Commentary. Edinburgh: T. & T. Clark, 1994.

Toorn, K. van der. 'The Iconic Book: Analogies Between the Babylonian Cult of Images and the Veneration of the Torah'. In idem, ed., *The Image and the Book: Iconic Cults, Aniconism, and the Rise of Book religion in Israel and the Ancient Near East*, 229–48. Contributions to Biblical Exegesis and Theology 21. Leuven: Peeters, 1997.

Travis, S.H. 'Paul's Boasting in 2 Corinthians 10–12'. In E.A. Livingstone, ed., *Studia Evangelica VI*, 527–32. Berlin: Akademie, 1973.

Treggiari, S. 'Social Status and Social Legislation'. In A.K. Bowman, E. Champlin, and A. Lintott, eds., *The Cambridge Ancient History, X: The Augustan Empire, 43 B.C.–A.D. 69*, 873–904. Cambridge: Cambridge University Press, 1996.

Turner, M. 'Approaching "Personhood" in the New Testament, with Special Reference to Ephesians'. *Evangelical Quarterly* 77 (2005): 211–33.

Unnik, W.C. van. '"With Unveiled Face", An Exegesis of 2 Corinthians iii 12–18'. *Novum Testamentum* 6 (1963): 153–69.

Vanhoye, A. 'L'interprétation d'Ex 34 en 2 Co 3,7–14'. In L. de Lorenzi, ed., *Paolo Ministro del Nuovo Testamento (2 Co 2,14–4,6)*, 159–96. Benedictina 9. Roma: Abbazia di S. Paolo, 1987.

Walbank, M.E.H. 'The Foundation and Planning of Early Roman Corinth'. *Journal of Roman Archaeology* 10 (1997): 95–130.

_____. 'What's in a Name? Corinth under the Flavians'. *Zeitschrift für Papyrologie und Epigraphik* 139 (2002): 251–64.

Walker, D.D. *Paul's Offer of Leniency (2 Cor 10.1): Populist Ideology and Rhetoric in a Pauline Letter Fragment*. Wissenschaftliche Untersuchungen zum Neuen Testament 2/152. Tübingen: Mohr Siebeck, 2002.

Walker, H.J. *Valerius Maximus. Memorable Deeds and Sayings: One Thousand Tales from Ancient Rome*. Indianapolis: Hackett, 2004.

Wallace-Hadrill, A. 'The Emperor and His Virtues'. *Historia* 30 (1981): 298–323.

_____. '*Mutatio morum*: The Idea of a Cultural Revolution'. In T. Habinek, ed., *The Roman Cultural Revolution*, 3–22. Cambridge: Cambridge University Press, 1997.

Wardle, D. '"The Sainted Julius": Valerius Maximus and the Dictator'. *Classical Philology* 92 (1997): 323–45.

_____. *Valerius Maximus: Memorable Deeds and Sayings, Book I*. Clarendon Ancient History Series. Oxford: Clarendon Press, 1998.

_____. 'Valerius Maximus on the *Domus Augusta*, Augustus, and Tiberius'. *Classical Quarterly* 50 (2000): 479–93.

Watson, F. '2 Cor. X–XIII and Paul's Painful Letter to the Corinthians'. *Journal of Theological Studies* 35 (1984): 324–46.

_____. 'In the Image of God'. In *Text and Truth: Redefining Biblical Theology*, 277–304. Edinburgh: T. & T. Clark, 1997.

_____. *Paul and the Hermeneutics of Faith*. London: T. & T. Clark, 2004.

Weaver, P.R.C. 'Epaphroditus, Josephus, and Epictetus'. *Classical Quarterly* 44 (1994): 468–79.

Weileder, A. *Valerius Maximus: Spiegel kaiserlicher Selbstdarstellung*. Münchener Arbeiten zur Alten Geschichte 12. München: Editio Maris, 1998.

Weissenrieder, A. 'Der Blick in den Spiegel: II Kor 3,18 vor dem Hintergrund antiker Spiegeltheorien und ikonographischer Abbildungen'. In A. Weissenrieder, F. Wendt, and P. von Gemünden, eds., *Picturing the New Testament: Studies in Ancient Visual Images*, 313–43. Wissenschaftliche Untersuchungen zum Neuen Testament 2/193. Tübingen: Mohr Siebeck, 2005.

Welborn, L.L. 'On the Discord in Corinth: 1 Corinthians 1–4 and Ancient Politics'. *Journal of Biblical Literature* 106 (1987): 85–111.

Welch, K. 'Negotiating Roman Spectacle Architecture in the Greek World: Athens and Corinth'. In B. Bergmann, and C. Kondoleon, eds., *The Art of Ancient Spectacle*, 125–45. Studies in the History of Art 56. New Haven: Yale University Press, 1999.

West, A.B. *Corinth – Latin Inscriptions 1896–1920*. Corinth: Results 8.2. Cambridge: Harvard University Press, 1931.

Westerholm, S. 'Letter and Spirit: The Foundation of Pauline Ethics'. *New Testament Studies* 30 (1984): 229–48.

White, L.M., and J.T. Fitzgerald. 'Quod est comparandum: The Problem of Parallels'. In J.T. Fitzgerald, T.H. Olbricht, and L.M. White, eds., *Early Christianity and Classical Culture: Comparative Studies in Honor of Abraham J. Malherbe*, 13–39. Supplements to Novum Testamentum 110. Leiden: Brill, 2003.

Whitmarsh, T. *The Second Sophistic*. Greece & Rome. New Surveys in the Classics 35. Oxford: Oxford University Press, 2005.

Williams, C.K., and N. Bookidis, eds. *Corinth: The Centenary, 1896–1996*. Corinth Vol. XX. Princeton: American School of Classical Studies at Athens, 2003.

Windisch, H. *Der zweite Korintherbrief*. Kritisch-exegetischer Kommentar über das Neue Testament 69. Göttingen: Vandenhoeck & Ruprecht, 1924.

Winter, B.W. 'The Public Honouring of Christian Benefactors, Romans 13.3–4 and 1 Peter 2.14–15'. *Journal for the Study of the New Testament* 34 (1988): 87–103.

_____. 'Civil Litigation in Secular Corinth and the Church: The Forensic Background to 1 Corinthians 6.1–8'. *New Testament Studies* 37 (1991): 559–72.

_____. 'The Entries and Ethics of Orators and Paul (1 Thessalonians 2:1–12)'. *Tyndale Bulletin* 44 (1993): 55–74.

_____. *Seek the Welfare of the City: Christians as Benefactors and Citizens*. First-Century Christians in the Graeco-Roman World. Grand Rapids: Eerdmans, 1994.

_____. '*Christentum und Antike*: Acts and Paul's *Corpus* as Ancient History'. In T.W. Hillard, R.A. Kearsley, C.E.V. Nixon, and A.M. Nobbs, eds., *Ancient History in a Modern University*, II:121–30. Grand Rapids: Eerdmans, 1998.

_____. *After Paul Left Corinth: The Influence of Secular Ethics and Social Change*. Grand Rapids: Eerdmans, 2001.

_____. *Philo and Paul Among the Sophists: Alexandrian and Corinthian Responses to a Julio-Claudian Movement*. 2nd ed. Grand Rapids: Eerdmans, 2002.

_____. 'The Imperial Cult and Early Christians in Roman Galatia (Acts XIII 13–50 and Galatians VI 11–18)'. In T. Drew-Bear, M. Taslialan, and C.M. Thomas, eds., *Actes du Ier Congrès International sur Antioche de Pisidie*, 67–75. Paris: de Boccard, 2002.

_____. 'Roman Law and Society in Romans 12–15'. In P. Oakes, ed., *Rome in the Bible and the Early Church*, 67–102. Carlisle: Paternoster Press, 2002.

_____. 'The Toppling of Favorinus and Paul by the Corinthians'. In J.T. Fitzgerald, T.H. Olbricht, and L.M. White, eds., *Early Christianity and Classical Culture: Comparative Studies in Honor of Abraham J. Malherbe*, 291–306. Supplements to Novum Testamentum 110. Leiden: Brill, 2003.

_____. 'Philodemus and Paul on Rhetorical Delivery (ὑπόκρισις)'. In J.T. Fitzgerald, D. Obbink, and G.S. Holland, eds., *Philodemus and the New Testament World*, 323–42. Supplements to Novum Testamentum 111. Leiden: Brill, 2004.

_____. 'A Cambridge Lexical Handbook of New Testament Greek: Social Settings, Semantic Domains and First-Century Synonyms'. Paper presented at *Lexicography and Lexical Semantics: Questions at Issue in the Making of a Greek Lexicon*. Lisbon, November 2006.

Winterbottom, M. 'W. Martin Bloomer, *Valerius Maximus and the Rhetoric of the New Nobility* (1992)'. *Classical Review* 44 (1994): 50–2.

Wire, A.C. 'Reconciled to Glory in Corinth? 2 Cor 2:14–7:4'. In A.Y. Collins, and M.M. Mitchell, eds., *Antiquity and Humanity: Essays on Ancient Religion and Philosophy. Presented to Hans Dieter Betz on His 70th Birthday*, 263–75. Tübingen: Mohr Siebeck, 2001.

Wirth, T. 'Arrians Erinnerungen an Epiktet'. *Museum Helveticum* 24 (1967): 149–89, 197–216.

Wiseman, J. 'Corinth and Rome I: 228 BC–AD 267'. In H. Temporini, ed., *Aufstieg und Niedergang der römischen Welt* II.7.1, 438–548. Berlin: de Gruyter, 1979.

Wiseman, T.P. *Clio's Cosmetics: Three Studies in Greco-Roman Literature*. Leicester: Leicester University Press, 1979.

Witherington, B. *Conflict and Community in Corinth: A Socio-Rhetorical Commentary on 1 and 2 Corinthians*. Grand Rapids: Eerdmans, 1995.

_____. *Grace in Galatia: A Commentary on Paul's Letter to the Galatians*. Grand Rapids: Eerdmans, 1998.

_____. *Paul's Letter to the Romans: A Socio-Rhetorical Commentary*. Grand Rapids: Eerdmans, 2004.

Wolff, C. *Der zweite Brief des Paulus an die Korinther*. Theologischer Handkommentar zum Neuen Testament 8. Berlin: Evangelische Verlagsanstalt, 1989.

_____. 'Humility and Self-Denial in Jesus' Life and Message and in the Apostolic Existence of Paul'. In A.J.M. Wedderburn, ed., *Paul and Jesus. Collected Essays*, 145–60. Journal for the Study of the New Testament Supplement Series 37. Sheffield: Sheffield Academic Press, 1989.

Woolf, G. 'Becoming Roman, Staying Greek: Culture, Identity and the Civilising Process in the Roman East'. *Proceedings of the Cambridge Philological Society* 40 (1994): 116–43.

Wright, N.T. 'Reflected Glory: 2 Corinthians 3'. In *The Climax of the Covenant: Christ and the Law in Pauline Theology*, 175–92. Edinburgh: T. & T. Clark, 1991.

Wuellner, W. 'The Sociological Implications of 1 Corinthians 1.26–28 Reconsidered'. In E.A. Livingstone, ed., *Studia Evangelica VI*, 666–72. Berlin: Berlin Academy, 1973.

_____. 'Ursprung und Verwendung der σοφός-, δυνατός-, εὐγενής- Formel in 1 Kor 1,26'. In E. Bammel, C.K. Barrett, and W.D. Davies, eds., *Donum Gentilicium: New Testament Studies in Honour of David Daube*, 165–84. Oxford: Clarendon Press, 1978.

_____. 'Tradition and Interpretation of the "Wise-Powerful-Noble" Triad in 1 Cor 1,26'. In E.A. Livingstone, ed., *Studia Evangelica VII*, 557–62. Berlin: Berlin Academy, 1982.

Yieh, J.Y.-H. *One Teacher: Jesus' Teaching Role in Matthew's Gospel Report*. Beihefte zur Zeitschrift für die neutestamentliche Wissenschaft 125. Berlin: de Gruyter, 2004.

Young, F.M., and D.F. Ford. *Meaning and Truth in 2 Corinthians*. Biblical Foundations in Theology. London: SPCK, 1987.

Zanker, P. *The Power of Images in the Age of Augustus*. Translated by A. Shapiro. Ann Arbor: University of Michigan Press, 1988.

Zimmermann, R. *The Law of Obligations: Roman Foundations of the Civilian Tradition*. Oxford: Clarendon Press, 1996.

Zulueta, F. de. *The Institutes of Gaius. Part II: Commentary*. Oxford: Clarendon Press, 1953.

Index of Ancient Sources

1. Old Testament

2. New Testament

3. Other Greek and Latin Sources

Index of Modern Authors

Index of Subjects and Key Terms

Wissenschaftliche Untersuchungen zum Neuen Testament

Alphabetical Index of the First and Second Series

Bieringer, Reimund: see *Koester, Craig.*

Bittner, Wolfgang J.: Jesu Zeichen im Johannesevangelium. 1987. *Vol. II/26.*

Bjerkelund, Carl J.: Tauta Egeneto. 1987. *Vol. 40.*

Blackburn, Barry Lee: Theios Aner and the Markan Miracle Traditions. 1991. *Vol. II/40.*

Blanton IV, Thomas R.: Constructing a New Covenant. 2007. *Vol. II/233.*

Bock, Darrell L.: Blasphemy and Exaltation in Judaism and the Final Examination of Jesus. 1998. *Vol. II/106.*

Bockmuehl, Markus N.A.: Revelation and Mystery in Ancient Judaism and Pauline Christianity. 1990. *Vol. II/36.*

Bøe, Sverre: Gog and Magog. 2001. *Vol. II/135.*

Böhlig, Alexander: Gnosis und Synkretismus. Vol. 1 1989. *Vol. 47* – Vol. 2 1989. *Vol. 48.*

Böhm, Martina: Samarien und die Samaritai bei Lukas. 1999. *Vol. II/111.*

Böttrich, Christfried: Weltweisheit – Menschheitsethik – Urkult. 1992. *Vol. II/50.*

– */ Herzer, Jens* (Ed.): Josephus und das Neue Testament. 2007. *Vol. 209.*

Bolyki, János: Jesu Tischgemeinschaften. 1997. *Vol. II/96.*

Bosman, Philip: Conscience in Philo and Paul. 2003. *Vol. II/166.*

Bovon, François: Studies in Early Christianity. 2003. *Vol. 161.*

Brändl, Martin: Der Agon bei Paulus. 2006. *Vol. II/222.*

Breytenbach, Cilliers: see *Frey, Jörg.*

Brocke, Christoph vom: Thessaloniki – Stadt des Kassander und Gemeinde des Paulus. 2001. *Vol. II/125.*

Brunson, Andrew: Psalm 118 in the Gospel of John. 2003. *Vol. II/158.*

Büchli, Jörg: Der Poimandres – ein paganisiertes Evangelium. 1987. *Vol. II/27.*

Bühner, Jan A.: Der Gesandte und sein Weg im 4. Evangelium. 1977. *Vol. II/2.*

Burchard, Christoph: Untersuchungen zu Joseph und Aseneth. 1965. *Vol. 8.*

– Studien zur Theologie, Sprache und Umwelt des Neuen Testaments. Ed. by D. Sänger. 1998. *Vol. 107.*

Burnett, Richard: Karl Barth's Theological Exegesis. 2001. *Vol. II/145.*

Byron, John: Slavery Metaphors in Early Judaism and Pauline Christianity. 2003. *Vol. II/162.*

Byrskog, Samuel: Story as History – History as Story. 2000. *Vol. 123.*

Cancik, Hubert (Ed.): Markus-Philologie. 1984. *Vol. 33.*

Capes, David B.: Old Testament Yaweh Texts in Paul's Christology. 1992. *Vol. II/47.*

Caragounis, Chrys C.: The Development of Greek and the New Testament. 2004. *Vol. 167.*

– The Son of Man. 1986. *Vol. 38.*

– see *Fridrichsen, Anton.*

Carleton Paget, James: The Epistle of Barnabas. 1994. *Vol. II/64.*

Carson, D.A., O'Brien, Peter T. and *Mark Seifrid* (Ed.): Justification and Variegated Nomism.

Vol. 1: The Complexities of Second Temple Judaism. 2001. *Vol. II/140.*

Vol. 2: The Paradoxes of Paul. 2004. *Vol. II/181.*

Chae, Young Sam: Jesus as the Eschatological Davidic Shepherd. 2006. *Vol. II/216.*

Chester, Andrew: Messiah and Exaltation. 2007. *Vol. 207.*

Chibici-Revneanu, Nicole: Die Herrlichkeit des Verherrlichten. 2007. *Vol. II/231.*

Ciampa, Roy E.: The Presence and Function of Scripture in Galatians 1 and 2. 1998. *Vol. II/102.*

Classen, Carl Joachim: Rhetorical Criticsm of the New Testament. 2000. *Vol. 128.*

Colpe, Carsten: Iranier – Aramäer – Hebräer – Hellenen. 2003. *Vol. 154.*

Crump, David: Jesus the Intercessor. 1992. *Vol. II/49.*

Dahl, Nils Alstrup: Studies in Ephesians. 2000. *Vol. 131.*

Daise, Michael A.: Feasts in John. 2007. *Vol. II/229.*

Deines, Roland: Die Gerechtigkeit der Tora im Reich des Messias. 2004. *Vol. 177.*

– Jüdische Steingefäße und pharisäische Frömmigkeit. 1993. *Vol. II/52.*

– Die Pharisäer. 1997. *Vol. 101.*

Deines, Roland and *Karl-Wilhelm Niebuhr* (Ed.): Philo und das Neue Testament. 2004. *Vol. 172.*

Dennis, John A.: Jesus' Death and the Gathering of True Israel. 2006. *Vol. 217.*

Dettwiler, Andreas and *Jean Zumstein* (Ed.): Kreuzestheologie im Neuen Testament. 2002. *Vol. 151.*

Dickson, John P.: Mission-Commitment in Ancient Judaism and in the Pauline Communities. 2003. *Vol. II/159.*

Dietzfelbinger, Christian: Der Abschied des Kommenden. 1997. *Vol. 95.*

Dimitrov, Ivan Z., James D.G. Dunn, Ulrich Luz and *Karl-Wilhelm Niebuhr* (Ed.): Das Alte Testament als christliche Bibel in orthodoxer und westlicher Sicht. 2004. *Vol. 174.*

Dobbeler, Axel von: Glaube als Teilhabe. 1987. *Vol. II/22.*

Dryden, J. de Waal: Theology and Ethics in 1 Peter. 2006. *Vol. II/209.*

Du Toit, David S.: Theios Anthropos. 1997. *Vol. II/91.*

Dübbers, Michael: Christologie und Existenz im Kolosserbrief. 2005. *Vol. II/191.*

Dunn, James D.G.: The New Perspective on Paul. 2005. *Vol. 185.*

Dunn , James D.G. (Ed.): Jews and Christians. 1992. *Vol. 66.*

– Paul and the Mosaic Law. 1996. *Vol. 89.*

– see *Dimitrov, Ivan Z.*

–, *Hans Klein, Ulrich Luz* and *Vasile Mihoc* (Ed.): Auslegung der Bibel in orthodoxer und westlicher Perspektive. 2000. *Vol. 130.*

Ebel, Eva: Die Attraktivität früher christlicher Gemeinden. 2004. *Vol. II/178.*

Ebertz, Michael N.: Das Charisma des Gekreuzigten. 1987. *Vol. 45.*

Eckstein, Hans-Joachim: Der Begriff Syneidesis bei Paulus. 1983. *Vol. II/10.*

– Verheißung und Gesetz. 1996. *Vol. 86.*

Ego, Beate: Im Himmel wie auf Erden. 1989. *Vol. II/34.*

Ego, Beate, Armin Lange and *Peter Pilhofer* (Ed.): Gemeinde ohne Tempel – Community without Temple. 1999. *Vol. 118.*

– and *Helmut Merkel* (Ed.): Religiöses Lernen in der biblischen, frühjüdischen und frühchristlichen Überlieferung. 2005. *Vol. 180.*

Eisen, Ute E.: see *Paulsen, Henning.*

Elledge, C.D.: Life after Death in Early Judaism. 2006. *Vol. II/208.*

Ellis, E. Earle: Prophecy and Hermeneutic in Early Christianity. 1978. *Vol. 18.*

– The Old Testament in Early Christianity. 1991. *Vol. 54.*

Endo, Masanobu: Creation and Christology. 2002. *Vol. 149.*

Ennulat, Andreas: Die 'Minor Agreements'. 1994. *Vol. II/62.*

Ensor, Peter W.: Jesus and His 'Works'. 1996. *Vol. II/85.*

Eskola, Timo: Messiah and the Throne. 2001. *Vol. II/142.*

– Theodicy and Predestination in Pauline Soteriology. 1998. *Vol. II/100.*

Fatehi, Mehrdad: The Spirit's Relation to the Risen Lord in Paul. 2000. *Vol. II/128.*

Feldmeier, Reinhard: Die Krisis des Gottessohnes. 1987. *Vol. II/21.*

– Die Christen als Fremde. 1992. *Vol. 64.*

Feldmeier, Reinhard and *Ulrich Heckel* (Ed.): Die Heiden. 1994. *Vol. 70.*

Fletcher-Louis, Crispin H.T.: Luke-Acts: Angels, Christology and Soteriology. 1997. *Vol. II/94.*

Förster, Niclas: Marcus Magus. 1999. *Vol. 114.*

Forbes, Christopher Brian: Prophecy and Inspired Speech in Early Christianity and its Hellenistic Environment. 1995. *Vol. II/75.*

Fornberg, Tord: see *Fridrichsen, Anton.*

Fossum, Jarl E.: The Name of God and the Angel of the Lord. 1985. *Vol. 36.*

Foster, Paul: Community, Law and Mission in Matthew's Gospel. *Vol. II/177.*

Fotopoulos, John: Food Offered to Idols in Roman Corinth. 2003. *Vol. II/151.*

Frenschkowski, Marco: Offenbarung und Epiphanie. Vol. 1 1995. *Vol. II/79* – Vol. 2 1997. *Vol. II/80.*

Frey, Jörg: Eugen Drewermann und die biblische Exegese. 1995. *Vol. II/71.*

– Die johanneische Eschatologie. Vol. I. 1997. *Vol. 96.* – Vol. II. 1998. *Vol. 110.* – Vol. III. 2000. *Vol. 117.*

Frey, Jörg and *Cilliers Breytenbach* (Ed.): Aufgabe und Durchführung einer Theologie des Neuen Testaments. 2007. *Vol. 205.*

– and *Udo Schnelle (Ed.):* Kontexte des Johannesevangeliums. 2004. *Vol. 175.*

– and *Jens Schröter* (Ed.): Deutungen des Todes Jesu im Neuen Testament. 2005. *Vol. 181.*

–, *Jan G. van der Watt,* and *Ruben Zimmermann* (Ed.): Imagery in the Gospel of John. 2006. *Vol. 200.*

Freyne, Sean: Galilee and Gospel. 2000. *Vol. 125.*

Fridrichsen, Anton: Exegetical Writings. Edited by C.C. Caragounis and T. Fornberg. 1994. *Vol. 76.*

Gäbel, Georg: Die Kulttheologie des Hebräerbriefes. 2006. *Vol. II/212.*

Gäckle, Volker: Die Starken und die Schwachen in Korinth und in Rom. 2005. *Vol. 200.*

Garlington, Don B.: 'The Obedience of Faith'. 1991. *Vol. II/38.*

– Faith, Obedience, and Perseverance. 1994. *Vol. 79.*

Garnet, Paul: Salvation and Atonement in the Qumran Scrolls. 1977. *Vol. II/3.*

Gemünden, Petra von (Ed.): see *Weissenrieder, Annette.*

Gese, Michael: Das Vermächtnis des Apostels. 1997. *Vol. II/99.*

Gheorghita, Radu: The Role of the Septuagint in Hebrews. 2003. *Vol. II/160.*

Gordley, Matthew E.: The Colossian Hymn in Context. 2007. *Vol. II/228.*

Gräbe, Petrus J.: The Power of God in Paul's Letters. 2000. *Vol. II/123.*

Gräßer, Erich: Der Alte Bund im Neuen. 1985. *Vol. 35.*

– Forschungen zur Apostelgeschichte. 2001. *Vol. 137.*

Grappe, Christian (Ed.): Le Repas de Dieu / Das Mahl Gottes.2004. *Vol. 169.*

Green, Joel B.: The Death of Jesus. 1988. *Vol. II/33.*

Gregg, Brian Han: The Historical Jesus and the Final Judgment Sayings in Q. 2005. *Vol. II/207.*

Gregory, Andrew: The Reception of Luke and Acts in the Period before Irenaeus. 2003. *Vol. II/169.*

Grindheim, Sigurd: The Crux of Election. 2005. *Vol. II/202.*

Gundry, Robert H.: The Old is Better. 2005. *Vol. 178.*

Gundry Volf, Judith M.: Paul and Perseverance. 1990. *Vol. II/37.*

Häußer, Detlef: Christusbekenntnis und Jesus-überlieferung bei Paulus. 2006. *Vol. 210.*

Hafemann, Scott J.: Suffering and the Spirit. 1986. *Vol. II/19.*

– Paul, Moses, and the History of Israel. 1995. *Vol. 81.*

Hahn, Ferdinand: Studien zum Neuen Testament.
Vol. I: Grundsatzfragen, Jesusforschung, Evangelien. 2006. *Vol. 191.*
Vol. II: Bekenntnisbildung und Theologie in urchristlicher Zeit. 2006. *Vol. 192.*

Hahn, Johannes (Ed.): Zerstörungen des Jerusalemer Tempels. 2002. *Vol. 147.*

Hamid-Khani, Saeed: Relevation and Concealment of Christ. 2000. *Vol. II/120.*

Hannah, Darrel D.: Michael and Christ. 1999. *Vol. II/109.*

Hardin, Justin K.: Galatians and the Imperial Cult? 2007. *Vol. II /237.*

Harrison; James R.: Paul's Language of Grace in Its Graeco-Roman Context. 2003. *Vol. II/172.*

Hartman, Lars: Text-Centered New Testament Studies. Ed. von D. Hellholm. 1997. *Vol. 102.*

Hartog, Paul: Polycarp and the New Testament. 2001. *Vol. II/134.*

Heckel, Theo K.: Der Innere Mensch. 1993. *Vol. II/53.*

– Vom Evangelium des Markus zum viergestaltigen Evangelium. 1999. *Vol. 120.*

Heckel, Ulrich: Kraft in Schwachheit. 1993. *Vol. II/56.*

– Der Segen im Neuen Testament. 2002. *Vol. 150.*

– see *Feldmeier, Reinhard.*

– see *Hengel, Martin.*

Heiligenthal, Roman: Werke als Zeichen. 1983. *Vol. II/9.*

Heliso, Desta: Pistis and the Righteous One. 2007. *Vol. II/235.*

Hellholm, D.: see *Hartman, Lars.*

Hemer, Colin J.: The Book of Acts in the Setting of Hellenistic History. 1989. *Vol. 49.*

Hengel, Martin: Judentum und Hellenismus. 1969, ³1988. *Vol. 10.*

– Die johanneische Frage. 1993. *Vol. 67.*

– Judaica et Hellenistica. Kleine Schriften I. 1996. *Vol. 90.*

– Judaica, Hellenistica et Christiana. Kleine Schriften II. 1999. *Vol. 109.*

– Paulus und Jakobus. Kleine Schriften III. 2002. *Vol. 141.*

– Studien zur Christologie. Kleine Schriften IV. 2006. *Vol. 201.*

– and *Anna Maria Schwemer:* Paulus zwischen Damaskus und Antiochien. 1998. *Vol. 108.*

– Der messianische Anspruch Jesu und die Anfänge der Christologie. 2001. *Vol. 138.*

Hengel, Martin and *Ulrich Heckel* (Ed.): Paulus und das antike Judentum. 1991. *Vol. 58.*

– and *Hermut Löhr* (Ed.): Schriftauslegung im antiken Judentum und im Urchristentum. 1994. *Vol. 73.*

– and *Anna Maria Schwemer* (Ed.): Königsherrschaft Gottes und himmlischer Kult. 1991. *Vol. 55.*

– Die Septuaginta. 1994. *Vol. 72.*

–, *Siegfried Mittmann* and *Anna Maria Schwemer* (Ed.): La Cité de Dieu / Die Stadt Gottes. 2000. *Vol. 129.*

Hentschel, Anni: Diakonia im Neuen Testament. 2007. *Vol. 226.*

Hernández Jr., Juan: Scribal Habits and Theological Influence in the Apocalypse. 2006. *Vol. II/218.*

Herrenbrück, Fritz: Jesus und die Zöllner. 1990. *Vol. II/41.*

Herzer, Jens: Paulus oder Petrus? 1998. *Vol. 103.*

– see *Böttrich, Christfried.*

Hill, Charles E.: From the Lost Teaching of Polycarp. 2005. *Vol. 186.*

Hoegen-Rohls, Christina: Der nachösterliche Johannes. 1996. *Vol. II/84.*

Hoffmann, Matthias Reinhard: The Destroyer and the Lamb. 2005. *Vol. II/203.*

Hofius, Otfried: Katapausis. 1970. *Vol. 11.*

– Der Vorhang vor dem Thron Gottes. 1972. *Vol. 14.*

– Der Christushymnus Philipper 2,6–11. 1976, ²1991. *Vol. 17.*

– Paulusstudien. 1989, ²1994. *Vol. 51.*

– Neutestamentliche Studien. 2000. *Vol. 132.*

– Paulusstudien II. 2002. *Vol. 143.*

– Exegetische Studien. 2008. *Vol. 223.*

– and *Hans-Christian Kammler:* Johannesstudien. 1996. *Vol. 88.*

Holmberg, Bengt (Ed.): Exploring Early Christian Identity. 2008. *Vol. 226.*

– und *Mikael Winninge* (Ed.): Identity Formation in the New Testament. 2008. *Vol. 227.*

Holtz, Traugott: Geschichte und Theologie des Urchristentums. 1991. *Vol. 57.*

Hommel, Hildebrecht: Sebasmata.

Vol. 1 1983. *Vol. 31.*
Vol. 2 1984. *Vol. 32.*
Horbury, William: Herodian Judaism and New Testament Study. 2006. *Vol. 193.*
Horst, Pieter W. van der: Jews and Christians in Their Graeco-Roman Context. 2006. *Vol. 196.*
Hvalvik, Reidar: The Struggle for Scripture and Covenant. 1996. *Vol. II/82.*
Jauhiainen, Marko: The Use of Zechariah in Revelation. 2005. *Vol. II/199.*
Jensen, Morten H.: Herod Antipas in Galilee. 2006. *Vol. II/215.*
Johns, Loren L.: The Lamb Christology of the Apocalypse of John. 2003. *Vol. II/167.*
Jossa, Giorgio: Jews or Christians? 2006. *Vol. 202.*
Joubert, Stephan: Paul as Benefactor. 2000. *Vol. II/124.*
Judge, E. A.: The First Christians in the Roman World. 2008. *Vol. 229.*
Jungbauer, Harry: „Ehre Vater und Mutter". 2002. *Vol. II/146.*
Kähler, Christoph: Jesu Gleichnisse als Poesie und Therapie. 1995. *Vol. 78.*
Kamlah, Ehrhard: Die Form der katalogischen Paränese im Neuen Testament. 1964. *Vol. 7.*
Kammler, Hans-Christian: Christologie und Eschatologie. 2000. *Vol. 126.*
– Kreuz und Weisheit. 2003. *Vol. 159.*
– see *Hofius, Otfried.*
Karakolis, Christos: see *Alexeev, Anatoly A.*
Karrer, Martin und *Wolfgang Kraus* (Ed.): Die Septuaginta – Texte, Kontexte, Lebenswelten. 2008. *Vol. 219.*
Kelhoffer, James A.: The Diet of John the Baptist. 2005. *Vol. 176.*
– Miracle and Mission. 1999. *Vol. II/112.*
Kelley, Nicole: Knowledge and Religious Authority in the Pseudo-Clementines. 2006. *Vol. II/213.*
Kieffer, René and *Jan Bergman (Ed.)*: La Main de Dieu / Die Hand Gottes. 1997. *Vol. 94.*
Kierspel, Lars: The Jews and the World in the Fourth Gospel. 2006. *Vol. 220.*
Kim, Seyoon: The Origin of Paul's Gospel. 1981, ²1984. *Vol. II/4.*
– Paul and the New Perspective. 2002. *Vol. 140.*
– "The 'Son of Man'" as the Son of God. 1983. *Vol. 30.*
Klauck, Hans-Josef: Religion und Gesellschaft im frühen Christentum. 2003. *Vol. 152.*
Klein, Hans: see *Dunn, James D.G.*
Kleinknecht, Karl Th.: Der leidende Gerechtfertigte. 1984, ²1988. *Vol. II/13.*
Klinghardt, Matthias: Gesetz und Volk Gottes. 1988. *Vol. II/32.*
Kloppenborg, John S.: The Tenants in the Vineyard. 2006. *Vol. 195.*

Koch, Michael: Drachenkampf und Sonnenfrau. 2004. *Vol. II/184.*
Koch, Stefan: Rechtliche Regelung von Konflikten im frühen Christentum. 2004. *Vol. II/174.*
Köhler, Wolf-Dietrich: Rezeption des Matthäusevangeliums in der Zeit vor Irenäus. 1987. *Vol. II/24.*
Köhn, Andreas: Der Neutestamentler Ernst Lohmeyer. 2004. *Vol. II/180.*
Koester, Craig and *Reimund Bieringer* (Ed.): The Resurrection of Jesus in the Gospel of John. 2008. *Vol. 222.*
Konradt, Matthias: Israel, Kirche und die Völker im Matthäusevangelium. 2007. *Vol. 215.*
Kooten, George H. van: Cosmic Christology in Paul and the Pauline School. 2003. *Vol. II/171.*
Korn, Manfred: Die Geschichte Jesu in veränderter Zeit. 1993. *Vol. II/51.*
Koskenniemi, Erkki: Apollonios von Tyana in der neutestamentlichen Exegese. 1994. *Vol. II/61.*
– The Old Testament Miracle-Workers in Early Judaism. 2005. *Vol. II/206.*
Kraus, Thomas J.: Sprache, Stil und historischer Ort des zweiten Petrusbriefes. 2001. *Vol. II/136.*
Kraus, Wolfgang: Das Volk Gottes. 1996. *Vol. 85.*
– see *Karrer, Martin.*
– see *Walter, Nikolaus.*
– and *Karl-Wilhelm Niebuhr* (Ed.): Frühjudentum und Neues Testament im Horizont Biblischer Theologie. 2003. *Vol. 162.*
Kreplin, Matthias: Das Selbstverständnis Jesu. 2001. *Vol. II/141.*
Kuhn, Karl G.: Achtzehngebet und Vaterunser und der Reim. 1950. *Vol. 1.*
Kvalbein, Hans: see *Ådna, Jostein.*
Kwon, Yon-Gyong: Eschatology in Galatians. 2004. *Vol. II/183.*
Laansma, Jon: I Will Give You Rest. 1997. *Vol. II/98.*
Labahn, Michael: Offenbarung in Zeichen und Wort. 2000. *Vol. II/117.*
Lambers-Petry, Doris: see *Tomson, Peter J.*
Lange, Armin: see *Ego, Beate.*
Lampe, Peter: Die stadtrömischen Christen in den ersten beiden Jahrhunderten. 1987, ²1989. *Vol. II/18.*
Landmesser, Christof: Wahrheit als Grundbegriff neutestamentlicher Wissenschaft. 1999. *Vol. 113.*
– Jüngerberufung und Zuwendung zu Gott. 2000. *Vol. 133.*
Lau, Andrew: Manifest in Flesh. 1996. *Vol. II/86.*
Lawrence, Louise: An Ethnography of the Gospel of Matthew. 2003. *Vol. II/165.*

Lee, Aquila H.I.: From Messiah to Preexistent Son. 2005. *Vol. II/192.*

Lee, Pilchan: The New Jerusalem in the Book of Relevation. 2000. *Vol. II/129.*

Lichtenberger, Hermann: Das Ich Adams und das Ich der Menschheit. 2004. *Vol. 164.*

– see *Avemarie, Friedrich.*

Lierman, John: The New Testament Moses. 2004. *Vol. II/173.*

– (Ed.): Challenging Perspectives on the Gospel of John. 2006. *Vol. II/219.*

Lieu, Samuel N.C.: Manichaeism in the Later Roman Empire and Medieval China. ²1992. *Vol. 63.*

Lindgård, Fredrik: Paul's Line of Thought in 2 Corinthians 4:16–5:10. 2004. *Vol. II/189.*

Loader, William R.G.: Jesus' Attitude Towards the Law. 1997. *Vol. II/97.*

Löhr, Gebhard: Verherrlichung Gottes durch Philosophie. 1997. *Vol. 97.*

Löhr, Hermut: Studien zum frühchristlichen und frühjüdischen Gebet. 2003. *Vol. 160.*

– see *Hengel, Martin.*

Löhr, Winrich Alfried: Basilides und seine Schule. 1995. *Vol. 83.*

Luomanen, Petri: Entering the Kingdom of Heaven. 1998. *Vol. II/101.*

Luz, Ulrich: see *Alexeev, Anatoly A.*

–: see *Dunn, James D.G.*

Mackay, Ian D.: John's Raltionship with Mark. 2004. *Vol. II/182.*

Mackie, Scott D.: Eschatology and Exhortation in the Epistle to the Hebrews. 2006. *Vol. II/223.*

Maier, Gerhard: Mensch und freier Wille. 1971. *Vol. 12.*

– Die Johannesoffenbarung und die Kirche. 1981. *Vol. 25.*

Markschies, Christoph: Valentinus Gnosticus? 1992. *Vol. 65.*

Marshall, Peter: Enmity in Corinth: Social Conventions in Paul's Relations with the Corinthians. 1987. *Vol. II/23.*

Martin, Dale B.: see *Zangenberg, Jürgen.*

Mayer, Annemarie: Sprache der Einheit im Epheserbrief und in der Ökumene. 2002. *Vol. II/150.*

Mayordomo, Moisés: Argumentiert Paulus logisch? 2005. *Vol. 188.*

McDonough, Sean M.: YHWH at Patmos: Rev. 1:4 in its Hellenistic and Early Jewish Setting. 1999. *Vol. II/107.*

McDowell, Markus: Prayers of Jewish Women. 2006. *Vol. II/211.*

McGlynn, Moyna: Divine Judgement and Divine Benevolence in the Book of Wisdom. 2001. *Vol. II/139.*

Meade, David G.: Pseudonymity and Canon. 1986. *Vol. 39.*

Meadors, Edward P.: Jesus the Messianic Herald of Salvation. 1995. *Vol. II/72.*

Meißner, Stefan: Die Heimholung des Ketzers. 1996. *Vol. II/87.*

Mell, Ulrich: Die „anderen" Winzer. 1994. *Vol. 77.*

– see *Sänger, Dieter.*

Mengel, Berthold: Studien zum Philipperbrief. 1982. *Vol. II/8.*

Merkel, Helmut: Die Widersprüche zwischen den Evangelien. 1971. *Vol. 13.*

– see *Ego, Beate.*

Merklein, Helmut: Studien zu Jesus und Paulus. Vol. 1 1987. *Vol. 43.* – Vol. 2 1998. *Vol. 105.*

Metzdorf, Christina: Die Tempelaktion Jesu. 2003. *Vol. II/168.*

Metzler, Karin: Der griechische Begriff des Verzeihens. 1991. *Vol. II/44.*

Metzner, Rainer: Die Rezeption des Matthäusevangeliums im 1. Petrusbrief. 1995. *Vol. II/74.*

– Das Verständnis der Sünde im Johannesevangelium. 2000. *Vol. 122.*

Mihoc, Vasile: see *Dunn, James D.G..*

Mineshige, Kiyoshi: Besitzverzicht und Almosen bei Lukas. 2003. *Vol. II/163.*

Mittmann, Siegfried: see *Hengel, Martin.*

Mittmann-Richert, Ulrike: Magnifikat und Benediktus. 1996. *Vol. II/90.*

Miura, Yuzuru: David in Luke-Acts. 2007. *Vol. II/232.*

Mournet, Terence C.: Oral Tradition and Literary Dependency. 2005. *Vol. II/195.*

Mußner, Franz: Jesus von Nazareth im Umfeld Israels und der Urkirche. Ed. von M. Theobald. 1998. *Vol. 111.*

Mutschler, Bernhard: Das Corpus Johanneum bei Irenäus von Lyon. 2005. *Vol. 189.*

Nguyen, V. Henry T.: Christian Identity in Corinth. 2008. *Vol. II/243.*

Niebuhr, Karl-Wilhelm: Gesetz und Paränese. 1987. *Vol. II/28.*

– Heidenapostel aus Israel. 1992. *Vol. 62.*

– see *Deines, Roland*

– see *Dimitrov, Ivan Z.*

– see *Kraus, Wolfgang*

Nielsen, Anders E.: "Until it is Fullfilled". 2000. *Vol. II/126.*

Nissen, Andreas: Gott und der Nächste im antiken Judentum. 1974. *Vol. 15.*

Noack, Christian: Gottesbewußtsein. 2000. *Vol. II/116.*

Noormann, Rolf: Irenäus als Paulusinterpret. 1994. *Vol. II/66.*

Novakovic, Lidija: Messiah, the Healer of the Sick. 2003. *Vol. II/170.*

Obermann, Andreas: Die christologische Erfüllung der Schrift im Johannesevangelium. 1996. *Vol. II/83.*

Öhler, Markus: Barnabas. 2003. *Vol. 156.*

– see *Becker, Michael.*
Okure, Teresa: The Johannine Approach to Mission. 1988. *Vol. II/31.*
Onuki, Takashi: Heil und Erlösung. 2004. *Vol. 165.*
Oropeza, B. J.: Paul and Apostasy. 2000. *Vol. II/115.*
Ostmeyer, Karl-Heinrich: Kommunikation mit Gott und Christus. 2006. *Vol. 197.*
– Taufe und Typos. 2000. *Vol. II/118.*
Paulsen, Henning: Studien zur Literatur und Geschichte des frühen Christentums. Ed. von Ute E. Eisen. 1997. *Vol. 99.*
Pao, David W.: Acts and the Isaianic New Exodus. 2000. *Vol. II/130.*
Park, Eung Chun: The Mission Discourse in Matthew's Interpretation. 1995. *Vol. II/81.*
Park, Joseph S.: Conceptions of Afterlife in Jewish Insriptions. 2000. *Vol. II/121.*
Pate, C. Marvin: The Reverse of the Curse. 2000. *Vol. II/114.*
Pearce, Sarah J.K.: The Land of the Body. 2007. *Vol. 208.*
Peres, Imre: Griechische Grabinschriften und neutestamentliche Eschatologie. 2003. *Vol. 157.*
Philip, Finny: The Origins of Pauline Pneumatology. 2005. *Vol. II/194.*
Philonenko, Marc (Ed.): Le Trône de Dieu. 1993. *Vol. 69.*
Pilhofer, Peter: Presbyteron Kreitton. 1990. *Vol. II/39.*
– Philippi. Vol. 1 1995. *Vol. 87.* – Vol. 2 2000. *Vol. 119.*
– Die frühen Christen und ihre Welt. 2002. *Vol. 145.*
– see *Becker, Eve-Marie.*
– see *Ego, Beate.*
Pitre, Brant: Jesus, the Tribulation, and the End of the Exile. 2005. *Vol. II/204.*
Plümacher, Eckhard: Geschichte und Geschichten. 2004. *Vol. 170.*
Pöhlmann, Wolfgang: Der Verlorene Sohn und das Haus. 1993. *Vol. 68.*
Pokorný, Petr and *Josef B. Souček:* Bibelauslegung als Theologie. 1997. *Vol. 100.*
– and *Jan Roskovec* (Ed.): Philosophical Hermeneutics and Biblical Exegesis. 2002. *Vol. 153.*
Popkes, Enno Edzard: Das Menschenbild des Thomasevangeliums. 2007. *Vol. 206.*
– Die Theologie der Liebe Gottes in den johanneischen Schriften. 2005. *Vol. II/197.*
Porter, Stanley E.: The Paul of Acts. 1999. *Vol. 115.*
Prieur, Alexander: Die Verkündigung der Gottesherrschaft. 1996. *Vol. II/89.*
Probst, Hermann: Paulus und der Brief. 1991. *Vol. II/45.*

Räisänen, Heikki: Paul and the Law. 1983, ²1987. *Vol. 29.*
Rehkopf, Friedrich: Die lukanische Sonderquelle. 1959. *Vol. 5.*
Rein, Matthias: Die Heilung des Blindgeborenen (Joh 9). 1995. *Vol. II/73.*
Reinmuth, Eckart: Pseudo-Philo und Lukas. 1994. *Vol. 74.*
Reiser, Marius: Bibelkritik und Auslegung der Heiligen Schrift. 2007. *Vol. 217.*
– Syntax und Stil des Markusevangeliums. 1984. *Vol. II/11.*
Rhodes, James N.: The Epistle of Barnabas and the Deuteronomic Tradition. 2004. *Vol. II/188.*
Richards, E. Randolph: The Secretary in the Letters of Paul. 1991. *Vol. II/42.*
Riesner, Rainer: Jesus als Lehrer. 1981, ³1988. *Vol. II/7.*
– Die Frühzeit des Apostels Paulus. 1994. *Vol. 71.*
Rissi, Mathias: Die Theologie des Hebräerbriefs. 1987. *Vol. 41.*
Roskovec, Jan: see *Pokorný, Petr.*
Röhser, Günter: Metaphorik und Personifikation der Sünde. 1987. *Vol. II/25.*
Rose, Christian: Theologie als Erzählung im Markusevangelium. 2007. *Vol. II/236.*
– Die Wolke der Zeugen. 1994. *Vol. II/60.*
Rothschild, Clare K.: Baptist Traditions and Q. 2005. *Vol. 190.*
– Luke Acts and the Rhetoric of History. 2004. *Vol. II/175.*
Rüegger, Hans-Ulrich: Verstehen, was Markus erzählt. 2002. *Vol. II/155.*
Rüger, Hans Peter: Die Weisheitsschrift aus der Kairoer Geniza. 1991. *Vol. 53.*
Sänger, Dieter: Antikes Judentum und die Mysterien. 1980. *Vol. II/5.*
– Die Verkündigung des Gekreuzigten und Israel. 1994. *Vol. 75.*
– see *Burchard, Christoph*
– and *Ulrich Mell* (Hrsg.): Paulus und Johannes. 2006. *Vol. 198.*
Salier, Willis Hedley: The Rhetorical Impact of the Semeia in the Gospel of John. 2004. *Vol. II/186.*
Salzmann, Jorg Christian: Lehren und Ermahnen. 1994. *Vol. II/59.*
Sandnes, Karl Olav: Paul – One of the Prophets? 1991. *Vol. II/43.*
Sato, Migaku: Q und Prophetie. 1988. *Vol. II/29.*
Schäfer, Ruth: Paulus bis zum Apostelkonzil. 2004. *Vol. II/179.*
Schaper, Joachim: Eschatology in the Greek Psalter. 1995. *Vol. II/76.*
Schimanowski, Gottfried: Die himmlische Liturgie in der Apokalypse des Johannes. 2002. *Vol. II/154.*
– Weisheit und Messias. 1985. *Vol. II/17.*

Schlichting, Günter: Ein jüdisches Leben Jesu. 1982. *Vol. 24.*

Schließer, Benjamin: Abraham's Faith in Romans 4. 2007. *Vol. II/224.*

Schnabel, Eckhard J.: Law and Wisdom from Ben Sira to Paul. 1985. *Vol. II/16.*

Schnelle, Udo: see *Frey, Jörg.*

Schröter, Jens: Von Jesus zum Neuen Testament. 2007. *Vol. 204.*

– see *Frey, Jörg.*

Schutter, William L.: Hermeneutic and Composition in I Peter. 1989. *Vol. II/30.*

Schwartz, Daniel R.: Studies in the Jewish Background of Christianity. 1992. *Vol. 60.*

Schwemer, Anna Maria: see *Hengel, Martin*

Scott, Ian W.: Implicit Epistemology in the Letters of Paul. 2005. *Vol. II/205.*

Scott, James M.: Adoption as Sons of God. 1992. *Vol. II/48.*

– Paul and the Nations. 1995. *Vol. 84.*

Shum, Shiu-Lun: Paul's Use of Isaiah in Romans. 2002. *Vol. II/156.*

Siegert, Folker: Drei hellenistisch-jüdische Predigten. Teil I 1980. *Vol. 20* – Teil II 1992. *Vol. 61.*

– Nag-Hammadi-Register. 1982. *Vol. 26.*

– Argumentation bei Paulus. 1985. *Vol. 34.*

– Philon von Alexandrien. 1988. *Vol. 46.*

Simon, Marcel: Le christianisme antique et son contexte religieux I/II. 1981. *Vol. 23.*

Smit, Peter-Ben: Fellowship and Food in the Kingdom. 2008. *Vol. II/234.*

Snodgrass, Klyne: The Parable of the Wicked Tenants. 1983. *Vol. 27.*

Söding, Thomas: Das Wort vom Kreuz. 1997. *Vol. 93.*

– see *Thüsing, Wilhelm.*

Sommer, Urs: Die Passionsgeschichte des Markusevangeliums. 1993. *Vol. II/58.*

Sorensen, Eric: Possession and Exorcism in the New Testament and Early Christianity. 2002. *Vol. II/157.*

Souček, Josef B.: see *Pokorný, Petr.*

Southall, David J.: Rediscovering Righteousness in Romans. 2008. *Vol. 240.*

Spangenberg, Volker: Herrlichkeit des Neuen Bundes. 1993. *Vol. II/55.*

Spanje, T.E. van: Inconsistency in Paul? 1999. *Vol. II/110.*

Speyer, Wolfgang: Frühes Christentum im antiken Strahlungsfeld. Vol. I: 1989. *Vol. 50.*

– Vol. II: 1999. *Vol. 116.*

– Vol. III: 2007. *Vol. 213.*

Sprinkle, Preston: Law and Life. 2008. *Vol. II/241.*

Stadelmann, Helge: Ben Sira als Schriftgelehrter. 1980. *Vol. II/6.*

Stenschke, Christoph W.: Luke's Portrait of Gentiles Prior to Their Coming to Faith. *Vol. II/108.*

Sterck-Degueldre, Jean-Pierre: Eine Frau namens Lydia. 2004. *Vol. II/176.*

Stettler, Christian: Der Kolosserhymnus. 2000. *Vol. II/131.*

Stettler, Hanna: Die Christologie der Pastoralbriefe. 1998. *Vol. II/105.*

Stökl Ben Ezra, Daniel: The Impact of Yom Kippur on Early Christianity. 2003. *Vol. 163.*

Strobel, August: Die Stunde der Wahrheit. 1980. *Vol. 21.*

Stroumsa, Guy G.: Barbarian Philosophy. 1999. *Vol. 112.*

Stuckenbruck, Loren T.: Angel Veneration and Christology. 1995. *Vol. II/70.*

– , *Stephen C. Barton* and *Benjamin G. Wold* (Ed.): Memory in the Bible and Antiquity. 2007. *Vol. 212.*

Stuhlmacher, Peter (Ed.): Das Evangelium und die Evangelien. 1983. *Vol. 28.*

– Biblische Theologie und Evangelium. 2002. *Vol. 146.*

Sung, Chong-Hyon: Vergebung der Sünden. 1993. *Vol. II/57.*

Tajra, Harry W.: The Trial of St. Paul. 1989. *Vol. II/35.*

– The Martyrdom of St.Paul. 1994. *Vol. II/67.*

Theißen, Gerd: Studien zur Soziologie des Urchristentums. 1979, ³1989. *Vol. 19.*

Theobald, Michael: Studien zum Römerbrief. 2001. *Vol. 136.*

Theobald, Michael: see *Mußner, Franz.*

Thornton, Claus-Jürgen: Der Zeuge des Zeugen. 1991. *Vol. 56.*

Thüsing, Wilhelm: Studien zur neutestamentlichen Theologie. Ed. von Thomas Söding. 1995. *Vol. 82.*

Thurén, Lauri: Derhethorizing Paul. 2000. *Vol. 124.*

Thyen, Hartwig: Studien zum Corpus Iohanneum. 2007. *Vol. 214.*

Tibbs, Clint: Religious Experience of the Pneuma. 2007. *Vol. II/230.*

Tolmie, D. Francois: Persuading the Galatians. 2005. *Vol. II/190.*

Tomson, Peter J. and *Doris Lambers-Petry* (Ed.): The Image of the Judaeo-Christians in Ancient Jewish and Christian Literature. 2003. *Vol. 158.*

Trebilco, Paul: The Early Christians in Ephesus from Paul to Ignatius. 2004. *Vol. 166.*

Treloar, Geoffrey R.: Lightfoot the Historian. 1998. *Vol. II/103.*

Tsuji, Manabu: Glaube zwischen Vollkommenheit und Verweltlichung. 1997. *Vol. II/93.*

Twelftree, Graham H.: Jesus the Exorcist. 1993. *Vol. II/54.*

Ulrichs, Karl Friedrich: Christusglaube. 2007. *Vol. II/227.*

Urban, Christina: Das Menschenbild nach dem Johannesevangelium. 2001. *Vol. II/137.*

Vahrenhorst, Martin: Kultische Sprache in den Paulusbriefen. 2008. *Vol. 230.*

Vegge, Ivar: 2 Corinthians – a Letter about Reconciliation. 2008. *Vol. II/239.*

Visotzky, Burton L.: Fathers of the World. 1995. *Vol. 80.*

Vollenweider, Samuel: Horizonte neutestamentlicher Christologie. 2002. *Vol. 144.*

Vos, Johan S.: Die Kunst der Argumentation bei Paulus. 2002. *Vol. 149.*

Wagener, Ulrike: Die Ordnung des „Hauses Gottes". 1994. *Vol. II/65.*

Wahlen, Clinton: Jesus and the Impurity of Spirits in the Synoptic Gospels. 2004. *Vol. II/185.*

Walker, Donald D.: Paul's Offer of Leniency (2 Cor 10:1). 2002. *Vol. II/152.*

Walter, Nikolaus: Praeparatio Evangelica. Ed. von Wolfgang Kraus und Florian Wilk. 1997. *Vol. 98.*

Wander, Bernd: Gottesfürchtige und Sympathisanten. 1998. *Vol. 104.*

Waters, Guy: The End of Deuteronomy in the Epistles of Paul. 2006. *Vol. 221.*

Watt, Jan G. van der: see *Frey, Jörg*

Watts, Rikki: Isaiah's New Exodus and Mark. 1997. *Vol. II/88.*

Wedderburn, A.J.M.: Baptism and Resurrection. 1987. *Vol. 44.*

Wegner, Uwe: Der Hauptmann von Kafarnaum. 1985. *Vol. II/14.*

Weissenrieder, Annette: Images of Illness in the Gospel of Luke. 2003. Vol. II/164.

–, *Friederike Wendt* and *Petra von Gemünden* (Ed.): Picturing the New Testament. 2005. *Vol. II/193.*

Welck, Christian: Erzählte ‚Zeichen'. 1994. *Vol. II/69.*

Wendt, Friederike (Ed.): see *Weissenrieder, Annette.*

Wiarda, Timothy: Peter in the Gospels. 2000. *Vol. II/127.*

Wifstrand, Albert: Epochs and Styles. 2005. *Vol. 179.*

Wilk, Florian: see *Walter, Nikolaus.*

Williams, Catrin H.: I am He. 2000. *Vol. II/113.*

Wilson, Todd A.: The Curse of the Law and the Crisis in Galatia. 2007. *Vol. II/225.*

Wilson, Walter T.: Love without Pretense. 1991. *Vol. II/46.*

Winninge, Mikael: see *Holmberg, Bengt.*

Wischmeyer, Oda: Von Ben Sira zu Paulus. 2004. *Vol. 173.*

Wisdom, Jeffrey: Blessing for the Nations and the Curse of the Law. 2001. *Vol. II/133.*

Wold, Benjamin G.: Women, Men, and Angels. 2005. *Vol. II/2001.*

– see *Stuckenbruck, Loren T.*

Wright, Archie T.: The Origin of Evil Spirits. 2005. *Vol. II/198.*

Wucherpfennig, Ansgar: Heracleon Philologus. 2002. *Vol. 142.*

Yeung, Maureen: Faith in Jesus and Paul. 2002. *Vol. II/147.*

Zangenberg, Jürgen, Harold W. Attridge and *Dale B. Martin* (Ed.): Religion, Ethnicity and Identity in Ancient Galilee. 2007. *Vol. 210.*

Zimmermann, Alfred E.: Die urchristlichen Lehrer. 1984, ²1988. *Vol. II/12.*

Zimmermann, Johannes: Messianische Texte aus Qumran. 1998. *Vol. II/104.*

Zimmermann, Ruben: Christologie der Bilder im Johannesevangelium. 2004. *Vol. 171.*

– Geschlechtermetaphorik und Gottesverhältnis. 2001. *Vol. II/122.*

– see *Frey, Jörg*

Zumstein, Jean: see *Dettwiler, Andreas*

Zwiep, Arie W.: Judas and the Choice of Matthias. 2004. *Vol. II/187.*

For a complete catalogue please write to the publisher
Mohr Siebeck • P.O. Box 2030 • D–72010 Tübingen/Germany
Up-to-date information on the internet at www.mohr.de